Luxemburg International Studies in Political Economy

Series Editors

Jan Toporowski
School of Oriental and African Studies
University of London, UK

Frieder Otto Wolf
Free University of Berlin
Germany

The Rosa Luxemburg Foundation is one of the largest political education institutions in Germany today. The Foundation's book series, Luxemburg International Studies in Political Economy, publishes serious academic studies in political economy, broadly conceived to cover critical research in the social sciences on capitalism, as well as feminist and environmental political economy.

More information about this series at
http://www.springer.com/series/15118

Judith Dellheim • Frieder Otto Wolf
Editors

Rosa Luxemburg: A Permanent Challenge for Political Economy

On the History and the Present of Luxemburg's 'Accumulation of Capital'

palgrave
macmillan

Editors
Judith Dellheim
Rosa Luxemburg Foundation
Berlin, Germany

Frieder Otto Wolf
Free University of Berlin
Germany

Translated by Loren Balhorn and Jan-Peter Herrmann

Luxemburg International Studies in Political Economy
ISBN 978-1-137-60107-0 ISBN 978-1-137-60108-7 (eBook)
DOI 10.1057/978-1-137-60108-7

Library of Congress Control Number: 2016946835

Printed on acid-free paper

This Palgrave Macmillan imprint is published by Springer Nature
The registered company is Macmillan Publishers Ltd. London

Foreword

This book has a very specific history, dating back to the year 2011. It began with the idea for a conference to mark the 100th anniversary of Rosa Luxemburg's foundational *The Accumulation of Capital: A Contribution to an Economic Explanation of Imperialism*. The discussion of this idea at the Rosa Luxemburg Foundation ended with a clear provisional conclusion: that there would be no such conference. The main reason for this decision was to avoid a vulgar reflection of the historical debate surrounding the book, as it was conducted by the German Social Democrats in the year before the beginning of World War I and in the first war years on the one hand, and by the Stalinists on the other hand. Luxemburg's opponents were much more interested in defaming Rosa Luxemburg's personality than in discussing her theoretical insights. For those purposes, however, they were able to make use of some real mistakes and weaknesses in Luxemburg's book. The main point of this 'treatment' of Luxemburg by these two groups (and their later, more or less conscious followers) was to misuse Luxemburg for their own political and ideological designs, without truly addressing her theoretical achievements—simply because she was a revolutionary, a co-founder of the Communist Party of Germany, and, ultimately, a murder victim. The Social Democrats made use of Luxemburg's harsh criticism of the Bolsheviks, while the Stalinists insisted on the fact that her murder had been indirectly caused and condoned by a few Social Democrats.

There were strong concerns among leading members of the foundation that an event returning to a discussion of *Accumulation of Capital* could turn into a highly ideological confrontation and a mere re-enactment of fruitless historical debates.

Nevertheless, contemporary theoretical and political discussions, both internationally and within the German Left, have brought about a renewal of Luxemburg studies as an attempt to make her impressive theoretical potential accessible to ongoing research and critical discussions. Moreover, her work stands out as a historical example of a Marxist position which had escaped the crippling dichotomy of Stalinism and Social Democracy—comparable to Antonio Gramsci on the Communist, and the 'Austro-Marxists' on the Social Democratic side. The growing interest in Luxemburg as a resource for an emancipatory renewal of Marxism as it emerged in the New Left in the 1960s (with its components and echoes both in the East and in the West) has been further strengthened by the growing importance of global and European issues in the real world, as has it been reflected within Left politics.

At the same time, comparison of present-day conjunctures with political constellations similar to some of those existing before World War I has become much more plausible and much more frequently pursued in recent years. This has inevitably brought a renewed relevance to Rosa Luxemburg's attempts to produce a theoretical reconstruction of such dynamics. Young people in particular, struggling with theory in order to understand the economic background of emerging critical political problems of our times, and of the difficulties of the Left to self-organise in a sustainable way, have raised many questions linked to Rosa Luxemburg's theoretical achievements.

For Rosa Luxemburg represents a unique combination of political activism, scientific study and teaching. Although she published only a few 'academic' books in her lifetime, all of her speeches, articles and brochures are grounded in a deep theoretical understanding of society. Against the backdrop of a traditional liberal-bourgeois education, she was able to see and to feel the main tendencies within modern bourgeois society that continuously undermined both economic and cultural structures. As political activist and intellectual, it was important for her to understand emerging elements in the framework of contradictions of the capitalist mode of production as the core of bourgeois society. Thus, her criticism of Marx was a consequence of the Marxian scientific approach itself. The understanding of the emergence, resolution and re-emergence of basic contradictions was the key not only to understanding society, but to creating political strategies and to building alliances. Thus, it is impossible to divide the 'academic' *Accumulation of Capital* from the other aspects of her work.

We can confidently state that *The Accumulation of Capital* is a kind of 'conclusion', made by Luxemburg on the basis of experiences in all fields of her activities. The year 1913, when the book was published, saw a change in the mode of rule in Germany, which she connected to the establishment of the property tax as an instrument of financing military expansion. She labelled this a 'turning point' and 'milestone' in the political development of Germany. In the years preceding she had already written about and spoken out against the dangers posed by war, colonial expansion and the militarisation of society. In *Accumulation of Capital* she described the scientific background of her own political activities. Luxemburg tried to find answers concerning the mode of reproduction of modern capitalism in the form of imperialism, as well as the driving forces and the resources of its development. In the Marxian tradition, she employed the instrument of critique both of given theoretical doctrines and of reality itself. This approach qualifies the book not only as a theoretical text, but also a textbook for students and politicians alike. Even today, the analysis of the destruction of non-capitalist (or non-capitalised) elements within bourgeois society as a source of accumulation and of the role of the state is an inspiration for both scientists and political activists. But Luxemburg also emphasised that capitalism does not break down automatically. Political activists and the masses must understand the social contradictions and find a historically specific way to solve them. Otherwise the sharpening of contradictions will only deepen the social and political crisis of civilisation. Accordingly, her book is on the one hand a call for using the Marxian approach as a social scientific tool and, on the other hand, a call for action.

This is why many emancipatory and solidarity-oriented partners of the Rosa Luxemburg Foundations both in Germany and especially abroad have asked for an event to be held on occasion of the 100th anniversary of *The Accumulation of Capital*, in order to begin a new, constructive debate based on a continuous study of the reflections on Luxemburg's work as they are emerging in international discussions. The supporters of the conference argued that outside Germany recent discussions on Luxemburg's work have left behind both the old divisions and also the attempts to instrumentalise her legacy. The contemporary discussion instead refers to and makes use of her inspiring ideas and her research method. Within the international debate, Luxemburg's legacy is used in a much more broadly minded and productive way.

Inspired by this ongoing international debate, the Rosa Luxemburg Foundation chose to issue a call for papers[1] entitled '100th Anniversary of *The Accumulation of Capital*: A century-old work remains current, provocative and seminal'.[2] This call was published in the beginning of 2013, intending to highlight two dramatic commemoration dates in 2014 which were both connected to the theoretical work and political struggle of Rosa Luxemburg: the start of the Berlin Conference in 1884, with its brutal and blood-stained consequences for the peoples of Africa, and the beginning of the terrible World War I in 1914. The call extended an invitation to an international workshop to be held on 7–9 March 2014, around the birthday of Rosa Luxemburg.

The text began with the following paragraph: 'A hundred years since the first Berlin edition of *The Accumulation of Capital: A Contribution to an Economic Explanation of Imperialism*, no one needs a commemorative address to introduce the work. The work is still being referred to by scholars, writers and people all around the world who fight for democracy nd justice; for a life of dignity, solidarity and ecological responsibility; and for socialism. Its continued prominence is a tribute to its author, her academic methodology and the topicality of the questions she posed, yet it also demonstrates a corresponding weakness in the modern Left, particularly among socialists.

[1] Invitation to an international discussion: '100th anniversary of *The Accumulation of Capital: A Contribution to an Economic Explanation of Imperialism*: A century-old work remains current, provocative and seminal, http://kapacc.blog.rosalux.de/2013/05/19/100th-anniversary-of-the-accumulation-of-capital-a-contribution-to-an-economic-explanation-of-imperialism-a-century-old-work-remains-current-provocative-and-eminal/

[2] This call was formulated on the occasion of Frieder Otto Wolf's 70th birthday.

Rosa Luxemburg, one of the most fascinating characters in the struggle for freedom in equality, has radically criticised capitalism's underlying social relations and capital accumulation, and she has fought equally radically against the resulting outcomes in terms of human oppression and natural destruction. After her murder on 15 January 1919 by her political enemies, her legacy lived on, as it still does today.'

The call focused on three priorities: *firstly*, to 'initiate discussion about today's globalised (financial) capital accumulation, the economy's increasing financialisation and the main players involved—modern oligarchies of capital. *Secondly*, it is relevant to examine how the debate on land grabbing has been, or may be used, to support efforts for a social and ecological transformation by local and regional EU, European and global movements/alliances against social and ecological destruction. *Thirdly*, we ask what lessons can be learned from the fact that a concept which should be subjected to critique is promoted as theoretical, political insight. *In this connection methodical and methodological questions are of highest interest, especially the work using mathematic models.*'

The call's resonance far exceeded the expectation of its organisers. The workshop proved to be a powerful and illuminating event.[3] During the workshop, participants were guided by two distinct, yet closely linked aims: to make use of Luxemburg's *Accumulation of Capital* as a source of inspiration to deal with contemporary social problems, and to improve one's own research methodology. The vital aspects of Rosa Luxemburg's theoretical (and political) heritage for overcoming a dogmatic or orthodox 'Marxism' which has crippled Marxist debates (particularly on the Stalinist side) were highlighted and taken up in all of the contributions.

As a result of this successful workshop, the publication of a book (which had been discussed from the outset of the project) has become feasible. This is not conceived as a mere 'scrapbook' of conference papers, but rather represents the further discussion and elaboration of conference contributions, in order to help clarify three main theoretical issues:

- from whom and from what had Luxemburg taken her inspiration,
- who was been inspired by her work and why and to what extent,

[3] See also the workshop blog at http://kapacc.blog.rosalux.de/

- what can explain the ongoing worldwide attraction of an apparently failed and tragic politician, who authored a number of books and articles which indisputably include serious theoretical mistakes and contradictions.

These questions can all be considered to be questions of a living methodology, of a method of research and of action, elaborated within real processes of deliberation and action. It has therefore been of central interest to fully understand how Rosa Luxemburg criticised theories, including Marxian ones, while looking for a solution to specific theoretical problems with very specific consequences for political activity. She always sought possibilities of dealing with contradictions within social and political practice, and for possibilities of making use of them in an emancipatory modality. Accordingly, the workshop and the work on this book have focused on the role of Rosa Luxemburg for the development of a dissident, critical strand of socialist thinking—not only historically, but in the present as well.

All of these considerations and developments have been relevant for the choice of texts: James D. White explains Maxim Kovalevsky as 'a key figure in the history of Marxism' and how Marx and Luxemburg used his book on the dissolution of communal landownership to explain colonisation by capitalist forces. Paul Zarembka reconstructs value as a concept elaborated by Marx and clarifies how Luxemburg's concept of the penetration of pre-modern strata of modern society by capitalist accumulation is determined by it. Michael R. Krätke has produced a very comprehensive account of Luxemburg's critique of Marx and its productive impact in transforming Marx' reproduction schemes 'into a cornerstone of Marxian macroeconomics'. Sharing such an approach, Greg Albo argues against an excessively polarised account of Luxemburg's 'great book in economics' and for taking 'better account of insights on capitalism as a monetary economy'. Doing so proved quite courageous in the Poland of the 1950s and 60s. As Jan Toporowski shows, Tadeusz Kowalik does exactly this: he discovers an 'important link between the analysis of Marx, in his schemes of reproduction … and the theories of Michal Kalecki (and the Keynesian Revolution in general)' in Luxemburg's *Accumulation*.

In the 1970s, feminists like Veronika Bennholdt-Thomsen used Luxemburg's findings to explain the relation between accumulation of capital and unpaid housework performed by women. Tove Soiland appreciates that and argues that with the relationship between paid and unpaid reproduction labour a new form of the subsumption of subsistence production by capitalist logic has emerged that does not disappear as long as the economy is dominated by an ongoing capitalist mode of production. Such insights can be developed only when research is focused on the everyday lives of real people. Its analysis could help to understand how the 'silent compulsion' of capital discovered by Marx and the aggressive essence of finance capital explained by Luxemburg shape the everyday lives of all people. Judith Dellheim analyses this and demonstrates the close interrelationship between financialisation and privatisation processes within pension systems and housing schemes, which is of strategic relevance for actual politics. Hanna K. Szymborska is also interested in financialisation. She discusses the relevance of Rosa Luxemburg's ideas, as outlined in her *Accumulation of Capital*, in understanding the shift in the balance of power inspired by the transformation of the financial sectors since the second half of the 20th century. Financialisation, in turn, is a specific kind of *Landnahme*,[4] driving growth as well as its destructive social and ecological consequences. Klaus Dörre analyses this and illuminates the debate on alternatives. Pursuing a similar theme, Julian Francis Park 'sets out to establish the relevance of Rosa Luxemburg's *The Accumulation of Capital* for present anti-imperial socialist struggle by studying the historical conditions … of its writing'. Michael Brie shares Park's interest in the issue. He shows how Third World theoreticians, feminists, ecologists, and the theoreticians of the alter-globalisation movements have reshaped the Luxemburg model in new ways. They all find themselves confronted

[4]Translator's note: Literally translated, *Landnahme* means land grabbing, land appropriation, or territorial gain (in German: 'land taking'). It refers to internal as well as external capitalist expansion. The concept of *Landnahme* espoused, for example, by Klaus Dörre, argues that in the long run capitalist societies cannot reproduce themselves entirely of their own accord. In order to reproduce themselves, they continuously have to occupy and commodify a non-capitalist 'Other' (i.e. regions, milieus, groups, activities) in, so to speak, ceaseless repetition of the act of primitive accumulation. Owed to the difficulty of finding a conclusive exact translation, the term *Landnahme* will be used throughout the book.

with the challenge to understand the structural interrelationships and interlinkages between capitalist accumulation and social reproduction, and by the historical task of finding ways of making their combination and articulation effective for actual political change.

Our many thanks go to the authors Greg Albo, Michael Brie, Klaus Dörre, Michael R. Krätke, Julian Francis Park, Tove Soiland, Hanna K. Szymborska, Jan Toporowski, James D. White, Paul Zarembka, and to our translators and lectors Jan-Peter Herrmann und Loren Balhorn—who have been so fantastically patient. And of course a very special thanks to Rachel Sangster and Gemma Leigh from Palgrave Macmillan.

This book owes its publication within this new series to the initiative of Jan Toporowski in particular. This series, edited in common by Jan Toporowski and Frieder Otto Wolf, seeks to broaden and to deepen the debate on the renewal of a living Marxism. It should help to invite interested people to an ongoing process of renewing Marxist analysis, which shall have a new high point in 2018: the 200th birthday of Karl Marx.

Judith Dellheim
Frieder Otto Wolf
Lutz Brangsch

The original version of this book was revised.
An erratum to this chapter can be found at
DOI 10.1057/978-1-137-60108-7_12

Contents

Notes on the Contributors

Greg Albo teaches political economy at York University in Toronto, is co-editor of the annual *Socialist Register*, and also coordinates the Centre for Social Justice. He has also published widely on the economic crisis, the political economy of Canada, international relations and democratisation.

Lutz Brangsch was born in 1957 in Berlin and worked as a researcher at the Academy of Social Sciences in Berlin. He was employed by the National Executive of the Party of Democratic Socialism from 1990 to 1999 and has worked at the Rosa Luxemburg Foundation since then. He has served as a senior research fellow at the Institute for Critical Social Analysis of the Rosa Luxembourg Foundation since 2009, where he specialises in economics, economic and social policy, and democratic theory.

Michael Brie is a social philosopher. He studied in Leningrad and Berlin and works as a researcher at the Institute for Critical Social Analysis of the Rosa Luxemburg Foundation in Berlin. The main topics of his research are the theory and history of socialism, concepts of the socio-ecological transformation of modern societies and strategic questions for the Left in the crisis of neoliberalism. His most recent publications are on Karl Polanyi as a socialist thinker and on Robert Owen. He is editor of the series *Beiträge zur kritischen Transformationsforschung*, published by VSA, Hamburg.

Judith Dellheim earned her PhD in 1983. She worked as a freelance scientific consultant from 2004 to 2010 and has served as a Senior Researcher at the Rosa Luxemburg Foundation since 2011. Her main research interests are concepts of the socio-ecological transformation of modern societies, the solidarity economy, the political economy of the European Union, and alternative economic policy.

Klaus Dörre is Professor of Sociology at the Friedrich-Schiller-University of Jena (Germany) where he chairs the Department of Labour, Industrial and Economic Sociology. He specialises in the Sociology of Labour as well as industrial and economic sociology. His areas of research include the theory of capitalism, finance capitalism, flexible and precarious employment, and labour relations, among others. He is the current director of the German Research Foundation (DFG) research group 'Post-Growth Societies' and a research associate at the Society, Work and Development Institute (SWOP) at the University of the Witwatersrand, Johannesburg, where his research topics include the politics of precarious society and decent work.

Michael R. Krätke is Professor and Chair of Political Economy at the University of Lancaster, UK. He is one of the leading academic experts on Marx's and Engels's critique of political economy and on the history of Marxist political economy and has been a collaborator of the new complete edition of the works of Marx and Engels ($MEGA^2$) for many years. He has edited and is still editing unpublished works by Rosa Luxemburg, Otto Bauer, Natalie Moszkowska, Karl Kautsky and Rudolf Hilferding. In many articles, published in leading academic journals in several languages, he has dealt with various topics of political economy—from the theory of money to crisis theory and modern public finance. As an economic journalist and leading specialist on world money and finance, he regularly publishes articles on current events in the world economy.

Julian Francis Park tries to write from where race treason, class suicide, and gender abolition might eventually meet. Recently he completed a book length poem entitled *Every Breath You Take* against literal and figurative policing in Oakland, CA (USA), amid intensifying social contradictions and within the movement to abolish the police. Recent publications include an essay-length review of Fred Moten's The Feel Trio & Claudia Rankine's Citizen in Tripwire: a journal of poetics and a long poem on (social) hygiene at a writers' conference, entitled "Ass Wipe Practice," in Entropy. He lives in Oakland where he recently got an MFA in Creative Writing at Mills College.

Tove Soiland is a historian concentrating on feminist theory. She lectures at various universities and conducts seminars on feminist economics and political theory for the VPOD trade union in Zürich. She completed her PhD at the University of Zürich in 2008. In 2003 she initiated a major debate on the theoretical foundations of gender in the German-speaking world (the so-called 'Gender-Streit'). In 2009 she authored the theatrical reading of 'Nehmen Sie Ihr Gender selbst in die Hand, Madam!' She is a member of the advisory committee of the journal *Widerspruch. Beiträge zur sozialistischen Politik*. Her current research focus consists of feminist theory and the connection between Francophone psychoanalysis and Marxism. She authored the 2013 entry on 'Lacanism' for the *Historical-Critical Dictionary of Marxism* (8/1).

Hanna K. Szymborska is a postgraduate researcher at the University of Leeds. Her research interests lie in the areas of inequality, social justice and the history of economic thought.

Jan Toporowski is Professor of Economics and Finance at the School of Oriental and African Studies, University of London, UK, and Visiting Professor of Economics at the University of Bergamo, Italy. He is the author of *Michal Kalecki: An Intellectual Biography: Volume 1, Rendezvous in Cambridge 1899–1939* (London: Palgrave 2013).

James D. White is Professor Emeritus at the University of Glasgow, Scotland. He has written on various aspects of the history of revolutionary movements in the Russian Empire and on the history of Marxism. His publications include *The Russian Revolution: A Short History* (1994), *Karl Marx and the Intellectual Origins of Dialectical Materialism* (1996) and *Lenin: The Practice and Theory of Revolution* (2001). He has also published articles on modern Russian, Chinese and Baltic history in journals including *Europe–Asia Studies, Revolutionary Russia*, the *Slavonic and East European Review* and *Research in Political Economy*. He is currently working on an intellectual biography of Alexander Bogdanov.

Frieder Otto Wolf is Honorary Professor of Philosophy at the Freie Universität Berlin. Born in Kiel, Germany in 1943, between 1962 and 1966 he studied philosophy and political science (at Kiel, Paris, and Edinburgh). He has been a lecturer in Philosophy at the Freie Universität Berlin since 1973, and became Honorary Professor in 2007. Active in European politics as a member of the German Green Party from 1984 to 1999 and member of the European Parliament from 1994 to 1999. He has served as Fellow at the Research Institute of the Rosa-Luxemburg-Foundation Member since 2013 and sits on the advisory boards of *Das Argument*, *Historical Materialism*, and *Cosmopolitiques, Écologie et Politique*.

Notable publications include *Die neue Wissenschaft des Thomas Hobbes* (1969), *Radikale Philosophie* (2002) and *Arbeitsglück* (2005). He co-edited *Das Kapital neu lesen* (2006). His English-language contributions have appeared in *New Left Review*, *Socialist Register*, and *Capitalism, Nature, Socialism*.

Paul Zarembka is Professor of Economics at the State University of New York at Buffalo. He has served as general editor of *Research in Political Economy*, an annual series based upon the class analysis of society, since 1977. One of his main research projects has been to conceptualise the meaning of 'accumulation of capital' within the Marxist tradition, including Luxemburg's understanding. He has also edited *The Hidden History of 9/11*, which undermines the US government's narrative concerning responsibility for September 11th, beginning with its utter failure to establish that the alleged hijackers were even on board the four planes. On the activism side, he has been president and is currently grievance officer for academics in his union.

List of Figures

List of Tables

1

On the Historical Conditions of *Accumulation*

Julian Francis Park

In 1903, twenty years after the death of Karl Marx, Rosa Luxemburg published an essay on the 'Stagnation and Progress of Marxism'. This should serve as a guide to our return to *The Accumulation of Capital* on the centennial anniversary of its publication. In 'Stagnation', Luxemburg notes that despite the publication of the second and third volumes of Marx's *Capital*, in 1885 and 1894 respectively, political agitation and Marxist doctrine in Germany and elsewhere had been popularised on the basis of the incomplete conclusions of Volume I. As she writes regarding the second and third volumes – and as we today might extend to her *Accumulation of Capital* – 'the splendid new weapon rusts unused' except amongst 'the restricted circles of the experts'. Rather than concluding that Marx's last elaborations were inflexible, or that the movement's intellectual talents were insufficient, Luxemburg argues that 'our needs are not yet adequate for the utilization of Marx's ideas' and that only as

J.F. Park (✉)
Causa Justa: Just Cause Tenant's Right Clinic
Bay Area Public School, Oakland, CA, USA

J. Dellheim, F.O. Wolf (eds.), *Rosa Luxemburg: A Permanent Challenge for Political Economy*, DOI 10.1057/978-1-137-60108-7_1

proletarian struggle encounters new practical problems will we return to the rusting weaponry (Luxemburg 1903).

In one of his few prison notes on the writings of Luxemburg, Antonio Gramsci claims that these conclusions in the 'Stagnation and Progress of Marxism' are a form of historical mysticism insofar as they 'present an abstract formulation of the fact to be explained as an explanation of the fact itself'. Nonetheless, Gramsci acknowledges that there is a kernel of truth in them that must be dialectically developed. One articulation of this development is that the stagnation of Marxist theory comes from the historical necessity of Marxist orthodoxy's alliance with undialectical – that is, positivist – materialisms 'in order to combat the residues of the pre-capitalist world that still exist among the popular masses' (Gramsci 1971, p. 392). And yet from the perspective of the totality, Gramsci's development seems to merely elevate Luxemburg's alleged abstraction to a higher level. For the claim that dialectical materialism expresses itself less dialectically out of the practical necessities of the ideological struggle to educate the masses reifies as necessary one set of mediations between proletarian class consciousness and so-called pre-capitalist consciousness. Admittedly, Gramsci poses his solution more concretely only a few pages later – the stagnation of Marxism, the dilution of the dialectical element of its materialism, would only ever be completely resolved when the petit bourgeois character of the Marxist intelligentsia was overcome by the emergence of an organically proletarian intelligentsia. Succinctly: 'Only after the creation of the new State does the cultural problem impose itself in all its complexity and tend towards a coherent solution'; prior to this solution, Marxism can at best be a 'critico-polemical' 'romanticism' (Gramsci 1971, pp. 397–8). Ironically, this is more or less the same solution that Luxemburg herself prescribes for the stagnation of Marxism: as she writes, 'The working class will not be in a position to create a science and an art of its own until it has been fully emancipated from its present class position' (Luxemburg 1903). Given the difference between the abstractions of Luxemburg and Gramsci and the nature of their concrete solutions, the mediation of their contradiction demands discovery.

If Luxemburg's abstract formulation on the one hand is referring to the inadequacy of historical needs for *Capital*, Volumes II and III, and Gramsci's on the other is affirming that dialectical materialism necessarily becomes diluted in order to win over the masses, then the historical intersection of the two explanations is the emergence of opportunistic socialism and its growing influence in the Second International. The classic text addressing the problem of opportunism is Luxemburg's own *Social Reform or Revolution*, published in 1899. Already in her critique of Eduard Bernstein's articles on the 'Problems of Socialism' for German Social Democracy, Luxemburg outlines an historical tendency largely responsible for the stagnation of Marxism, and thereby indicates the conditions for its resolution. According to Luxemburg, opportunism emerges (with Bernstein as its flag bearer) as the ideology of the petit bourgeois elements of the party seeking to replace the struggle for social reforms from being the *means* of Social Democracy to being the goal itself – that is, abandoning the aim of social revolution. According to this ideology, the collapse of capitalism becomes improbable because of its increasing adaptability and variation – in other words, general crises tend to disappear and segments of the proletariat are integrated into the middle class, while the most egregious proletarian conditions are ameliorated by the trade-union struggle (Luxemburg 1899, pp. 129–31). Thus, the growth of opportunism in the Second International implies that only the Marxian problem of capitalist exploitation, formulated most rigorously in *Capital*, Volume I is of concern. The dialectical twists of surplus value on its path to realisation through expanded reproduction and into the tendency of the rate of profit to fall leading the totality toward greater and greater crises, as discussed in Volumes II and III, have little to offer for petit bourgeois socialism – as Luxemburg puts it, 'Bernstein's theory of adaptation is nothing but a theoretical generalization of the conception of the individual capitalist' (Luxemburg 1899, p. 145). Furthermore, Bernstein's claim to popularise socialism by shifting its concern from the relations between capital and labour to those between rich and poor abandons the analysis of the structure of productive relations for the superstructure of property relations – moving from the dialectical basis of scientific socialism to that of utopian socialism (Luxemburg 1899, p. 148). Indeed, Bernstein attacks the dialectic itself (Luxemburg 1899, p. 162). But to consign the second and third volumes of *Capital* to the dustbin of history is to discard the scientific unity of theory and practice that transforms proletarian consciousness of the exploitative basis of capitalism and the tendency towards generalised crises into the necessity of social revolution. Thus opportunism teaches us that the nexus of Luxemburg and Gramsci's abstract formulations concerning the stagnation of Marxism find the conditions of their concrete solution in the historical necessity of preserving the fundamentally proletarian revolutionary character of the socialist struggle even before the conquest of political power. What at first seemed like a question of Marxist theory was already coinciding with the necessities of proletarian revolutionary practice – of keeping particular social reformist means of struggle subordinate to the universal ends of revolution.

In *History and Class Consciousness* (1971) Georg Lukács argues that Luxemburg's *The Accumulation of Capital* is one of two books of its era that mark the 'theoretical rebirth of Marxism' (p. 35). To understand this assertion in its fullness we must conceive of *The Accumulation of Capital* as depicting the concrete totality of capitalism from the proletarian revolutionary perspective of the conditions of its overthrow. In other words, not only does it scrape the rust off of the weaponry contained in volumes II and III of *Capital*, it puts them to use as historically necessary theoretical weapons for new historical conditions of the practice of class war. This rust removal has not been without controversy, neither in its time nor since then. The controversy has mostly centred on several aspects of two sides of the dialectic of the argument in Luxemburg's book: on the one hand, that Marx's scheme of expanded reproduction in *Capital*, Volume II, cannot explain the actual, historical accumulation of capital since it includes only capitalists and workers, neither of whom (as a class) can be the purchasers within the totality of capitalist society necessary to realise surplus value and thus accumulate it as capital. This necessitates the sale of surplus product to non-capitalist social strata, particularly in the form of imperialism. On the other hand, insofar as capitalism tends toward universality, while simultaneously depending on the destruction of non-capitalist social organisations, the elimination of this dependency is guaranteed, bringing its end all the more near (Luxemburg 1913, p. 332).

Ernest Mandel will be our first guide to these controversies. In his introduction to the second volume of *Capital*, Mandel addresses Luxemburg's argument on three levels, moving from the most abstract to the most concrete. His first point is that it is methodologically incorrect to pose the matter of reproduction on an expanded scale in terms of the totality of capital, since it is really only a problem for the competitive relations of many capitals. The second level considers the discontinuity of accumulation as a process, that is, whether full realisation of surplus value can be modelled using the schemes in a purely capitalist context – a context that Luxemburg did not think possible. Nonetheless, the ridiculousness of those who claim that the scheme itself proves that there is no limit to capital accumulation is made clear by the regularity of crises throughout the history of capitalism. At the third level of actual historical capital accumulation, Mandel maintains the essential correctness of Luxemburg (Mandel 1978, pp. 66–8).

Luxemburg's most important contemporary critic was Otto Bauer. By rewriting Marx's reproduction schemes so as to include elements only elaborated in the third volume of *Capital* such as the comparatively faster development of Department I, the rising organic composition of capital, the falling rate of profit and the rising mass of profit, Bauer produces a formula that claims to economico-theoretically demonstrate Bernstein's earlier conclusions. As Luxemburg summarised in her *Anti-Critique*, Bauer depicts capitalist production as capable of acting 'without restriction [*schrankenlos*] as its own consumer' and thereby becomes '(objectively) unrestricted [*schrankenlos*] once capitalist production has built a sufficient market for itself.' Bauer's conception thus renders the crises created by capitalism's tendency to exceed the limits of its market incomprehensible, thereby eliminating an understanding of the objective tendencies out of which proletarian consciousness and class struggle emerges and grows – in other words eliminating the scientific basis of the necessity of socialist revolution (Luxemburg 1921, 374–5). Lukács's defence of Luxemburg is particularly indicative with regard to Bauer, as Lukács points to the exclusively methodological usefulness of Marx's schematised purely capitalist society. Marx's positing of a society consisting of only capitalists and workers is an attempt to clarify, as he writes in Volume II, that the 'conditions for the normal course of reproduction, whether simple or on an expanded scale… turn into an equal number of conditions for an abnormal course' and thus necessitate 'possibilities of crisis, since, on the basis of the spontaneous pattern of this production, this balance is itself an accident' (Marx 1885, p. 571). But Marx's hypothetical society by no means serves to conceive accumulation as the concrete totality of the problem but rather, to quote Lukács (1971), 'to see the problem more clearly, before pressing forward to the larger question of the place of this problem within society as a whole' (p. 31). Bauer's attempt to demonstrate the opportunist claim that class antagonisms tend to weaken bases itself in a deeply undialectical or pseudo-dialectical method by bringing problems Marx addresses in Volume III into the accumulation schemes of Volume II.

Dialectical materialism undoubtedly demands determining not only the place of the partial problem within the totality of society, but also the discovery of the determination of the totality within each part. But Bauer only appears to do this by abstractly formulating his solution, or rather dissolution, of the problem of accumulation as the totality of capitalist society. Luxemburg's *Anti-Critique* thus brings us back towards concrete totalisation by reminding us of Marx's own placement of the schemes as a precursor to the elaboration of his theory of crises. Moreover, following the lines laid out in *The Accumulation of Capital*, Luxemburg argues contra Bauer not only that his formulae make the historical reality of crises incomprehensible, but that they also render the growth of imperialistic competition for foreign markets incomprehensible. On this point it might seem correct when Lukács asserts that the opportunists 'suppressed the fact that on this issue *Capital* is an incomplete fragment which stops short at the point where this problem should be opened up' (1971, p. 31). But it appears that the perspective Luxemburg elaborates from the 'Stagnation and Progress of Marxism' through *The Accumulation of Capital* to *Anti-Critique* that, at least in the case of Bernstein and Bauer, the opposite is true: the opportunists treat *Capital* as incomplete fragments to be sampled from and reorganised at will, while the hallmark of Luxemburg's orthodoxy is that, as she writes in 'Stagnation', 'Marx, in his scientific creation, has outstripped us as a party of practical fighters.' This is to say that today we can most adhere to Luxemburg's conception by conceding Mandel's second point – that Marx's reproduction schemes work for a purely capitalist society – and arguing that the confusion of the methodological levels addressed in Mandel's first point can be sorted out by considering the necessary presupposition that pure capitalism concerns the competition of many capitals as a formulation of the abstract totality of capitalist society. In Lukács's terms and in Luxemburg's in *Social Reform or Revolution*, this abstract totality is still the total conception of society belonging to the individual capitalist and the political economist – including opportunistic socialists. It is only from the proletarian revolutionary perspective on crises and imperialism that we can gain a concrete conception of the capitalist totality.

When (in the closing chapter of *The Accumulation of Capital*) Luxemburg introduces militarist production as the only sphere of accumulation that appears to be viable without limits and brings Marx's schemes back into use in her analysis, this must be understood as an historical realisation of their place of in a capitalist totality. It is worth quoting her at some length:

> Whereas the expansion of markets into other spheres as a basis on which capital can operate depends to a large extent on historical, social, and political factors beyond the control of capital, militaristic production constitutes a sphere whose regular surges of expansion appear to be determined in the first instance by the volition of capital itself.
>
> The historical exigencies of capital's intensified competition on a world scale for the conditions of its accumulation are thus transformed into a sphere of accumulation of the highest order for capital itself. The more forcefully capital uses militarism in order to assimilate the means of production and labor-power of noncapitalist countries and societies through foreign and colonial policy, the more powerfully the same militarism works progressively to wrest purchasing power at home, in the capitalist countries themselves, from the noncapitalist strata – i.e. from those engaged in simple commodity production, and from the working class. It does this by robbing the former of their forces of production on an increasing scale, and by reducing the standard of living of the latter, in order to increase the rate of the accumulation of capital enormously at the expense of both. From both sides, however, once a certain level has been reached, the conditions for the accumulation of capital turn into conditions for its demise.
>
> The more violently capital uses militarism to exterminate noncapitalist strata both at home and abroad, and to worsen living standards for all strata of workers, the more the day-to-day history of capital accumulation on the world stage is transformed into a continuous series of political and social catastrophes and convulsions, which, together with the periodic economic cataclysms in the form of crises, will make it impossible for accumulation to continue, and will turn the rebellion of the international

> working class against the rule of capital into a necessity, even before the latter has come up against its natural, selfcreated economic constraints. (Luxemburg 1921, p. 341)

Though it will undoubtedly be necessary to return to a discussion of the details of these conclusions on militarist production, imperialism and socialist revolution, it is with their introduction that we will for now shift attention to the matter of the historical conditions of their emergence as the solution to the problem of accumulation. These conditions will be considered along two lines: first, and more extensively, the theoretical, and second, and more briefly, the practical. It has already been argued that *The Accumulation of Capital* puts to use the neglected conclusions of the first, but also the second and third volumes of Marx's *Capital* – to quote above – 'as historically necessary theoretical weapons for new historical conditions of the practice of class war'. The matter at hand now is to complete this proof beyond the one-sided context of Luxemburg's engagement with opportunism. Theoretically, we see much of the groundwork for the final section of Luxemburg's volume on accumulation laid in her research on the dissolution of primitive communism undertaken during the decade between her essay on stagnation and the publication of her masterpiece. Two texts are of chief concern here, one originally intended as an early chapter in her unfinished *Introduction to Political Economy*, titled by the Anglophone editors of *The Rosa Luxemburg Reader* 'The Dissolution of Primitive Communism' and the second, drawn from the same *Reader* entitled 'Slavery'. These texts represent a period of research elaborating upon the closing section of *Capital*, Volume I to establish the conditions of capitalist primitive accumulation more concretely.

Beginning with 'Slavery,' a number of conclusions from this research are worth considering. Luxemburg draws attention to the uniqueness of slavery as 'the oldest form of class domination and economic exploitation', but finds Friedrich Engels's explanation of the emergence of slavery in his *Anti-Dühring* wanting. Engels argues that following the establishment of private property, war supplied an enslaved workforce to meet the new demand for foreign labour. Luxemburg finds this insufficient. Since slavery emerged subsequent to primitive communism – or the *mark* community, in her generalisation of the German term – it is there that its conditions must be found, rather than in the form of private property as such (Luxemburg 1909–13, p. 111). As Luxemburg demonstrates with reference to the Inca Empire and also to Ancient Greece, prior to the emergence of private property exploitation and servitude had resulted from the conquest of one mark community by another. The grafting of a foreign mark onto another allows for and creates a relationship of exploitation and servitude *toward the outside* preserved by the dominant mark's military aristocracy (p. 112). Thus, slavery and private property intersect with the growing militaristic dissolution of primitive communism, though slavery itself begins as a mode of subjugating conquered labourers to a state of communal property (p. 114). With reference to Aristotle's *Politics* Luxemburg argues that slavery effectuates a complete split between mental and manual labour (p. 120), a split that was initiated with the formation of a militaristic and priestly aristocracy, and that will finally be overturned with the realisation of socialist society (pp. 121–2).

In 'The Dissolution of Primitive Communism' Luxemburg elaborates on the preconditions of slavery and the emergence of military apparatuses as permanent structures. For her, the domination of one mark by another demonstrates that primitive communism has no basis in a general principle of freedom and equality, but merely in the solidarity among the membership of the marks whose traditions of communal property and production hold them together (Luxemburg 1925, p. 78). War functions as a method of solving conflicts of interest between social communities (p. 79), while the military apparatus itself only emerges from the imperative to establish exploitation as a permanent structure (p. 81). On the one hand, war is a method of overcoming limits to production by economic exploitation and subjugation. On the other, those modes of production that must persistently overcome their own limits develop a military aristocracy through which war may become permanent. The demands of intersocietal trade upon the militarily exploitative community bring slavery as a private property form into being, as in Greece (p. 82). In the Americas, Spanish colonialism introduces the debt systems, coerced labour, land grabbing and taxation that crushed the indigenous mark communities, even those that depended upon the military exploitation of other marks (p. 88). European colonialism represents the highest achievement of militarism up to that point by introducing the wholly new phenomena of expropriating the means of production of other societies, completing the collapse of those societies, and subjugating the members of those societies to a new one in which their alternatives are enslavement or extermination (p. 110). Altogether, Luxemburg's 'Slavery' and 'The Dissolution of Primitive Communism' stress militarism rather than private property as the main lever of the drive of the mode of production towards an increasing systemisation of exploitation. As she states in *The Accumulation of Capital*, 'political violence is nothing but a vehicle for the economic process' (Luxemburg 1913, p. xxvi). Indeed, she shows that her orthodoxy exceeds even that of Engels at times, by demonstrating that the origination of class domination and exploitation in slavery is not at all a superstructural effect of private property, but rather a structural effect of the limitations of productive capacity.

Turning now to the practical historical conditions for Luxemburg's *The Accumulation of Capital*, her participation in the 1907 Stuttgart Congress of the Second International will be one of two elements considered. In 1904 a resolution of the Amsterdam Congress of the International called for member parties to study the conditions of colonialism in order to establish the policy of the International. These studies came to fruition in Stuttgart with three days of lengthy reports and debates over the matter (Braunthal 1967, pp. 318–19). At this Congress a Colonial Commission was appointed to draft a majority report highlighting the so-called positive sides of colonialism and resolving for the advocacy of reforms and legal protections for and education of colonised indigenous populations. Though the resolution was defeated by a slim margin, it was made clear that half of those organised endorsed at least the ideological premise upon which the European imperialist powers competed for control over regions of Africa and Asia (Cliff 1958). Thus, an Anti-Militarist Commission was formed that drafted a new resolution, the first draft of which determined militarism to be an extension of capitalism, the end of which would only come with capitalism's own end (Yen-Shih 1965, p. 54). This first draft, as V.I. Lenin wrote on the matter, 'failed to indicate the active tasks of the proletariat' and thereby permitted this orthodox proposition to be viewed through an opportunistic lens (Lenin 1907, p. 80). Georg Heinrich Vollmar demonstrated just this lens when declaring that parliamentary struggle ought to be the exclusive mode of applying pressure on political authority and public opinion (Yen-Shih 1965, p. 53). Luxemburg submitted the following counter-proposal:

> In the event of a threat of war it is the duty of the workers and their parliamentary representatives in the countries involved to do everything possible to prevent the outbreak of war by taking suitable measures, which can of course change or be intensified in accordance with the intensification of the class struggle and the general political situation.
>
> In the event of war breaking out nevertheless, it is their duty to take measures to bring it to an end as quickly as possible, and to utilise the economic and political crisis brought about by the war to arouse the masses of the people and accelerate the overthrow of capitalist class rule. (Quoted in Cliff 1958)

The resolution was passed.

The first chapter to Luxemburg's Junius Pamphlet on *The Crisis in German Social Democracy* (1915) describes the general circumstances leading up to the publication of *The Accumulation of Capital* as well as those that led to her arrest and imprisonment under charges of inciting German soldiers to mutiny against the imperialist military apparatus. It is from prison that she writes:

> Business is flourishing upon the ruins. Cities are turned into shambles, whole countries into deserts, villages into cemeteries, whole nations into beggars, churches into stables… Hunger revolts in Venetia, in Lisbon, in Moscow, in Singapore; pestilence in Russia, misery and desperation is everywhere….And in the midst of this orgy a world tragedy has occurred; the capitulation of the Social Democracy. (Luxemburg 1915, p. 313)

The beginnings of this capitulation could be seen in the opportunist elements of the Second International securing a near-victory in 1907. Nonetheless, the efficacy of the Stuttgart anti-imperialist resolution for securing proletarian revolutionary consciousness and solidarity seems indubitable. In 1911 the official handbook for German socialist voters still maintained the notion that a world war would 'be, in all probability, the last war'. When that summer German imperialists nearly brought on said war by sending the warship *Panther* to Agadir, Morocco, an international socialist meeting in London declared the European labour movement prepared to oppose a declaration of war by any means necessary. A year later, in September on the floor of the German Reichstag, the Social Democratic deputies conveyed the masses' refusal to be instruments of war profiteering, while at the International Peace Congress in November allegiance to the International was maintained as the moral force against the war, with complete willingness to make any sacrifice necessary for the socialist struggle (Luxemburg 1915, pp. 318-19).

According to some accounts, as, for example, in the introduction to the most recent English edition (published by Routledge), *The Accumulation of Capital* represents the product of a 'sudden revelation' that led Luxemburg to unorthodoxy. Even Lukács, in the context of his relocation of the question of orthodoxy from the matter of Marx's system as developed in *Capital* to the method of dialectical materialism, asserted that Luxemburg solves Marx's unfinished problem of accumulation. At the level of theoretical conditions, I have already argued that militarism and imperialism concretise the notion of the abstract totality conceived by Marx – establishing military production as both the site of the reproduction schema's most perfect application and also the pre-eminent social method from primitive communism to capitalism for overcoming even the firmest internal limits to productive expansion. At the level of historical conditions we have seen that, despite the opportunists' claims that capitalist reproductive expansion within its own market becomes increasingly limitless, European militarism marches on while proletarian opposition remains apparently solid. It is here then that we find *The Accumulation of Capital*, perhaps as a revelation, but as the revelation of the derusted theoretical weaponry of scientific socialism, as the utilisation of Marx's ideas in the adequate, which is to say concrete, historical context of Luxemburg's publication. So, though we have found that it was correct of Gramsic to characterise Luxemberg's 'Stagnation and Progress of Marxism' as abstractly formulated, so too do we find the kernel of truth in these formulations concretely realised with the publicication of *The Accumulation of Capital*.

Returning to the longer quote above, the uniqueness of the providence of militarist production should be clear. If militarism is most significantly a motor of economic expansion and a destroyer of the limits posed by non-capitalist social organisation, then it is also necessarily the site of capitalism's purest reproductive form. Insofar as imperialism on the one hand robs simple commodity producers of their means of production while depressing the proletariat's quality of life on the other, it produces capitalism's grave on two counts. On the one hand, imperialism progressively destroys the basis of capital's apparently limitless expansion outside of itself, and on the other it creates the conditions of possibility for its internally productive classes becoming conscious of their fate within the totality. Consequently, Luxemburg's conclusion points to the necessary resolution of these two sides of the dialectic in a socialist revolution. The historical crisis of German Social Democracy indicates precisely this. To quote from the Junius pamphlet,

> The real problem that the world war has placed before the socialist parties, upon whose solution the future of the working class movement depends, *is the readiness of the proletarian mass to act in the fight against imperialism*. The international proletariat suffers, not from a dearth of postulates, programs, and slogans, but from a lack of deeds, of effective resistance, of the power to attack imperialism at the decisive moment, just in times of war. It has been unable to put its old slogan, war against war, into actual practice. Here is the Gordian knot of the proletarian movement and of its future. (Luxemburg 1915, p. 337, emphasis in original)

Luxemburg refuses to accept that the failure to stop the war is a consequence of a failure of the leadership of the proletariat – of Social Democracy's flagging readiness to continue class war against world war. Thus returns Gramsci's initial solution to the problem of the stagnation of Marxist theory – that it encounters its most significant difficulties in combat with the residues of pre-capitalist ideology and that the consciousness of the proletarian mass had not caught up with the imperialist historical reality of capitalism. If this is so, then it is not only a failure to recognise the consequences of imperialism for its own class, but also a failure to recognise the destructive realities of imperialism for non-capitalist social strata at home and abroad – a failure of the mediation of proletarian and non-capitalist social classes (especially peasants) to be realised in a concrete alliance. It is in this very recognition of a historically necessary alliance that the Bolshevik revolution triumphs. In her text on *The Russian Revolution* Luxemburg again invokes the classical image of the Gordian knot, but this time as cut by the conquest of power by the workers and peasants in alliance against imperialist war and for the equitable redistribution of the land (Luxemburg 1922, p. 287).

On the question of land redistribution – as with the question of national self-determination, which shall be dealt with later – we must side with Luxemburg against Lenin and his spokesperson Lukács. Luxemburg acknowledges the tactical excellence of the Bolshevik seizure and distribution of the land by and for the peasants, but criticises it strategically, arguing that this move cannot lead to socialist agriculture on several counts. First, the new socialist economy depends upon the largest estates as those practicing most advanced method of agricultural production (Luxemburg 1922, p. 290), but, most importantly, second, that this immediate seizure and distribution establishes the relatively unassailable barricade of a 'new form of private property' in the form of 'medium and small estates' multiplying rather than eliminating class antagonisms among the peasants by creating a 'newly developed and powerful mass of owning peasants who will defend their newly won property with tooth and nail against every socialist attack' (p. 292). Lukács responds to this argument, stating that Luxemburg overemphasises to the point of misrecognition the conscious proletarian character of the revolution and fails to acknowledge the ideological significance of the party sufficiently. Accordingly, Lukács argues that Luxemburg does not comprehend the significance of the participation of non-proletarians (and especially peasants) in the Bolshevik revolution, because she overestimates the organic, spontaneous forces of the revolution (Lukács 1971, pp. 274–5). On the contrary, what we must now demonstrate is that the question of spontaneity vis-à-vis socialist revolution is one of the socialist revolutionary consciousness of the masses rather than the organised consciousness of the party. In other words, the problem is the maintenance of dialectical materialism in and through popular combat with pre- and non-capitalist ideologies.

On this subject, it is necessary to make a detour through the theory of two of the foremost anti-imperialist dialectical materialists of the 20th century – Mao Tse-tung and Aimé Césaire. Let us begin with Tse-tung's classic essay 'On Contradiction' (1937). The overarching reminder here is that the universal dimension of a given contradiction resides in its particularity (p. 72). Tse-tung elaborates this by introducing the notions of the principal contradiction and the principal aspect of the contradiction. In the case of capitalist society the principal contradiction – that which determines all other contradictions – is the relationship between labour and capital. But in a colonial or semi-colonial society the principal contradiction may shift – when the nation is united against imperialism, the principal contradiction is between the colonisers and the colonised, but in conditions of neo-colonialism, wherein the imperialists are in alliance with an indigenous ruling class, the principal contradiction is between the indigenous masses and rulers. The principal aspect in any case is the dominant and therefore determining side of a given contradiction, while the overturning of a given contradiction produces a qualitatively new contradiction by means of the determinations of the newly ascended principal aspect. In these terms, we defend Luxemburg against Lukács by arguing that the tactical success but strategic failure of Bolshevik land policy is not an underestimation of the non-proletarian participation in the revolution, but rather the failure to resolve the contradiction between socialist industry and agriculture by allowing the principal contradiction between the feudal landlords and the peasants to resolve into a new, more complex and distributed principal contradiction between the medium estate owning peasant-capitalists and the small estate-owning peasants. In Paul Mattick's 1935 essay 'Luxemburg Versus Lenin' he terms this 'the capitalisation of agriculture'. Put differently, Luxemburg does not fail to see the significance of the party but rather appropriately estimates the significance of the contradictions of Russian agricultural society for Russian socialism as a whole.

We turn to Aimé Césaire's 1956 resignation from the French Communist Party next, as a fundamental text of anti-imperialist socialist theory, particularly on the question of consciousness. Césaire was, to those who do not know him or his work, the author of both the masterpiece of modernist African diasporic poetry entitled *Notebook of a Return to the*

Native Land, published in 1939, and the classic of anti-imperialist literature *Discourse on Colonialism*, published in 1955, as well as the secondary school teacher of Frantz Fanon, and, finally, a communist politician of note in his indigenous Martinique. As Césaire writes in his resignation 'Letter to Maurice Thorez', racialised peoples in their struggles against colonial powers 'have come to grasp, in [their] consciousness, the full breadth of [their] singularity, and are ready to assume on all levels and in all areas the responsibilities that flow from this coming to consciousness' asserting that in their anti-colonial and anti-racist – their anti-imperial – struggle their historical consciousness and practice cannot be relegated to outside the principal contradiction (Césaire 1956, p. 147), as it had not been only in capitalist but also in the Communist International's ideology – the latter according to which metropolitan-centred worker's anti-capitalist struggle was principal (Césaire 1956, p. 150). Typical of this Eurocentrism was Jean Paul-Sartre's essay 'Black Orpheus' concerning the poetry of Césaire and others associated with the concept of 'Négritude'. Sartre writes of Négritude 'as the minor moment of a dialectical progression' in which it is a purely negative phenomenon posed against white supremacist imperialism. Négritude is thus a 'subjective, existential, ethnic notion' to be surpassed 'into the objective, positive and precise, notion of the *proletariat*' in the class struggle with capitalism (Sartre 1948, p. 137).

Césaire's resignation reminds us then and now of the consequences of segregating particulars and universals by asserting a need to think their mediation – his 'conception of the universal is that of a universal enriched by all that is particular' – according to which he 'consider[ed] it our duty to combine our efforts with those of all men with a passion for justice and truth, in order to build organizations susceptible of honesty and effectively helping black peoples in their struggle for today and for tomorrow' – in other words, to build 'organizations capable…of preparing them' to operate in an 'autonomous manner' (Césaire 1956, p. 152). The question at hand is precisely that of the proper mediation between socialist revolutionary consciousness and that of so-called pre- or non-capitalist consciousness. In 'rural and peasant societies… in which the working class is tiny and… the middle classes have a political importance out of proportion', is 'effective action by communist organizations acting in isolation' possible at all (Césaire 1956, p. 147)? In the anti-imperial context Césaire proposes that Marxists ought to operate so as to inspire and focus rather than divide popular organising (Césaire 1956, p. 148). This inspiration and focus must aid rather than oppose popular unity formulated along lines of cultural consciousness since it is precisely the unity of colonised peoples that conditions an overthrow of imperialism in the colonies. In other words, it could be said that Sartre has merely abstractly formulated the facts and presented this abstraction as a solution to the problem at hand.

By conceiving the question of socialist revolutionary consciousness in the struggle of colonised peoples as a historical problem of effectuating the proper mediation between Marxism and predominantly peasant popular organising, Césaire presents a dialectical materialist conception of the problem Gramsci described for us earlier and which Luxemburg and Lenin debated. At the conclusion of his *Discourse on Colonialism*, Césaire asserts that the salvation of Europe and all of the metropole depends upon the success of the universal mission of the proletariat (Césaire 1955, p. 78). This success is only possible based on the practice of solidarity between the working classes and rural colonised peoples, since alongside industrial production there is what Césaire terms 'the factory for the production of lackeys' at work 'spitting out its cinders in the hearts of our forests or deep in the bush' (Césaire 1955, p. 77). Just as Luxemburg articulates for us the internal contradictions of capital that create imperialism, whereby 'Capital increasingly employs militarism for implementing a foreign and colonial policy to get hold of the means of production and labour power of non-capitalist countries and societies', Césaire describes the parallel movement of imperialism's ideological and practical degradation of colonised peoples, an ideology and practice that produces a 'boomerang effect' with the rise of fascism in Europe (Césaire 1955, p. 36, 41). In the name of solidarity, Césaire asserts the need for a European proletarian 'policy of *nationalities*... founded on respect for peoples and cultures' (Césaire 1955, p. 77), while Luxemburg in her Junius pamphlet presciently reminds us that although 'International Socialism recognizes the right of free independent nations with equal rights... Socialism alone can create such nations', for in the context of the capitalist totality 'imperialistic world policies determine and regulate the inner and the outer life of a nation' (Luxemburg 1915, p. 325). The contradiction of the two positions is quite easily resolved with support from each. On the one hand, respect for peoples and cultures demands, among other things, recognition of the real achievement of solidarity belonging to so-called 'primitive' communist or communalist societies – even if this solidarity has at times confined itself to within said communities. On the other hand, international socialism is based on degrees of but also creates conditions for the independence of peoples and cultures insofar as the destruction of capitalism from within itself is nothing more than the destruction of imperialism from without. In short, solidarity and autonomy are as distinct as they are inextricable – not merely in the communist future, but also in the struggles of the present, historically variant as the manner of their mediation may be. The importance of autonomy, among other things, may explain why Luxemburg never proposed concrete policies to colonised peoples abroad, though she persistently referred to imperialism to motivate socialist struggle in Europe (Nettl 1966, p. 535).

All of this returns us to where we left the debate between Bolshevism and Luxemburg. For as Lenin, Lukács and the history of the Communist International would indicate, Bolshevism commits itself to a form of solidarity with peasants and other non-proletarian exploited classes whose opportunism makes a show of promoting self-determination while not taking seriously the principality of contradictions other than those between organised capital and industrial labour. Before returning to Luxemburg, it is worth addressing Lenin directly. Consider *What Is to Be Done?*, published in 1902 several years before the events in Russia that would inspire Luxemburg to write *The Mass Strike* in 1906. Lenin's book develops the critique of spontaneism that would become, along with its inverse of economism, one of the main charges levelled against Luxemburg, but pays particular attention to the strike and imperialism especially. Lenin criticises what he calls the 'worship of spontaneity' on the basis of the historical necessity to revise socialist revolutionary tactics. Since the then present form of workers' struggle – predominantly trade-unionist – is deemed insufficient, the basis of socialist unity must start with drawing distinctions of principle and practice (Lenin 1902, p. 365). Though, as Lenin writes following Marx's *Critique of the Gotha Programme*, entering 'into agreements to satisfy the practical aims of the movement' must at times be necessary to maintain unity, scientific socialism ought to make no theoretical compromises since '[w]ithout revolutionary theory there can be no revolutionary movement' (Lenin 1902, p. 369). The similarity here between Lenin and Luxemburg on opportunism should come as no surprise, since Lenin attributed both economism and the worship of spontaneity to Bernstein and other opportunists in this very book, as well as elsewhere.

It is from the importance of theory and the historical emergence of scientific socialism that Lenin underlines the significance of party organisation. Though workers' struggle arises out of the antagonism with capital, Lenin argues that scientific socialism not only was but had to be brought to workers from without. Since trade union consciousness is the extent of workers' spontaneous self-knowledge, bourgeois intellectuals like Marx and Engels could have only synthesised the philosophical, historical, and economic theories into the form we know as Marxism. Similarly, the formation of a revolutionary socialist intelligentsia in Russia committed to scientific socialism could not spontaneously emerge out of the workers' movement (Lenin 1902, p. 364). At this point the difference between Lenin and Luxemburg becomes clearer – for it will be recalled from the discussion of her 'Stagnation' essay, that her position (which I have asserted to be one of the hallmarks of her orthodoxy) is that the conditions of struggle push forward the refurbishing of Marxist theory, even if it is true that revolutionary theory itself is a precondition for revolutionary struggle. Lenin's assertion that 'there can be no talk of an independent ideology formulated by the working masses themselves in the process of their movement' (Lenin 1902, p. 384) is actually assumed by Luxemburg when she provides her historical analysis of the causes of Marxist theoretical stagnation – recall, after all, her agreement with Gramsci that it is only with the overthrow of class conditions that a true workers' science, or for that matter art, will be possible. One could only assume that Luxemburg would agree with Lenin when he writes of the necessity of Social Democracy to 'take up actively the political education of the working class and the development of its political consciousness' (Lenin 1902, p. 164). What would seem to be the danger, and which undoubtedly resonates in hindsight, is that socialist revolutionary leadership – that is, the party – comes to mistake itself for general socialist revolutionary consciousness, whether among the urban workers or any other exploited class. This danger should by no means paralyse socialist struggle 'since', as Luxemburg reminds us in *Social Reform or Revolution*, 'the proletariat is absolutely obliged to seize power "too early" once or several times before it can enduringly maintain itself in power' and as such continue the withering away of the state and class society. It is for this reason that we must not seek to validate, or for that matter demonise, one particular form of socialist revolutionary organisation – whether in control of the state or not – but instead historicise them. As Luxemburg also points out in the same passage, the transition to socialist society will not begin with 'one act, by a victorious blow of the proletariat' (Luxemburg 1899, p. 15). Against Lukács, who in defence of Lenin's brand of orthodoxy claims Luxemburg overvalues mass spontaneity and undervalues party organisation, we must take seriously her writing on mass strikes.

We have now seen how Lukács's critique of Luxemburg's distinction between the tactical success and the strategic failure of Bolshevik land policy may be rejected. For it is not merely in hindsight that Luxemburg sought to insist on this distinction. Lukács writes that 'Luxemburg overlooks the choice between "impure" socialist necessities which fate forced upon the proletarian revolution right from the start' insofar as the ascendance of the revolutionary party demanded a specific consolidation of forces. The point is that the overemphasis on organisation and a certain kind of decisive action risks undermining socialist revolutionary principles and the growth of socialist revolutionary consciousness among all exploited classes such that anything more than an opportunistic consolidation of forces may be possible. In other words, Luxemburg criticises Bolshevist policy from the perspective of future socialist strategy – not out of a desire to invalidate proletarian state power, but so as to be wary of creating and recreating an intractable situation of state capitalism that garbs itself in socialist ideology. Acknowledging this, Luxemburg's largely positive appraisal of the Russian Revolution emphasises the 'driving force… of the mass of the urban proletariat' that the Bolsheviks had managed to galvanise in solidarity with the peasants to cut through the Gordian knot of imperialism (Luxemburg 1922, pp. 285–7).

Turning to the matter of mass strikes, it is important to clarify the relationship between Luxemburg's discussion of strikes and the publication of *The Accumulation of Capital.* From the perspective of her biographer J.P. Nettl, following the Russian Revolution of 1905 Luxemburg's conception of the role of the party moved towards considering organisation 'a potential hindrance, cohesion a factor of immobility, [and] tradition a dead weight', all of which she believed the revolution demonstrated could be brought back into dynamism when confronted by enthusiastic mass action (Nettl 1966, p. 513). According to the view I have sought to articulate, since at least 1903 Luxemburg had attributed a propulsive force to the practice of struggle as orthodox as the *Theses on Feuerbach* at least as early as 1903, though undoubtedly *The Mass Strike* took her conception thereof to a new level. Of particular interest today is Nettl's claim that Luxemburg's 'preoccupation with imperialism... arose directly out of the mass-strike discussion' (Nettl 1966, p. 519). One connection between imperialism and the mass strike has already been alluded to in the above citation of Luxemburg's resolution at the 1907 Stuttgart Congress – wherein it was resolved that any means necessary should be deployed by the workers and their party to prevent the threat of an oncoming imperialist war. The chronology of conception that Nettl lays out is as follows: 'we first have a mass-strike doctrine, then a struggle for its application, next a dissatisfaction with party policy against a background of personal disenchantment, and finally the development of a doctrine of imperialism in order to overcome the party's recalcitrance' (Nettl 1966, pp. 519–20). Much like the introduction to the current Routledge English edition of *Accumulation*, Nettl describes Luxemburg's concern with imperialism as 'visionary' and an 'inspiration' (Nettl 1966, p. 493) – a glowing appraisal that nonetheless, next to the 'background of personal disenchantment', risks implying that Luxemburg's so-called 'preoccupation' with imperialism exceeds the bounds of an orthodox reading of Marx.

It has already been demonstrated how Luxemburg's analysis of imperialism historically arrives at a conception of the concrete totality – passing from the practical concern with militarism at Stuttgart to the theory thereof that emerges out of her research on slavery and the dissolution of primitive communism to the historical political economy of *The Accumulation of Capital* and thereafter. This work arrives amid an internal struggle in Social Democracy to withstand the bourgeois imperialist influence of opportunism by putting to use Marx's once-rusted weaponry. Imperialism is precisely the capitalist totality in its militaristic destruction of non-capitalist social strata, at home as much as abroad, including the immobilisation of the revolutionary potential of Social Democracy. Though it may not have been framed in these terms initially, it is the mass strike that appears in Luxemburg as the proletarian counterforce to this immobilisation and to imperialism as a whole (Nettl 1966, pp. 519–47). Nonetheless, Luxemburg insisted that '[i]f anyone were to undertake to make the mass strike generally as a form of proletarian action the object of methodical agitation' it would be as much of a waste of effort as to reify any other form of revolution and proselytise them.

What was to be propagandised is not a strategic analysis of the tactical form, but the historical contexts of intensifying class struggle which have informed it. 'The mass strike has now become the center of the lively interest of the German and the international working class because it is a new form of struggle, and as such is the sure symptom of a thoroughgoing internal revolution in the relations of the classes and in the conditions of class struggle', Luxemburg writes (Luxemburg 1906, p. 171). Mass strikes make possible an awakening of class feeling and consciousness because they themselves are a spectacular expression of it – in them 'undercurrents of the social process of the revolution cross one another, check one another, and increase the internal contradictions of the revolution' through an overall intensification of circumstances (Luxemburg 1906, pp. 181–2). The most lasting repercussion of the mass wave is not a particular form of action but an enlivening intellectualisation of the necessity and conditions of action, a consciousness that lays the basis for further economic and political struggle (Luxemburg 1906, p. 185). Contrary to accusations of economism, Luxemburg's argument is that the political mass actions that emerge from socialist revolutionary consciousness dissolve after their pinnacle into a mass of economic strikes, that the refinement of political struggle effectuates a further spread and formalisation of the economic struggle–as she writes in short, 'the economic struggle is the transmitter from one political center to another; the political struggle is the periodic fertilization of the soil for the economic struggle' (Luxemburg 1906, pp. 194–5). The theory of the mass strike is that it in practice effectuates a consciousness amenable to dialectical materialism insofar as the reciprocal action of the economic and the political is precisely what it displays.

For scientific socialism to be efficacious, Marxists must work within the class struggle to support the formation of class-consciousness in and through mass action by themselves taking principled and consistent action–for it is our project to inspire 'in the masses a feeling of security, self-confidence and desire for struggle' (Luxemburg 1906, p. 199). The basis of this action must of course be our knowledge of the concrete totality of capitalism–and the dialectic of solidarity and autonomy this knowledge demands in the face of imperialism. *The Accumulation of Capital* is a crucial weapon in our struggle, for it elaborates to us the conditions that have made necessary a commitment to internationalist anti-imperialist struggle. Just as it emerges thoroughly out of the historical conditions it analyses, so too does it remind us that our work today demands an orthodoxy based in the international intensification of the class struggle–not only the lengths capital goes to avoid its ever more gaping grave, but also those mass actions of all the exploited that dig it.

Bibliography

Braunthal, J. (1967). *History of the international: Volume 1: 1863–1914.* New York: Frederick A. Praeger.

Césaire, A. [1955] (2000). *Discourse on colonialism.* New York: Monthly Review Press.

Césaire, A. [1956] (2010). Letter to Maurice Thorez. *Social Text, 28*(2), 145–152.

Cheng, Y.-S. (1965). The struggle at the Stuttgart Congress. In *Lenin's fight against revisionism and opportunism.* Peking: Foreign Language Press.

Cliff, T. [1958] (2008). *Rosa Luxemburg.* London: Bookmarks. https://www.marxists.org/archive/cliff/works/1959/rosalux/

Gramsci, A. (1971). *Selections from the prison notebooks.* New York: International Publishers.

Lenin, V. I. [1902] (1960). What is to be done? In *Lenin: Collected works* (Vol. 5). Moscow: Progress Publishers.

Lenin, V. I. [1907] (1962). The International Socialist Congress in Stuttgart In *Lenin: Collected works* (Vol. 13). Moscow: Progress Publishers.

Lukács, G. (1971). *History and class consciousness*. London: The Merlin Press.
Luxemburg, R. [1899] (2004). Social reform or revolution. In P. Hudis and K. Anderson (Eds.), *The Rosa Luxemburg reader*. New York: Monthly Review Press.
Luxemburg, R. [1903] (2000). *Stagnation and progress of Marxism in Rosa Luxemburg Internet archive*. https://www.marxists.org/archive/luxemburg/1903/misc/stagnation.htm
Luxemburg, R. [1906] (2004). The mass strike, the political party, and the trade unions. In P. Hudis and K. Anderson (Eds.), *The Rosa Luxemburg reader*. New York: Monthly Review Press.
Luxemburg, R. [1909–13] (2013). Slavery. In P. Hudis (Ed.), *The complete works of Rosa Luxemburg. Volume I, Economic writings 1* (pp. 301–329). London: Verso.
Luxemburg, R. [1913] (2013). The accumulation of capital. In P. Hudis and P. LeBlanc (Eds.), *The complete works of Rosa Luxemburg volume II, Economic writings 2* (pp. 89–300). London: Verso.
Luxemburg, R. [1915] (2004). The Junius Pamphlet: The crisis in Germany social democracy. In P. Hudis and K. Anderson (Eds.), *The Rosa Luxemburg reader*. New York: Monthly Review Press.
Luxemburg, R. [1921] (2015). The accumulation of capital–An anti-critique. In P. Hudis and P. LeBlanc (Eds.), *The complete works of Rosa Luxemburg. Volume II, Economic writings 2* (pp. 345–449). London: Verso.
Luxemburg, R. [1922] (2004). The Russian revolution. In P. Hudis and K. Anderson, (Eds.), *The Rosa Luxemburg reader*. New York: Monthly Review Press.
Luxemburg, R. [1925] (2004). The dissolution of primitive communism. In P. Hudis and K. Anderson (Eds.), *The Rosa Luxemburg reader* (pp. 71–109). New York: Monthly Review Press.
Mandel, E. [1978] (1992). Introduction. In K. Marx, *Capital, volume II*. London: Penguin Books.
Marx, K. [1885] (1992). *Capital, volume II*. London: Penguin Books.
Mattick, P. [1935] (2005). *Luxemburg versus Lenin*. London: Merlin Press. https://www.marxists.org/archive/mattick-paul/1935/luxemburg-lenin.htm
Nettl, J. P. (1966). *Rosa Luxemburg, volume 2*. London: Oxford University Press.
Sartre, J.-P. [1948] (2001). Black orpheus. In R. Bernasconi (Ed.), *Race* (pp. 115–141). Oxford: Blackwell Publishers.
Tse-Tung, M. [1937] (2007). On contradiction. In *On practice and contradiction*. Brooklyn: Verso.

2

Rosa Luxemburg and Contemporary Capitalism

Greg Albo

Introduction

Rosa Luxemburg (1871–1919) occupies an unusual place in the traditions of the western, and indeed, global Left, being met variously by scorn, silence and veneration. This is a response, in the first instance, to her powerful political interventions and ceaseless invocation of revolution to break the hammerlock of capitalism on democracy and development. But it is also a reflection of the reaction that greeted her major economic text, *The Accumulation of Capital* (1913), when it was first published just over a hundred years ago, and the abjuration that still greets that text among social scientists and militants today.

For modern social democracy, it has been all but impossible to avoid judging Luxemburg with scorn: hopelessly insurrectionist and naively idealist in the face of a necessary political realism. Her masterpiece

G. Albo (✉)
Department of Political Science, York University, Toronto, ON, Canada

J. Dellheim, F.O. Wolf (eds.), *Rosa Luxemburg: A Permanent Challenge for Political Economy*, DOI 10.1057/978-1-137-60108-7_2

polemic, *Reform and Revolution* (1900), remains, even for readers today, a blistering assault on revisionism, and for modern social democracy an unforgivable breach. For them, its political determinism misread political evolutions in the same way that *The Accumulation of Capital* misunderstood the changing dynamics of accumulation.

Although the official communist parties, from the Bolsheviks after Lenin onwards, turned her into a heroine, Luxemburg's actual political and economic writings were met with silence. The searing critique of democracy within the post-revolutionary context was too filled with minefields for open discussion; and they had to be sealed off as these parties Stalinised and theoretically ossified (Josef Stalin himself linked Luxemburg with Leon Trotsky's theories of uneven development, which was for him the ultimate heresy). *The Accumulation of Capital*, moreover, rivalled V.I. Lenin's *Imperialism* (1917) as the pre-eminent critique of imperialism and yielded fewer certainties that capitalism had reached its highest stage, was now over-ripe and losing its economic dynamism. In any case, the thesis of state monopoly capitalism – claiming that the capitalist economy was becoming absorbed into the state – came to dominate the theoretical perspective of the communist parties. Little theoretical space remained for the political and market turbulence that Luxemburg theorised, and her texts, in turn, left no allowance for an evolutionary transformation from state capitalism to socialism.

In contrast, within the Trotskyist movement (or at least most of it), Luxemburg gained a place in the pantheon of great thinkers as the revolutionary alternative to both the imperialist countries and Stalinism in the Soviet Union, and as a thinker coming to grips with the thesis of uneven development. This status revolved around her political writings: *Reform and Revolution* (1900) and *The Junius Pamphlet: The Crisis of Social Democracy* (1915), of course, but also *Organizational Questions of Russian Social Democracy* (1904) and *The Mass Strike, the Political Party and Trade Unions* (1906). The last, despite often being characterised crudely and erroneously by sympathisers and detractors alike as support for spontaneous resistance without regard for political strategy, actually subtly combined the insistence on the capacity for revolt and organisation of the masses with the recognition of the necessary role of the socialist party. But even in the Trotskyist political tendencies where Luxemburg has become an authoritative figure, *The Accumulation of Capital* remained little mentioned, except in passing as a forerunner to Lenin's *Imperialism*, and usually only for pointing to the historical passages on primitive accumulation and to the role of militarism in supporting capital accumulation.

With the New Left in the 1960s, however, a quite different assessment of Luxemburg began to emerge that broke out of these political frames. The appeal of Luxemburg was, at least initially, quite obvious: her political position outside of the ever more imprisoning polarities of authoritarian communism and social democracy; the emphasis on radical democracy to upset the organisational sclerosis of unions and leftist parties; the resounding trumpet for participatory democracy; and the focus, found in the *Accumulation of Capital*, on imperialism and colonial occupations (a theme converging directly with the mass attention given to the decolonisation revolts and dependency theory at the time). As the New Left embarked on a highly charged re-assessment of all the major thinkers of socialism, from Karl Marx and Lenin to Georg Lukács, Karl Kautsky and Antonio Gramsci, to Paul Sweezy and Maurice Dobb, among others, it was impossible not to confront – and be surprised by – Luxemburg. She was, after all, a thinker deeply embedded in the Second International, with its direct lineages in organisation and theory to Marx and Frederick Engels; politically lionised for her resolute stance against Social Democracy's acquiescence to the debacle of World War 1, for her prescient critique of Bolshevik ruling practices in post-1917 Russia, and, moreover, her martyrdom in the failed German revolution.

The reclamation of Luxemburg's theoretical and strategic legacies by the New Left, however, still largely ignored her economic writings. Even the *Monthly Review* school, the foremost defenders of modern underconsumption theory (as a secular trend in capitalism toward stagnation), kept its distance, in line with Sweezy's sharp critique of Luxemburg's economic theory in his *Theory of Capitalist Development* (1942). Dependency theorists did pick up some of the themes of Luxemburg, but in keeping with what Robert Brenner (1977) accurately described as their 'neo-Smithian' approach, they focused on what Luxemburg wrote about the inequalities of exchange, and were less concerned with her theoretical points of departure rooted in value theory, analysis of capitalist reproduction schemes and of the economic forces driving inter-imperial rivalries.

For the New Left, Luxemburg's economics were too associated with the theory of economic breakdown, and her famous counter-position between socialism and barbarism also struck a discordant chord in the face of the long post-war boom, the rise of mass consumption and the absorption of working-class citizenship into parliamentary proceduralism. Moreover, as the crisis of the 1970s emerged amidst an accelerating pace of inflation and the intense distributional struggles over wages and social benefits, its characteristics seemed to have little to do with Luxemburg's identification of the sources and limits on effective demand in capitalist economies. As the crisis wore on, the theoretical and political diagnosis of the 'contradictions of Keynesianism', Luxemburg's political writings once again provided political validation for the extra-parliamentary union and political struggles sweeping across the core capitalist states. But there was still little incentive to withdraw the negative verdict on her economics.

The dichotomy in assessment between Luxemburg's political strategising and her economic theory has been long-standing within Marxian political economy. But this is, we will argue following recent re-readings of Luxemburg, somewhat partial and one-sided and underestimates the way Luxemburg's intervention advanced socialist economic theory. The *Accumulation of Capital* was published in 1913 and falls in the middle of her economic writings. It came after her PhD thesis on Polish capitalism (1897), and her extensive writing in the SPD (*Sozialdemokratische Partei Deutschlands*) press on the changing structure of the world market as Britain declined and the USA and Germany rose to prominence. These were themes carried over into her polemic with Eduard Bernstein over the ways that the 'new' capitalism was transforming both crises and classes; and later contentions that the capitalist world market was far from being superseded or in a final crisis, as the imperialist powers were re-dividing the world market. And it came before the *Anti-Critique* response to her critics and her *Introduction to Political Economy* (both published posthumously in 1921 and 1925 respectively) where she more thoroughly lays out the key questions about capitalism she is concerned with and vigorously defends her answers against both her critics and rival interpretations.[1] When these texts are laid out together, rather than

[1] The *Introduction to Political Economy* was based on lecture notes drafted for her teaching in the SPD party school before she wrote *The Accumulation of Capital*, and only part of the manuscript was located when published. It is clear that she is following Marx in being engaged, in the famous subtitle to *Capital*, in a critique of political economy.

partitioned to the side, the themes of her theoretical project – and its importance – gain clarity.

Capitalism, for Luxemburg, is an economic system that takes hold across the world market and remorselessly draws new sectors into it; as a monetary economy, capitalism is animated by the accumulation of capital in its money-form, intertwining the sphere of circulation with the sphere of production but with its own dynamics and requisites for circulation to sustain itself on an expanded basis. As such, the money-commodity and loan-capital are, for capitalism, central conditions for economic reproduction. Capitalism, in itself as an economic system driven by competition to expansion, had to continually find mechanisms to resolve the problem of adequate effective demand and to compel capitalists to invest their money-balances into productive inputs. In this way, Luxemburg returned to a core theme of classical political economy, but now restated it as a fundamental dilemma for the capitalist system, which could be subjected to historical investigation and probed for its political implications. '[H]ow is the capitalist economy possible?' she asked in her *Introduction to Political Economy*: '[T]he capitalist economy, which in view of its total lack of planning, its lack of any conscious organisation, is at first sight something impossible, an inextricable puzzle, can nevertheless exist and function as a whole' (1925, p. 293). For Luxemburg, this was also, to be sure, to pose the question in reverse: what would make a capitalist economy 'impossible' (p. 295)?

The Accumulation of Capital

Written in just a span of months (Frolich 1939), *The Accumulation of Capital* is one of the classic books in Marxian political economy, alongside those of Hilferding, Kautsky, Bauer, and Lenin, among others – that emerged from the milieu of the Second International and attempted to address the many paradoxes and silences left in Marx's notoriously incomplete project. While Marx identified the competitive imperatives of capital accumulation that form the basis for the economic divisions of the world market, he did not propose any theory of imperialism to explain the competitive processes or the forms of interdependence and rivalry between states that the divisions of the world market generate. By the turn to the 20th century, the foremost Marxist thinkers during the Second International could not avoid taking these issues up (Barone 1985; Brewer 1980). The new theories of the economics of imperialism that emerged addressed the 'organised capitalism' of monopolies, cartels, banks and finance, alongside new mass production factory-centred labour processes; an emerging state capitalism in the form of tariffs and regulations spreading across the entire spectrum of economic activity, including military production; and the internationalisation of capital in its various forms from commodities to bank-capital to direct investments.

Rudolph Hilferding contended that competition in 'organised capitalism' was characterised by banks fusing with industry to form finance capital which, in turn, exported capital in search of markets for investment and trade. For Lenin, the export of capital defined imperialism as the monopoly stage of capitalism as competition between rival firms transformed into inter-state conflict over control of markets and territory. Whereas Kautsky suggested that the cartels and national states might cooperate in a policy of imperialism, Lenin held the view that uneven development compelled continual competition. For Nikolai Bukharin, however, the 'world economy as a system of production relations and, correspondingly of exchange relations on a world scale' produced not one but two tendencies forming imperialism. As he put it, 'together with… the internationalisation of capital, there is going on a process of "national" intertwining of capital, a process of "nationalising" capital' (1917, pp. 25–6, 80).

Luxemburg's historical excavations of colonialism were also very much concerned with dissecting the evolution of the forces driving the militarism and imperialism of her time, arguing that capitalist social relations restricted the basis for realisation and thus necessitated the search for external trade outlets in pre-capitalist societies (and thus *Accumulation*'s subtitle – *A Contribution to an Economic Explanation of Imperialism*). But if Hilferding's *Finance Capital* (1901) garnered widespread praise and emulation, Luxemburg's book was subject to vigorous 'scientific critique' for its errors, not least from Otto Bauer and Bukharin. This began the long neglect of her economic contribution, as a result of which there has been an unfortunate failure to recognise the theoretical space opened up by Luxemburg through the crucial questions she posed about capitalist development.[2] A brief summary is in order.

The *Accumulation of Capital* is laid out in three parts: Part I provides the initial thesis on the problem of effective demand and outlets for commodities produced as capital accumulates and productive capacity expands; in the second part, she surveys various approaches to effective demand and how limits to demand might be resolved; and in the third, she advances her own argument (moving from abstract reproduction schemes to concrete mechanisms) on how the problem of adequate effective demand in the capitalist sector and core zones of accumulation has been resolved historically through 'external outlets'.

The architecture of the text alone suggests that Luxemburg's purpose is not about revising Marx's problematic pertaining to the production of capital as set out in Volume I of *Capital*. Instead, the *Accumulation of Capital* addresses and attempts to elaborate, as she sees it, the circulation of capital and the necessary conditions for expanded reproduction as set out in Volume II. In Volume I of *Capital*, Marx demonstrates the production of capital – and the capital-relation – from the generation of surplus labour and values from the exploitation of the waged-labour working class through the commodity-form, the *differentia specifica* of capitalism as an economic system. From this thesis, Marx attempts to specify the determinants of the magnitude of surplus value; the pre-conditions that allow the continual expanded reproduction of capital through technological change and the expansion of fixed capital (dead labour displacing living labour) through an accumulation of the means of production; and the production of new value from living labour stemming from an ever-expanding and readily-available supply of workers who are dependent upon the sale of their labour-power in the market to attain their means of subsistence.[3]

[2] An exception was Lukács (1924, pp. 131–32). He linked Kautsky's 'strategy of attrition' to his political compromises leading into World War I and his thesis of imperialism as 'chance development'. In contrast, Luxemburg's writings on the necessity of imperialism were matched by her strategy of the mass strike.

[3] Trincado (2010, pp. 153–54) argues that Luxemburg also departs from important aspects of Marx's positions on the surplus in Volume I.

In Volume II, Marx turns to the circulation of capital (the theoretical issues of the production of capital being proposed in Volume I), and the necessary conditions of exchange that would make capital accumulation possible; but he also considers the possibility of economic breakdown. To do so, Marx develops a two-sector model of capitalist production, wherein Department I is posited to produce the means of production and Department II the means of consumption. From here, it is possible to lay out the conditions for simple reproduction (that is to say, where there is no accumulation) by determining the exchange between the two departments of means of consumption and means of production in both physical and value terms. All that is produced is consumed between the two departments in a given period of the turnover of capital.[4]

But as Luxemburg and others pointed out, the highly abstract and restrictive conditions of simple reproduction only clarify certain conditions for stability: it hardly represents capitalism as we know it theoretically as a system of endless accumulation and historically as it has existed on the world market. The conditions for expanded reproduction as developed by Marx, however, begin to clarify the issues at hand and the continual chaos and adjustments that are essential to capitalist production. In this case, there is a need for a surplus in the production of means of production that can be exchanged for a portion of the surplus value of the capitalist classes and capitalised into 'new capital'. If capitalist competition continually forces new investments in fixed capital (via relative surplus value techniques), the value of means of production and the output of Department I will tend to increase relative to Department II. That is, there are conditions of exchange that will provide stable expanded reproduction but these cannot be guaranteed. Capitalist development is moreover characterised by an increasing proportion of annual output (and thus labour-power) being absorbed into the production of means of production. This is the thesis presented in Volume I as the tendency

[4] In Volume 3, Marx in particular addressed the transformation of direct values into prices of production, the formation of the average rate of profit, the division of new value-added into their various revenue forms and the falling rate of profit and its counter-tendencies. It needs recalling that the falling rate of profit theory as the 'orthodox' interpretation of Marx's crisis theory emerged after the end of the Second International with the work of Henryk Grossman, and developed by Joseph Gillman, Shane Mage, Ernest Mandel and Anwar Shaikh.

for 'dead labour' to displace 'living labour' as relative surplus value techniques are deployed, and in the schemas of Volume II that capitalist competition drives ahead the development of the forces of production in Department I to create the economic conditions for expanded reproduction. But, from the standpoint of circulation, these same conditions are made more difficult to attain and more dependent on means of exchange, credit-money and so forth.

If Marx presents in Volume II, across his numerous schemas, the conditions of possibility for both accumulation and crisis, for Luxemburg he nevertheless fails to address a crucial question. If capitalism is a monetary economy, and if it is individual capitalist agents who must invest in new capital, where does the increase in effective demand that will take up the expanded output of means of production come from? For Luxemburg, this is not a problem of classical underconsumptionism in which the workers lack the income to purchase the goods produced, or of the limited capacity of capitalists for sufficient increased consumption to compensate for this; it is a problem of the effective demand for the realisation of the surplus value that is to come from reinvestment in means of production. Who would purchase the new means of production? This could not be, she insisted, production for production's sake via other capitalists and an ever-increasing expansion of Department I production. In reworking Marx's reproduction schemes in *The Accumulation of Capital*, Luxemburg contended: 'From the capitalist point of view it is absurd to produce more consumer goods in order to maintain more workers, and to turn out more means of production merely to keep this surplus of workers occupied' (1913: 132). At some point, capitalists would stop investing, for additional investment would only serve as a support to existing investment, and adequate demand for the existing productive capacity would dry up. In this sense, for Luxemburg, even the abstract *pure capitalism* without reference to the turbulence of concrete history, as posited in Volume II by Marx, raised immense contradictions for accumulation. Expanded reproduction would be wracked by increasing disproportions between surpluses of goods in Department II and deficits in Department I.

For Luxemburg, two further fundamental questions emerged – questions central to modern capitalist economies in a phase of crisis – from this framing of the problem of accumulation. If capitalists are driven by the pursuit of profits and exchange-value, what happens to the incentive to invest in conditions of stagnation? And where does the money-commodity come from to validate the new commodities and provide profits? In the focus on the conditions for circulation and adjustment in Volume II of *Capital*, these questions animated Luxemburg in her dissatisfaction with Marx's treatment. As she put it: 'Realisation of the surplus value is doubtless a vital question of capitalist accumulation. It requires as its prime condition. .. that there should be a strata of buyers outside of capitalist society.' On this startling and paradoxical conclusion Luxemburg is quite emphatic: that 'The decisive fact is that the surplus value cannot be realised by sale either to workers or to capitalists, but only if it is sold to such social organisations or strata whose own mode of production is not capitalistic' (1913, pp. 351–52). In other words, the surplus that is to be re-capitalised (and thus accumulated) depends for its realisation on outlets 'external' to the capitalist market (a third sector in terms of her and Marx's abstract two sector model).[5]

It follows from this model of accumulation that imperialism is an inherent tendency of capitalist accumulation, given in its most general laws of development and exhibited concretely in its historical features. As she defines its dynamics: 'Imperialism is the political expression of the accumulation of capital in its competitive struggle for what remains still open of the non-capitalist environment.... [W]itness the immense masses of capital accumulated in the old countries which seek an outlet for their surplus product and strive to capitalise their surplus value, and the rapid change-over to capitalism of the pre-capitalist civilizations. With the high development of the capitalist countries and their increasingly severe competition in acquiring non-capitalist areas, imperialism

[5] Sweezy (1942, p. 179) pointed out that Kautsky had in 1902 described the crisis theory of Marxists in terms of the market for consumption growing less rapidly than accumulation: 'Capitalist industry must, therefore, seek an additional market outside of its domain in non-capitalist nations and strata of the population.' Kautsky and others also saw crises growing more severe through time. This was a theme Luxemburg would also adopt. In his introduction to Luxemburg's economic writings, Peter Hudis (1913, p. X) observes that in her 1897 dissertation on the economic development of Poland, she had already had formed the theoretical theme that any exclusively national development path was closed by capitalism striving to ‚materially bind together the most distant places... to make them economically dependent on each other.'

grows in lawlessness and violence, both in aggression against the non-capitalist world and in ever more serious conflicts among the competing capitalist countries. Though imperialism is the historical method for prolonging the career of capitalism, it is also a sure means of bringing it to a swift conclusion' (1913, p. 446).

For Luxemburg, a 'third sector' that might provide an outlet and thus sustain accumulation could also include military spending, state economic policies to increase trade such as international loans and protectionist policies that maintain the home market for national capitals. Thus the 'so-called primitive accumulation', with which Marx concludes Volume I, is not limited to the genesis of capital as 'capitalism in its full maturity also depends in all respects on non-capitalist strata and social organisations existing side by side with it' (1913, p. 365). All these possibilities, it hardly needs underlining, were central to the confluence of forces gaining momentum across the classical age of imperialism leading to the interwar crisis.

If the impossibility of pure capitalism made up of only workers and capitalists and existing in a closed system was made possible by an 'external' sector, the very process of capitalist expansion brought these zones into capitalist social relations. For Luxemburg, this occurred in stages: the pre-capitalist 'natural economy' is first destroyed as commodity production is imposed by colonialism; the remnants of simple commodity production dominated by peasants is steadily eroded with colonial policies actively tearing apart the linkages between agriculture and industry as capitalist social relations form; and, finally, the imperialist stage as capitalist industrialisation takes hold in the peripheries with capital imports financing the building of railroads, manufacturing sectors, and so forth. This final stage, however, is wracked with contradictions: on the one hand, 'the achievement of capitalist autonomy in the hinterland…is attained amidst wars and revolutions' and the creation of 'a modern state machinery adapted to the purposes of capitalist production'; on the other hand, there is increased 'aggression against the non-capitalist world and…ever more serious conflicts among the competing capitalist countries' (1913, p. 419, 446). What Luxemburg suggested theoretically to be unattainable would eventually manifest itself in capitalist crisis and breakdown in practice. Luxemburg concluded *The Accumulation of Capital* with these words: 'Capitalism is…a mode which tends to engulf the entire globe and stamp out all other economies, tolerating no rival at its side. Yet at the same time it is also the first mode of economy which is unable to exist by itself… Although it strives to become universal, and, indeed, on account of this its tendency, it must breakdown' (1913, p. 467).

In her *Anti-Critique* (written in prison in 1915 but published after her death), she reiterated her thesis of capitalist breakdown in somewhat blunter terms, and tied it even more tightly to the exhaustion of the external non-capitalist sector necessary for the realisation of surplus value: 'As it approaches the point where humanity only consists of capitalist and proletarians, further accumulation will become impossible. At the same time, the absolute and undivided rule of capital aggravates class struggle…to such an extent, that, long before the last consequences of economic development, it must lead to the rebellion of the international proletariat against the existence of the rule of capital. This, in brief, is my conception of the problem and its solution' (1921, p. 60).

It is necessary to reassert, against the standard readings, the fundamental points clarified by *The Accumulation of Capital.* These are, for example, that the spheres of production, circulation and money and credit are interdependent but not identical thereby allowing specific dynamics of imbalanced production to emerge; that the decisions and processes which translate the economic surplus into actual investments (the savings that equal investment in Say's Law) are separated in time, formed in uncertainty and entered into in specific historical settings; that from the outset the internationalisation of capital is a necessary feature forming capitalism into a world market; and that the processes of territorialisation and state formation become intertwined with trade flows, capital exports and colonisation in a continually shifting division of the world market.

It has been a habit to treat Luxemburg's political writings apart from her economic texts. But *Reform and Revolution* and *The Accumulation of Capital*, for example, carry common themes, above all the insistence that there can be no steady evolution toward socialism on a national scale by incremental reforms or by extending state coordination over individual capitals. Even Bukharin, the harshest critic of *The Accumulation of Capital* at the time, recognised these points, as well as the contribution of the book in highlighting the historical expansion of imperialism from primitive accumulation to modern imperialism as capitalist states attempted to absorb colonies within their economic zones.

Critiques and Retrievals

Although Luxemburg's mapping of capitalist exchange relations through both the schemas of reproduction and the international flows of capital, especially the role of money-capital, influenced all subsequent writings on imperialism, it was the critiques that prevailed in the reception of *The Accumulation of Capital.* And the critics have been many, from its own time to this day, including not only Bukharin and Bauer but also Lenin, Anton Pannekeok, Kautsky, Sweezy, and Ernest Mandel, and, notably, even a number of Marxists that have themselves been prone to the theory of underconsumptionism. The critiques pivoted around a few basic points, which may be briefly summarised.

First, it has been charged from the outset that Luxemburg's models of expanded reproduction conceived effective demand in too static a manner. A basic feature of capitalist markets is that capitalists themselves are, in part, each other's market 'as the demand for that part of the social product which is destined for accumulation comes from capitalists intent upon increasing their employment of constant and variable capital' (Howard and King 1989, p. 112). The capital advanced in a new round of accumulation, it was noted, can absorb the increased productive capacity of the previous investment by even more investment in new plants and new workers as the market expands (Bleaney 1976, Ch. 9; Kalecki 1971, pp. 148–55). In confronting this, Luxemburg retorted that the realisation of surplus value in this way means that capitalists become 'fanatical supporters of an expansion of production for production's sake…an increasing production of producer's goods to no purpose whatever (Luxemburg 1913, pp. 334–45). But critics from Bukharin (1924, pp. 168–69) onward have argued that this is to give a 'purpose' to the 'capitalist system'. At the level of the circulation of total social capital (the level of analysis the reproduction schemes are posited), the conditions for realisation are feasible. It is only a possibility that they may not hold and a crisis erupt, and this requires no attribution of motive to capitalists other than the competitive imperative to accumulate.

Second, it has also been pointed out against Luxemburg that investment in means of production also increases the volume of variable capital employed. This will, of course, given constant real wages, expand the consumption volume of workers and thus positively affect the conditions for realisation of surplus value in Department II output of consumption goods. As the new investment increases productivity, moreover, the level of real wages may also increase and extend the market. Indeed, if the ratios between productivity, the real wage and the surplus remain constant, then the conditions for accumulation expand proportionate to the increase in accumulation. This is (and not just in the 'golden age' conditions) the very basis for expanded reproduction and the positing of a static volume of variable capital (and consumption) reproduced conditions akin to simple reproduction. As Bauer suggested, Luxemburg (re)posed a problem for capitalist expansion, but one that was neither insoluble abstractly in reproduction schemas nor historically in particular patterns of regulating the distribution of output.[6]

Third, Luxemburg assumed that investment is taken up in the same sectors where the profit is gained and that the exchange between departments is the only means by which the surplus is realised. But exchange between production units in the same department producing different commodities also serves as a means to realise a surplus – a maker of socks exchanging with producers of bread; and many production units will produce commodities that serve as both Department I and II output. More fundamentally: Luxemburg's assumption violates the market imperatives toward profit equalisation that surplus capital flows into the sectors of highest profit and demand. Thus Department I deficits and Department II surpluses would bring a restructuring of industry as surplus capital flowed from one to the other to restore proportionality (Cliff

[6] Numerous critiques at the time raised this issue, but it was Bauer's that gained the most attention and was the basis for subsequent responses. See: Gaido and Quiroga (2013); Howard and King (1989, Ch. 6); and Darity (1979). Sweezy (1942, pp. 202–07) suggested she posed, in this part of her analysis, 'a false solution to a specious problem' in the assumptions made about variable capital being resolved by an external third sector. He saw this as inadequate to account for secular stagnation, and the role of monopolies in restricting investment and attempting to spur effective demand through other mechanisms.

1959, pp. 71–73). There is, then, the possibility that proportionality will hold between sectors, but this may well involve in actual economies, as Luxemburg suggested, a continual chaotic process of adjustment through penetration of non-capitalist formations.

Fourth, in positing non-capitalist territories as essential outlets for the expanded reproduction of capital, a number of conceptual – and, indeed, historical – limitations arise. It is not possible, for example, to sell into non-capitalist zones without them also exporting to gain the means of payment to purchase imports. Moreover, any production capacity forming in non-capitalist zones, particularly gained from loan-capital from the imperialist countries, will also require a net export surplus relative to the dominant countries to pay-off the loan. This can form a deepening interdependence in the division of labour between the two markets, but not a source of net effective demand to serve as an outlet (Howard and King 1989, pp. 113–14; Lee 1971, pp. 859–61).

Fifth, Luxemburg identifies the source of new money-capital as a crucial limit on the sources of effective demand that compel the search for 'outside' markets. This issue needs to be separated from the question of money hoards or the production of commodity-money in the form of gold (something Luxemburg also poses). Either might raise conjunctural problems, but pose no serious structural issues for flows of money-capital that would obstruct effective demand. All that has to be noted, in the first instance, is that in the processes of circulation at the level of total social capital there is a continual process of converting money-capital into production inputs and consumption goods. Moreover, the circuits of bank capital and credit can meet the demand for money-capital for the circulation of new value added, and the expansion of credit-money is not necessarily constrained by the gold-commodity, as bank credit, even in the gold system, expands in proportion to gold reserves.

Although differing in their particularities, these critiques all take offence to Luxemburg's abstract reproduction schemes as containing a series of analytical flaws (which she never comes to terms with). They insist that, at least conceptually, a 'pure capitalism' that does not rely on a third sector is theoretically conceivable, even if in practice imperialist penetration was a central historical characteristic. Imperialism still emerges out of the dynamics of an over-accumulation of capital that intensifies competition and gives rise to particular state economic policies supporting 'national' capitals in the competition for world markets.

From the 1930s on, however, Marxian influenced 'left-Keynesians' (as they became, somewhat misleadingly, known), such as Michał Kalecki, began to offer a more generous interpretation. In their view, Luxemburg posed powerfully some of the fundamental questions regarding the dilemmas of capitalist accumulation, if not always providing complete and adequate answers, as they lay in the sources of effective demand, the concrete incentives that transformed market imperatives into actual investments by capitalists and the monetary conditions for accumulation.

Kalecki in fact explicitly took off from Luxemburg's reproduction schemes to formulate his 'class-theoretic' conceptualisation of effective demand, captured in the famous Kaleckian aphorism that 'workers spend what they get, while capitalists get what they spend'. This was the unmistakable lesson of *The Accumulation of Capital*. In her somewhat ambiguous appraisal in the 1951 introduction to the English translation to the book, Joan Robinson pointed out that Luxemburg clarified, in a way that Keynes had not, the inherent uncertainty in a monetary economy of the capitalist's 'inducement to invest'. Robinson did not skirt the difficulties in the appraisal of the text, with its sometimes confused and incomplete theoretical excursions.[7] Still, as Robinson endorsed Luxemburg's concerns (echoing the key question of the *Introduction to Political Economy*): 'What motive have the capitalists for enlarging their stock of real capital? How do they know that there will be demand for the increased output of goods which the new capital will produce, so that they can "capitalise" their surplus in profitable form?' (1951, p. 20). Luxemburg helped clarify that 'Investment can take place in an ever-accumulating stock of capital only if the capitalists are assured of an ever-expanding market for the goods which the capital will produce' (p. 21). While admitting that Luxemburg neglected the competitive imperatives to invest and rising wages that widen the space of the market, Robinson contended that she got right the role of imperialism and the world market in helping resolve the problem of outlets for capitalist production, if sometimes through the practices of neo-mercantilist economic policies.

[7] See the comments of Maurice Dobb (1955) on both Robinson and Luxemburg.

Ironically, despite the decline of the Left and the generalisation of capitalist exchange relations across the globe over the last three decades, a number of new, and even more generous, readings of Luxemburg's political economy have appeared. This undoubtedly stems from her political writings, with her distinct position within Western Marxism as an early critic of the democratic limits of the Russian Revolution, the cautions on the strategic sclerosis of unions and socialist parties, and her impassioned warnings that all reformist gains, including democratic reforms, are subject to challenges from the capitalist classes and competitive pressures. These are themes that no socialist today can avoid addressing in confronting neoliberalism. But a few of the particular themes of *The Accumulation of Capital*, which we expand on below, also bear relevance for today: the role of international loan capital in the disciplining states via the IMF and structural adjustment policies; the competitive austerity dynamic in the world market limiting global effective demand; the pillaging of non-capitalist sectors and state enterprises to open up new spaces for accumulation; the role of militarism and the security apparatuses in the capitalist economy and state; and the hollowing out of democracy.

The most prominent retrieval of *The Accumulation of Capital* has come from David Harvey (2003, 2005). This stems not so much from his adhering to Luxemburg's theory of crisis and breakdown, as from the emphasis he places on the fragility of the conditions for realisation and the constant search for new outlets for surplus capital outside of the existing built environment and means of production, that is to say, the search for 'a third sector'. [8] For Harvey, as with Luxemburg, this is an ever-constant need of capitalism – one of the laws of capital accumulation – that is not limited to the emergence of capitalism via the primitive accumulation of money-capital and commodification of land and labour. As he states in *The New Imperialism* (2003, p. 141): 'The idea that some sort of 'outside' is necessary for the stabilisation of capitalism therefore has relevance. But capitalism can either make use of some pre-existing outside (non-capitalist social formations or some sector within capital-

[8] Fine (2012) takes a quite distinct view arguing that there is no need for a 'third sector'. Capitalism, he suggests, actually tends to encourage the expansion of non-capitalist production (some of it in the form of commodities for sale in the market) and also the socialisation of social life through the agency of the state. Both of these act as sources of effective demand.

ism – such as education – that has not yet been proletarianised) or it can actively manufacture it.' In discussing the conditions for realisation, Harvey contends that the structural problem of effective demand is a crucial factor in driving the expansion of the credit-money system.

But Harvey also makes a stronger claim about the need for capital to continually find new spaces and outlets for surplus capital *external* to existing circuits of capital. Indeed, in Harvey's theory of imperialism this process of 'accumulation by dispossession' comes to dominate as it 'release[s] a set of assets (including labour power) at very low (and in some cases zero) cost. Overaccumulated capital can seize hold of such assets and immediately turn them to profitable use' (2003, p. 149). In a manner running parallel to *The Accumulation of Capital*, he identifies a series of quite specific mechanisms by which the dispossessions of modern imperialism, guided by neoliberal ideology, occurs – new forms of 'land grabs' that alienate peasants form their land; privatisation of common spaces and public assets; the loans of money-capital turned against debtors through IMF-led structural adjustment policies; the restructuring of states under neoliberal policies to generalise market compulsions; and the new scramble of the countries of the core capitalist states to exploit the natural resources of peripheral zones. As non-capitalist modes of production are assimilated into capitalism forming new class structures and social relations in the imperialised zones, they have to be examined, Harvey suggests, in their own right and as embedded in the hierarchy of the inter-state system.

A more radical repositioning of Luxemburg's political economy, while still pivoting around *The Accumulation of Capital* and demand instabilities, is offered by Riccardo Bellofiore (2009) and his colleagues. There is less a direct lineage here to Luxemburg's themes than to Harvey's reworking of primitive accumulation, or her 'third sector' account of the forces propelling imperialism. Instead, Luxemburg's 'underconsumptionism' (for Bellofiore especially, this is not read as restrained wages but as investment instability) is re-read through a Kaleckian lens. Disproportionalities emerge between different sectors in general if wages consistently lag productivity; and they emerge cumulatively in sectors in the specific form of the chaotic market adjustments. These tendencies lead to systematic problems (quite beyond Keynesian formulations) of effective demand relative to potential output in conditions of capitalist competitions and monetary exchange. According to Bellofiore, Luxemburg properly posed the economic issues at hand in insisting that the production and circulation spheres are interrelated; that the capitalist incentives to invest are concretely determined based on profit expectations; that effective demand shortfalls become cumulative and destabilising; that monetary economies tend to exacerbate these shortfalls; and that the processes by which profits are monetised always need concrete examination. As he summarises her point: 'Although capitalists are always able to receive back the finance they advance to start production and to support their demand, they cannot possibly find inside their sector a source of more money…. Capital needs to find a demand that is an *external* source of more money, i.e. a demand that does not originate from capital itself, because it is a strict impossibility for the capitalist class as a whole to gain an excess of money receipts over the money injected into the system' (Bellofiore 2009, pp. 9–10).

For Bellofiore, the linkage Luxemburg makes between the weakness of national effective demand and imperialism provides a central theoretical insight, left out of conventional accounts of globalisation, into the contemporary world configuration. The weakness of demand from policies of austerity over the period of neoliberalism has been relieved by a hyperextension in the monetary circuits of capital in the form of an asset-based Keynesian lending that fuels financialisation. If loan-capital sustains effective demand, when transposed onto the world market it reinforces imperialist hierarchies. As with Luxemburg, financial disciplines enforced by both economic and political power are used to break open markets in peripheral states.

Beginning from the same starting point as Luxemburg, theorising capitalism as a specifically monetary economy, and thus potential market instabilities being consistently registered in aggregate demand failures, others revisiting Luxemburg have stressed her contribution to specifying the mechanisms that sustain effective demand. This is a theme that traverses all her economic writings, but figures most prominently in *The Accumulation of Capital* and the *Anti-Critique*. For 'left-Keynesians' like Geoff Harcourt, Peter Kriesler (2012) and Jan Toporowski (2013) this has meant, following Robinson's critique, drawing out more carefully Luxemburg's analysis of the material and political conditions that determine the 'incentive to invest' for individual capitalists and compositional implications for the capitalist class as a whole. This is found, for them, in contemporary capitalism in the extra-market institutional conditions that shape corporate behaviour. Not the least of these being the role of the economic policies of the capitalist state and, in particular, the institutional and regulatory forms of modern finance.

From within Marxism, Ingo Schmidt redeploys the economic and political writings of Luxemburg to dissect the current phase of capitalism and the impasse of working-class politics. 'Luxemburg's accumulation theory', Schmidt argues, 'recognizes the role of political intervention by the ruling classes at all stages of capitalist development and, at the same time, explores working-class capacities to act as an anti-capitalist force' (Schmidt 2012a, p. 254). Following Luxemburg's lead, Schmidt attempts to trace the new sources of effective demand, for example, militarism and welfare state spending across the post-war boom, and the massive expansion of credit and opening up of new markets to capitalist penetration by the collapse of the East Bloc, the transformation of China and in the Global South, over the neoliberal period. But these are not just value flows, as Schmidt's analysis utilises the historical forms of generating demand to dissect the dynamics of class formation in the vein of Luxemburg's political writings.

Schmidt reworks, in a sense, the modalities Luxemburg emphasises in *The Accumulation of Capital* such as militarism, the impact of cartels, the extent of loan-capital and trade policy. 'Luxemburg's demand-side Marxism offers an explanation... [of how] cyclical recessions turn into structural crises of capitalism. The defeats labour movements suffered after World War I and again during the 1970s were crucial for de-linking wages and productivity for decades and the subsequent build up for structural crises' (Schmidt 2014, p. 4).[9] For Schmidt, it is the differentiated political-economic conditions that permit capital accumulation – the concrete forms the expanded reproduction of the circuits of capital and class exploitation take – that is the key to understanding the world market of neoliberalism.[10]

---

[9] These themes are further developed in Schmidt (2010, 2012b).

[10] Hudis (2012, 2014) takes up many of the same themes but rejects the Keynesian interpretation of these reclamations. Instead, he places emphasis on Luxemburg's critique of the irrationality of capitalism as always open to economic crises and, thus, bearing insights into the current crisis.

Luxemburg and Contemporary Imperialism

These reclamations offer a quite different interpretation of Luxemburg's political economy, while leaving to the side her particular thesis of capitalist breakdown. The contribution of *The Accumulation of Capital* to a theory of imperialism centres on the structural deficiencies of effective demand within capitalism leading to a search for a compensating 'third sector', with an emphasis on the direct political mechanisms of appropriation and realisation of value through colonial subordination. But contemporary imperialism is in fact primarily reproduced through formally equal exchanges in the world market, guided by a negotiated 'rules-based', 'contract-centred' framework for trade, and equal relations between states – the law of value and the rule of law – in a universalised capitalism. Harry Magdoff famously labelled this new phase of imperialism, from the post-war period onwards, as 'imperialism without colonies' in which competitive economic rivalry was now intertwined with economic and political interdependency and subordination through formally equal states.

This shift in the dynamics of the world market helps to clarify a theoretical point obscured in the classical formulations; that is, the expanded reproduction of capitalism creates a world market through new processes of valorisation, with quite distinct economic and political mechanisms, while extending the differentiation and integration of increasingly complex particular units of capital and states where the production of value and class relations are located and materialised. This formulation implies – and this is consistent with Luxemburg – an international division of labour in the production and exchange of commodities. But it also suggests the necessary role of the state, and its economic policy practices, in mediating between local production and world circulation – a hierarchy of states and value relations. Imperialism, therefore, always emerges in the configurations of the world market as produced by the internationalisation of capital and the economic policies adopted by states, and in particular as dominated by the states at the centre of world capitalism. This theorisation of the new imperialism is quite removed from the stance of departure of Luxemburg's *The Accumulation of Capital*. Yet it is still possible to identify a number of lineages from her text to central concerns today.

1. *Interdependence and differentiation.* For Luxemburg, imperialism is not defined in terms of a given geography, but by the continual transformation of the core capitalist economies in its relationship to 'non-capitalist social organizations as the setting for its development' (Luxemburg 1913, p. 366). In this sense, the circulation of capital is a continual process of uneven geographical differentiation. As she insisted: 'Accumulation is more than an internal relationship between the branches of capitalist production; it is primarily a relationship between capital and a non-capitalist environment... From this we get most complicate relations, divergencies in the speed and direction of accumulation for the two departments, different relations with non-capitalist modes of production as regards material elements and elements of value' (Luxemburg 1913, p. 417). This is the sense that tendencies toward equalisation and differentiation are understood today as inherent in capitalist competition and world market. These processes, while creating global interdependence, simultaneously partition the imperialist bloc from the dominated bloc, and also make differentiation an attribute of inter-imperial relations.
2. *International competition.* A consequence of focusing on the need for an 'outside' for capital to accumulate in its central zones was that Luxemburg had to examine competition not just as sectoral or national but international. In *The Accumulation of Capital*, Luxemburg presented some of the mechanisms by which this occurred – new zones of demand, displacement and migration increasing the supplies of exploitable labour; the advance of international loans and the creation of international commodity markets. Luxemburg, moreover, problematised the origins and formation of money-capital – the credit integral to both national and international exchanges – invested before the output is sold that permits accumulation. These points remain integral to modern propositions that the local and particular forms of value production are connected with the abstract and universal flows of money in the world market. International competition is, in this reading, a central, and historically specific, aspect of inter-imperialist relations (Worth 2012; Desai 2004, pp. 93–96).
3. *Competition through states.* In defining imperialism as the 'political expression of the accumulation of capital in its competitive struggle

for what remains open of the non-capitalist environment' (Luxemburg 1913, p. 446), Luxemburg exposed the foreign economic policies of the core capitalist states. These states, she argued, engaged in a competitive struggle for spheres of influence not as a result of the actions of a single state but as a product of their rivalry. She supported this by detailing the state policies building up armaments, providing international loan supports and implementing tariffs. Her contentions remained theoretically underdeveloped, but they did rightly suggest that the competition between 'many capitals' makes for multiple power centres and a particular geo-political configuration of the inter-state system (Basso 1975, pp. 42–43; LeBlanc 2010, pp. 169–70). Capital accumulation is characterised by processes of both internationalisation and nationalisation (meaning state-building) as international competition does not occur apart from or against states but through states.

4. *The 'internalisation' of foreign capital.* A theoretical result of *The Accumulation of Capital* is that what might begin as 'external' becomes 'internalised' as capitalism develops and the circulation of capital integrates the world market. But if the analysis intends 'not any single country but the capitalist world market', Luxemburg proposed, 'there can be no foreign trade: all countries are "home"' (Luxemburg 1913, p. 136). This is not a contention that trade does not exist, but methodologically treating political-economic spaces as closed entities to be formed around a national bourgeoisie is a misconception. This methodological edict is important to the study of the imperialism today given that the tendencies to intensification, concentration and centralisation of capital all increase the scale of operations, the technical division of labour and the territorial complexity of capitalist firms. Transnational firms, for example, have a 'home' base in that the dominant agents who possess and allocate these assets have a specific location. But they also become important agents of accumulation, and become an internalised part of the power bloc in the places they invest in. As opposed to a 'national bourgeoisie' organising a national economic space for itself, the state actively reproduces, ideologically, politically and through competitive supports both domestic and foreign capital.

5. *Internationalisation and the circuits of capital.* A central thesis of *The Accumulation of Capital* is that capitalist penetration of the periphery evolves in a struggle against the 'natural economy', the extension of the commodity economy and the dissolution of the peasant economy with the spread of capitalist industry. Each phase involves particular flows of surplus capital to the periphery and pattern of political domination (Bieler et al. 2014). International loans, for example, 'widen the scope for the accumulation of capital; but at the same time they restrict it by creating new competition for the investing countries. These inherent conflicts of the international loan system are a classic example of spatio-temporal divergences between the conditions for the realisation of surplus value and the capitalisation thereof' (Luxemburg 1913, p. 421). This theme foreshadows the core contention today that different phases of internationalisation will be dominated by a varying matrix of the circuits of capital, different modalities of uneven development and, hence, a unique configuration in the pattern of international competition.
6. *The internal reorganisation of states.* Although *The Accumulation of Capital* identifies state economic policy as an integral aspect of imperialism, the specific organisation of the state in either the imperialist centres or the colonised peripheries is left unexamined. The economic role of the state with respect to industrial policies or the state management of money and credit is quite perfunctory. The integration of militarism as an integral aspect of imperialism, however, forcefully raises a series of questions (Rowthorn 1980; Kowalik 1987). Militarism not only serves as another 'third sector' to absorb surplus output, but also imposes itself on state organisation and extending commodification. What is the outcome, Luxemburg asks, of 'diverting purchasing power…to the state for militarist purposes[?]… Capital will now produce an equivalent of war materials for the state instead of producing large quantities of means of production and subsistence for peasant consumers… Taxation pressures the produce of peasant economy into circulation and compels the peasants to become buyers of capitalist products' (Luxemburg 1913, p. 465). This is suggestive of the means by which the internal economic policy apparatuses of the state become increasingly subordinate to those dealing with the internationalisation

of capital, and the domination of the military and foreign policy branches of the state in mediating and protecting the circulation of capital in the world market. The capacities of each state to mediate international competition are determined, in turn, by its administrative and diplomatic capacities, its place in the imperialist chain and internal class relations.

7. *Contradictions in inter-imperial relations.* The organisational structure of *The Accumulation of Capital* marches toward the conclusion that the dominant imperialist states struggle over control of peripheral zones as they are integrated into a matrix of competing blocs. '[W]ith the international development of capitalism the capitalisation of surplus value becomes ever more urgent and precarious', Luxemburg argued. 'Hence the contradictory phenomena that the old capitalist countries provide ever larger markets for, and become increasingly dependent upon, one another, yet on the other hand compete ever more ruthlessly for trade relations with non-capitalist countries' (Luxemburg 1913, p. 367). In the conjuncture before World War I, she presciently observed the economic competition between the monopolies being inexorably displaced into competitive imperial rivalry between states and into military competition. But as the volume and complexity of the internationalisation of capital increased through time, the unity and contradictions in the international circulation of capital meant that conflict and cooperation, competitive rivalry and interdependency, became equally embedded in the world market. Only in particular historical conjunctures will inter-firm and inter-state competitive rivalries spill over into imperial rivalry in the sense of military conflict over political leadership of the imperialist bloc (Panitch and Leys 2004).

Luxemburg and the Socialist Project

Luxemburg's political economy, and *The Accumulation of Capital* in particular, defended the thesis that capitalist development inexorably moved toward an economic breakdown. This position was never in support, as so often charged, of a politics of fatalism or a proclamation of the inevitability of socialism. Quite the contrary: her economics served as a warning. The working-class gains made in economic struggles for wages and welfare are always subjected to the capitalist imperatives to increase the rate of exploitation; just as the democratic freedoms workers had won in political struggle were always subject to erosion in capitalist efforts to maintain their rule.[11] As Luxemburg so often repeated in argument against revisionist views of a steady evolution toward socialism, no ruling class in history simply gave up its hold on power by argument. There was little reason to expect otherwise of the capitalist classes.

In Luxemburg's judgement, the bourgeoisie was all too willing to sacrifice liberal political freedoms in defence of their property and rule: a sense of political urgency, as so powerfully presented in *The Mass Strike*, was necessary to avert a fatalism that could only serve to prepare the ground for political disaster. Socialism not only spontaneously emerges from the laws of social development or in a singular moment of radical political rupture. It is only from the self-initiative and growing self-confidence of the working classes that a new democratic order can gain a secure footing. This is a theme, more implicit than explicitly stated, of *The Accumulation of Capital*, if still here tethered to her conclusions on a breakdown in accumulation: '[A]fter a certain stage the conditions for the accumulation of capital both at home and abroad turn into their very opposite – they become conditions for the decline of capitalism.... At a certain stage of development there will be no other way out than the application of socialist principles' (Luxemburg 1913, pp. 466–67).

There is a particular resonance to these themes, a century after they were written, for the Left today. The 'general crisis' that capitalism entered into in 2008 (a conjuncture of breakdown in Luxemburg's usage) has not been met by a political upsurge of the Left or anti-market policy departures from the citadels of power in the state. Indeed, neoliberalism has undergone a remarkable renovation, and continues to retain its place as the all but exclusive economic policy practice guiding capitalist states, certainly in the capitalist core, but to one degree or another across the world market. In this phase of the crisis, neoliberal austerity is backed

[11] Some of the best attempts to engage both Luxemburg's political economy and economic strategy in her time, with its relevance for making the new socialism for today, are Geras (1976), Eley (1980), Schütrumpf (2008) and Schulman (2013).

by the armour of an increasingly authoritarian state, ever more willing to encroach upon democratic freedoms.

The Left has experienced little else but setbacks over the period of neoliberalism, every small victory or organisational initiative running up against another significant defeat, from marginalisation as a parliamentary force to the fracturing of the networks initially nurturing a new social movement politics into ever smaller, ever looser social coalitions. With liberal democracy now reduced to the most ritualistic electoralist legitimation of ruling class agendas, it is not surprising that Luxemburg's political slogan of 'socialism or barbarism' is again in wide circulation in political discussions.[12] The phrase was never meant as a hard and fast 'drawing out' of exclusive alternate development trajectories. It rather attempted to capture, in one dramatic expression, that the chaotic market processes that were an inevitable part of capital accumulation are always pregnant with the possibility of an assault on democracy in the absence of working-class mobilisation armed with its own organisation, alternative programme and vision. And it is this deficiency that explains the sense of political fatalism that pervades the Left today – 'there is no alternative' – as the lived experience of socialist opposition to neoliberalism.

The Accumulation of Capital still has many lessons to teach on the dynamics of contemporary capitalism and, thus, of contemporary imperialism. But like all her contributions to socialist theory and strategy, *Accumulation* is also adamant on the political limitations of what postwar reformers came to call, in what is now so clearly a completely misguided term, democratic capitalism. That is a theoretical insight that is painfully being relearned today. And as we learn it, it will also be necessary to retrieve one of Luxemburg's most penetrating – and controversial – strategic pointers on the overriding importance on the democratic exploration of alternatives, which always needs to be done 'step by step' so as 'to feel out the ground, tryout, experiment, test now one way now another.' For Luxemburg, a 'program is nothing but a few main signposts…there is no key in any socialist party program or textbook… Only experience is capable of correcting and opening new ways' (1918, p. 390).

[12] The phrase originates with Karl Kautsky's commentary on the Erfurt Programme written in 1888, and subsequently widely published in English as *The Class Struggle*.

Bibliography

Barone, C. (1985). *Marxist thought on imperialism*. Armonk: M.E. Sharpe.

Basso, L. (1975). *Rosa Luxemburg: A reappraisal*. London: André Deutsch.

Bellofiore, R. (Ed.) (2009). *Rosa Luxemburg and the critique of political economy*. New York: Routledge.

Bieler, A., et al. (2014). The enduring relevance of Rosa Luxemburg's *The accumulation of capital*. *Journal of International Relations and Development*, 17, on-line, 1–28.

Bleaney, M. (1976). *Underconsumption theories*. London: Lawrence and Wishart.

Brewer, A. (1980). *Marxist theories of imperialism*. London: Routledge.

Brenner R. (1977). The Origins of Capitalist Development: A Critique of Neo-Smithian Marxism. New Left Review, *104*, 25–92.

Bukharin, N. [1917] (1972). *Imperialism and world economy*. London: Merlin.

Bukharin, N. [1924] (1972). *Imperialism and the accumulation of capital*. New York: Monthly Review Press.

Cliff, T. (1959). *Rosa Luxemburg*. London: Bookmarks.

Darity, W. A. (1979). Kalecki, Luxemburg and Imperialism. *Journal of Post-Keynesian Economics, 2*(2), 223–230.

Desai, M. (2004). *Marx's revenge*. London: Verso.

Dobb, M. (1955). *'The accumulation of capital'. In Id., On economic theory and socialism*. London: Routledge and Kegan Paul.

Eley, G. (1980). The legacy of Rosa Luxemburg. *Critique, 12*(1), 139–150.

Fine, B. (2012). Revisiting Rosa Luxemburg's political economy. *Critique Journal of Socialist Theory, 40*(3), 449–456.

Frolich, P. [1939] (1972). *Rosa Luxemburg: Her life and work*. New York: Monthly Review Press.

Gaido, D., & Quiroga, M. (2013). The early reception of Rosa Luxemburg's theory of imperialism. *Capital and Class, 37*(3), 437–455.

Geras, N. (1976). *The legacy of Rosa Luxemburg*. London: Verso.

Harcout, G. C., & Kriesler, P. (2012). *Michal Kalecki and Rosa Luxemburg on Marx's schemes of reproduction: Two incisive interpreters of capitalism*. UNSW Australian School of Business Research Paper No. 2012-34.

Harvey, D. (2003). *The new imperialism*. Oxford: Oxford University Press.

Harvey, D. (2005). *A brief history of neoliberalism*. Oxford: Oxford University Press.

Howard, M. C., & King, J. E. (1989). *A history of Marxian economics: Volume I, 1883–1929*. London: Macmillan.

Hudis, P. (2012). New perspectives on Rosa Luxemburg's critique of global capitalism. *Perspectives on Global Development and Technology, 11*(1), 27–37.

Hudis, P. (2013). Introduction: The multidimensionality of Rosa Luxemburg. In P. Hudis (Ed.), *The complete works of Rosa Luxemburg: Volume I, Economic Writings 1*. London: Verso, xii-xxiii.

Hudis, P. (2014). The dialectic of the spatial determination of capital: Rosa Luxemburg's *accumulation of capital* reconsidered. Logos, *13*, 1.

Kalecki, M. (1971). *Selected essays on the dynamics of the capitalist economy, 1933–1970*. Cambridge: Cambridge University Press.

Kowalik, T. (1987). Rosa Luxemburg. In *The new Palgrave: Marxian economics.* New York: W.W. Norton.

LeBlanc, P. (2010). Rosa Luxemburg and the global violence of capitalism. *Socialist Studies, 6*(2), 1–8.

Lee, G. (1971). Rosa Luxemburg and the impact of imperialism. *Economic Journal, 81*, 847–862.

Lukács, G. (1924/1972). *Political Writings, 1919–1929.* London: New Left Books.

Luxemburg, R. (1913/1963). *The accumulation of capital.* London: Routledge and Kegan Paul.

Luxemburg, R. (1918/1970). The Russian revolution. In M.-A. Waters (Ed.), *Rosa Luxemburg speaks.* New York: Pathfinder.

Luxemburg, R. (1921/1972). *The accumulation of capital – An anti-critique.* New York: Monthly Review Press.

Luxemburg, R. (1925/2013). Introduction to political economy. In P. Hudis (Ed.), *The complete works of Rosa Luxemburg: Volume I, Economic Writings 1.* London: Verso.

Panitch, L., & Leys, C. (Eds.) (2004). *The new imperial challenge: Socialist register 2004*. London: Merlin Press.

Robinson, J. [1951] (1963). Introduction. In *R. Luxemburg the accumulation of capital*. London: Routledge and Kegan Paul.

Rowthorn, B. (1980). Rosa Luxemburg and the political economy of militarism. In *Capitalism, conflict, inflation*. London: Lawrence and Wishart.

Schmidt, I. (2010). Rosa Luxemburg's *accumulation of capital*: New perspectives on capitalist development and American Hegemony. *Socialist Studies, 6*(2), 92–117.

Schmidt, I. (2012a). Rosa Luxemburg and the critique of political economy. *Historical Materialism, 20*(1) 253–266.

Schmidt, I. (2012b). Rosa Luxemburg's *accumulation of capital*: A centennial update with additions from long wave theory and Karl Polanyi's *great transformation*. *Critique, 40*(2), 337–356.

Schmidt, I. (2014). Rosa Luxemburg: Economics for a new socialist project. *New Politics, 15*(1).

Schulman, J. (Ed.) (2013). *Rosa Luxemburg – Her life and legacy*. New York: Palgrave.

Schütrumpf, J. (2008). *Rosa Luxemburg or: The price of freedom*. Berlin: Rosa Luxemburg Foundation.

Sweezy, P. (1942). *The theory of capitalist development*. New York: Monthly Review Press.

Toporowski, J. (2013). Tadeusz Kowalik and the accumulation of capital. *Monthly Review, 64*(8), 33–44.

Trincado, E. (2010). The current relevance of Rosa Luxemburg's thought. *Socialist Studies, 6*(2), 141–159.

Veneziani, R. (2009). Global capitalism and imperialism theory: Methodological and substantive insights from Rosa Luxemburg. *Review of Political Economy, 21*(2), 195–211.

Worth, O. (2012). Accumulating the critical spirit: Rosa Luxemburg and critical IPE. *International Politics, 49*, 136–153.

3

Value: Marx's Evolution and Luxemburg's Legacy[1]

Paul Zarembka

Introduction

Conceptions of classical political economists appear quite unchallenged in Marx's early work. Within his unpublished *1844 Manuscripts* 'capital, accumulation, competition, division of labour, wages, profit, etc...

P. Zarembka (✉)
Department of Economics, SUNY at Buffalo, Buffalo, NY, USA and
General Editor, Research in Political Economy.

[1] Work on this topic originated more than a decade ago for several conferences. An early draft, considerably different, was prepared under a distinct title for the Japan Society for Political Economy's 51st Annual Conference "Political Economy Now - Marxist Reappraisal", 18-19 October 2003, Musashi University, Tokyo; as well as for Rethinking Marxism's 5th International Gala Conference "Marxism and the World Stage", 6-8 November 2003, University of Massachusetts at Amherst. A subsequent draft was prepared for the conference, "Like a Candle Burning at Both Ends: Rosa Luxemburg and the Critique of Political Economy", 16-18 December 2004, University of Bergamo, Italy. After a long pause, it was then extensively revised for the Workshop on "100th Anniversary of The Accumulation of Capital: A Contribution to an Economic Explanation of Imperialism: A Century-Old Work Remains Current, Provocative and Seminal", Berlin, March 7-9, 2014 and finally revised for the IIPPE conference "The Crisis: Scholarship, Policies, Conflicts and Alternatives", Naples, 16-18 September 2014.

J. Dellheim, F.O. Wolf (eds.), *Rosa Luxemburg: A Permanent Challenge for Political Economy*, DOI 10.1057/978-1-137-60108-7_3

are concepts of Classical Political Economy, which Marx borrows *just as* he finds them there, without changing them one iota, without adding to them any new concept, and without modifying anything at all of their theoretical organization' (Althusser 1974, p. 109, fn. 4, emphasis in original). Just one year (1845), Marx begins to introduce new conceptions: mode of production, relations of production, and productive forces. Further development of his conceptual categories, at least based on the written evidence available to us, would require another 12 years. Marx's evolving conceptual construction is more than a mere elaboration of his understanding from 1844, but rather represents a shift of focus that initially culminates in Volume I of *Capital*, but continues to develop further even after this.

Value is the foundation of Marx's understanding of the capitalist mode of production, it is the theoretical heart of *Capital*. In the following, we seek to reconstruct the intellectual development of Marx's understanding of what constitutes value as such. Fundamentally, we do not find that Marx holds the same theory at age 23 (at the time of his doctoral dissertation), at age 26 (*Economic and Philosophical Manuscripts of 1844*, unpublished by him) or at age 54 (*Capital*, 2nd edition). Thus, we cannot agree with authors such as Baronian (2013), who argues otherwise in his book *Marx and Living Labour*, concluding that 'From 1844, Marx established the two tasks of the critical method which show the profound continuity of his writings from his doctoral dissertation onwards' (p. 6). Rather, as Marx matures, we find that his emphasis changes and the fulcrum of his thought moves as well.

We will focus on works that were published by Marx himself, rather than those he did not publish (notably, the *1844 Manuscripts* and *Grundrisse*). Following a survey of Marx's evolving understanding of value, we turn to the question of whether his conception of value would be 'contaminated' were we to expand the theoretical object of investigation to include, along with the understanding of the capitalist mode, the implications of the ongoing destruction of non-capitalist modes of production as part and parcel of the capitalist mode itself. Or, instead, must we exclude penetration as part of the inherent object of discussion so that it remains ancillary to the main topic? Marx did not foresee a potential theoretical problem for value, nor did Luxemburg. Yet both of them moved towards said problem as none before them had.

Poverty of Philosophy (1847): Economic Concepts Are Historically Conditioned

Marx's intellectual project truly begins in 1847 when he publishes *The Poverty of Philosophy* as a critique of Proudhon. In this work there is no direct criticism of the classical economist he most respected, David Ricardo, except for a remark on his tendency to eternalise economic concepts ahistorically. Ricardo's value theory is the 'scientific interpretation of actual economic life' (1847, p. 124), in contrast to Proudhon's utopianism. Twelve years later, Marx continues to cite the importance of his 1847 work. The salient points of our conception were first outlined in an academic, although polemical, form in my *Poverty of Philosophy* Marx (1859, p. 264). Only later in life does he refer to Ricardo's scientific 'inadequacy' while drafting *Theories of Surplus Value* (Marx 1905b, p. 390; in *Capital*, see the longer footnotes toward the end of the section on the fetishism of commodities, Marx 1867a, pp. 174–177).

The most important distinction in *Poverty* is the recognition by Marx that economists eternalise the categories they use, that is to say they are applied analytically to all modes of production: 'Economists express the relations of bourgeois production, the division of labour, credit, money, etc., as fixed, immutable, eternal categories ... but what they do not explain is how these relations themselves are produced.' 'Economic categories are only the theoretical expressions, the abstractions of the social relations of production.' Economists such as Smith and Ricardo 'have no other mission than that of showing how wealth is acquired in bourgeois production relations, of formulating these relations into categories, into laws, and of showing' their superiority to those of feudal society. All (sic) economists 'represent the bourgeois relations of production as eternal categories' (Marx 1847, p. 162, 165, 176, 202).

This weakness of classical economists proves fundamental to all of Marx's subsequent reconsiderations of political economy. In the following, we follow Marx as he develops his new understanding of value – an understanding that ultimately does not correspond to those of the classical economists.[2]

[2] Oishi (2001) claims that *Poverty of Philosophy* is fundamental to understand Marx's critique of political economy and that it implicitly targets Ricardo in addition to the obvious target of

Contribution (1859): Abstract Labour as the Substance of Value

After years of work and hints in Marx's 1857–58 *Grundrisse*, the crucial new concept of 'abstract labour' is finally introduced in the *Contribution to the Critique of Political Economy*, often expanded as 'abstract universal labour'. An example of Marx's use in the *Contribution* is the following:

> ...the labour which posits exchange value is a specific social form of labour. For example, tailoring if one considers its physical aspect as a distinct productive activity produces a coat, but not the exchange value of the coat. The exchange value is produced by it not as tailoring as such but as *abstract universal labour*, and this belongs to a social framework not devised by the tailor. Women in ancient domestic industry, for instance, produced coats without producing the exchange value of coats. Labour as source of material wealth was well known both to Moses, the law-giver, and to Adam Smith, the customs official. (Marx 1859, p. 278, emphasis is ours)

Rubin (1927) argued for the importance of the 'abstract labour' concept early on and, furthermore, considered Marx's emphasis on 'universal' in the *Contribution* to be an essential component and an appropriate carryover from Hegelian language. Rubin (p. 119) does recognise, however,

---

Proudhon. Marx had witnessed the development of private property through litigation surrounding theft of wood from what had been common land. So, according to Oishi, Marx focused thereafter on the essence of private property leading to the importance of estranged labour in his earlier *1844 Manuscripts*. In *Poverty* Marx understands Proudhon as eternalising economic categories in the same way as the classical economists (albeit via a detour), and, for Marx, this represents a contradiction to the actual historical emergence of private property in the then recent times. Having witnessed the emergence of private property in Germany, Marx breaks with such an eternalisation, and thereby with the analytical method used by the classical economists.

Oishi's primary theme is the continuity and unity of Marx's thought centred upon the principle of estranged or alienated labour. For Oishi, the importance of alienated labour had been negated by Soviet Marxists and Western followers when, for him, there was no rupture or break in Marx's own thought as he matures. White (1996), like Oishi, sees little change in Marx's basic scheme after the emphasis on alienated labor and private property in the 1844 Manuscripts; the later 'abstract labour' is little more than a substitution for alienated labour, and 'surplus value' a substitution for private property (pp. 146–147; see also p. 199). Unlike Oishi, however, White sees a major shift in Marx's late thought away from the importance of Hegel. We shall return to White, as we argue major conceptual changes by Marx as his thought evolves. Returning to Oishi (p. 135), he does equate alienated labour to labour under the control of others. How capitalism would be distinguished from slavery is thus not clear.

that most of the Hegelian language disappears from *Capital* in Marx's second edition, a point driven home by White (1996, Chapter 4) who describes, among other changes, the dropping of the word 'universal' throughout much of Marx's text, including from the phrase 'abstract universal labour' (see also Zarembka 2014).

Without Hegelian language, we determine Marx's meaning to be as follows: commodities have all kinds of use-values, that is, useful qualities. Abstracting 'from the material constituents and forms which make it a use value [it is] no longer a table, a house, yarn, or any other useful thing. All its sensuous characteristics are extinguished. Nor is it any longer the product of the labour of the joiner, the mason, the spinner, or of any other particular kind of productive labour' (Marx 1867a, p. 128). Although Marx himself did not make the analogy, it is rather like in physics: objects of all different shapes, sizes and colours are pulled towards a heavier mass. Newton abstracted from those differing qualities to arrive at 'gravity' as the commonality to describe this pull, a fact we all still learn in school today. In Marx's case, a commodity has value 'only because human labour in the abstract has been embodied or materialized in it'. Labour in the abstract is essential to the capital–wage-labour relation.

Value is the *objectification of abstract labour, which itself is a product of capitalism*. In Cleaver's words,

> to make abstraction from [any commodity's] use-values is to make abstraction from their particular attributes. That, in turn, is to make abstraction from the special characteristics of the human labour which created those attributes and made them different from other commodities.... In abstraction from their material reality as use-values and as products of particular forms of useful labour, these commodities emerge as only products of human labour in abstraction from any particularity. This human labour that is common to them Marx calls abstract labour. As products of abstract human labour they are qualitatively equivalent and as such he calls them *values*.... [Abstract labour is] meaningful because capital itself, in its continual struggle with labour to create and maintain the division of labour which is the basis for commodity production, exchange, and social control, tries to continually make labour more malleable to its needs. (Cleaver 1979, pp. 110–112, emphasis in original, paragraphing not indicated; also, Mohun 1991 and Milios et al. 2002, pp. 17–21)

Thus, value is expanded beyond Ricardo's ahistorical usage. Value, based upon abstract labour within capitalism, is not transhistorical, but is rather a concept only applicable to the capitalist mode of production. Like Cleaver, Postone (1993) also says that the '*essential* difference between Marx's critique of political economy and classical political economy is precisely the treatment of labour' and that 'a trans-historical conception of value-constituting labour. .. hinders an adequate analysis of the capitalist social formation' (pp. 54–55, emphasis in original).

Turning to another aspect of his *Contribution*, Marx surveyed the history of political economy for the problems other economists had with the classical (especially Ricardian) determination of exchange-value by labour time. Suggesting where he himself fits in, the relevant portion begins:

> *David Ricardo*, unlike Adam Smith, neatly sets forth the determination of the value of commodities by labour time, and demonstrates that this law governs even those bourgeois relations of production which apparently contradict it most decisively. Ricardo's investigations are concerned exclusively with the *magnitude of value*, and regarding this he is at least aware that the operation of the law depends on definite historical preconditions. He says that the determination of value by labour time applies to 'such commodities only as can be increased in quantity by the exertion of human industry, and on the production of which competition operates without restraint' [as corrected to Ricardo's actual words, rather than the re-translation back from Marx's German. P.Z.].
>
> This in fact means that the full development of the law of value presupposes a society in which large-scale industrial production and free competition obtain, in other words, modern bourgeois society. For the rest, the bourgeois form of labour is regarded by Ricardo as the eternal natural form of social labour. (Marx 1859, p. 300, emphasis in original)

Marx then offered four points of comparison of which the following is most relevant:

> If the exchange value of a product equals the labour time contained in the product, then the exchange value of a working day is equal to the product it yields, in other words, wages must be equal to the product of labour. But in fact the opposite is true. *Ergo*, this objection amounts to the problem,

> – how does production on the basis of exchange value solely determined by labour time lead to the result that the exchange value of labour is less than the exchange value of its product? This problem is solved in our analysis of capital. (Marx 1859, pp. 301–302)

Marx promises an analysis to solve the problem of the origin of surplus value. He takes confidence from personal clarifications conducted in his notes, which were published after his death as the *Grundrisse*. The *Grundrisse* is, in fact, where Marx originally develops many of the new theoretical concepts which would appear in the first volume of *Capital*. Nevertheless, the concept of labour power is not even hinted at.

Baronian's (2013) book addresses 'living labour' in Marx and could be considered an alternative to our argument, even though we are in agreement concerning Marx's break with the classical economists. Where some have emphasised 'alienation' as decisive for Marx (Oishi is discussed in our fn. 1), political economy 'builds on phenomena arising in the sphere of circulation, in which economic agents relate to each other only as possessors of commodities' (p. 8). Marx had seen that Hegel had incorrectly conceived 'real productive labour in the same way as political economy, as alienated labour or commodity producing labour' (p. 4). Marx overcomes that conception by instead focusing on living labour:

> … Although political economy always grasps the commodity in its twofold nature, i.e. as use value and exchange value, it conceives living labour itself just as labour that creates use values. … Had the economists defined the living labour both as concrete labour and abstract labour, the exchange of products as commodities would have immediately appeared to them as a very particular way under which society coordinates and exchanges producers' various activities. (Baronian 2013, p. 7)

In successive chapters, issues addressed by Baronian include the transition to capitalism, the Cambridge controversy regarding Ricardian versus neoclassical capital theory, the transformation problem, the process of abstraction of labour (including Taylorism and cognitive labour), surplus population and the claim of working-class immiseration, circuits of capital and Keynesian monetary theory, as well as the role of constant capital in crisis (the topic which concludes his book). When

Baronian first gives attention to the transition to capitalism and includes discussion of well-known works by Sweezy, Dobb, Hilton, Wood and Brenner, he sides with Dobb and Hilton. Unfortunately, he fails to show explicitly how living labour is evident in some authors and missing in others. At least to this reader, a similar problem occurs in later chapters.

Baronian's last chapter begins by stating that the failure to realise that constant capital is sustained by living labour is at the root of inadequate theories of crisis, be they falling rate of profit or over-accumulation theories (he does not mention other possibilities). Noting Marx's polemic against Adam Smith that constant capital is an element of gross product in capital's reproduction (p. 172), Baronian makes the point that constant capital can only be sustained when living labour operates on those materials – those use-values – that constant capital represents. The living labour represented in those values can be carried over into the production process, which would otherwise be useless. So far, so good. Yet further into the chapter, the relevance of pointing to living labour no longer seems clear, and his inadequate consideration of the complexities of the composition of capital (see Zarembka 2015a) undermines his discussion.

Capital (1867): Labour Power Distinguished from Ricardian Labour

> Suddenly the voice of the labourer, which had been stifled in the storm and stress of the process of production, rises: The commodity that I have sold to you [my beloved employer] differs from the crowd of other commodities, in that its use creates value, and a value greater than its own. That is why you bought it. Marx (1867a, p. 342)

Contemporary Marxists often take the concept of 'labour power' for granted and consider it easy to grasp. Yet an important theoretical development in this regard occurred after 1847. Indeed, even Marx's *Contribution*, published in 1859, fails to mention 'labour power'. When presenting a copy of his *Poverty of Philosophy* to Natalia Utina in 1876, Marx pens in the word 'power' after 'labour' in the following original sentence (the first of only four corrections he made anywhere in the book): 'Labour, inasmuch as it is bought and sold, is a commodity like any other commodity, and has, in consequence, an exchange value' (Marx 1847, p. 130).

Although Marx 'had yet to grasp its analytical significance more fully' (Oakley 1984, p. 173), Oakley claims that a first reference by Marx to 'labour power' can be found in his *Grundrisse*, written in 1857–58 but published long after his death (Marx 1939–41a, pp. 282–3). A later translation of the *Grundrisse*, unavailable to Oakley, notes, however, that the German original speaks of *Arbeitsvermögen*, or labour capacity. Not until *Capital*, Volume I did Marx use this term interchangeably with *Arbeitskraft*, that is, labour power (see Marx 1939b–41b, p. 212 and 554, fn. 85). While 'labour power' thus remains unclearly defined, other concepts emerge in the *Grundrisse*, such as constant and variable capital and absolute and relative surplus value (Marx 1939–41a, p. 389 and 407–08; see also Oakley, p. 180). Clearly, a theoretical project is in progress.

In the Ricardian understanding of political economy, the labour time required for the commodity's production determines its value (and thus exchange value).[3] If the worker were selling his or her labour directly to the capitalist and selling a commodity which is itself labour time (value), how could surplus value (profit) be created at all? If 'the value of a commodity is determined by the labour time required for its production; how does it happen that this law of value does not hold good in the greatest of all exchanges, which forms the foundation of capitalist production, the exchange between capitalist and wage worker? Why is the quantity OF REALISED LABOUR received by the worker as WAGES not equal to the quantity of IMMEDIATE LABOUR which he gives in exchange for his WAGES?' (Marx 1910, p. 279, written about 1863, while commenting on James Mill's *Elements of Political Economy* (1824) emphasis in the original).

[3] For determining value, Ricardo does not actually refer to *labour time*, but rather to time *and* labour: 'the value of [hunted] animals would be regulated, not solely by the time and labour necessary to their destruction, but also by the time and labour necessary for providing the hunter's capital, the weapon' (Ricardo 1821, p. 23). A few pages earlier Ricardo nevertheless cites Smith, for whom labour time seems to be uniquely at stake, favourably: 'what is usually the produce of two days', or two hours' labour, should be worth double of what is usually the produce of one day's, or one hour's labour' (p. 13). Smith, it might be noted, neglected the weapon mentioned by Ricardo.

Marx was in the process of realising the full implications of the fact that labour itself is not produced nor sold. Rather, what is produced and becomes an expense for capitalists is the cost of workers' subsistence needs. Marx therefore develops a new theoretical concept: *labour power*. The capitalist purchases *labour power* at its exchange-value, the labour time required to produce the worker's subsistence needs. We now have a consistent theoretical system: the capitalist confronts the labourer on the market – a living human being with material needs (which must in turn be produced): 'not labour which directly confronts the possessor of money on the commodity-market, but rather the worker. What the worker is selling is his labour power. As soon as his labour actually begins, it has already ceased to belong to him; it can therefore no longer be sold by him' (Marx 1867a, p. 677). The expression *Arbeitskraft* was well known within German working-class culture in his time: Biernacki (1995, pp. 42–3, 272–4) says that it was common by 1848. Perhaps this facilitated Marx's theoretical development?

Does the addition of 'power' to 'labour', when appropriate, contain the solution to the problem? By purchasing labour power, the capitalist obtains a very specific, and unique, use-value: the workers' ability to produce value. While the use-value of a light bulb is to provide light, the use-value to the capitalist purchasing labour power is the value the worker produces (not specific items like light bulbs, toothpaste, and cars, which are of no interest to the capitalist).

> In order to extract value out of the consumption of a commodity, our friend the money-owner must be lucky enough to find within the sphere of circulation, on the market, a commodity whose use-value possesses the peculiar property of being a source of value, whose actual consumption is therefore an objectification [*Vergegenständlichung*] of labour, hence a creation of value. (Marx 1867a, p. 270)

Luckily for the money-owner, the use-value of labour power is precisely its ability to produce value.[4]

[4] See also Foley (1991) who notes that labour power 'requires the separation of the direct producers from means of production so that they cannot produce and sell the product of their own labour' and that 'the use value of labour power is its capacity to produce value' (p. 296). Contrast this to

Furthermore, the value produced is above cost. Thus, we read:

> For the use value of labour capacity to the capitalist as a capitalist does not consist in its *actual* use value, in the usefulness of this particular concrete labour – that it is spinning labour, weaving labour, and so on. He is as little concerned with this as with the use value of the product of this labour as such, since for the capitalist the product is a commodity (even before its first metamorphosis), not an article of consumption [...] the use value of the labour is, for him, that he gets back a greater quantity of labour time than he has paid out in the form of wages. (Marx 1905b, p. 12, emphasis in original)
>
> For it [capital], the use-value of labour-power is precisely the excess of the quantity of labour which it performs over the quantity of labour which is materialized in the labour-power itself and hence is required to reproduce it.... [The] concrete character, which is what enables it to take the form of a commodity, is not its *specific use-value* for capital. Its specific use-value for capital consists in its quantity as labour in general, and in the difference, the excess, of the quantity of labour which it performs *over* the quantity of labour which it costs. (Marx 1905b, p. 400, emphasis in original)[5]

Marx is now able to show the weakness of Ricardo's system. Ricardo can only demonstrate that the value of 'labour' depends upon the means of subsistence, which depends, in turn, upon supply and demand. However,

(Sinha 1996, p. 207) who writes that the 'use-value of labour-power happens to be the working activity itself', or to (Hunt 2002, p. 217) who says that the use-value of labour power is 'simply the performance of work—the actualizing of the potential labour'. Yet, since working activity or the performance of work occurs in all modes of production, there is no recognition in these sentences by Sinha and Hunt for labour in the abstract as a property of the capitalist relations of production. While a formulation such as Sinha's or Hunt's could be thought to find a support in Marx by citing 'the use-value supplied by the labourer to the capitalist is not, in fact, his labour-power, but its function, some definite useful labour, the work of tailoring, shoemaking, spinning, etc.'; however, it is more easily swallowed if its following sentence is ignored: 'That this same labour is, on the other hand, the universal value-creating element, and thus possesses a property by which it differs from all other commodities, is something which falls outside the frame of reference of the everyday consciousness' (Marx 1867a, p. 681).

[5] Also, a couple of remarks in Marx (1910):

> [T]he specific feature of this commodity [labour-power] is that its use value is itself a factor of exchange value, its use therefore creates a greater exchange value than it itself contained. (p. 280)
>
> The use value of labour-power is labour, the element which produces exchange value... the value which the capitalist receives from the worker in exchange [for labour-power] is greater than the price he pays for this labour. (p. 363, emphasis in original)

> Instead of *labour*, Ricardo should have discussed labour *capacity*. But had he done so, *capital* would also have been revealed as the material conditions of labour, confronting the labourer as power that had acquired an independent existence. And capital would at once have been revealed as a *definite social relationship*. Ricardo thus only distinguishes capital as "ACCUMULATED LABOUR" from "IMMEDIATE LABOUR". And it is something purely physical, only an element in the *labour process*, from which the relation between the worker and capital, WAGES AND PROFITS, could never be developed. (Marx 1910, pp. 36–37, emphasis in original).

In other words, by referring to the sale of 'labour', Ricardo skips over the fact that workers work with means of production they do not own. Ricardo's conception ignores that the workers do *not* have labour to sell, which would require means of production, but rather the worker sells only the *capacity for labour*:

> [T]he worker is compelled to sell, instead of a commodity, his own labour capacity as a commodity, because he is confronted on the other side by the whole of the means of production, by the whole of the objective conditions of labour, as well as by the whole of the means of subsistence, money, means of production and means of subsistence as alien property... [T]he *conditions of his labour confront* him as *alien property*. (Marx 1933, p. 410, emphasis in original)

In sum, the class character of capitalism and the social relations of production of capitalism cannot be theorised adequately without distinguishing between labour and labour power, as we would limit ourselves to the terrain of commodity transactions. Political economists after Ricardo struggled with the problem of what it is that workers sell. This problem, however, could not be solved without distinguishing labour power from labour. It took someone like Marx, with his intellectual powers and commitment to working-class struggle, to do so. Other economists either did not share his commitment to the working-class, or were explicitly committed to the capitalist class.[6]

---

[6]A comment by E.K. Hunt (2002, p. 282) suggests that the classical labour theory of value originated from the struggle of the industrial capitalist against landlords and merchants, not from within the class character of capitalism itself: commodity prices (setting aside scarce or one-of-a-

Engels recognised the great significance of the concept of labour. Following Marx's death, Engels compared Marx's discovery of 'labour-power' to Lavoisier's discovery of 'oxygen' in his preface to the second volume of *Capital*. Posing the question of what separates Marx from classical economics, Engels recalls the theoretical revolution Lavoisier triggered in chemistry through the discovery of a new chemical element, oxygen. While the phlogistic theorists Priestley and Scheele had discovered the *fact* of oxygen without recognising what an innovation it was, Lavoisier created a new category, that is, discovered the new element, and thereby placed 'all chemistry, which in its phlogistic form had stood on its head, squarely on its feet'. Engels then says that Marx stands in the same revolutionary relationship to his predecessors in classical economics. Although the existence of surplus-value was known long before him (albeit under different names), Marx understood that he had to *explain* this fact, explain what value was, and critique Ricardian theory: according to Engels, 'By substituting labour-power, the value-producing property, for labour he solved with one stroke one of the difficulties which brought about the downfall of the Ricardian school, viz., the impossibility of harmonising the mutual exchange of capital and labour with the Ricardian law that value is determined by labour' (Marx 1885, pp. 20–21).[7]

---

kind commodities (Ricardo 1821, p. 12)) are determined by quantity of labour. Distinguishing between productive and unproductive labour within the labour theory thus became a weapon of the industrial capitalists against the landlords (even manufacturing capitalists of the time often undertook labour which they could describe as productive).

As capitalism developed in the 19th century, such a theory was no longer useful for bourgeois interests as the struggle against workers rose in importance. So, bourgeois interests found their own solution: dump labour as the creator of the value of commodities. In its place came marginalism and its inaccurate individualism (pp. 283–84) and an abandonment of a class-based political economy. Ricardo's theory had fulfilled its mission for capital. To drive it further required a transformation of the object of political economy to the interests of the working class.

[7] Althusser (1965) has pointed out the significance of this passage, since Engels is describing how Marx revolutionised the theoretical object of classical economics by recognising the *relations of production* as a concept. Marx's distinction 'does not lie in his having claimed or even demonstrated the primacy of production (Ricardo had already done this is his own way), but in his having transformed the *concept of production* by assigning to it an object radically different from the object designated by the old concept' (Althusser, p. 170, emphasis in original). Marx saw the importance of the material conditions of production belonging to the concept of production—hence constant capital and variable capital, hence Department I and Department II, hence Marx writing to Engels that he 'attributed much more importance to *the category of use-value*' than his predecessors. Where Smith has reduced wealth exclusively to labour, Marx broke 'with this idealism of labour by think-

Capital (1867): Value as Socially Necessary Labour Time and Exchange Value as the Form of Value

By Volume I of *Capital*, Marx emphasises *socially necessary labour time* as the only commonality between commodities exchanged on the market, and which is not the same as the *actual* labour time contained in the production of a specific commodity being sold in. Sieber saw the importance of this concept very early on:

> The introduction into science of this concept [of socially necessary labour time] once and for all eliminates any possibility of discussing the question of value within those narrow, atomistic, confines in which very many economists speak of it: once and for all the ground is cut from under the feet of those objections to Ricardo's theory (Walras, Bastiat, Macleod, etc.), who try to show its falsity in specific instances of exchange.... The value of a specific product is aligned here with the average value.... A product may cost less, but until this relative cheapness of production has become social the owner of the product enjoys on the market a certain advantage, which also does not infringe the law of the average, social value, because it is a special, individual phenomenon. (Sieber 1871, pp. 32–3)

Relative cheapness also pushes all capitalists to innovate, such as by developing technological improvements in production – an insight that

---

ing the concept of the material conditions of every labour process and by providing the concept of the *economic forms of existence* of these material conditions: in the capitalist mode of production, the decisive distinctions between constant and variable capital on the one hand, and between Department I and Department II on the other' (p. 172, emphasis in original). In turn, this leads to the recognition that the social relations of production must include the material elements of the production process.

Labour power as a concept has been subject to counter-attack. Steedman has a six-page discussion stating that no problem is solved by introducing the concept. Surprisingly, however, his position amounts to no more than an assertion, not a demonstration (Steedman 1982, p. 149). Workers are like land, a fixed resource utilised in production. Although workers are reproduced when obtaining their subsistence needs, thereby permitting them to stay alive and work (for capitalists), Steedman does not consider that their reproduction (survival) requires any production at all. He is followed later by Sinha (1996, pp. 210–213) who refers explicitly to a fixed resource and argues that '*the market for labor-power does not exist*' (p. 213, emphasis in original).

Marx incorporates into his concept of the production of relative surplus value.

The concept of 'value-form' – including 'relative' and 'equivalent' forms – emerges in the first published edition of *Capital* in 1867.[8] Upon the advice of both Engels and Kugelman, a special appendix entitled 'The Value-Form' was added while Marx worked on proofs for that edition (Marx and Engels 1948, p. 105). Marx must have been sufficiently satisfied with his new 'non-dialectical' language, as he used much of the language from the appendix in the body of the next edition (also removing most of the remaining Hegelian language from *Capital* – see White 1996, Chapter 4). The third section of Chapter 1 becomes 'The Form of Value or Exchange-Value'. While the title arguably suggests that value-form and exchange-value are the same, the wording of the actual explanation of value-form does not.[9]

---

[8] In drafting *Theories of Surplus Value*, written around 1862, Marx's chapter 'Disintegration of the Ricardian School' cannot be said to introduce this concept, as there is but one use of it within the text: 'The point of departure in the process of the production and circulation of capital, is the independent *form of value* which maintains itself, increases, measures the increase against the original amount' (Marx 1910, p. 318, emphasis is ours).

[9] Ranganayakamma (1999, Part I, Chapter 3) provides a straightforward understanding of the value-form, describing it with examples such as the 'value of the cloth, that did not appear before the exchange [with a coat], appears in the form of a coat' (p. 81; N.B., the coat, not a value of the coat). Thus, the 1867 Appendix to his first edition gives an example of linen exchanging for a coat, the 'linen is the commodity *which expresses its value in the body of a commodity different from it*, the coat' (1867b, p. 134, emphasis in original). The linen's value is expressed in a coat, the linen's value is seen in the coat (while value itself is not seen). In later editions we find that a commodity's function in consideration of the relative form of value is 'only provides the material in which the value of the first commodity is expressed' (1867a, p. 140). And when a material such as gold monopolises a position as universal equivalent, the money-form becomes the general form of value. This reading of the value-form is sustained in Arthur's (2004) work.

Interpretations of the value-form include works by the Uno school in Japan, specifically, Itoh and Sekine, as well as elsewhere in works by Arthur, Lapavitsas, Reuten, Smith, and Williams. Discussing their works would take us afield with little use for present purposes, except to say that a critique by Weeks (1990) appears consistent with the understanding of the present author: 'the law of value must derive from the insight that capitalism is primarily a commodity *producing* society, and only secondarily a commodity *exchanging* society' (p. 18, emphasis in original). The value-form seems to drop from any further role for Marx after Part I of Volume I, other than permitting Marx to denominate values and surplus values in pounds sterling, that is, in units of money.

Kliman's (2000) article, following upon Rubin and Dunayevskaya, relates to the value-form, but with a subtle change. Standing upon a phrase 'intrinsic value' used only once by Marx, Kliman says that value is the 'third thing' present in each commodity exchanged. Thus, '*living* labour *creates* value, is the 'value-forming substance', while the commodity considered as the container of this labour in objective form, *dead* labour, *is* value'. It is not transhistorical but 'an alienated and fetish-

In the 1859 *Contribution*, Marx had not distinguished value from exchange-value:

> The labour time objectified in the use-values of commodities is both the substance that turns them into exchange values and therefore into commodities, and the standard by which the precise magnitude of their value is measured. The corresponding quantities of different use-values containing the same amount of labour time are equivalents; that is, all use-values are equivalents when taken in proportions which contain the same amount of expended, objectified labour time. Regarded as exchange-values all commodities are merely definite quantities of *congealed labour time*. (Marx 1859, p. 272, emphasis in original)

That is to say, there is no way to separate exchange-value from value itself. By August 1862, Marx begins to address the problem of how values are translated into prices (see, for example, Marx's letter to Engels: Marx and Engels 1948, pp. 74–78). The distinction between value and exchange-value could not easily be ignored. This translation problem was later to become a tool of Marx's bourgeois critics. Part of the subsequent debate actually originated, however, in errors in Engels's editorship of the third volume of *Capital* and, subsequently, Bortkiewicz's alteration of textual evidence for his own purposes (see Ramos 1998–99).

Volume I is interspersed with such comments as 'we assume here that the capitalist sells the commodities he has produced at their value, and we shall not concern ourselves with their later return to the market, or the new forms that capital assumes in the sphere of circulation, or the

istic relation between subject and object' (pp. 106–7, emphasis in original). By distinguishing value from exchange-value in this manner, Kliman asserts that a domination of dead labour over living labour is thereby expressed—value is contained in dead objects (commodities), having been previously created by living labour. Similar argumentation appears in Dunayevskaya's conceptual discussion of the organic composition of capital. Her argumentation centres wholly upon her one point: Marx's concept of alienation 'broke through all criticism' of bourgeois society (see Zarembka 2001, p. 360). Marx's discussion of the value-form is not closely followed, and 'intrinsic value' seems offered as a substitute concept.

concrete conditions of reproduction hidden within those forms' (Marx 1867a, p. 710).[10] To make it absolutely clear, he says.

> We have in fact assumed that prices = values. We shall, however, see, in Book III, that even in the case of average prices the assumption cannot be made in this very simple manner. (p. 229, fn. 2)

Subsequently, Marxist political economy, as well as bourgeois economics, seem obsessed with this issue of the relationship between labour time in production and the pricing of commodities. Sinha's (2010) wide-ranging criticism of Marx includes a focus on this concern (pp. 181–8, 205–13, 222–58) and follows a path led by Böhm-Bawerk whose well-known 1896 critique of Marx, according to Sinha, 'is among the best and most forceful to date' (p. 205). This issue can even be argued to be an important conceptual argument against Marx taken up by Keynes after reading McCracken's (1933) book. Keynes wrote to McCracken stating, 'I have found it [the book] of much interest, particularly perhaps the passages relating to Karl Marx, with which I have never been so familiar as I ought to have been' (Kates 2010, p. 44). McCracken (1933, pp. 53–4) considered the introduction of the concept of socially necessary labour time to be one of Marx's three weaknesses, albeit a necessary one if goods are to be exchanged at their actual value. McCracken refers the reader to Böhm-Bawerk's 'admirable' treatment of the question.

To assume that price reflects value for individual commodities, as Marx does in the first volume of *Capital*, was his way of dispensing with the issue for the sake of arriving at his fundamental analysis of the capitalist mode of production. More in keeping with such methodology, but not within Marx's own attempt to do so in Volume III, would be to limit one's analysis to a collection of commodities regularly consumed by workers. The total price of the collection of commodities must cor-

[10] Marx even said in Chapter 1, first edition, fn. 9: 'when we employ the word value with no other additional determination, we refer always to exchange value'. As this footnote is absent in later editions, Dussel (2001, p. 19, citing himself in 1990) claims that Marx 'at the very earliest, in 1872, distinguished between "value" and "exchange-value".' Yet, how then does Dussel understand Marx's earlier work on the transformation problem and was not the footnoted sentence left out merely because the Appendix to the first edition was used as the basis for the re-write of Chapter 1 for the next edition?

respond to its value. Such an approach may address many of the technical concerns that have been raised regarding individual commodity pricing, including the difficult problem of 'joint production'. With this approach we would find surplus value to be the difference between the overall value that workers produce compared to the value of their labour power. One could suspect that some room would still be left for further criticism of Marx, though not as compelling (except perhaps for those who identify every gap in Marx's analysis as sufficient reason to dismiss him entirely).

Marx's 1868 Retrospective on Value: Luxemburg's Later Retrospective

A critical comment on *Capital* in an 1868 Leipzig publication led Marx to write a sharp defence of the concept to his friend Louis Kugelmann:

> … if there had been no chapter at all on 'Value' in my book, then the analysis of the real relations which I provide would contain the proof and evidence of the real relation of value. All the gossip about the necessity of proving the concept of value is based only on the most complete ignorance, as much of the problem under discussion as of the scientific method…. It is self-evident that this *necessity* of the *division* of social labour in certain proportions is not at all negated by the *specific form* of social production…. [When] the connection of social labour asserts itself as a *private exchange* of the individual products of labour, [the form] is precisely the exchange-value of those products. (Marx and Engels 1948, p. 148, emphasis in original)

Value is directly connected to labour and may be considered to confirm what Marx wrote Engels in 1851, namely that 'Value as such has no other "material" than labour itself' (p. 58). Astonishingly, Marx is saying that his first chapter could be dropped entirely without negating the rest of his work (though this is of course not what he advocated)!

After some remarks on the form of value, Marx then turns to the scientific question, writing:

> Science consists precisely in working out *how* the law of value asserts itself. So if one wishes to 'explain' all the phenomena which appear to contradict

> the law from the very start, then one would have to provide the science *before* the science. This is exactly Ricardo's mistake.... (p. 148, emphasis in original)

This remark can be illustrated with a simple example. If we are studying the rate of acceleration of a falling object near the surface of the earth, we do not explain the effect of air resistance *before* we establish the law of acceleration as being 32 feet per second. From another angle, we can understand why Marx wrote in Volume I that 'We have in fact assumed that prices = values' (already discussed above), and why he wrote Domela-Nieuwenhuis in 1880 that 'the connection between "value" and "production price" ... does not belong at all to the theory of value as such' (1948, p. 198).

Marx goes on to explain Ricardo's mistake. We, however, prefer the language he uses with Engels in 1877 to make the same point, 'Ricardo's great sin, which made him indigestible from the start, was precisely the attempt to prove the correctness of his theory of value by those economic facts which seemed to contradict it most' (1948, p. 187).

Luxemburg broke off working on her *Introduction to Political Economy* to write and publish *The Accumulation of Capital.* Her remarks on value here are centred on a discussion of Marx's correction of Adam Smith to include that the value of commodities must include not only living labour but also the dead labour time embodied in constant capital. For Smith, 'the total annual production of commodities by society could also be divided without remainder in terms of their total value into these two parts: wages and surplus value. Here the category of capital has suddenly completely disappeared: society produces nothing but revenue, nothing but articles of consumption, which are also completely consumed by society' (1913, p. 32). She elaborates:

> That this posed an extremely difficult theoretical problem is demonstrated by the extent to which Marx himself burrowed deep into the matter without at first making any progress or finding a way out; these attempts can be retraced in *Theories of Surplus Value*. However, he did finally manage to provide a brilliant solution, and this came precisely on the basis of his theory of value. Smith was perfectly right: the value of each individual commodity, and of the total production of commodities, represents noth-

> ing other than labor. Furthermore, he was right when he stated that, from the capitalist point of view, all labor can be divided into paid labor (which replaces wages) and unpaid labor (which accrues to the various classes of owners of the means of production). However, he forgot (or rather he overlooked) the fact that labor, alongside its characteristic of creating new value, has also the attribute of transferring the old value contained in the means of production to the commodities newly produced with the latter. (Luxemburg 1913, p. 34)

The theoretical understanding of the renewal of social capital was at stake. Marx's solution was to point out that living labour is not only newly created value, but also the source for transferring past labour (having been engaged in creating means of production) into the value of current commodities, that is, an amalgamation of old, transferred value and newly created value. Thus, where Smith had neglected to incorporate the means of production into commodity values, Marx did not. Furthermore, it becomes 'of decisive importance, for using it, whether the commodity is itself a means of production or a consumer good' (p. 44). This distinction in turn underpins, for her, the importance of Marx's schemes of reproduction in which production of the means of production is separated from production of the means of consumption.

Here we see Luxemburg's recognition of a deep theoretical problem that Marx had to work very hard in order to solve. Intellectual labour is difficult labour indeed.

Marx's 1873 Appreciation of Sieber's Discussion of Value: *Capital*, Volume I, First Edition

> [O]nly a short step separates the approach to the question of the Smith-Ricardo school from the definition of the subject [of value], which left nothing to be desired in terms of clarity, precision and certitude. The credit... should be given to the German economist K. Marx. Sieber (1871, p. 17)

> N. Sieber ... referred to my theory of value, of money and capital as in its fundamentals a necessary sequel to the teaching of Smith and Ricardo. What astonishes a Western European when he reads this excellent piece of work is the author's consistent and firm grasp of the purely theoretical position. Marx (1867a, p. 99, 'Postface' to the second German edition)

N. I. Sieber (1871) analysed the first edition of *Capital* during Marx's lifetime, claiming that 'Marx's method is the deductive method of the whole English school' (p. 30). Marx (1867a, pp. 99–100) cited this sentence from Sieber in his 1873 Postface to the second edition of *Capital* – without objection. Indeed, a few sentences earlier in the same Postface, Marx describes Sieber's work as 'excellent' on the theoretical issue of value.

In 1874 Marx read and commented upon Sieber's article 'Marx's Economic Theory', published that same year (Sieber 1874). This article contained some criticisms of Marx, yet did not dissuade Marx from his approval of Sieber. In 1881 Marx continued to judge Sieber's work positively, to the point that Sieber's work could be considered an alternative to his own: 'Mr. Wagner could have familiarized himself with the difference between me and Ricardo both from *Capital* and from *Sieber's work* (if he knew Russian)' (Marx 1930, p. 534, emphasis in original).

Sieber was well aware that a definition of value was at stake; he even prefaced his chapter with the question 'what exactly is value?' (1871, p. 17). He begins by meticulously summarising Marx's first chapter. He then undertakes his own comparison of Marx to Ricardo in order to show how Marx's theory contained 'new and important scientific propositions, which impart to Ricardo's theory a fuller and more complete form, and also endorse its validity with new proofs' (p. 30). These new propositions, in Sieber's order, are the following:

(i) Rather than being only a 'regulator' of exchange, labour itself is value. It is 'the only *social* creator of those proportions in which acts of exchange take place' (p. 31, emphasis in original). Labour in its universal form only exists in exchange economies (a point also made by Sieber a few pages earlier, pp. 24–25).
(ii) Marx's concept of socially necessary labour time solves a problem raised by those objecting to Ricardo's theory on narrow, individual grounds (pp. 32–33).

(iii) The money form is a necessity for commodities to pass to the stage of being 'fully a value' (p. 36). By contrast,

> ... neither Ricardo himself nor his followers, being concerned as they were solely with investigations into the magnitude of value and conditions upon which it depended, paid any attention to the qualitative difference between the labour contained in money and that contained in other products, and did not notice that only labour of the first type was labour of the directly social form.... The money form, [Marx] says, is indispensable for every commodity, because only by manifesting itself in monetary material can each concrete type of labour become social labour. (pp. 41–42, emphasis in original)

Marx himself, following his 1881 re-statement of appreciation for Sieber, confirms Sieber's reading when saying that 'Ricardo did indeed concern himself with labour solely as a *measure of the magnitude of value*, and was therefore unable to find any link between his theory of value and the nature of money' (Marx 1930, p. 534, emphasis in original). Note that Marx made the same point in his *Contribution* discussed above.

(iv) Money is not merely a convenience (as J. S. Mill had argued). Rather, 'a profound and many-sided division of labour is impossible without money' (p. 40), says Sieber in interpreting Marx. Indeed, economists prior to Marx ignored 'the form of value', and 'the determination of those specific particularities which characterize monetary exchange in economies with the division of labour' (p. 43).

In reading Sieber, one can on the one hand join Marx in appreciating the depth of Sieber's analysis. Both White (2001, p. 13) and Smith (2001, p. 59) are complimentary of Sieber's understanding of Marx's first edition. Marx certainly had no reason to say of Sieber what he said later of Rodbertus, who 'has neither examined nor grasped the substance of value any more than Ricardo did' (Marx 1930, p. 552). On the other hand, despite Sieber's suggestion that Marxist value theory represents a mere 'short step', does it not actually represent a major break with Ricardo – a break that signifies a different class position in the production of theory? Sinha has suggested correctly that the 'concept of *value* in the discourse of *Capital* refers to its object, the *capitalist mode of production*, and does not take shape without the introduction of the capital-wage labour relation, an element... that is explicitly absent' from the beginning discussion of simple commodity production (1990, p. 42, emphasis in original).[11]

'Notes on Wagner' (1881)

We have already mentioned that Marx compliments Sieber in his 1881 notes on Adolph Wagner's *Lehrbuch der Politischen Ökonomie*. The notes are, of course, reactions to Wagner's writings, but also reaffirm his conclusions about value:

> As for 'Labour', Mr. Wagner does not distinguish between the *concrete character of each kind of labour* and the *expenditure of labour power* common

[11] Milios et al. (2002) have argued that Marx's value concept (and, thus, surplus value) is a monetary one, determined in exchange. Value is only indirectly measurable through its monetary form, through its appearance therein, so that value itself, they say, is *conceptually non-measurable*: 'In Marx's system, value does not belong to the world of empirically detectable (and measurable) quantities; only money does… Exchange value is the sole *objective materialisation* (form of appearance) of value' (p. viii and 21, emphasis in original).

While they do not happen to cite the passage, the observation that exchange-value is the sole appearance of value appears very early in *Capital*: 'The progress of our investigation will show that exchange-value is the only form in which the value of commodities can manifest itself or be expressed'. To begin, however, 'we must consider the nature of value independently of its form of appearance' (Marx 1867a, p. 128). Presumably, therefore, Milios et al., would not be disturbed by the passage which quickly follows regarding the measurement of value:

> How, then, is the magnitude of this value [of human labour in the abstract] to be measured? By means of the quantity of the 'value-forming substance', the labour, contained in the article. This quantity of labour is measured by its duration and the labour-time is itself measured on the particular scale of hours, days, etc. (p. 129)

Yet, and more significantly, reference to value being associated with labour time is frequent, even past all of Part I of *Capital*. Where they find that the first half-dozen pages of *Capital*, Volume I (i.e., Section 1 of Chapter 1) are thoroughly Ricardian and that the next hundred-plus pages of Volume I after Section 1 '*theoretically recast*' (Milios et al. 2002, p. 17, emphasis in original) those first pages, we find that the measurability of value is sustained throughout *Capital*. Part II says that the value of labour power 'is determined, as in the case of every other commodity, by the labour-time necessary for the production, and consequently also the reproduction, of this specific article' (p. 274). This passage goes on to illustrate a calculation of the value of labour power, and repeats that 'the value of every commodity is determined by the labour-time required to provide it in its normal quality' (p. 277). In Part III, reference is made to 'determining the value of the yarn, or the labour-time required for its production' (p. 294). In Part IV, we find 'the value of labour-power, i.e., the labour-time requisite to produce labour-power' (p. 297), and the 'law of the determination of value by labour-time' (p. 436). In Part V, 'the value-product in which a day of labour is embodied increases with the length of that day' (p. 663); etc. We, therefore, cannot follow Milios, et al. in claiming value's non-measurability for Marx.

> to all these concrete types of labour.... [I]n this duality of the commodity there presents itself the dual *character* of the labour whose product it is: of *useful* labour, i.e. the concrete modes of the labours which create use-values, and of abstract *labour*, of labour *as expenditure of labour power*, regardless of the "useful" way in which it is expended... (Marx 1930, p. 531, 546, emphasis in original, paragraphing not indicated)
>
> What I proceed from is the simplest social form in which the product of labour presents itself in contemporary society, and this is the '*commodity*'. This I analyse, initially, in the *form in which it appears*. Here I find... a *use-value* [and] a *bearer of exchange-value*.... Further analysis of the latter shows me that exchange-value is merely a '*form* of expression', an independent way of presenting the *value* contained in the commodity... [T]he *concrete social form* of the product of labour, the '*commodity*', is on the one hand, use-value and on the other, 'value', not exchange value, since the mere *form* of expression is not its own *content*. (pp. 544–5, emphasis in original)
>
> [W]hen analysing the commodity I do not immediately drag in definitions of 'capital', not even when dealing with the 'use-value' of the commodity. Such definitions are bound to be sheer nonsense as long as we have advanced no further than the analysis of the elements of the commodity.... [M]y *analytic* method... does not proceed from *man* but from a given economic period of society... (pp. 546–7, emphasis in original, paragraphing not indicated)

The first comment illustrates the importance of clearly recognising 'abstract labour'. The next extract confirms the necessity of illuminating the nature of exchange-value to get to its substance, value.[12] The last statement defends, at least implicitly, the correctness of *Capital*'s study of the capitalist mode of production by starting with 'Commodities', rather than a definition of humanity.

A Problem: Value Alongside Accumulation of Capital

Marx began his theoretical work by recognising that economic categories are socially determined. Later, he introduced the concept of abstract

[12] Kristjanson-Gural (2005) asks whether, for individual commodities, value is solely defined in production prior to exchange, or whether exchange has a role in the determination of value. But his question seems inconsistent with Marx's conception of value insofar as exchange is a form of value, not a determination thereof.

labour. They were followed in *Capital* by the introduction of labour power as a concept and the argument that value is the substance of exchange-value, but distinct from it. Little of his analysis of value was changed thereafter. Yet Marx's developing understanding retains a presumption, dating to at least as early as 1858, that leads to a problem. In that year, Marx sent Engels an outline of the work he was preparing at the time, and included a significant comment concerning value:

> *Value*. This is reduced entirely to the quantity of labour; time as a measure of value.... Value as such has no other 'material' than labour itself.... It already presupposes 1. the destruction of natural communism (in India etc.); 2. the destruction of all undeveloped, pre-bourgeois modes of production which are not governed in their totality by exchange. Although it is an abstraction, it is an abstraction which can only be assumed on the basis of a particular economic development of society. (Marx and Engels 1948, p. 58)

In the *Grundrisse*, he says that 'The economic concept of value does not occur in antiquity.' The 'concept of value is entirely peculiar to the most modern economy, since it is the most abstract expression of capital itself and of the production resting on it' (Marx 1939–41a, p. 776).

This presumption is continued in the first volume of *Capital*. In a footnote on the accumulation of capital, Marx states: 'In order to examine the object of our investigation in its integrity; free from all disturbing subsidiary circumstances, we must treat the whole world of trade as one nation, and assume that capitalist production is established everywhere and has taken possession of every branch of industry' (1867a, p. 727, fn. 2). Luxemburg (1913) reviews several other statements Marx makes in this regard, notably in Volume II, concluding: 'no doubt, therefore, that Marx's aim was to give an exposition of the process of accumulation in a society under the general and exclusive domination of the capitalist mode of production, and consisting exclusively of capitalists and workers' (p. 238). This appears even as late as 1878 in the last draft of Marx's schemes of reproduction (discussed in Zarembka 2009, p. 67). This is to be understood as an assumption on the part of Marx that is necessary to simplify and clarify his analysis, particularly as we know full well that he knew the world to be much more complex. But this presumption is nevertheless problematic within the internal logic of his work, and risks destabilising the concept of value as such.[13]

The problem arises from the fact that the separate concept of 'accumulation of capital' is not consistent with the presumption of a fully capitalist social formation. Though the theoretical relevance thereof is often underappreciated (see Zarembka 2000), Marx's accumulation of capital must include *continuous* penetration of non-capitalist modes. As Marx himself expressed, 'a part of the annual surplus-labour must have been applied to the production of additional means of production and subsistence. [...] Now, in order that these components may actually function as capital, the capitalist class requires additional labour. [...] Accumulation of capital is therefore multiplication of the proletariat' (Marx 1867a, pp. 727–8, 764). While population increase could be a partial element of this increase, it cannot be the essential aspect of an understanding of capital accumulation. Thus, presumption of a fully capitalist world undermines the understanding of capital accumulation found in *Capital*. Marx's presumption of a fully capitalist world does not mesh with his understanding of accumulation.

'Results of the Immediate Process of Production', drafted for Volume I, already contained the seed of the problem:

> The *accumulation process* is itself an immanent moment of the capitalist production process. It includes the *creation* of new *wage labourers* [...] Capital therefore does not just produce capital, it produces a growing mass of workers, the material which alone enables it to function as additional capital. [...] Capitalist production is not only the reproduction of the relation, it is its reproduction on an ever growing scale [...]
>
> The *growth of capital* and the *increase of the proletariat* therefore appear as associated *products* of the same process, even if they are polar opposites. (Marx 1933, p. 463, emphasis in original)

Marx excluded 'Results' when Volume I went to the publisher in 1867. The published edition of Volume I shows that 'Very little remained of the argument that in its cycle of reproduction capital created its own preconditions on an ever increasing scale' (White, p. 201).

[13] Much of this paragraph and the next are drawn from Zarembka (2009, pp. 64–5).

Value is developed in *Capital* as the foundation of Marx's theoretical understanding of the capitalist mode of production. Since *Poverty*, economic categories were to be understood as socially conditioned. What then is to be the appropriate object of analysis leading to the concept of value – simply the capital/wage-labour relation, or that relation as well as the penetration of non-capitalist modes of production corresponding to accumulation of capital? The former has been universally presumed, based upon Marx's simplifying assumption that 'capitalist production is everywhere established'. But if penetration must be included in the object of analysis, is value left unaffected?[14]

Reconsidering Value

> As a concrete, historical process, capitalist accumulation as a whole thus has two different facets. The first of these consists in the process that occurs at the point of production of surplus value – in the factories, the mines, the farms [...]
>
> The other dimension of capital accumulation consists in a process that takes place between capital and noncapitalist forms of production. [...] Here violence, fraud, oppression, and plunder are displayed quite openly, without any attempt to disguise them, and it requires a lot of effort to uncover the strict laws governing the economic process beneath this turmoil of political violence and trials of strength. Luxemburg (1913, p. 329)

Marx spent many years after the publication of Volume I studying pre-capitalist societies, reading much Russian literature on the topic:

> Just as Marx was about to publish the first volume of *Das Kapital* he had run into serious problems with the section of his projected work which

[14]Without concern for penetration of non-capitalist modes of production, Weeks (1982) claimed that without full realisation of all production, Marxist theory of value must be rejected. With a focus on underconsumptionism, he says that 'if one postulates that a "pure" capitalist system is endemically afflicted by the inability to sell all that is produced, then the Marxian concept of value *must* be rejected' (Weeks 1982, p. 61, emphasis in original). Weeks' argument is addressed in Zarembka (2009, pp. 73–5).

> would deal with the circulation of capital. He had hitherto assumed that capital would spread throughout the world carrying all before it, but he had overlooked the fact that even in his own native Hunsrücken despite the development of capitalism, the older, collective, social and economic system still survived. Capitalism, apparently, did not necessarily erode traditional peasant society, but coexisted with it. Marx removed much of the philosophical underpinnings for his earlier view of capitalist development from the published version of *Das Kapital*, continuing the excisions in the second and French editions, and he embarked on a lengthy empirical investigation of how capital actually began to circulate. He had an excellent example to hand in Russia, which had just embarked on the capitalist road, having abolished serfdom a few years earlier. In 1870 Marx learnt Russian and got down to the serious job of collecting materials on Russian economic development. (White 2001, pp. 12–13, summarising a major result of his own 1996 book)

Marx (1948, p. 165) writes Engels in 1870 that the most important work published since Engels' own *Condition of the Working Class in England* is Flerovsky's *Condition of the Working* [*Peasant*] *Class in Russia* (published in 1869). What a recommendation! Flerovsky's book focuses precisely upon the proletarianisation process and the role of taxation in it: 'The main reason which compels the worker [peasant] to resort to the capitalist is to pay his taxes' (as translated by White 1996, p. 249, who also explains that a 'worker' for Flerovsky is a 'peasant' in our usage). It is fair to say that Marx is trying to understand the forms of – and limitations to – the penetration of capital, which became an ongoing focus to the end of his life and included extensive correspondence with Russians.[15]

Consider a later example: in the late 19th century, Rhodesian gold mines were in desperate need of waged labourers. These were supplied by the British colonial authorities through the institution of extraordinarily high taxation on peasant land in Nyasaland (now Malawi), thereby forcing young men from peasant families off the land and into waged employment. Working in the mines could aid families in paying land taxes or provide a market for cash crops, the profit from which could be

[15] The foregoing two paragraphs are borrowed from Zarembka (2009, pp. 66–7), while the next two are borrowed from p. 76.

used to pay taxes (van Onselen 1976). Nevertheless, as peasant land continued to go into receivership, remaining family members were driven into waged labour on large capitalist farms producing subsistence crops, ultimately converting nearly all subsistence peasant farmers into value-producing proletarians. Such a process is clearly a case of the accumulation of capital. (In cases like this occurring after capitalism had been established as a mode of production, such a result is often, unfortunately, mislabelled as 'primitive accumulation' – see Zarembka 2002.)

But what to make of the intermediate step, in which some peasants produce cash crops, which are in turn purchased by those working in the mines? The miners, working waged jobs, produce value. But what of the peasants selling cash crops to pay taxes? This process involves coercion – namely, the power of the state to expropriate land for non-payment of taxes – much more so than it involves any kind of 'free market'. Where in the traditional analysis of waged labour as producer of value is the coercion involved in proletarianisation captured?

Marx's late interest in capital's penetration finds its successor in Luxemburg's interest in the same question, evidenced most concretely by her *Introduction to Political Economy* (1925), a posthumously published draft (although some chapters were never found). Her work uses many of the same sources Marx had studied, but concludes with a more complete destruction of the Russian commune than Marx had foreseen.

A Conundrum highlighted by Luxemburg

Although their connections are deep, Marx's *Capital* and Luxemburg's *Introduction to Political Economy* have distinct points of departure. Marx begins with 'Commodities'. Luxemburg does not arrive at this subject until several chapters later, namely, those on 'What is Political Economy?', 'Social Labour' (of which no copy exists), and two on 'Material on Economic History', which includes primitive communism, the feudal system, and medieval city and guilds (a portion of which we have already cited). Her draft chapter on commodity production is followed by one on 'Wage-Labour'. For Luxemburg, the capitalist mode of production arises in an historical context, which she chooses to elaborate first.

Luxemburg's chapter on wage-labour addresses the cost of labour power and the concept of surplus value. It neglects to mention the concept of *abstract labour*. She also neglects to mention the concepts of *production of absolute surplus value* and of *relative surplus value*, although both are very clearly discussed indirectly. In other words, other than labour power, value, and surplus value, Luxemburg's *Introduction* is not interested in reprising concepts developed by Marx so much as in utilising what can be gained from Marx's expositions.

With regard to the concept of value – which comes after the historical discussion – a problem surfaces. Toward the end of her chapter on commodity production, Luxemburg offers a statement on Marx's contribution to the concept of value compared to Smith's and Ricardo's:

> In the second half of the eighteenth and the early nineteenth century, the Englishmen Adam Smith and David Ricardo made the great discovery that the value of each commodity is nothing other than the human labour it contains, so that with the exchange of commodities equal quantities of different kinds of labour are exchanged for one another. Money is simply the mediator here.... At the time when the shoemaker and the baker exchanged their respective products, as I said, it was still obvious and visible that exchange came into being because, despite their different uses, each of these took the same amount of labour as the other, and each was therefore worth the same as the other in so far as they both took the same amount of time. (1925, p. 257)

Labour time regulates exchange. This suggests that the concept of value would apply to exchange before capitalism, although she does not quite use the word *value*. A passage in *Accumulation* (1913, p. 183) reads similarly, but a passage explicating Marx's scheme of simple reproduction is unambiguous even while connecting the concepts of value and labour power transhistorically:

> The above is merely the expression in value relations of the foundation not only of capitalist reproduction, but of reproduction in every society. In every productive society, regardless of its social form – whether this be the primitive small village community of the Bakairí of Brazil, the *oikos* of a Timon of Athens with its slaves, or the imperial *feudal estates* of Charlemagne – the mass of labor at society's disposal must be allocated such that means of

> production and means of consumption are produced in sufficient quantities. (pp. 49–50)

She argues that the concept of value is as applicable to a pre-capitalist society engaging in trading as to the capitalist mode of production.

This theoretical practice does not correspond to Marx's position that concepts are applicable to the mode of production being analysed (the capitalist mode in this case), but not across modes. As we have noted, Marx emphasises in *Poverty of Philosophy* and repeats in the *Grundrisse* that economic concepts arise under concrete historical conditions. We do not have evidence that he ever changed his opinion on this matter.[16] Therefore, Luxemburg's work itself is not directly helpful with regard to deepening an understanding of the concept of value.

Setting this issue aside, Luxemburg moves on in her *Introduction*, taking a different direction regarding Marx's contribution on value. Smith and Ricardo's discovery:

> is only a half-truth. The other half of the truth consists in the explanation of how and why it is that human labor then assumes the strange form of exchange-value, and the puzzling form of money at that. The English founders of political economy did not even raise this question…
>
> … Only Karl Marx … made comparisons between present relations and earlier ones at other times. He showed in this way that people had lived for thousands of years without knowing much about money and exchange.… This meaningless invention [money, being without itself any particular use] is thus a necessity without which no exchange would be possible, i.e. the entire history of culture since the dissolution of primitive communism. (1925, p. 258)

---

[16] There may be an example in his work that value may fail to be defined clearly by Marx around wage-labour, even if not enough to call Marx's overall usage of the concept of value into question. Consider the following from his unpublished 'Results' (removed by Marx before publication of Volume I):

> The distinctive character of the *formal* subsumption of labour under capital appears at its sharpest if we compare it to situations in which capital is to be found in certain specific, subordinate functions, but where it has not yet emerged as the direct purchaser of labour and as the immediate owner of the process of production, and where in consequence it has not yet succeeded in becoming the dominant force, capable of determining the form of society as a whole. In India, for example, the capital of the *usurer* advances raw materials or tools or even both to the immediate producer in the form of money. The exorbitant interest which it attracts, the interest which, irrespective of its magnitude, it extorts from the primary producer, is just another name for surplus-value. (Marx 1933, pp. 1022–3, emphasis in original)

This insightful passage comes after a long discussion of money. Luxemburg first points out that humans lived without trade for a long time. Trade is then described by her as developing over time, as illustrated by the cobbler producing shoes and the baker producing bread and each requiring the product of the other. Thus, they exchange. As exchanging products becomes more complex, the need for some product that is universally required is very useful, so that the desire for this product and the awareness that it can be utilised for trade is met simultaneously. This product is cattle, which can provide all of life's necessities – 'they supply meat, milk, hides, plowing service, etc.' (p. 244). Cattle, 'a product of labour that was desired by everyone and at all time', became money because they were extremely useful. But, subsequently, 'the more that cattle were used as mediator in universal exchange, the more the immediate use of cattle as a means of subsistence fell into the background' (p. 246). Thus, a metal (notably useless for sustaining life) later replaced cattle as money. As a coda to her explanation, she notes that 'the old Roman word *pecunia*, meaning money, stems from *pecus*, meaning cattle' (p. 248).

Money, whether cattle or a dead piece of metal, takes on the form of wealth. But money is not the basis of wealth, labour is. We can see the same redirection away from money when Marx refers to the *real accumulation* of capital: 'it may also happen that surplus-value must be converted into money and this money hoarded for a much longer time before this process, i.e. real accumulation, expansion of production, can take place' (Marx 1885, p. 489). From this remark, likely one of the last that he wrote for any portion of *Capital*, it seems clear that money is not accumulation as such, presumably because money itself does not produce any value. Rather, money in capitalism is a kind of holding mechanism to be used for value creation when workers are hired in exchange for it.[17]

[17] Baronian (2013) claims that Luxemburg 'forgets that money is not only the form in which surplus value is realized, but the starting point of the production and reproduction process itself'. The accumulation process, says Baronian, has as its aim 'money itself as the absolute form of value' (p. 158). Yet, Luxemburg says regarding *Capital*, Volume 2 that production of surplus value is, in fact, the underlying focus of Marx's work:

> *Volume 2 deals with the process of circulation of capital.* The circulation of capital is the total process that capital as a whole goes through. This encompasses the purchase of raw materials, and of means of production, the actual production process itself, and the sale of the goods produced. The circulation process is the entire circuit completed by capital.

Returning to the unpublished *Grundrisse*, Marx writes:

> In every form of society there is a particular [branch of] production which determines the position and importance of all the others, and the relations obtaining in this branch accordingly determine those in all other branches. It is the general light tingeing all other colours and modifying them in their specific quality; it is a special ether determining the specific gravity of everything found in it. (Marx 1939b–41b, p. 43)

For Althusser (1965) this is an important passage, used by him in the conclusion of many prior pages of discussion. Marx's theoretical object was the capitalist mode of production and it required new concepts appropriate to that object in order 'to think the determination of the elements of a whole by the structure of the whole' (p. 187). Althusser, however, was unaware of any difficulty with the concept of accumulation of capital.

It is Luxemburg, not Althusser, who has most clearly thrust this theoretical challenge upon us, particularly, but not exclusively with her *Accumulation of Capital*. She is the more remarkable in that many of Marx's unpublished works cited here were unavailable to her but can been used to confirm the similarity between her theoretical conception and his. Unconsciously, both were advancing toward a significant theoretical problem regarding the conception of value in Marxist theory.

> Volume 1 deals with the middle phase, which is the decisive one, the most important, because it shows where surplus value comes from. (Luxemburg 2013b, p. 421, emphasis in original)

While much discussion within Part 3 of the second volume of *Capital* focuses on monetary questions and questions of hoarding, is not Luxemburg correct? Baronian's second chapter discusses the necessity of money in Marx, but without a clear conclusion. By contrast, Karimzadi (2013) addresses the question of the origin of money over the history of thought in political economy, and is somewhat critical of Marx for failing to get to the bottom of the issue. He does credit Marx with an emphasis on the necessity of exchange occurring in an historical context, while failing to recognise that money is not synonymous with a generally accepted medium of exchange, whether as a commodity such as cattle, gold or silver, or as paper currency mandated by the state. This author has reviewed Karimzadi's book (see Zarembka 2015b).

Bibliography

Althusser, L. [1965] (1970). The object of *capital.* In L. Althusser & E. Balibar (Eds.), *Reading capital* (pp. 71–198). London: New Left Books.

Althusser, L. [1974] (1976). Elements of self-criticism. In L. Althusser (Ed.), *Essays in self-criticism* (pp. 105–149). London: New Left Books.

Arthur, C. J. (2004). Money and the form of value. In R. Bellofiore & N. Taylor (Eds.), *The constitution of capital: Essays on volume 1 of capital,* (pp. 35–62). Basingstoke/New York: Palgrave Macmillan.

Baronian, L. (2013). *Marx and living labour.* London/New York: Routledge.

Biernacki, R. (1995). *The fabrication of labor: Germany and Britain, 1640–1914.* Berkeley: University of California Press.

Cleaver, H. [1979] (2000). *Reading capital politically* (2nd ed.). Leeds/Edinburg: AK Press.

Dussel, E. (2001). The four drafts of capital: Towards a new interpretation of the dialectical thought of Marx. *Rethinking Marxism, 13*(1), 10–26.

Foley, D. (1991). Labour power. In T. Bottomore (Ed.), *A dictionary of Marxist thought* (2nd ed., pp. 296–297). Oxford/Cambridge, MA: Blackwell.

Hunt, E.K. (2002). *History of economic thought* (2nd ed.). Berkeley: University of California Press.

Karimzadi, S. (2013). *Money and its origins.* London/New York: Routledge.

Kates, S. (2010). Influencing Keynes: The intellectual origins of the *general theory. History of Economic Ideas,, XVIII*(3), 33–64.

Kliman, A. J. (2000). Marx's concept of intrinsic value. *Historical Materialism, 6,* 89–113.

Kristjanson-Gural, D. (2005). Exchange, demand and the market-price of production: Reconciling traditional and monetary approaches to value and price. In P. Zarembka (Ed.), *The capitalist state and its economy: Democracy in socialism, research in political economy* (Vol. 22, pp. 137–169). Amsterdam: JAI/ Elsevier Science.

Luxemburg, R. [1913] (2015). The accumulation of capital. In *The complete works of Rosa Luxemburg: Volume II, Economic writings* (Vol. 2). London: Verso.

Luxemburg, R. (1925). *Introduction to political economy* in Luxemburg 2013a, pp. 89–300.

Luxemburg, R. (2013a). Notes About the Economic Form of Antiquity/Slavery. In P. Hudis (Ed.), *The complete works of Rosa Luxemburg: Volume I: Economic writings.* London/New York: Verso, pp. 331–338.

Luxemberg, R. (2013b). Practical economics: Volume 2 of Marx's *Capital.* In Luxemburg 2013a, pp. 421–460.

Marx, K. [1847] (1975). The poverty of philosophy. In *Marx-Engels collected works* (Vol. 6, pp. 105–212). New York: International Publishers.

Marx, K. [1859] (1975). A contribution to the critique of political economy. In *Marx-Engels collected works* (Vol. 29, pp. 257–417). New York: International Publishers.

Marx, K. [1867a] (1982). *Capital. A critique of political economy* (Vol. I). New York: Penguin Books.

Marx, K. [1867b] (1978). The value-form. *Capital and Class 2*(1), 130–150.

Marx, K. [1885] (1992). *Capital. A critique of political economy* (Vol. I1). New York: Penguin Books.

Marx, K. [1905a] (1988). Theories of surplus value, Part I. In *Marx-Engels collected works* (Vol. 30, pp. 348–451). New York: International Publishers.

Marx, K. [1905b] (1989). Theories of surplus value, Part II. In *Marx-Engels collected works* (Vol. 31, pp. 6–581). New York: International Publishers.

Marx, K. [1910] (1991). Theories of surplus value, Part III. In *Marx-Engels collected works* (Vol. 32, pp. 7–545). Nework: International Publishers.

Marx, K. [1930] (1989). Marginal notes on Adolph Wagner's Lehrbuch der Politischen Oekonomie. In *Marx-Engels collected works* (Vol. 24, pp. 531–559). New York: International Publishers.

Marx, K. [1933] (1982). Results of the direct production process in Marx [1867c] (1982), pp. 949–1083.

Marx, K. [1939a] (1973). *Grundrisse.* New York/Toronto: Vintage Books.

Marx, K. [1939b] (1986). Grundrisse. In *Marx-Engels collected works* (Vol. 28). New York: International Publishers.

Marx, K., & F. Engels [1948] (1983). *Letters on capital.* London: New Park Publications.

McCracken, H. L. (1933). *Value theory and business cycles.* Binghamton: Falcon Press.

Milios, J., Dimoulis, D., & Economakis, G. (2002). *Karl Marx and the classics: An essay on value, crises and the capitalist mode of production.* Hampshire/Burlington: Ashgate.

Mohun, S. (1991). Value. In T. Bottomore (Ed.), *A dictionary of Marxist thought* (2nd ed., pp. 564–568). Oxford/Cambridge, MA: Blackwell.

Oakley, A. (1984). *Marx's critique of political economy: Intellectual sources and evolution* (Vol. I, pp. 1844–1861). London: Routledge & Kegan Paul.

Oishi, T. (2001). *The unknown Marx: Reconstructing a unified perspective.* London/Sterling: Pluto.

Postone, M. (1993). *Time, labor and social domination: A reinterpretation of Marx's critical theory.* Cambridge/New York: Cambridge University Press.

Ramos, M. A. (1998–99). Value and price of production: New evidence on Marx's transformation procedure. *International Journal of Political Economy, 28*(4), 55–81.

Ranganayakamma. (1999). *An introduction to Marx's capital (in 3 Volumes)* (Vol. I). Hyderabad: Sweet Home Publications.

Ricardo, D. [1821] (1951). *On the principles of political economy and taxation.* Cambridge: Cambridge University Press.

Rubin, I. I. [1927] (1978). Abstract labour and value in Marx's system. *Capital and Class, 5*, 107–139.

Sieber, N. I. [1871] (2001). Marx's theory of value and money. In P. Zarembka (Ed.), *Marx's* capital *and capitalism*; *Markets in a socialist alternative, research in political economy* (Vol. 19, pp. 17–45). New York: JAI/Elsevier Science.

Sieber, N. I. [1874] (2011). Marx's economic theory. In P. Zarembka & R. Desai (Eds), *Revitalizing Marxist theory for today's capitalism, research in political economy* (Vol. 27, pp. 155–190) Bingley: Emerald Publishing Group Limited.

Sinha, A. (1990). The concept of value in Marx: A reinterpretation. In P. Zarembka (Ed.), *Research in political economy* (Vol. 12, pp. 41–79). Greenwich: JAI Press.

Sinha, A. (1996). A critique of part one of *capital* volume one: The value controversy revisited. In P. Zarembka & A. Sinha (Eds.), *Recent developments in Marxist theory, research in political economy* (Vol. 15, pp. 195–222). Greenwich: JAI Press.

Sinha, A. (2010). *Theories of value from Adam Smith to Piero Sraffa.* New Delhi: Routledge.

Smith, D. N. (2001). The spectral reality of value: Sieber, Marx, and Commodity Fetishism. In P. Zarembka (Ed.), *Marx's* capital *and capitalism*; *Markets in a socialist alternative, research in political economy* (Vol. 19), pp. 47–66. New York: JAI/Elsevier Science.

Steedman, I. (1982). Marx on Ricardo. In I. Bradley & M. Howard (Eds.), *Classical and Marxian political economy*: *Essays in Honour of Ronald L. Meek* (pp. 115–156). London/Basingstoke: Macmillan.

van Onselen, C. (1976). *Chibaro: African mine labour in Southern Rhodesia, 1900–1933.* London: Pluto.

Weeks, J. (1982). A note on underconsumptionist theory and the labor theory of value. *Science & Society, 46*(1), 60–76.

Weeks, J. (1990). Abstract labor and commodity production. In P. Zarembka (Ed.), *Research in political economy* (Vol. 12, pp. 3–19). Greenwich/London: JAI Press.

White, J. D. (1996). *Karl Marx and the intellectual origins of dialectical materialism*. London: Macmillian.

White, J. D. (2001). Nikolai Sieber and Karl Marx. In P. Zarembka (Ed.), *Marx's capital and capitalism; markets in a socialist alternative, research in political economy* (Vol. 19, pp. 3–16). New York: JAI/Elsevier Science.

Zarembka, P. (2000). Accumulation of capital, its definition: A century after Lenin and Luxemburg. In P. Zarembka (Ed.), *Value, capitalist dynamics and money, research in political economy* (Vol. 18, pp. 183–241). New York: JAI/Elsevier Science.

Zarembka, P. (2001). The declining importance of Hegel for Marx: J. D. White's provocative work. *Historical Materialism, 8*, 355–365.

Zarembka, P. 2002, "Primitive Accumulation in Marxism, Historical or Trans-historical Separation from Means of Production?", The Commoner, A Web Journal for Other Values (Debate: on Primitive Accumulation at http://www.commoner.org.uk). Reprinted as amended in Subverting the Present, Imagining the Future, W. Bonefeld, ed., Autonomedia,. Brooklyn, 2008, pp. 67–75.

Zarembka, P. [2002] (2008). Primitive accumulation in Marxism, historical or trans-historical separation from means of production? In W. Bonefeld (Ed.), *Subverting the present, imagining the future* (pp. 67–75). Brooklyn: Autonomedia.

Zarembka, P. (2009). Late Marx and Luxemburg: Opening a development within political economy. In R. Bellofiore (Ed.), *Rosa Luxemburg and the critique of political economy.* (pp. 64–80). Milton Park/Abingdon: Routledge.

Zarembka, P. (2014). Marxist political economy without Hegel: Contrasting Marx and Luxemburg to Plekhanov and Lenin. In J. Toporowski, E. Karwowski, & R. ellofiore (Eds.), *Legacy of Rosa Luxemburg, Oskar Lange and Michal Kalecki: Essays in honour of Tadeusz Kowalik* (pp. 58–77). Houndmills/Basingstoke/Hampshire/New York: Palgrave Macmillan.

Zarembka, P. (2015a). Materialized composition of capital and its stability in the United States: Findings stimulated by Paitaridis and Tsoulfidis (2012). *Review of Radical Political Economy*. 47(1), pp. 106–111.

Zarembka, P. (2015b). Review of S. Karimzadi, "Money and its origins". *Review of Keynesian Economics*. 3(3), pp. 438–441.

4

Rosa Luxemburg and Maxim Kovalevsky

James D. White

Introduction

One does not have to be a particularly observant reader of Rosa Luxemburg's chief economic works to notice the references to Maxim Kovalevsky's book on *Communal Landownership*. Mention of the work is most frequent in the *Introduction to Political Economy*, where Luxemburg draws on it to illustrate how the dissolution of primitive communities in Latin America, India and Algeria serves as the precondition to the emergence of commodity relations. In *The Accumulation of Capital* Luxemburg uses Kovalevsky's findings to support her central theme, namely, that the capitalist economy achieves expanded reproduction by drawing pre-capitalist societies into its orbit.

In his day Kovalevsky was a scholar of international standing and a prolific writer on law, politics, ethnology, economic history and, above

J.D. White (✉)
Department of Central and East European Studies, University of Glasgow,
8-9 Lilybank Gardens, Glasgow, G12 8RZ, Scotland, UK

J. Dellheim, F.O. Wolf (eds.), *Rosa Luxemburg: A Permanent Challenge for Political Economy*, DOI 10.1057/978-1-137-60108-7_4

all, sociology, of which he was a pioneer in his native Russia. From 1878 he held the chair of Civil Law and Comparative Government at Moscow University until his expulsion in 1887 due to his liberal views. In exile Kovalevsky lectured in London, Oxford, Paris, Stockholm and other universities Western Europe and the United States. The political upheaval of 1905 brought Kovalevsky back to his native country, where he became a member of the first Duma. Disqualified as a candidate for election to the second Duma, he was elected by the Russian Academy and the universities as their representative in the upper chamber, the Council of the Empire, where he remained until his death in 1916. By that time Kovalevsky's intellectual standing was such that one of his biographers could compare him to Tolstoy (Pasvolsky 1916, p. 1).

Not only did Kovalevsky provide Luxemburg with a source of information on the dissolution of primitive communities, he also collaborated with Karl Marx in the 1870s, when the latter had been engaged in studies of the Russian economy and the evolution of the Russian peasant commune in particular. Through Kovalevsky, therefore, there exists a continuity between Marx and Luxemburg that is instructive to reconstruct and examine.

Kovalevsky's Early Years

Maksim Maksimovich Kovalevsky was born on 27 August (8 September in the Gregorian calendar) 1851 in Kharkov as the son of a wealthy landowner. His early education was conducted at home with French and German governesses and tutors from whom he acquired his facility with languages that he would later employ in his scholarly research. At the age of 14 Kovalevsky transferred to the third year of Kharkov *gimnaziia*, from which he graduated with a gold medal in 1868. He then entered Kharkov University to study for a law degree. His main teacher was D. I. Kachenovskii, an Anglophile and an admirer of the British form of government. Since he could not openly campaign for parliamentary government in Russia, Kachenovskii did this indirectly by publishing studies on the constitutional history of Britain and other European countries. This would be a method that was later to be adopted by Kovalevsky himself.

It was also Kachenovskii who introduced Kovalevsky to the Positivist philosophy of Auguste Comte. Comte's works were banned in Russia, but expositions of them by his English followers John Stuart Mill and George Lewes were available even in Russian translation (Mokievsky 1890, p. 155). It is easy to see what the attraction of Positivism would be for people like Kachenovskii, who anticipated a time when Russia would have a constitutional government. According to Comte, humanity passed through three stages of intellectual development: the Religious, the Metaphysical and the Positive. This was a progression from the times when people's views were determined by superstition and fetishism to modern times when the outlook of humanity was derived from scientific methods of empirical observation and experiment. Corresponding to these intellectual stages was societal progression from the feudal or militaristic society to industrial society and its institutions based on order and progress (Lewes 1853, p. 269; Mill 1865, p. 105). Comte, therefore, provided Kachenovskii and his pupil with the assurance that the laws of history derived from objective empirical observation would eventually lead to the establishment of the kind of regime they so desired in Russia. Comte's influence was to be a lasting one in determining the direction of Kovalevsky's later research. As he stated in his memoirs: 'I was interested then, as I am now, in the close interdependence between the development of state institutions and the changes in the social order, which, in its turn, is brought about by the evolution of the economic orders. The history of institutions and the history of society – these were the themes that attracted me most.' (Kovalevskii 2005, p. 78).

Kachenovskii's death in 1872 deprived Kovalevsky of his preferred supervisor for his master's degree. Accordingly, he left Kharkov to continue his postgraduate studies at Moscow University. In order to collect material for his dissertation Kovalevsky took an extended trip to Western Europe. Having spent the winter semester of 1872 in Berlin, Kovalevsky went on to Paris, where he began research on the history of French administrative law. He set out to show that, contrary to current academic opinion, England and Germany were not the only countries with administrative courts able to act as an independent check on the actions of the bureaucracy – France had them, as well. The monograph which resulted from this research (Kovalevskii 1876b) was entitled *Studies in the History of the Jurisdiction of Taxes in France from the XIV Century to the Death of Louis XIV*, and was published in Moscow in 1876.

Henry Sumner Maine

While in Paris, Kovalevsky made contact with émigré Russians living there, including the writer Ivan Turgenev and fellow Positivist Grigorii Vyrubov. In 1867 Vyrubov, together with Emile Littré, one of the most eminent of Comte's followers, had founded the journal *La philosophie positiviste* to promote Positivist teachings (Simon 1963, p. 22). In 1875 Kovalevsky contributed a review of Sir Henry Sumner Maine's book *Lectures on the Early History of Institutions* to Vyrubov's journal (Kovalevskii 1875). Kovalevsky was deeply impressed by Maine's book and recommended it to the journal's readership because 'the questions of the origin of private property, classes and kingship cannot be a matter of indifference to people who are seriously interested in the progress of sociology; and every book which aims to cast new light on the subject cannot but provoke a lively interest on the part of Positivists' (Kovalevskii 1875, p. 310). Maine had already written two books, *Ancient Law* and *Village Communities in the East and West*. There, drawing together existing accounts of rural communities in the Classical world, Germany, Russia and India, Maine had shown that all of them displayed remarkably similar modes of social organisation. In *Lectures on the Early History of Institutions*, Maine analysed the ancient Irish legal codes to confirm that the Irish had possessed similar kinds of social institutions prior to English conquest. To Kovalevsky, Maine's studies signified an increased certainty that all societies, at least those of the Indo-European peoples, passed through the same social stages. The most primitive of these stages was tribal nomadic society characterised by ties based on blood relationships. This stage gave way to a settled existence with social relations based on the village community. Increased economic inequality allowed feudalism to develop out of the village community while, subsequently, the spread of private property prepared the way for the emergence of modern society. As Kovalevsky indicated, the scheme of historical development that emerged from Maine's research was important for Positivists, because it added substance to the world historical perspective that Comte had outlined.

Maine was to be an important influence on Kovalevsky's own work, and several of Maine's ideas were developed in Kovalevsky's writings on sociology. One of these was the transition from the blood ties of nomadic society to the social relations of the village community. The source for this conception of Maine's was American scholar Lewis Morgan's *Systems of Consanguinity and Affinity of the Human Family* (1871), which incorporated research on the social relations of American Indians. Morgan's work impressed Kovalevsky deeply and he used it extensively in his major study of village communities, *Communal Landownership* (*Obshchinnoe zemlevladenie*).

From Vyrubov Kovalevsky received letters of introduction to representatives of Positivism in England. In London Kovalevsky's first contact was George Lewes, the author of the book on Comte's philosophy with which Kovalevsky was already familiar. Lewes's partner was the famous novelist George Eliot, whose *Silas Marner* and *Mill on the Floss* Kovalevsky had read in Russian translation. On meeting her, Kovalevsky was captivated by her extraordinary personality. She was, he records, the most remarkable woman he had ever met (Kovalevskii 2005, pp. 153–154).

Around Lewes and Eliot revolved the wider circle of English Positivists. Among these, Frederic Harrison was of especial interest to Kovalevsky, because he had been a pupil of Henry Sumner Maine and had encouraged his former tutor to publish his lectures as *Ancient Law*. Harrison saw in Maine's legal categories a parallel with the Comtean stages of the religious, the metaphysical and the scientific (Vogeler 1984, p. 50). Along with his friends Edward Beesly and John Bridges, Harrison had been introduced to Comte's ideas by Richard Congreve, their tutor at Wadham College, Oxford. The four men formed the nucleus of the orthodox wing of the Comtists in England. Taking a volume each, they had translated Comte's *Système de politique positive* into English. Through Harrison Kovalevsky got to know Bridges, Beesly and Congreve, all of whom he met at the home of John Cotter Morison, a wealthy member of the Comtist community and author of a life of St Bernard of Clairvaux, reflecting Comte's high regard for the Catholic Church as a model for his own, secular, 'Religion of Humanity' (Kovalevskii 1997, p. 193).

The most eminent figure in Lewes and Eliot's circle of friends was the philosopher Herbert Spencer. Although his ideas had many similarities with those of Comte, he dissociated himself from his French counterpart. Kovalevsky claims he only spoke to Spencer once, and that was in response to a request to suggest his name for a membership in the Athenaeum Club. It is notable that when Kovalevsky came to write the essay 'Two Lives' comparing Spencer and Marx, the material for Spencer was taken almost entirely from printed sources, whereas for Marx it came from personal reminiscences. It seems that while he admired Spencer as a thinker, he found him uncongenial as a person.

As Kovalevsky's reminiscences imply, there was no hermetic separation between the English Positivists and Marx's circle of followers. Although ideological differences persisted, a considerable amount of cooperation took place between Marx and the Positivists, particularly with Beesly (Harrison 1959, pp. 22–58). This was reinforced by the Paris Commune, when both Marxists and Positivists provided aid and shelter to refugees from France (Wright 1986, p. 113). And, in terms of radicalism, the Positivists could compete with the Marxists in both domestic as well as foreign politics.

In London Kovalevsky worked on his second dissertation, *The History of the Police Administration and Police Courts in the English Shires from the Earliest Times to the Death of Edward III, On the Origins of Local Government in England*, which was published in Prague in 1877 (Kovalevskii 2005, pp. 166–167). But his first scholarly publication was a short pamphlet influenced directly by Henry Sumner Maine and encouraged by the Belgian economist Emile Laveleye on the dissolution of communal landownership in the Swiss Canton of Vaud (Kovalevskii 1876a). The pamphlet was published in London in Russian in 1876 and in Switzerland in German in the following year. Lest anyone imagine that this was an insignificant subject, Kovalevsky hastened to disabuse them in the preface of the Russian edition, explaining that:

> In the present work the reader will find the first attempt to distinguish the essential elements in the process of the gradual dissolution of communal landownership, at least in its latest form, the collective exploitation of meadows, pastures and woods.

> Although the author has limited his field of investigation to the agrarian relations in a single French canton of Switzerland, he permits himself to express the conviction that the same elements will necessarily be found by students of the history of agrarian relations in all countries where the village community has given way to the manor.

For the German edition Kovalevsky took the opportunity to write a new preface making explicit the relevance his research on the Swiss Canton of Vaud had for the future of Russia.

> Among the questions which occupy Russia at the present time scarcely any is of greater importance than the one to enquire whether the government should continue to guarantee the share of all the members of the peasant commune in the common land, or whether it should devote all its efforts to enabling the Russian peasant to gradually develop private property out of common property. If one considers what consequences the dissolution of common property had almost everywhere in Europe, and if one also bears in mind that a population of more than 35 million is waiting in suspense to see what measures the government will take, it is legitimate to presume that for the future history of Russia a great deal depends on the manner in which this question will be decided. (Kovalevskii 1877, p. 1)

Kovalevsky presented Lewes with a copy of the German translation of his pamphlet on the Canton Vaud (Kovalevskii 2005, p. 157). Lewes, as the biographer of Goethe, and Eliot, as the translator of Strauss's *Life of Jesus* and Feuerbach's *Essence of Christianity*, were both well versed in German. Lewes, obviously impressed by Kovalevsky's work, passed the book on to Spencer, who was working on his multi-volume *Principles of Sociology*. Kovalevsky recalls that he was most gratified when Spencer quoted from his book in his account of the history of primitive forms of property in the second volume of *Principles of Sociology* (Kovalevskii 1997, p. 109).

It was through Harrison that Kovalevsky was able to meet Maine, and through Maine's influence that Kovalevsky was able to gain access to the archive and library of the India Office, where he found rich and little-used material on the Indian agrarian commune and the role played by British colonial policy in its fate. Kovalevsky would use this material in the production of a comparative study of the destruction of the agrarian commune by the British in India, the Spanish in South America and the French in Algeria. He also met regularly with Maine, who divided his time between the India Office and lecturing at Oxford, and discussed his research with him. The result would be the book *Communal Landownership* which was published in 1879.

Communal Landownership

In his introduction to *Communal Landownership*, Kovalevsky writes that it is in some ways a continuation of his *Canton Vaud*. It is true that the theme of the dissolution of communal landownership is further developed there, but the later work has the additional feature of dealing with territories under foreign occupation: Mexico and Peru under the Spaniards, India under the British and Algeria under the French. This is a feature that is to be explained by the intellectual environment in which the book was written, especially by the influence of the English Positivists. In the *Système de politique positive*, which had been translated by Richard Congreve and his friends, Comte had insisted that politics should be subordinated to morals. This applied not only to domestic politics, but to international relations as well. Comte condemned the colonial conquests of his own country and expressed the hope that the Arabs would expel the French from Algeria. On Comte's suggestion, Congreve launched a campaign for the return of Gibraltar to Spain, and subsequently published a pamphlet demanding the withdrawal of the British from India (Congreve 1874, p. 69). He regarded the British occupation of India as immoral and compared it to the cruelty and avarice of the Spanish conquerors of Mexico and Peru in the 16th century (Congreve 1874, pp. 87–88. Congreve repeated this comparison in his essay in *International Policy*, a symposium in which he and his Positivist friends condemned British colonialism (Congreve et al. 1866, p. 9). In his chapter on 'England at Sea' Beesly also argued that justice required the British to recognise their duty to withdraw from India and shape their policy towards that end. He indicated that this course of action was in accordance with what Comte would have wished, since Comte had urged that France abandon not just Algeria, but Corsica as well (Congreve et al. 1866, p. 210). This aspect of Positivist doctrine is prominent in Kovalevsky's *Communal Landownership*.

In *Communal Landownership* Kovalevsky introduces his subject of study by rehearsing the phases through which it had progressed. These are the familiar Positivist phases of the Theological, the Metaphysical and the Positive. In Kovalevsky's opinion, the works of Georg Maurer (Maurer 1854) had pointed the way to the Positivist approach to the question by showing the dependence of this or that form of landownership on the degree of social development of a people. Maurer had believed that private property in land had evolved out of collective property, and this had been shown to be a world phenomenon by the comparative-historical method that Henry Sumner Maine had employed in his studies of village communities.

Kovalevsky went on to declare that he himself had adopted the comparative-historical approach to the study of the evolution of property relations under the influence of Maine and from conversations with him. But despite the basic similarity of views, Kovalevsky disagreed with Maine on the question of the influence of artificial causes on the disintegration of communal forms of landownership. He thought that Maine completely ignored the role played by the agrarian policy of the European states in the process of the disintegration of communal landownership among peoples who had fallen under their rule.

It was, Kovalevsky explained, the aim of his book to study the development of private property in countries that, until now, had not been subject to comparative-historical investigation. The project had begun three years earlier with his work on the dissolution of communal property in one of the cantons of French Switzerland. In his view, the findings of that research were valid on an international scale. Kovalevsky contended that common ownership of land and its replacement by private property was undermined by the 'conflict of interests' within the community: the conflict between the wealthier among the agrarian population who advocated for the dissolution of communal property, and the less wealthy who sought to retain it. This was a process, Kovalevsky believed, which sooner or later would take place in all countries. The emergence of private property out of common ownership was a universal phenomenon.

But whereas the action of 'internal necessity' was likely to be a gradual one, in colonial countries the individualisation of property in land and also its centralisation in the hands of an elite few had been effected within some two or three decades. This was the consequence of the legislative and administrative measures of this or that foreign government, which was likely to be unfamiliar with local conditions and the social structure of the native populations. Nevertheless, although the artificial and fortuitous causes brought about by colonial rule served to accelerate the dissolution of common landownership, in the end it led to the same results as the spontaneous ones, that is, to the rapid transformation of small property into larger property and the concentration of landownership in the hands of a small class of capitalist-usurers (Kovalevskii 1879, p. 20).

From Maine's work and the research of Lewis Morgan Kovalevsky had formed a conception not only of how communal landownership came to an end, but also how it had originated in the first place. The agrarian commune had arisen out of the clan commune, whose sense of kinship rested on the conception that every member of the community was descended from a common ancestor. This conception was preserved in the course of centuries and survived even after the transition of the clan commune to the village community. Kovalevsky also followed Maine in viewing the emergence of feudal relations as one of the consequences of the break-up of communal landownership. This too was a process which took place much more rapidly in colonial countries.

In surveying the phenomenon of communal landownership in countries subject to foreign domination, Kovalevsky was able to show its evolution through different stages. The first chapter dealt with the most primitive types of social organisation, those observed among the American Indians by Morgan as well as the tribes of Mexico and Peru before the Spanish conquest. He then turned to the agrarian organisation of India and the influence upon it by Mogul and subsequently British rule. The final section was devoted to how French rule in Algeria had transformed traditional Islamic society by replacing the common ownership of land by individual property. Throughout the book Kovalevsky made references to the situation in his own country, where processes of a comparable kind were at work to undermine the collective ownership of land in the Russian peasant commune. Readers of Kovalevsky's work would have little doubt as to where the author's chief concerns lay.

Collaboration with Marx

According to Kovalevsky, his first meeting with Marx, which took place in the winter of 1874–75, was inauspicious. Marx spent most of the time denouncing émigré Russians – Herzen and Bakunin in particular. But later in the year, when Kovalevsky and Marx met up in Karlsbad where both had taken up residence for health reasons, a lasting friendship was established on the basis of common scholarly interests. Kovalevsky, however, had doubts about the validity of Marx's methodology, as he mentioned in a letter to the economist I. I. Ianzhul, dated 15 October 1875:

> In Karlsbad I spent many happy hours in Marx's company. He is a most noble and a most gifted person. It is a great pity that he was and remains a Hegelian, and that therefore his scientific constructions are built on sand. While in Karlsbad I read well over half of his book which he presented me with, and I found in it fresh proof that any departure from the Positive method and, most of all the application of the maxim: '*les grandes idées viennent du coeur*,' inevitably lead to frequent unconscious misconceptions. (Kazakov 1969, p. 100).

In London Kovalevsky visited Marx practically every week, ending only in 1876 when Kovalevsky obtained a professorship at Moscow University and returned to Russia. A correspondence then began between the two men. Unfortunately, none of Marx's letters to Kovalevsky have survived, since they were burnt by Kovalevsky's associate I. I. Ivaniukov when he feared a raid on his home by the Tsarist police (Anon 1918, p. 17). Marx referred to Kovalevsky as one of his 'scientific friends' and Kovalevsky for his part emphasised in his memoirs the influence that Marx had exerted on his work:

> My appointment as a professor at Moscow University brought an end to my almost weekly exchange of ideas with the author of *Das Kapital*, which lasted for two years. At first we continued to exchange letters now and

> again. When I visited London I resumed my visits, generally on Sundays, and each time I would come away from the meetings with a new stimulus for scholarly work in the field of the history of the economic and social development of Western Europe. It is very likely that had I not known Marx I would not have studied the history of landownership or the economic growth of Europe, but would have concentrated my attention more on the development of political institutions, the more so since these themes corresponded directly to the subject I taught. Marx read my works and frankly gave his opinion on them. If I deferred the printing of my first extensive dissertation on administrative law in France with special reference to juridical tariffs, this was partly because of the unfavourable opinion Marx gave of my work. He expressed more approval of my attempt to investigate the history of the agrarian commune and to trace the development of family types from ancient times using the data from comparative ethnology and the comparative history of law. (Kovalevskii 1909a, p. 19).

Kovalevsky's additional claim that Marx had 'largely determined the direction' of his scholarly work is somewhat exaggerated. For Kovalevsky's interest in the history of agrarian communes had a dynamic of its own, and owed more of its inspiration to Maine than to Marx. Nevertheless, there is no reason to doubt that Marx encouraged him in this interest and, one may infer, influenced the direction the study took.

At the time he met Kovalevsky Marx was working on the second volume of *Capital*, concerned with the circulation and expanded reproduction of capital. In the drafts he had written prior to the publication of the first volume in 1867, Marx had assumed that capital eroded away earlier forms of social and economic organisation as it circulated, widening and deepening the sphere of capital's operation. But by 1868 he had come to believe that capital in its circuits did not carry all before it, and instead could coexist with traditional pre-capitalist societies. In March of that year he wrote to Engels, praising Maurer's studies of the *Mark* (the German village community) and adding that even in his own neighbourhood on the Hunsrücken the old Germanic system had survived until only a few years prior (White 1996, pp. 204–207). From that point on Marx consistently held that contact with the capitalist system did not automatically extend capitalist relations, a position reflected in his comments on Kovalevsky's book.

In his attempt to complete the second volume of his work, Marx embarked upon an intensive empirical study of how capital began to circulate and reproduce itself. He was fortunate in that he had a convenient example at hand in Russia, where serfdom had recently been abolished and capitalism was still in its early stages of development. Marx was also fortunate to have Russian contacts like N. F. Danielson and G. A. Lopatin, the translators of the first volume of *Capital*, who supplied him with materials on the Russian economy. Kovalevsky's research on the dissolution of village communities and the emergence of the capitalist economy had a direct bearing on Marx's preoccupations at the time. In his memoirs Kovalevsky confirms that this was the direction of Marx's studies. He says:

> At that time Marx was working on the second volume of his treatise, intending to devote in it considerable space to the way in which capitals accumulated in two comparatively new countries – America and Russia, and consequently received many books from New York and Moscow. (Kovalevskii 1909a, p. 11).

Kovalevsky himself was to be one of the people who dispatched books on Russian society and economy from Moscow for Marx to use. It was also Kovalevsky who loaned Marx his copy of Lewis Morgan's principal work *Ancient Society* (1877), which he had obtained during his first trip to the USA in 1881 (Kovalevskii 1909b, p. 11). Morgan's work was relevant to Marx's investigations because it dealt with the more primitive forms of society that had preceded the peasant communal organisations. Marx made extensive notes from it, which were later utilised by Engels in writing *The Origin of the Family, Private Property and the State* (1884).

Marx received a copy of *Communal Landownership* from Kovalevsky in 1879. His detailed notes on it are of considerable interest, as they show how he viewed the evolution of social and economic systems in the last years of his life. For the most part the notes follow Kovalevsky's text rather closely, often translating long passages from Kovalevsky's book into German or summarising individual chapters. The notes begin with the chapter on the American Indians, omitting Kovalevsky's Preface and Introduction, where he explains his methodological presuppositions.

Nevertheless, there are indications as to how Marx viewed these presuppositions from the marginal annotations on the pages of the book.

One may conveniently divide Marx's commentary on Kovalevsky's book into two categories: the aspects with which Marx agreed, and those to which he took exception. To the first category belong those sections of the book where Kovalevsky showed how the agrarian policies of the colonial powers had served to undermine communal landownership. Thus, in the case of the British in India, paraphrasing Kovalevsky, Marx observed:

> British officials in India, as well as the publicists, like Sir Henry Maine, who rely on them, describe the dissolution of communal ownership of land in the Punjab as if it took place as the inevitable consequence of economic progress despite the affectionate attitude of the British towards this archaic form. The truth is rather that the British themselves are the chief (active) culprits responsible for this dissolution – to their own danger. (Harstick 1977, p. 88)

As for the methods the British employed to dissolve common landownership and foster the emergence of private property, Marx noted:

> With the help of 'deposits' and the 'disposal of property' sanctioned by law the British government tries in the North-West provinces of India and in the Punjab to dissolve the collective property of the peasants, finally to expropriate them and encourage the transfer of communal land to the private property of usurers. (Harstick 1977, p. 107)

And in connection with the policies of French in Algeria, the same kind of manipulation of the local legal system was employed to destroy common landownership and deprive the peasants of their land:

> [In so far as the foreign, (non-European) law is 'profitable' for them the Europeans not only – immediately! – recognise it, as here, Islamic law, but also 'do not understand it' only to their own profit, as in the present case.] The French greed is completely obvious. (Harstick 1977, p. 101)

An aspect of Kovalevsky's work with which Marx disagreed was of a fundamental nature: namely, Kovalevsky's cherished conception that, sooner or later, communal landownership would be replaced by private property through 'conflicts of interest' that were generated within the community. It was this conception that led Kovalevsky to argue that legislation of the occupying powers only accelerated a process that would occur in any case. But why should conflicts of interest inevitably arise everywhere? This was something Kovalevsky did not explain, as was observed by Marx in a marginal annotation (Harstick 1977, p. 269).

In the case of the Spanish conquest of Mexico and Peru, Marx agreed with Kovalevsky's account of how the Spaniards had undermined the system of communal landownership, but diverged from Kovalevsky in the way he interpreted the role of internal conflicts amongst the Indians. He thought that these had weakened the Indians' ability to resist the Spanish conquest, which in turn was ultimately responsible for the collapse of communal landownership (Harstick 1997, p. 36).

In his notes on the body of the book, most of Marx's critical comments are made on passages where Kovalevsky attempted to put forward the Positivist idea that all countries shared the same pattern of historical development. For example, Marx found Kovalevsky's arguments justifying the existence of Western European-style feudalism in India unconvincing, and disputed Kovalevsky's evidence (Harstick 1977, p. 76).

With regard to the conceptions Kovalevsky had expounded in *Communal Landownership*, Marx agreed completely with Kovalevsky that government policy was capable of undermining communal landownership, but he did not agree that communal landownership would have inevitably been destroyed by more long-term natural causes. He believed that, without governmental interference, communal forms of ownership were resilient enough to survive.

One finds this position reflected fully in Marx's drafts of the letter he wrote in response to Vera Zasulich, enquiring whether Marx believed that Russia must inevitably pass through the capitalist stage before reaching socialism. Marx answered this question in terms of whether or not the Russian peasant commune could survive and become the basis for a socialist order in Russia. Here Marx deployed two kinds of argument: one to explain why he thought the commune could survive, and the other to explain under what circumstances it was likely to be destroyed.

In arguing for the survival of the peasant commune Marx emphasised that its demise was not decreed by historical inevitability. He pointed out that in the French edition of *Das Kapital* where he discussed expropriation of the peasants, he had 'expressly limited the "historical inevitability" of this process to the countries of Western Europe' (Marx 1985, p. 231). Although it might be said that institutions analogous to the peasant commune had disappeared in other European countries, this did not imply that the same had to occur in Russia. Even when the disappearance of village communities was attributed to spontaneous forces, in reality the cause had been deliberate policy. The example Marx gave was one he had found in Kovalevsky's book:

> When reading the histories of primitive communities written by bourgeois writers it is necessary to be on one's guard. They do not even shrink from falsehoods. Sir Henry Maine, for example, who was a keen collaborator of the British Government in carrying out the violent destruction of the Indian communes, hypocritically assures us that all the government's noble efforts to support the communes were thwarted by the spontaneous forces of economic laws! (Marx 1985, p. 230)

Marx contended that, unlike India, Russia had the considerable advantage of not being subject to colonial rule.

According to Marx, what was threatening the life of the Russian commune was the same thing that had undermined the commune in India: neither historical inevitability nor a specific theory were responsible, but rather oppression by the state and exploitation by capitalist intruders, who had been empowered at the expense of the peasants by the same state (Marx 1985, p. 233). In what might have been a veiled reference to Kovalevsky, Marx intimated that the Russian liberals were rather keen on establishing capitalism in Russia by abolishing communal property and expropriating the peasantry, but he did not think that their wish would necessarily become reality (Marx 1985, p. 231). Therefore, Marx reasoned, what was needed to protect the peasant commune was a revolution in Russia.

One prominent feature of the drafts of Marx's letter to Vera Zasulich was the attention paid to the dynamics of the peasant commune, to its evolution from more primitive types of social organisation. This was an element that Marx had adopted from Kovalevsky's book, and Kovalevsky, in turn, had borrowed from the studies of Henry Sumner Maine and Lewis Morgan. Drawing on Kovalevsky, Marx pointed out that the Russian peasant commune was a relatively modern example of the type, that whereas earlier communities had been based on blood relations between their members, the Russian peasant commune was the first social grouping of free men not held together by blood ties.

Kovalevsky and Sieber

Kovalevsky was not the only Russian scholar engaged in studying the evolution of peasant communities in connection with the emergence of capitalism. Nikolai Sieber, whose commentary on *Capital* (Ziber 1871) was greatly admired by Marx (White 2001, pp. 3–14), published a book on this subject in 1883 entitled *Studies in Primitive Economic Culture* (Ziber 1883). Besides drawing on a vast body of primary sources, the book used the works of Kovalevsky, Maine, Morgan and Lubbock to reconstruct the economic formations that had existed prior to capitalism. In the second edition of his commentary on Marx's *Capital*, entitled *David Ricardo and Karl Marx in their Socio-Economic Researches* and published in 1885 (Ziber 1885), Sieber incorporated material used in *Studies in Primitive Economic Culture* to present Marx's ideas in historical context.

Although Sieber's later works appeared after Marx's death, it is highly probable that Marx was familiar with their contents, as Sieber visited him in January 1881 while he was researching his book on primitive economic culture in the British Museum (Anon 1969, p. 78). It was immediately after this visit that Marx embarked on an intensive reading of Morgan, Maine and Lubbock – the writers featuring prominently in Sieber's work. Marx made very extensive notes on them (Krader 1974), but at the time of his death in 1883 he had not utilised them even in drafts. It is not absolutely clear how Marx intended to use them, but the context suggests it would have been to account for the emergence of capitalism from earlier collectivist society – that is, in connection with Volume II of *Capital*.

A major factor which obscured the connection between Marx's notes on Kovalevsky's and other works on village communities and the second volume of *Capital* was Engels' decision not to incorporate any of the Russian materials Marx had collected (White 1996, pp. 281–282). One can understand why this was done, as it would have complicated the task enormously, but it dismayed Marx's Russian contacts who had supplied the material and who knew the full extent of Marx's Russian studies. In the preface to the third volume of *Capital*, Engels claimed that Marx's Russian studies had sought to elucidate the question of ground rent. This is, however, contradicted by Kovalevsky's statement quoted above that the Russian material Marx collected was intended for the second volume of his work (which dealt with circulation) to research the question of the accumulation of capital – a much more significant topic. Once Engels had sent the second and third volumes to press, the impression was created that *Capital* was complete.

A second factor which severed the continuity between *Capital* and Marx's Russian and village community studies was the manner in which Engels presented Lewis Morgan's work. This was not in connection with the origins of capitalism, but the evolution of the family. Engels's *The Origin of the Family, Private Property and the State* does not mention Kovalevsky's *Communal Landownership*, though it does cite Kovalevsky's later work *Tableau des origines et de l'évolution de la famille et de la propriété* (Kovalevskii 1890). Engels's *Origin of the Family* provides very little indication of the direction Marx's studies had taken in the last decade of his life.

Kovalevsky is a key figure in Marx's intellectual biography and the history of Marx's ideas. He links Marx's economic studies to his research into village communities and their historical evolution. Establishing this continuity shows that Marx pursued his main project – that is, revealing the workings of the capitalist system – until the end. He was not someone who left his life's work unfinished while indulging a predilection for 'ethnology' as the title of the collection of Marx's notes on village communities implies. While Marx had begun his monumental analysis of capitalism using the methodology of Hegelian philosophy, his approach in later years had become more empirical, and took him into the field of study he shared with Maxim Kovalevsky.

Luxemburg's *Introduction to Political Economy*

Luxemburg did not read Marx's commentary on Kovalevsky, of course, but the fact that such a commentary existed had been revealed by Kovalevsky in a memoir published in 1895 (Kovalevskii 1895, pp. 61–80). From this memoir and one published in 1908 (Kovalevskii 1909a) Luxemburg could have learnt of Kovalevsky's close collaboration with Marx. Even if she had overlooked these sources, she was certainly familiar with at least one of them. On 27 July 1911 Luxemburg wrote to Jogiches, asking him to send her 'the issue of the journal which contained the letters of Engels to Nikolai-on' (Luxemburg 1971, p. 237). The journal in question was an issue of *Byloe* from 1908 containing a collection of letters from Marx and Engels to Danielson (whose pseudonym was 'Nikolai-on'); the collection was issued in the same year as a separate volume, which is the form in which Luxemburg refers to the letters (Luxemburg 1981, pp. 394–395). She made use of the collection both in the *Introduction to Political Economy*[1] and in *The Accumulation of Capital*. Several of the letters mention Kovalevsky, the most significant one being the reply to Danielson's offer to send Marx a copy of Kovalevsky's *Communal Landownership*. Marx writes that he already has received a copy from the author himself, who is one of his 'scientific friends' (Marx and Engels 1908, p. 25). In his introduction to the letters Danielson explains that he expected Marx to use the materials on the Russian economy that were sent to him to show the emergence of capitalist relations from earlier economic forms found in Russia. He was thus extremely disappointed when the second and third volumes of *Capital* were published in the same form as they had been written in the 1860s, the Russian materials from the 1870s being left unused (Marx and Engels 1908, Chap. IV–V). On receipt of Danielson's collection of letters Luxemburg would have been left in no doubt of the validity of the historical approach to Marx's economics.

References to Kovalevsky first appear in Luxemburg's *Introduction to*

[1] The editors of Luxemburg's *Complete Works Volume I* note the similarity between Luxemburg's rebuttal of Boris Chicherin's conception of the Russian peasant commune as a governmental creation in *Introduction* and Marx's views on the subject in his letter to Danielson of 22 March 1873 (p.220). The similarity is hardly surprising as Luxemburg possessed the letter in question.

Political Economy. This was a 'popularisation of Marx's economic doctrines' (Luxemburg 1925, p. 7) which grew out of her lectures at the SPD's school in Berlin compiled intermittently between 1907 and 1916. It was, however, never published in her lifetime and appeared in 1925 in a posthumous edition edited by her friend Paul Levi (Luxemburg 1925). One can see from the series of outlines that Luxemburg included in her correspondence with Jogiches that the character of the *Introduction* underwent a considerable evolution. Whereas in the published edition the exposition is largely historical, tracing the origins of the capitalist system from the dissolution of village communities, this was in all probability not Luxemburg's original intention. The earliest outline from 1907–8 does not contain a historical dimension; rather, it contains the sections: (1) What is Economics?; (2) Social Labour; (3) Exchange; (4) Wage Labour; (5) The Rule of Capital; (6) Contradictions in the Capitalist Economy (Luxemburg 2013). Clearly, this was intended to be an analytic study of the capitalist economy, perhaps something like Karl Kautsky's textbook on Marx's economic doctrines (Kautsky 1886).

That Luxemburg did not intend the *Introduction*'s structure to be historical is reflected in a letter she wrote to Alexander Bogdanov on 29 June 1909. Bogdanov was the author of a successful textbook on Marxist economics that *had* adopted a historical approach to the subject (Bogdanov 1902). Luxemburg wanted Bogdanov to use his influence with his publisher to have *Introduction* appear in Russian translation. Luxemburg explained that she needed Bogdanov's cooperation, 'as otherwise the publisher might think that my work in some way would compete with your "Economy", while both are differently set out, and rather successfully complement each other' (Luxemburg 1971, p. 37). Despite Bogdanov's assurance that 'the author's name alone guarantees the talent and interest of the work' (Antonova and Drozdova 1995, p. 164), the Russian translation of the *Introduction* did not materialise, since the publisher did not consider it financially viable.[2] The rejection, however, freed Luxemburg from any obligation to eschew the historical approach. Ultimately, the version of the *Introduction* that was published in 1925

[2] Paul Levi's edition of the *Introduction to Political Economy* contains the announcement that: 'The Russian edition of this book is appearing simultaneously in the "Krasnaia nov" publishing house in Moscow.'

did adopt a historical approach and thus would have been in competition with Bogdanov's book. As Luxemburg envisaged a Russian readership for the *Introduction*, a historical approach would have been appropriate, since the capitalist economy in Russia was still in the process of development and the peasant commune still very much alive. Both of these facts were mentioned by Luxemburg in her *Introduction* (Luxemburg 2013, pp. 104, 221). By February 1910 Luxemburg had included a section on 'Economic History' in her outline, and by the beginning of March 1910 the historical element had acquired the most prominent place in it. It now contained the following sections: (1) What Is the National Economy?; (2) Social Labour; (3) Economic Historical (Primitive Communist, Slave Economy, Serf Economy, Guild Handicraft); (4) Exchange; (5) Wage Labour; (6) The Rule of Capital (the Rate of Profit); (7) Crises; (8) Tendencies of the Capitalist Economy (Luxemburg 1971, pp. 94, 98).

At the time of Luxemburg's death in 1919 only six chapters were found among her papers: (1) What Is the National Economy?; (2) Economic Historical I; (3) Economic Historical II; (4) Commodity Production; (5) Wage Labour; (6) Tendencies of the Capitalist Economy. Levy thought that the work was incomplete, either because Luxemburg had been prevented from finishing it or because some parts of it had been stolen following her death. He believed a theoretical part was missing: the sections dealing with value, surplus value, profit – that is, what Marx in *Capital* had shown to be the workings of the capitalist system. (Luxemburg 1925). However, such sections are not explicitly mentioned in any of Luxemburg's outlines, and this kind of theoretical approach would not be in keeping with the mainly historical method adopted in the extant text. The work is probably more complete than Levy suspected, as the increased attention to the historical element presaged in the outlines is reflected in the two chapters devoted to the 'Economic Historical' topics. Moreover, the type of historical treatment employed is not the series of historical stages envisaged in the 1910 outline: primitive communism, slave economy, serf economy, guild handicraft; rather, it is largely in terms of the emergence of capitalism from the dissolution of the village community, or, as Luxemburg terms it, following Maurer, the '*Mark*.' It is an approach that is clearly in the tradition of Maurer, Henry Sumner Maine, Sieber and Kovalevsky, all of whom she cites in her notes to the

Introduction (Luxemburg 2013, pp. 539–554).

It is Kovalevsky who is the most important influence. This is obvious from the subject matter of the *Introduction* and the source material used. Kovalevsky is invoked constantly as the authority on the Spanish conquest of South America, British rule in India and the French conquest of Algeria. Luxemburg also accepts Kovalevsky's typology of the stages through which the village community evolved. The oldest form was that found among the American Indians and the Peruvian Incas, the clan community, which consisted entirely of blood relatives. The clan owned the land in common and cultivated it collectively. Here the land was unpartitioned, and only the fruits of the harvest were distributed. The second stage emerged when the original tribal community disintegrated and a new form of kinship community appeared which partitioned the land it owned according to the family's relationship to tribal ancestors. This was the stage the Indian village community had reached at the time of the British conquest. The final stage of the evolution of the village community's evolution was represented by the Russian peasant commune, whose method of equal division of the land among its constituent families Luxemburg described in great detail.

Luxemburg also accepted Kovalevsky's explanation of how the village commune disintegrated to give rise to capitalist relations. After mentioning the extraordinary vitality of the peasant commune and its ability to withstand every form of conquest, foreign rule, despotism and exploitation, she went on to say that there was only one contact it was unable to resist: 'the contact with European civilisation, with capitalism'. Like Kovalevsky, Luxemburg regarded this factor as 'simply the last and not the sole factor that brings about the inevitable decline of primitive society. The seeds of this lie within the society itself.' It was, she said, the division of labour at the heart of primitive society that inevitably led to the breakup of political and economic equality from within (Luxemburg 2013, pp. 226–228).

If contact with European civilisation – that is, with capitalism – could cause the disintegration of primitive communities and spread capitalist relations, then this had far-reaching implications, which Luxemburg made explicit. Namely: 'What particularly distinguishes the capitalist mode of production from all of its predecessors is that it has the inherent impetus to extend automatically across the whole of the earth, and drive out all other social orders' (Luxemburg 2013, p. 295). This was the position Marx had held until 1868, when he became convinced that traditional village communities were sufficiently resilient to withstand the onslaught of the capitalist system. It was this position that also made the treatment of the circulation of capital and expanded reproduction in Volume II of *Capital* so problematic, compelling Marx to leave it unfinished.

Of all the sources on village communities that Luxemburg used in her *Introduction*, Kovalevsky's book was unique; for only his book examined the impact of foreign capitalist powers on traditional societies. Because it lay outside the scope of his research, Luxemburg was bound to ask a question that Kovalevsky did not pose: namely, what impelled foreign capitalist powers to engage with non-capitalist countries, dissolve their traditional societies and draw them into the orbit of capitalism? The answer that Luxemburg proposed was that in its drive for expanded reproduction, capital drew new areas into the sphere of commodity relations. In other words, Kovalevsky had suggested the solution to the problem that Marx had failed to solve.

The Accumulation of Capital

It is quite understandable that Luxemburg chose to break off writing the *Introduction* to work on *The Accumulation of Capital*. It was certainly preferable to produce a serious contribution to Marxist theory than a mere popularisation of Marx's economic ideas. The unforeseen use to which Kovalevsky's work could be put accounts for the fact that the topic of the accumulation of capital is not mentioned in any of the outlines of the *Introduction* or in the *Introduction* itself (Kowalik 2012, p. 167). Yet Kovalevsky's work serves as a strong element of continuity between the *Introduction* and *The Accumulation of Capital*.

Much of Luxemburg's *Accumulation of Capital* is devoted to an analysis of the failure of previous writers to provide a satisfactory account of the expanded reproduction of capital. Her survey begins with Marx himself, whose mathematical reproduction schemes she analyses in considerable detail. She points out, however, that the second volume of *Capital* in which accumulation is discussed is not a finished work, but rather a manuscript that breaks off half-way through, and thus cannot be considered Marx's final word on the subject. Luxemburg then expounds the solutions proposed by later economic thinkers, such as Tugan-Baranovsky, Peter Struve, Sergei Bulgakov and Danielson, finding them unconvincing.

Luxemburg's own solution to the question of expanded reproduction of capital comes in the section of the book beginning with the chapter entitled 'The Struggle against the Natural Economy'. Here we again encounter Kovalevsky's conception of the two factors responsible for the dissolution of primitive communities: slow internal disintegration and rapid disruption caused by the interference of capitalist powers. Capitalism cannot wait for primitive communities to dissolve of their own accord; it must assimilate them in order to accumulate, but as the natural economy is a barrier to its progress, it conducts a war of annihilation against it. According to Luxemburg, the principal methods employed in this struggle are political force (revolution, war), oppressive taxation by the state and cheap goods (Luxemburg 1981, p. 317).

Luxemburg then proceeds to illustrate these processes with two case studies taken from Kovalevsky: those of the British in India and the French in Algeria. In both instances the resilience of the traditional communities with their common ownership of land had been broken by the persistent attacks of the occupying powers. Only with the arrival of the British did the Indian village community, which had survived centuries of war and conquest, finally capitulate to the blight of capitalist civilisation, which succeeded in disrupting the entire social organisation of the people. The British artificially created a landed aristocracy at the expense of the ancient property rights of the peasant communities. In Algeria, the French pursued a similar policy in their systematic and deliberate attempts to destroy communal property and establish private property in land, which could then become the object of speculation by the French colonists (Luxemburg 1981, pp. 320–333).

In generalising from these and other historical examples, Luxemburg concluded that non-capitalist organisations provided fertile soil for capitalism; capital fed on the ruins of such organisations. She believed that the non-capitalist milieu was indispensable to the accumulation of capital, that the accumulation of capital was a kind of metabolism between the capitalist economy and the pre-capitalist methods of production in which the latter were corroded and assimilated by the former. The implication was that: 'capital cannot accumulate without the aid of non-capitalist organisations, nor, on the other hand, can it tolerate their continued existence side by side with itself. Only the continuous and progressive disintegration of non-capitalist organisations makes accumulation of capital possible' (Luxemburg 1981, p. 364).

Marx and Luxemburg in a Kovalevsky Perspective

In terms of the evolution of Marx's thought, Luxemburg's economic writings are of great significance. By adopting a historical approach to the emergence of commodity relations from primitive communities, Luxemburg followed the direction that Marx's economic studies had taken him in the last decade of his life. Her *Introduction* incorporates the works of writers that Marx had studied and summarised but which he had not successfully incorporated into a systematic study (such as Maurer, Henry Sumner Maine, Lewis Morgan and Kovalevsky).

There is a great deal of consensus between Marx and Luxemburg concerning the evolution of the village community. They both accepted Kovalevsky's account of its evolution from clan relationships based on blood ties and both saw the Russian peasant commune as a relatively advanced stage of this evolution. The differences between Marx and Luxemburg concern the ability of capitalism to dissolve all previous types of economic formation. In the earlier drafts of *Capital*, Marx had assumed that capitalism was capable of such a dissolution, and that this would culminate in capitalism becoming the universal economic system. But after 1868 this ceased to be his opinion and became a serious obstacle to his completion of the second volume of his life's work. Luxemburg's stance on the question can be characterised as being in line with Kovalevsky and with Marx prior to 1868. She thought that capital could carry all before it and that village communities were powerless to halt its advance. This was the view she expressed in the *Introduction*, and is fundamental to her argument in *Accumulation*, where she explains the expansion of the capitalist system by its absorption of the primitive communities both at home and abroad.

The solution to the problem of expanded reproduction of capital that Luxemburg proposed had been available to Marx earlier. He had been in possession of Kovalevsky's book since 1879 and had studied it thoroughly. Moreover, he was extremely knowledgeable about the evolution of village communities and especially of the Russian peasant commune from his extensive reading on the subject. Why did he not use these materials to complete Volume II of *Capital* along the lines of Luxemburg's *Accumulation*?

Marx's notes on Kovalevsky's book suggest an answer to this question. For Marx, the lesson that emerged from Kovalevsky's study was that primitive communities were extremely resilient – they could even withstand contact with capitalism. Where disintegration had taken place, it was due to the deliberate actions of occupying powers. In other words, what destroyed pre-capitalist forms of organisation were political rather than economic processes. Moreover, all of Marx's drafts for Volume II indicate the kind of exposition he envisaged, namely, in terms of an internal dynamic or 'dialectic' of the economic categories. It would have defeated his purpose to resort to an explanation involving wars and revolutions, as Luxemburg had done. So long as his favoured approach remained inaccessible, Marx preferred to suspend the completion of Volume II entirely.

The question also arises: if Luxemburg had been familiar with Marx's notes on Kovalevsky and his drafts of the letter to Vera Zasulich, would this have influenced her approach to the question of the accumulation of capital? The answer must be: almost certainly not. One can observe from her earliest work on economics (her doctoral dissertation on the industrial development of Poland) that Luxemburg predicated her thinking on the continued expansion of the sphere of capital, which could involve the action of the state and the absorption of non-capitalist surroundings. In the opinion of one scholar there is a consistent logical thread running through all of Luxemburg's economic works (Dziewulski 1972, p. 290). She would have been most unlikely to sacrifice this consistency in response to Marx's notes. Moreover, while Luxemburg regarded Marx as a serious scholar whose work ought to be taken into account, as is clear from *The Accumulation of Capital*, she did not think of him as an infallible authority. In retrospect, one can say that Luxemburg's conception of the way capitalism extended throughout the world is an entirely credible one, and that in this respect her use of Kovalevsky's work served her well.

Bibliography

Anon. (1918). Maksim Kovalevskii 1851–1916. *Sbornik statei*. Petrograd.

Anon (1969). *Russkie sovremenniki o K. Markse i F. Engel'se*. Moscow: Politizdat.

Antonova, N. S., & Drozdova, N. V. (Eds.) (1995). *A. A. Bogdanov (Malinovskii) Stat'i, doklady, pis'ma i vospominaniia 1901–1928, Volume 1 of Neizvestnyi Bogdanov*. Moscow: ITs AIRO-XX.

Bogdanov, A. (1902). *Kratkii kurs ekonomicheskoi nauki* (3rd ed.). Moscow: S. Dorovatovskii i A. Charushnikov.

Congreve, R. (1874). *Essays political, social, and religious*. London: Longmans, Green & Co.

Congreve, R., Harrison, F., Beesly, E. S., Pember, E. H., Bridges, J. H., Cookson, C. A., et al. (1866). *International policy essays on the foreign relations of England*. London: Chapman and Hall.

Dziewulski, J. (1972). *Wokól pogladów ekonomicznych Róży Luksemburg*. Warsaw: Ksiażka i wiedza.

Harrison, R. (1959). E. S. Beesly and Karl Marx. *International Review of Social History, 4*(1), 22–58.

Harstick, H. (1977). *Karl Marx über Formen vorkapitalistischer Produktion. Vergleichende Studien zur Geschichte des Grundeigentums 1879–80*. Frankfurt/ New York: Campus Verlag.

Kautsky, K. (1886). *Karl Marx' ökonomische Lehren*. Stuttgart: Dietz.

Kazakov, A. P. (1969). *Teoriia progressa v russkoi sotsiologii kontsa XIX veka (P.L. Lavrov, N.K. Mikhailovskii, M.M. Kovalevskii*. Leningrad: Izd-vo Leningradskogo universiteta.

Kovalevskii, M. M. (1875). Review of *Lectures on the early history of institutions* by Sir Henry Sumner Maine. *La philosophie positive. Revue dirigée par E. Littré et G. Wyrouboff, 8*(15), 310–318.

Kovalevskii, M.M. (1876a). *Ocherk istorii raspadeniia obshchinnogo zemlevladeniia v Kantone Vaadt*. London.

Kovalevskii, M. M. (1876b). *Opyty po istorii iurisdiktsii nalogov vo Frantsii s XIV veka do smerti Liudvika XIV*. Moscow: Tipografiia A. I. Mamontova i Ko.

Kovalevskii, M. M. (1877). *Umriss einer Geschichte der Zerstückelung der*

Feldgemeinschaft im Kanton Waadt. Zürich: Druck und Verlag von Caesar Schmidt.

Kovalevskii, M. M. (1879). *Obshchinnoe zemlevladenie, prichiny, khod i posledstviia ego razlozheniia Chast' I. Obshchinnoe zemlevladenie v koloniiakh i vliianie pozemel'noi politiki na ego razlozheniie*. Moscow: Tipografiia F. B. Millera.

Kovalevskii, M. M. (1890). *Tableau des origines et de l'évolution de la famille et de la propriété*. Stockholm: Samson and Wallin.

Kovalevskii, M. M. (1895). Moe nauchnoe i literaturnoe skital'chestvo. *Russkaia mysl, 1*, 61–80.

Kovalevskii, M. M. (1909a). Dve zhizni. *Vestnik Evropy, 7*, 5–23.

Kovalevskii, M. M. (1909b). Dve zhizni. *Vestnik Evropy, 6*, 495–522.

Kovalevskii, M. M. (1997). *Sotsiologiia. Sochineniia v dvukh tomakh, 1, Seriia Rossiiskaia sotsiologiia*. Sankt-Peterburg: Izd-vo 'Aleteiia'.

Kovalevskii, M. M. (2005). *Moia zhizn'. Vospominaniia*. Moscow: ROSSPEN.

Kowalik, T. (2012). *Róża Luksemburg. Teoria akumulacji i imperializmu*. Warsaw: Ksiażka i Prasa.

Krader, L. (Ed.) (1974). *The ethnological notebooks of Karl Marx*. Assen: Van Gorcum.

Lewes, G. H. (1853). *Comte's philosophy of the sciences being an exposition of the principles of the cours de philosophie positive of Auguste Comte*. London: H.G. Bohn.

Luxemburg, R. (1925). *Einführung in die Nationalökonomie*. Berlin: E. Laub.

Luxemburg, R. (1971). *Listy do Leona Jogichesa-Tyszki Volume III*. Warsaw: Ksiażka i Wiedza.

Luxemburg, R. (1981). *Ökonomische Schriften* in *Gesammelte Werke, Volume 5*. Berlin: Dietz Verlag.

Luxemburg, R. (2013). *Collected works of Rosa Luxemburg. Volume 1: Economic writings*. London/New York: Verso.

Marx, K. (1985). *Werke. Artikel Entwürfe Mai 1875 bis Mai 1883* in *Gesamtausgabe*, Volume 25. Berlin: Dietz Verlag.

Marx, K., & Engels, F. (1908). *Pis'ma Karla Marksa i Fridrikha Engel'sa k Nikolaiu-onu*. St Petersburg: A. Benke.

Mill, J. S. (1865). *Auguste Comte and positivism*. London: Trübner.

Mokievsky, P. K. (1890). Philosophy in Russia. *Mind, 15*(57), 155–160.

Pasvolsky, L. (1916). M. M. Kovalevsky. *The Russian Review, 1*(5), 1–14.

Simon, W. M. (1963). *European positivism in the nineteenth century: An essay in intellectual history*. Ithaca: Cornell University Press.

Vogeler, M. S. (1984). *Frederic Harrison: the vocations of a positivist*. Oxford:

Clarendon Press.

von Maurer, G. L. (1854). *Einleitung zur Geschichte der Mark-, Hof-, Dorf- und Stadtverfassung und der öffentlichen Gewalt*. Munich: Kaiser.

White, J.D. (1996). Karl Marx and the intellectual origins of dialectical materialism. Basingstoke: Macmillan; New York: St. Martin's Press.

White, J. D. (2001). Nikolai Sieber and Karl Marx. In P. Zarembka (Ed.), *Marx's capital and capitalism; markets in a socialist alternative, research in political economy 19* (pp. 3–14). Oxford: Elsevier Science.

Wright, T. R. (1986). *The religion of humanity. The impact of Comtean positivism on Victorian Britain*. Cambridge: Cambridge University Press.

Ziber, N. I. (1871). *Teoriia tsennosti i kapitala Rikardo v sviazi s pozdneishimi dopolneniiami i raz'iasneniiami* (Kiev).

Ziber, N. I. (1883). *Ocherki pervobytnoi ekonomicheskoi kul'tury*. Moscow: Izd. K.T. Soldatenkova.

Ziber, N.I. (1885). *David Rikardo i Karl Marks v ikh obshchestvenno-ekonomicheskikh issledovanniiakh: opyt kritiko-ekonomicheskogo issledovaniia* (St. Petersburg).

5

On the Beginnings of Marxian Macroeconomics

Michael R. Krätke

The Imperialism Debate in German Social Democracy

Several years before World War I, the German Social Democratic Party (SPD), the leading party of the Second International, had shifted its attention from mere colonial politics towards the rather new phenomenon of 'imperialism', regarded as a revival of the 'world politics' of the great powers. Over several party congresses, for instance Mainz in 1900, Chemnitz at 1912, as well as at congresses held by the Socialist International, the politics of imperialism were clearly condemned. From the early years of the 20th century, leading party theorists in Germany and Austria had become engaged in debates on the explanation of imperialist politics – Karl Kautsky and the rising stars of Austro-Marxism, Otto Bauer and

M.R. Krätke (✉)
Department of Sociology/FASS, Lancaster University, Bowland North, Lancaster LA1 4YN, UK

J. Dellheim, F.O. Wolf (eds.), *Rosa Luxemburg: A Permanent Challenge for Political Economy*, DOI 10.1057/978-1-137-60108-7_5

Rudolf Hilferding, made the main contributions.[1] Rosa Luxemburg was the first Marxist economist to devote an entire book-length study to imperialism, joining the debate rather late, in 1913.[2] Unlike her predecessors, and very much in the mood and style of her old adversary Eduard Bernstein, she combined the explanation of imperialism with a harsh and thorough critique of Marx. In order to develop Marx's political economy further, one had to criticise its gaps and weaknesses with the same ruthlessness as he himself had criticised the classical political economists. So, in 1913, finally publishing the 'great work' that everybody expected from her, Rosa Luxemburg became a Marxist revisionist of sorts. Accordingly, she had to brace herself for a series of sharp responses.

Marx's *tableaux économiques*

From 1857 until 1881, Marx wrote several versions of what was to become one of his most famous achievements in political economy: his own *tableaux économiques*, better known as his reproduction schemes. It was in fact the second version of a macroeconomic analysis of the whole reproduction process in capitalist economies, drafted two hundred years after François Quesnay had first designed and published a model depicting the circulation of the national product between the three great economic classes of society in 1758. Quesnay and his followers (notably Nicolas Baudeau) produced several versions of the much-admired tableaux, but, unfortunately, neither Quesnay nor the other members of the thriving physiocratic school ever finished the job. After a short career, the *tableau économique* fell into oblivion.

In 1857–8, while writing the large economic manuscripts that are today known as the *Grundrisse*, Marx encountered the problem of the

[1] The theoretical debate on the further development of capitalism on a world scale, including its crisis tendencies, was actually triggered by two articles in the *Neue Zeit*, the first by Heinrich Cunow (1899), the second by Karl Kautsky (1902).

[2] Otto Bauer had already devoted several chapters of his seminal book on *The Question of Nationalities and the Social Democracy* to the analysis of imperialism, and Rudolf Hilferding analysed imperialism as a specific kind of economic policy pursued by the new economic and political elites in the advanced capitalist countries under the rule of 'finance capital' in his book on *Finance Capital*, published in 1910 (Bauer [1907](1975); Hilferding 1910).

reproduction of total social capital for the first time. He sought to explain the phenomenon of recurring cyclical crises, or, using the parlance of classical political economy, 'general gluts'. According to his original plan, the famous six-book plan of 1858, a book on crisis and the world market would provide the conclusion and culmination of his entire project, the 'critique of political economy'. The manuscript of 1857–8 is a research manuscript, intended not for publication but to achieve a clarification of the author's thoughts, remaining highly experimental throughout.[3] It is not a philosophical tract at all but rather a first effort to unify Marx's various efforts to criticise the main concepts and tenets of classical political economy from 1843–4 onwards in a coherent, systematic way as something that would and should become a treatise of critical political economy. Accordingly, Marx the political economist tried repeatedly to resolve the problems that classical political economy had left unsettled. Among them was the problem of the reproduction and accumulation of capital on a national or world scale – a problem that had troubled the classical economists and intrigued their first socialist critics.

In this manuscript, Marx starts with a series of examples – subdividing total social capital into no less than five different and particular capitals or industries – and struggles on with a lot of arithmetic illustrations. However, he does eventually arrive at a conclusion: the 'inner structure' of capital, any (industrial) capital, should somehow also determine the differentiation of total social capital – as well as the proportions in which the different parts of social capital would exchange with each other (MEGA² II/1.2, pp. 353, 354).[4]

In the next larger research manuscript, the manuscript of 1861–3, Marx took a decisive step forward. It was here that he first came up with his own version of a *tableau économique* for the first time. He sketched a graph – very much like the tableau of Francois Quesnay – based upon

---

[3] I have explained the status of the *Grundrisse* and its real place in the long story of the making of Marx's *Capital* elsewhere (Krätke 2008). The now-prevailing view, which turns it into an exercise of applied Hegelianism, is completely misguided. The abuse of the text (its very poor translation into English notwithstanding) as a quarry for citations serving as starting points for all sorts of lofty 'philosophical' exercises is a disgrace and divorced from serious scholarship, Marxist or not.

[4] There is no reliable English translation of the *Grundrisse* text, another reason not to trust the Anglo-Saxon philosopher's tales about it.

his own analytical categories, and divided it between three departments of social production and/or poles of societal exchange – consumption goods, production goods and the total social production. Confining himself to 'simple reproduction', he spent a lot of time analysing the intermediary movements of money and commodities (no less than seven intermediary flows of either money or commodities) and drafting various plans for the treatise of this topic – the analysis of the total process of the reproduction of capital – in his future work (MEGA² II/3.6, pp. 2270ff, 2337ff).

During the first half of 1865, Marx wrote the first full version of what he intended to become Volume II of *Capital*.[5] In this manuscript, he outlined a rather ambitious programme: he would present a full analysis of the circulation and reproduction of total social capital in the concluding Chap. (or section) 3 of this volume; an analysis which would comprise the examination of the process of expanded reproduction or accumulation, including money capital accumulation (or 'savings') and provide the necessary clues for the later analysis of crises or 'disturbances of the reproduction process' (MEGA² II/4.1, pp. 321ff, 381). This manuscript still very much bears the marks of a research manuscript, in which the author is experimenting with various devices. He had not yet made up his mind as to the right distinction of departments or fractions of total social capital, and although he had by now dropped the original graph, he had not yet found a way to replace it by another form of presentation. Nevertheless, the general direction of the investigation is already clear.

The decisive step forward was made in 1868–70, when Marx wrote the second full version of Volume II of *Capital* (known among Marxologists as manuscript II).[6] Although he was still experimenting to a certain extent, he had now found the algebraic form of presentation of his 'schemes of reproduction'. In writing, he followed his usual practice of drafting a variety of numerical examples, entangling himself in the arithmetic. But the basic concepts are present and quite clear. As the manuscript shows,

[5] These manuscripts were published for the first time in the second MEGA, more than a hundred years after the actual time of writing. Until today, there is no English translation of this very first draft of *Capital*, Volume II.

[6] This manuscript has been published for the first time, in MEGA², volume II/11. In print, it is more than 500 pages long.

Marx had not given up his ambitious plan to include all the intermediary movements of money and commodities in his analysis, which he still conceived of as an analysis of the total process of reproduction and circulation in terms of flows (of capital, of commodities, of money, or, in functional terms, of revenues and capital). Pondering his invention, he experimented with various divisions and subdivisions – in one version no less than five different departments plus two further subdivisions of departments – and discussed the problems of accumulation, including the accumulation of money capital, at length. Nonetheless, the manuscript was broken off and remained unfinished.

In 1877, Marx wrote a piece for Engels who was involved in a lengthy polemic against a then famous critic, Eugen Dühring. Marx supported him by criticising Dühring's *History of Economic Thought*. The centrepiece of Marx's contribution was a rather detailed exposition and explanation of Francois Quesnay's *tableaux économiques*. As we can see now from his drafts, published for the first time in the MEGA^2, volume I/27, he grasped the opportunity to engage himself in another intense study of Quesnay's work. The results of these renewed studies are included in his later manuscripts for *Capital*, Volume II.

In 1878–81, in his last manuscript for *Capital*, Volume II (among Marxologists better known as manuscript VIII), Marx tried again to find the adequate form to present his results.[7] But as the manuscript shows clearly, Marx was not yet done with his research. The bulk of the manuscript was actually dedicated to the analysis of the reproduction and circulation of total social capital (the third part or chapter of what was later to become Volume II) and to the analysis of the accumulation process in particular. Although his manner of presentation remained rather clumsy, he analysed not only the impact of accumulation on the structure of the surplus product, but also the interrelationship between money accumulation and what he then called 'real accumulation'.[8] As in the earlier

[7] This manuscript has been published for the first time, in MEGA^2 II/11. In print, it is more than 300 pages long.

[8] Capitalists' savings and investments (real or direct, not financial or portfolio) in today's economic parlance. In the second section of *Capital*, Volume II, Marx shows in much detail why (not always how) capitalists are bound to save money, that is to say to 'hoard', to build up reserve funds of various kinds serving different functions, due to the very 'mechanics' of capital turnover.

manuscripts, and still conforming to his plan of 1863, he deals with the production of gold as a source of additional money as well as with the hoarding of money by capitalists in both departments.[9] One can even find an analysis of the famous 'third persons' and their specific role in the total process of reproduction and circulation. Even if the manner of presentation is far from finished, elements of the solution of all the salient problems of the accumulation process are clearly present in this last manuscript. He left it unfinished due to another illness in the summer of 1881.

Rosa Luxemburg's Critique

Volume II of *Capital*, first published in 1885, had gone relatively unnoticed. It was only due to the debate among Russian radicals on the future capitalist development of that eventually some use was made of the Marxian schemes of reproduction.[10] Tugan-Baranowsky was the first to use them to prove the possibility of industrial growth without limits – and independent of foreign markets (Tugan-Baranowsky 1901). Danielson, well known as the first translator of Marx's *Capital*, Volume I into Russian, as well as an interlocutor whom both Marx and Engels held in high regard, was the first to argue the opposite case at length – that the development of capitalism in Russia, lacking colonies and surrounding 'non-capitalist' environments, was doomed to fail (Danielson 1893),[11] while the Marxists, legal or not, tried to prove the opposite. There were a few brief, rather hostile reactions to Tugan's first book on the theory and history of crises in Britain (Tugan-Baranowsky 1901) as well as to his later book on the theoretical foundations of Marxism

[9] Marx sticks to the abstraction from credit in all his manuscripts for this volume. So, the only sources of 'money' are either gold production or hoards. As his analysis of the turnover of capital shows, hoarding is a necessity for every industrial capital.

[10] For a history of this debate, see Rosdolsky ([1969] (1992)). Luxemburg devoted two chapters of the second section of her book, the section dealing with the history of economic thought on the problem of capital accumulation, to the debates between various kinds of radical economists in Russia, including the Marxists.

[11] Marx had read Danielson's articles on the development of capitalism in Russia, 'Our Post-Reform Economy', and had encouraged him to publish them as a book.

(Tugan-Baranowsky 1905) in the leading German socialist journals *Die Neue Zeit* and *Sozialistische Monatshefte* (Schmidt 1901; Kautsky 1902; Bauer 1904, 1906; Boudin 1907a, 1907b; Pannekoek 1910), but no extended debate on the matter.

Karl Kautsky was the first to combine and blend the issues of an explanation of the recent phenomena of 'imperialism' and the Great Depression, which had morphed into a long boom since 1895. His critique of Tugan's work triggered a debate, the first real debate on crisis theory in the history of Marxism (Krätke 2015). Louis Boudin, Anton Pannekoek, Conrad Schmidt, Otto Bauer, Heinrich Cunow, and even Eduard Bernstein contributed to it, but Rosa Luxemburg stayed out of the fray.[12] The debate lingered on for several years, but ended without any clear resolution. Some of the protagonists had become aware of the difficulties that the unresolved questions of the critique of political economy that Marx had bequeathed to them were more serious than they had presumed.[13] This left the ground well prepared for another 'revision' of Marx.

In 1913, after about 15 years of preparation, Rosa Luxemburg published her only major treatise on political economy, *The Accumulation of Capital*.[14] The book was meant to provide an explanation of imperialism, as she announced in the subtitle (*A Contribution to an Economic Explanation of Imperialism*). Implicitly, she launched an all-out attack against the prevailing Marxist orthodoxy in the German Social Democratic Party. The boldness with which she criticised Marx himself and introduced a far-reaching revision to one of the core parts of his economic theory, even dismissing the usually untouchable 'method' of Marx's economic analysis, stunned friends and foes alike. Rosa Luxemburg, the stalwart defender of Marxist orthodoxy against 'revisionist' heresies, did not hesitate to note and deplore Marx's 'great inconsistencies', the 'deficiencies' of his reasoning, his 'wrong approach' and 'many long-winded detours',

---

[12] During the debate on revisionism, when preparing her critique of Bernstein, she had already admitted in private correspondence that she found the issues of crisis and growth rather daunting.

[13] Richard Day and Daniel Gaido have recently published two volumes which make the main contributions to these debates available to an English speaking audience for the first time (see Day and Gaido 2011, 2012).

[14] It was followed by a response to her critics, at book length, the *Anti-Critique*, written in 1915, and published only after her death, in 1921 (Luxemburg 1925).

and eventually to dismiss outright his rather 'misleading formulation of the problem' - 'Thus the question itself has been wrongly formulated by Marx all along' (Luxemburg 1913b, pp. 93, 253, 113, 215). As she emphasised time and again, *Capital*, Volume II had remained unfinished, crucial parts of Marx's analyses were left 'quite incomplete' and simply broken off (Luxemburg 1913b, p. 116).

From 1907, she had worked as a lecturer in Political Economy and Economic History at the party school of the SPD, based in Berlin. Her lectures, covering a vast array of topics from the early history of mankind to the tendencies of modern industrial capitalism, were quite successful, so she started transforming them into a full-scale introductory textbook on political economy. The text was never completed, crucial chapters were never written and large parts of the manuscripts were lost, while some of the remaining parts were only published in 1925, six years after her death.[15] However, the fragments provide some hints as to her general conception of political economy and its critique. In the study of political economy, we look for explanations for the possibility of modern capitalism: how is an anarchic market economy on a world scale possible? How is continuous growth of such an economy sustainable in the long run? Eventually, as the development of capitalism has its distinct limits, the task is changed from the investigation of the preconditions of capitalism – how is capitalism possible, how is capitalist development possible? – to the investigation of the conditions – that render capitalism impossible and will bring capitalist development to its end. As Rosa Luxemburg saw it, the fine point of Marx's critique was the determination of capitalism's historical limits – in historical space and time. An investigation that went clearly further than the identification of 'inner' contradictions or the conditions of disequilibrium and crisis inherent to capitalism as such (Luxemburg 1925, pp. 235ff)[16].

When she wrote her critique of Marx's reproduction schemes, she had no idea of the variety of Marx's manuscripts dedicated to the mat-

---

[15] Several lecture notes and further manuscripts by Rosa Luxemburg have been published recently or are about to be published soon. Until very recently, most of the text of Luxemburg's introduction to political economy was not available in English (Luxemburg [1925] (2013)).

[16] That is what she emphasized in her short piece on Marx' Capital, volume II and III, that she wrote at about the same time for Franz Mehring's Karl Marx biography (cf. Mehring 1974).

ter at hand. In fact, in May 1900 she had refused to participate in the editing work on Marx's many unpublished papers and manuscripts when Kautsky invited her to help him with what he was later to publish as *Theories of Surplus Value* in 1905–10 (Krätke 2010).[17] Thus, she missed the opportunity to study Marx's unpublished manuscripts for the second volume of *Capital* to take a look at Marx's conceptual workshop from the inside.

In 1911, while working on her book, she provided some comments on the topic in the form of private letters where she did not restrict her language. To her close friend Kostja Zetkin she wrote in November of that year that the Marxian reproduction schemes had already perturbed her for a long time; now, upon closer examination, she found them full of unreliabilities ('Windbeuteleien' in German, which is actually a much harsher expression) (Laschitza 2000, p. 411). In other words, Marx did not only not finish the job of analysing the process of (expanded) reproduction of total social capital, he did a lousy job as well.

Her book starts with an examination of Marx's theory of the reproduction process of capital as expounded in Section III of *Capital*, Volume II. In several chapters – Chaps. 4–9 of the first section – she first examines Marx's schemes of simple reproduction of total social capital, raising just a few objections of minor importance, such as the way in which the reproduction of fixed capital (a difficulty that Marx avoided) or the way in which he deals with the production of gold, where she proposes putting gold production into a separate, third department of social production (Luxemburg 1915, pp. 356ff.). She then goes on to present and discuss Marx's schemes of expanded reproduction. What bothers her is the apparent smoothness of the accumulation process which – in accordance with the rules of proportionality between the two departments as expounded by Marx – could go on forever without any limits. She views this as an easy, 'fool-proof mathematical exercise' and asks whether Marx's scheme actually fits in the real world of capitalism (Luxemburg 1915, p. 367). Obviously, she thinks not. In her view, Marx's schemes are valid for a socialist planned economy, but not for a capitalist economy. What Marx does not explain in the last chapter of Volume II (largely

[17] In a private letter, Rosa Luxemburg commented upon Kautsky's proposal–which was actually quite an honour to her–and dismissed it as a trick to lure her into submission (Krätke 2010).

drawn from his unfinished last manuscript, manuscript VIII of 1880–1) is where the increasing additional demand that would induce capitalists in Departments I and II to invest and expand their production comes from. Who will buy the additional goods emanating from the expanded production apparatus of a continuously accumulating industrial capital (Luxemburg 1915, p. 368)? Upon closer examination of Marx's argument, she concludes that the abstraction from money, money circulation and hoarding is at the core of the matter. As Marx lifts this abstraction in the very same manuscript, she scrutinises his 'attempt to resolve the difficulty' (in Chaps. 8 and 9) and rejects it. In her view, Marx's solution – the additional amount of effective demand coming from the continuous hoarding of many capitalists in both departments, which is clearly in line with all of Marx's analyses of the turnover process of capital in the previous Section II of Volume II – can only be valid for one, highly specific and exceptional case: for the transition from simple to expanded reproduction (Luxemburg 1913b, pp. 114, 115). But it cannot serve as an explanation for the continued process of accumulation in the longer run and under 'normal' circumstances.

After a long detour through the history of political economy and the many debates on the role of 'third persons' in the reproduction process, Luxemburg returns to the examination of Marx's schemes (in Chap. 25), now taking issue with the core of Marx's argument: what Marx regards as an adequate solution to her problem is in fact insufficient, because the amounts of hoarded money capital will be too small to provide a sufficient amount of efficient demand for the growing production in the context of expanded capitalist reproduction (Luxemburg 1913b, pp. 240ff). This assertion is sufficient for her to reject Marx's schemes outright. Whatever their merits, they cannot 'explain the actual and historical process of accumulation' (Luxemburg 1913b, p. 250). Jumping from a theoretical argument into historical explanation, she spent the bulk of Section III of her book (Chaps. 26–32) outlining a correct historical explanation of the accumulation process in the European countries. To overcome the unsettled problem she had identified in Marx's theory of accumulation, she proposed a solution which would take into account another set of 'third persons', this time the large non- or pre-capitalist world as part of the real context of capitalist expansion and part of the capitalist world economy.

From the logic and context of her argument it is not self-evident that these 'non-capitalist' environments must necessarily be found 'outside' of the capitalist world in spatial terms. But that is the turn that she took. In these last chapters of her book, she presented her famous explanation of the historical phenomenon of imperialism and inter-imperialist rivalry between the advanced capitalist countries in particular. She made no further effort whatsoever to meet Marx on his own ground or, continuing and expanding the analysis on his terms, to provide an improved version of a scheme of expanded reproduction and accumulation. She even maintained that a contradiction existed between the theory of the accumulation process as outlined in the last chapters of *Capital*, Volume I and the third section of Volume III, and the rather barren analysis which Marx vainly tried to carry out in Capital, Volume II.

The Luxemburg Debate: Round One

Luxemburg's critique of Marx was as harsh as, if not harsher than most of the criticism that the protagonists of 'revisionism' had ever expounded. But in striking contrast to Bernstein, for instance, she argued in favour of the hypothesis of an inevitable 'breakdown' of the capitalist world economy. In the longer run, capitalist accumulation on a world scale would no longer be possible. It would come to a grinding halt, not a collapse but rather a long-lasting and worldwide stagnation.

This hypothesis triggered an international debate which lasted until the 1930s and was never formally concluded. Because the leading Marxist theorists of her day were provoked by her attack on Marx's theory, they began reworking and reformulating it. No one denied, as Engels had already stated quite frankly, that Marx had left his work unfinished and that something could and should be done about the unfinished and incomplete theory of accumulation which clearly was essential to a fully-fledged analysis of the dynamics of modern capitalism. As a matter of fact, Rosa Luxemburg had presented the Marxist economists with a real challenge: Marx's analysis of the reproduction process of capitalist societies was meant to be constructed from several interlinked analytical blocks. First, one had to deal with the apparently simple (and actually imaginary) case of 'simple reproduction' (when the whole of capitalist reproduction is reproduced in material and social terms, without any intrinsic changes, preserving the same size and the same proportions between its parts). Followed, second, by the analysis of the accumulation process of capital, in which the whole of capitalist production was reproduced on an ever larger scale, in both material and social terms. The analysis of the accumulation process was again subdivided – into the analysis of simple accumulation (when the whole system grows in scale while the proportions between its parts remain unchanged), and 'accelerated' accumulation, as Marx had already indicated in the second German and the French edition of *Capital*, Volume I. This was the most complicated issue – the analysis of the accumulation process in a capitalist economy when the production system not only grew in scale but also changed its proportions, both materially and socially. Accelerated accumulation, accumulation on an ever-increasing scale together with constant change of the proportions between its parts, was bound to occur in all capitalist economies and societies that had reached the stage of industrial capitalism (large-scale industry and the factory system). Accumulation of industrial capital would inevitably include rising levels of labour productivity due to innovation and technological change in the capitalist production process. Accordingly, the theory of accumulation and the theory of capitalist development (or intrinsic qualitative change) would become intertwined.

The issue at hand was simply whether this ambitious kind of dynamic analysis could be conducted under the specific assumptions Marx had made in order to construct his schemes – or whether these assumptions as well as the whole idea of studying capitalism in a 'pure form' had to be abandoned as Rosa Luxemburg had insisted. It was to become a long-winded and exhausting debate (Mandel 1978).[18]

Ultimately, the outcome of the debate was something Rosa Luxemburg had never wanted and never expected: a much more sophisticated and formalised version of Marxian macroeconomic analysis, the beginnings of the systematic study of capitalist macrodynamics which had impacted –

---

[18] Accounts of this debate by professed Marxists of some kind or the other have been distorted by the fatal habit of reading everybody's contributions as open or clandestine statements of political views–right, centrist, harmonist, reformist, revolutionary. That is, of course, nonsense.

mostly through the work of Michał Kalecki – Keynesian macro theory and modern growth theory.

Only a few reviews of Luxemburg's book in the socialist press were friendly, such as the reviews by Franz Mehring and Julian Marchlewski in the *Leipziger Volkszeitung*: both hailed her book as a true enlargement of Marxian economic theory (Marchlewski 1913; Mehring 1913). The two reviewers, however, had no expertise and certainly no reputation as political economists. Some reviews were quite hostile, like the one written by Max Schippel for the *Sozialistische Monatshefte*. This treated her very unfairly indeed, mocking her as a quack doctor who was inventing an 'imaginary disease' (Schippel 1913, p. 148).

Most of the reviewers in the socialist press were unconvinced by her effort to demonstrate the impossibility of equilibrium growth and the necessity of a breakdown of capitalism. Gustav Eckstein, in his very detailed and polite review in *Vorwärts*, accused her of simply misunderstanding the reproduction schemes and their purpose, of missing the logic of Marx' argument.[19] As he pointed out, Rosa Luxemburg had created an insuperable difficulty by tacitly introducing additional conditions into the reproduction schemes, assuming – instead of proving – a kind of 'law' of equal accumulation in both departments or an equal rate of accumulation (Eckstein 1913, p. 702ff, 707f). He was right, of course: accumulation rates could vary across industries, sectors and 'departments', hence the possibility of an equilibrium path of accumulation could not be excluded on purely logical grounds. And he was also right in refuting her argument that European or American surplus production was being sold to the peasant populations of non-capitalist countries on a large scale. Rosa Luxemburg's own insights into the ways in which these countries and their populations were actually exploited by the imperialist powers were incompatible with that assumption (Eckstein 1913, p. 711–2). Accordingly, Eckstein rejected her explanation of the limits of capitalism.

Another protagonist of the social democratic Left in Europe, the Dutch astronomer Anton Pannekoek, a man quite close to Rosa Luxemburg as

[19] A logic that was not unfamiliar to Rosa Luxemburg, as her lectures on *Capital*, Volume II clearly show (Luxemburg [1925] (2013), pp. 421ff.).

far as the actual policies of the Social Democratic Party in Germany were concerned, criticised and refuted the central thesis of her book in his review, published in the *Bremer Bürger-Zeitung* the very same year. He rejected her criticism of Marx's reproduction schemes outright, showing that the conditions of growth and increasing productivity of labour, hence the rising organic composition of capital, could be met within the confines of Marx's schemes. Marx's models could be enlarged and differentiated, completely in accordance with his own method (Pannekoek 1913, p. 685ff). Furthermore, Pannekoek did not even accept her explanation of imperialism, although he saw some value in her detailed description of the praxis of capitalist expansion in the last chapters of her book. But Luxemburg had failed to grasp the peculiarities of contemporary imperialist policies, for 'imperialism is a modern phenomenon' and not identical with the colonialism of the 17th and 18th centuries or with the capitalist world policy of the first half of the 19th century. In particular, Rosa Luxemburg had misunderstood the economic reasons for the new world politics of the great capitalist powers, which lay not in the search for new markets for selling surplus commodities but in the necessity of capital exports. Hilferding had done an excellent job of outlining this, while Luxemburg had missed his points – both in her critique of Marx and in her economic explanation of imperialism (Pannekoek 1913, pp. 691–3).[20] Rosa Luxemburg was apparently stunned by the lack of understanding for both the problem and the solution she put forward in her book, as she admitted in a private letter to Franz Mehring (Laschitza 2000, p. 420). Lenin, for his part, was quite pleased with Pannekoek's review. When he had read Luxemburg's book, he drafted an article against it, in which he again rejected her interpretation of Marx as completely wrong and her addition to his theory as an outright failure (Lenin 1985, pp. 105ff.).[21]

---

[20] Anton Pannekoek was a journalist working for German socialist newspapers at the time. He had come to Germany to teach at the SPD's party school in Berlin. By training, he was an astronomer (he later wrote a very remarkable history of astronomy after he had become chair of Astronomy at the University of Amsterdam) and a very well-versed mathematician.

[21] Lenin never finished his critique of Luxemburg's book. There have been various publications of publications of his notes and first drafts for his Luxemburg-critique in Russian, the last and most complete in the 1980s edition of his works (Lenin 1985).

Round Two: Otto Bauer's Critique

The leading German-speaking Marxist theorists of the time responded to Luxemburg's Marx-critique rather quickly.[22] The most substantial critique came from Otto Bauer in an article entitled 'The Accumulation of Capital', published in the leading theoretical journal of international socialism, the *Neue Zeit*, in 1913.[23] Politely but without any reservations, he attacked what he saw as just another version of the venerable 'third persons' theorem, albeit now in a Marxist guise. He took up Luxemburg's challenge and set out to defend what he regarded as an essential part of Marx' economic theory: the analysis of the conditions under which an equilibrium growth of a purely capitalist economy was possible. This growth nevertheless had certain objective limits, but was still possible.[24]

Bauer's critique of Luxemburg is different, as he dismissed her almost immediately and devoted little space to her argument or to a critique of her mistakes. Instead, he developed a more sophisticated and more complex model of accumulation and capitalist growth, including population growth (albeit at a steady rate) and technical progress, that is to say a rising organic composition of capital in both departments. Initially, he kept the rate of exploitation to surplus value constant, but he unfortunately failed to relax this assumption later on. Nevertheless, he demonstrated the possibility of equilibrium accumulation and growth in a purely capitalist economy in terms of a time sequence, over four periods/years. In Bauer's model, the capitalists' rate of savings increases steadily from one period to the next. Unfortunately, he did not follow Marx's example and ignored the distinction between money accumulation and real accumulation (or direct investment) which Marx actually makes.[25] Explicitly, Bauer allowed for the possibility of capital transfer between the two departments which

---

[22] With the remarkable exception of Rudolf Hilferding. He was urged by Otto Bauer to write a review of Luxemburg's book for the Austro-Marxist journal *Der Kampf*, but did not do so. Curiously enough, Rosa Luxemburg also kept silent about Rudolf Hilferding's widely discussed and highly influential book on *Finance Capital*, published a few years before, in 1910.

[23] Otto Bauer's article is one of the few contributions to the debate which has been translated to English by John E. King in 1986 (King 1986).

[24] Bauer was and remained quite critical of Tugan-Baranowsky's attempt to prove that unlimited industrial growth was possible.

[25] He did so in his later writings on the theory of crisis (Bauer 2015). Actually, the preceding section II of *Capital*, Volume II dealing with the turnover of capital had already shown the sources of an ever increasing 'accumulation funds' for capital–while still maintaining the abstraction from credit.

presupposes credit relations. In his model, capitalists can and do invest their savings (the parts of surplus value not privately consumed, but saved, that they have appropriated) outside of their own or home department, shifting investments from one department to the other so that accumulation and growth remains possible and on a path of equilibrium. Bauer rejected Luxemburg's solution to her problem, since, according to him, the accumulated part of surplus value can actually be realised inside a supposedly 'closed' capitalist economy. His objection was correct: selling surplus products in the guise of means of production abroad, exporting them to the non-capitalist world could never solve the problem. On the contrary, it would impair accumulation and make it impossible in the long run. Moreover, Luxemburg did not explain – and nor could she – how people in non-capitalist areas of the world would ever be able to provide for a rising amount of additional effective demand, providing an ever-expanding market for the capitalist industries in the core countries of capitalism. After all, historical imperialism depended upon a constant flow of capital exports from the capitalist countries to the non-capitalist parts of the world.

Otto Bauer understood Marx's intention to provide an additional ingredient to his theory of crisis perfectly well. Thus, he did what Rosa Luxemburg had completely forgotten and avoided: he engaged in a discussion of the cyclical movement of the capitalist accumulation process. A process by a periodical change between over-accumulation and under-accumulation that allowed for long-term growth of capitalist economies, crises notwithstanding. He did not disagree with the concept of 'limits to the accumulation of capital', but in his view Luxemburg had failed to determine what those limits were. Nevertheless, in Bauer's view her theory of imperialism contained a kernel of truth, as imperialism served to extend the limits of accumulation and to alleviate the crises that periodic over-accumulation of capital in the European heartlands of industrial capitalism would inevitably entail.

Bauer's growth model was 'the most sophisticated piece of macrodynamic analysis attempted by any Marxian economist before 1914' (Howard and King 1989, p. 120).[26] It exhibits close affinities with the

[26] Perhaps with the exception of Charasoff's study of 1910 which Otto Bauer had reviewed in the theoretical journal of the Austrian Social Democratic Party, *Der Kampf* (Bauer 1911). Bauer's first contribution to the debate, his article on 'Marx's theory of economic crises' (Marx's Theorie der Wirtschaftskrisen) in 1904, already showed some of the elements of a mathematical treatment of macroeconomic dynamics that he was to develop further in later writings.

modern Harrod–Domar growth model. Of course, it has its weaknesses as well, the largest being its reliance upon population growth as the one and only independent variable that determines the movements of capital accumulation. In the Bauer model, the full employment of the working class appears as an 'iron law' of capitalist development. However, assuming a closed and completely developed capitalist economy, the growth of the population itself becomes an important factor and precondition of overall economic growth (as Marx himself already knew).

Round Three: Rosa Luxemburg's Anti-Critique

When Luxemburg found herself in jail during World War I, she finally had the time to respond to her critics. She did so, writing a large *Anti-Critique*, mostly during the year 1915. Her papers were partly lost after the end of the war and her untimely death in January 1919, but the manuscript of *Anti-Critique* was recovered. The book was published in 1921, though it was no great success. It is a highly polemical text, in which Luxemburg attacks her critics on political grounds: in her eyes they are all reformists, adhering to a flawed, 'harmonist' view of the capitalist world system, denying the possibility of a 'breakdown' of capitalism (Luxemburg 1915).

She focused on Otto Bauer: most of the space in the book is devoted to ridiculing and refuting his elaborated version of a Marxist model of accumulation and growth, but she avoids any real engagement with the finer points of his model. Gustav Eckstein is attacked viciously and very unfairly; clearly, Rosa Luxemburg was unaware of his fine work as a Marxist historian and political analyst.[27] Of course, Anton Pannekoek, her political ally, could not be dismissed in this way, so in that case she preferred simply to ignore him. As she was in jail, she had no knowledge of two further critiques of her book, also published in 1915: one

[27] Her extremely unfair attacks on the Austro-Marxists, the group of young scholars and intellectuals to which Gustav Eckstein also belonged, is a rather strange phenomenon. Rosa Luxemburg hated Rudolf Hilferding, and she despised the Vienna Marxist crowd, although she should have been aware of the fact that these young theorists were as hostile to revisionism as she was. Bernstein, for one, immediately understood the meaning of the Austro-Marxist school in the making.

by Conrad Schmidt in *Sozialistische Monatshefte*, and the other by Sam de Wolff in the Dutch socialist journal *De nieuwe tijd*. Again, in these contributions two of the most capable Marxist economists of the time dismissed her argument outright (Schmidt 1915; de Wolff 1915).

She refused to enter the terrain of theoretical debate and does not engage in any further mathematical exercises. Any effort to improve or enlarge the Marxian schemes is futile. In her view, the Marxian reproduction schemes were fundamentally flawed and no reformulation could save them. There are only two substantial points she makes in her polemic against Otto Bauer: the assumption of a constant rate of exploitation is not compatible with a rising organic composition of capital and should be abandoned in order to develop a complete view of the capitalist accumulation process. The notion that the rate of capital accumulation would follow the rate of growth of the (working class) population is rather a strange one. However, her assertions against Otto Bauer's demonstration of a possible proportionate exchange between the two departments and hence the possibility of equilibrium accumulation and growth are simply incorrect. Of course, she is right when she stresses the double nature of accumulation as both a political and an economic process in historical time (Luxemburg 1915, p. 375). But her belief that she had provided a scientific proof for the inevitability of an overall breakdown of the capitalist world economy is simply wrong and completely misguided. In *Anti-Critique* she restated her core idea concerning political economy in its Marxian, critical guise: Marx's theory was meant to be a 'theory of capitalist development' (as she had already characterised it in 1903) (Luxemburg [1903] 1970, p. 370). Its main task was first to show why and how capitalism was possible at all, and, second, to demonstrate why and how capitalism as an economic and social system would ultimately become impossible to sustain. In other words, Marxists had to determine the specific, intrinsic limits to capitalist development in historical time and geographical space (Luxemburg 1915, p. 295). Again, she repeated her view that a theory of accumulation should explain the 'real historical process of capitalist accumulation' (Luxemburg 1915, p. 250).[28]

[28] In a footnote, she dismissed the famous 'law' of the general rate of profit to fall, today the shibboleth of all true Marxist believers, as irrelevant (Luxemburg 1915, p. 449, fn. 4).

Unfortunately, her defence only encouraged her followers to refuse any serious engagement with anything that a 'reformist' or 'centrist' such as Otto Bauer might have to say, perhaps with the exception of Henryk Grossmann, the only Marxist economist to provide a substantial criticism of Otto Bauer's model during the next round. Even Roman Rosdolsky, reassessing the debate decades later in the 1950s, was impressed by the political attack against the so-called 'neo-harmonists'. In the vein of Luxemburg, he simply ignored Bauer's effort to extend and develop the Marxian reproduction schemes into a fully-fledged theory of (cyclical) crisis (Rosdolsky [1969] (1992), p. 490ff).

Round Four

The debate continued into the 1920s, albeit in the shadow of a political struggle within the Communist movement against the current known as 'Luxemburgism'. Few Marxists dared to take Luxemburg's theory of imperialism as a frame of reference for their own work; indeed, only people outside of the world of the Communist and Social Democratic parties could. Of these, Fritz Sternberg provided the most prominent example, and will be discussed later in this section.

Writing from inside the heartland of the Communist movement, Nikolai Bukharin penned another critique of Luxemburg in the early 1920s, inspired by his desire to come to grips with the phenomenon of imperialism after World War I. Eventually he expanded his original article and transformed it into a small book, published in 1925 (Bukharin [1926] (1997)). Here, Bukharin provided another highly sophisticated example of a Marxian model of accumulation and growth, taking into account most of the variables that had been discussed until then and redressing the proportionalities between the departments in order to come to a fully dynamised growth model. In Bukharin's version we find rising rates of exploitation as well as rising organic compositions of capital in both departments, and we also encounter variable rates of accumulation (savings and investment) and output growth. Bukharin defends Marx's models on methodological grounds: such a device is required to demonstrate the sheer possibility of limitless equilibrium growth by illustrating the many possibilities of disequilibrium and unbalanced growth in capitalist development – but the modelling of such growth is not to be confused with assertions as to the likelihood that it will occur. Furthermore, he took Luxemburg's explanation of imperialism seriously and found it to be deeply flawed. Luxemburg fails to understand the implications of commodity exports to pre-capitalist markets. An export surplus can indeed provide a net increase in effective demand, but it will inevitably involve the export of capital to the pre-capitalist regions of the world – a reality that Luxemburg fails to grasp and explain and which is firmly rooted in the historical experience and practice of European colonialism and imperialism.

One of the few serious defences of Luxemburg came from Fritz Sternberg, who set out in the 1920s to give a new and comprehensive explanation of the phenomenon of imperialism (Sternberg 1926). Sternberg followed Rosa Luxemburg's lead with respect to her Marx-critique (some reservations notwithstanding). In his view, her criticism was correct and completely justified, although he did feel that she had overlooked some important points. In order to come to grips with imperialism, Marxist economists had to integrate the rise of the organic composition of capital in both departments as well as the difference of the organic composition of capital between them. Moreover, he tried to historicise most of the Marxian 'laws of movement' of modern capital in a radical manner. In his view, they were only valid for certain periods in the history of modern capitalism and had to be specified accordingly. Following Luxemburg, he was the first to try to integrate the non- or pre-capitalist areas into a long-term periodisation of capitalist development. He distinguishes between different eras and different stages of imperialism (early and late imperialism): depending upon the principal source of surplus labour and surplus population, one could identify different and subsequent periods of capitalist development – some of which, like his famous 'honeymoon period', were much more favourable to the working class than others. Recently, this 'honeymoon period' had come to an end, and the prospects of further capitalist development as well as the very nature of 'imperialism' were changing accordingly. Thus, Sternberg's work could be read as a defence as well as an extension of Luxemburg's original theory.

Curiously enough, the harshest attack on Sternberg came from Henryk Grossmann, who for his part sought to reformulate and defend Rosa Luxemburg's original theory about the inevitable breakdown of capitalism in a more rigorous and radical manner (Grossmann 1929). Grossmann, in his scathing review, ridiculed the lack of Marxist scholarship in Sternberg's approach.[29] In Sternberg's book there was no scheme of expanded reproduction, just some numerical examples which he did not analyse. So Grossmann and Helene Bauer, Otto Bauer's wife, had no difficulty demonstrating the inherent weakness of his theory of crisis, resting as it did upon assertions and a few historical illustrations rather than an extension of macroeconomic analysis. In her review Helene Bauer simply repeated the main arguments from her husband's article against Luxemburg (Bauer 1927). Sternberg, in his lengthy riposte to his various critics, tried to re-establish the necessity of a 'consumption rest' of unsold and unsaleable commodities in department I. His scheme, based upon Bauer's and Bukharin's contributions, was more sophisticated than that of Luxemburg. As some of his critics (such as Helene Bauer and Alfred Braunthal, one of the younger Austro-Marxist economists) pointed out, the conditions of a dynamic equilibrium in the case of 'accelerated accumulation' with technological progress and rising organic compositions of capital in both departments could still be met by an appropriate variation of the respective rates of accumulation (Braunthal 1927). Sternberg did not like the argument, but he was unable to refute it (Sternberg 1929).

The last major effort to buttress Rosa Luxemburg's original argument in favour of an inevitable limit to accumulation and an eventual breakdown of capitalism was to be made by Henryk Grossmann just three years later (Grossmann 1929). His starting point was not Luxemburg's but rather Otto Bauer's scheme of expanded reproduction, the very model that had been constructed in order to refute Rosa Luxemburg in the first place. Now Grossmann used it without changes; he simply extended it from the original four-period sequence to a sequence of 36 periods. Even under

[29] Actually, the polemic between Sternberg and Grossmann raged on. When Grossmann's book on the *Law of Accumulation* was published in 1929, Sternberg replied with a book-length critique (Sternberg 1930).

the original assumptions made by Otto Bauer, the model – or numerical example – landed in a severe crisis, as the path of accumulation could not be sustained in the longer run. Both capitalist consumption and accumulation would slow down and peter out due to an increasing lack of surplus value. A continuous rise of the rate of accumulation is only possible within certain time limits. In view of this central argument of the book, it is rather surprising that its author hardly mentions – and never incorporates – any rise of the rate of exploitation in his model.

Grossmann's book immediately came under heavy attack. Braunthal, for example, dismissed it outright as humbug (Braunthal 1929). Sternberg took his revenge on Grossmann (Sternberg 1930), arguing against Grossmann's core idea of a necessary breakdown of capitalism and demonstrating various deficiencies in Grossmann's argument. Helene Bauer joined the fray again, accusing Grossmann of merely playing with numbers (and words) (Bauer 1929). The most substantial criticism at the time came from Otto Benedikt, who published a long article in the leading theoretical journal of the Communist International, *Unter dem Banner des Marxismus*. In his view, Grossmann had fallen far behind Otto Bauer, as he had abandoned the distinction between two departments and ignored the effects of technical progress which would affect not only the organic composition of capital, but also labour productivity, real wages and the rate of exploitation. In order to prove a 'law' of a tendency towards breakdown, Benedikt argues, one has to develop a rigorous model of capitalist accumulation in algebraic terms, a model in which all the strategic variables determining the structure of the total social product and the total social capital are consequently treated as interdependent variables. That is precisely what he tried to do in his article, presenting all the relevant magnitudes: constant capital, variable capital, surplus value, rate of exploitation, organic composition of capital, rate of saving and the rate of accumulation varying over time in both departments (Benedikt 1929). Despite the clumsy notation, it represents a major step beyond the model sketched by Otto Bauer in 1913.[30]

[30] Another scathing critique of Grossmann's book came from Anton Pannekoek, who started with a brief review of the Luxemburg debate to date, defending both Luxemburg and Bauer against Grossmann (Pannekoek 1934).

There exists only one major effort to take stock of the debate as it had unfolded to this point, the book *Kampf um Marx* ('Struggle for Marx') by Werner Alexander (1932). This is a remarkable contribution, because its author saw himself not as a Marxist, but rather as an observer of quarrels *within* Marxist circles. At various points he tried to rescue Rosa Luxemburg's book because of its theoretical merits. First of all, he emphasised the importance of her attempt to further elaborate Marx's theory of accumulation (Alexander 1932, p. 85f). He was correct in this regard. Rosa Luxemburg had indeed been the first to take the step towards an analysis of 'accelerated' accumulation and thereby open up the vista on capitalist macrodynamics. Her critics had followed her onto this new and relatively uncharted terrain. It was Alfred Braunthal who, in a long article in the Austrian theoretical journal *Der Kampf*, reaffirmed the urgent necessity of further developing the theory of capitalist dynamics pioneered by Marx (Braunthal 1933). By that time, the world economic crisis which was to become known as the Great Depression had already been raging for nearly four years, and all Marxists worth mentioning were desperately trying to understand what was happening.

Round Five: Otto Bauer's Reformulation of Marxist Macroeconomics in the 1930s

Otto Bauer never made any formal response to Luxemburg's *Anti-Critique*. However, he continued his work on the theoretical core of the debate – the model of accumulation and growth which would, in accordance with Marx's intentions, provide a systematic clue for the explanation of all major and recurrent crises in capitalism. From his various manuscripts, only two pieces have survived. One short text, comprising only a few pages, has been published in exile as an appendix to Bauer's book on the present and future of world socialism, published under the title *Zwischen zwei Weltkriegen* ('Between Two World Wars') in 1936.[31] The much longer manuscript presenting a full-scale analysis of the Great

[31] Bauer (1936, 1976, pp. 327–31). In this appendix, Bauer did briefly mention, but not explain some of the conceptual innovations that he had made in his much larger manuscript, written in 1934–5.

Crisis of the 1930s and a diligent presentation of all the salient elements of Marx's theory of crisis, including some innovations made by Bauer himself, remains unpublished.[32]

The first short text is a fragment. It shows that Bauer had begun developing a dynamic growth model, perhaps following the example given by Otto Benedikt a few years prior. Bauer's intention was to specify in algebraic form the very conditions not of a breakdown, but of a state of overproduction and over-accumulation resulting from capitalist accelerated accumulation – expansion of the scale and scope of production plus technological innovation – in order to determine the conditions of a state of crisis that must regularly occur and reoccur in the course of capitalist development. In this model, Bauer deploys many variables, the growth rates of which vary temporally – more often than not at an accelerated pace. It is this simple, abridged version, presented without further differentiation between departments of social production and without any analysis of monetary circulation, changing amounts of money and credit (which can be found in the much larger, unpublished manuscript) which had, curiously enough, some impact upon the formation of a dynamic macroeconomic theory of growth. Not directly, but via the efforts of a young American economist by the name of Paul Malor Sweezy.

In the early 1940s, Paul Sweezy used Bauer's 1936 scheme, the only one known to him, as a starting point for his analysis of growth and crisis Sweezy (1942). Sweezy built his model referring to most of his forerunners, including Bukharin and Bauer.[33] In particular, Sweezy claimed to have improved Bauer's model of 1936 and hoped to have strengthened the case of the Marxist theory of accumulation leading to crisis with this amended version. Bauer's model had passed unnoticed, as by the second half of the 1930s his book was not being read by academic economists and Marxists were no longer interested in such matters. Sweezy's slightly amended version, however, was seriously discussed by economists, such as Evsey Domar in 1948 (Domar [1948] (1957)). During this brief exchange, mainstream (neoclassical) economists discovered, much to

[32] It has now been published last year in the original German version (Bauer 2015).

[33] Sweezy had spent a year studying at the London School of Economics. It is here that he made acquaintance with Bauer's work, probably thanks to Harold Laski, himself an admirer of the Austro-Marxists' work.

their surprise, the importance of Marx (and the Marxian school) as pioneers of a theory of accumulation and growth. Responding to his critics in 1949, Sweezy admitted that his aggregate dynamic model was a failure, because he – following Otto Bauer's sketch from 1936 – had given up Marx's original bisectoral scheme (Sweezy 1953). That is, however, not what Otto Bauer had done in his manuscript of 1935, unpublished and thus unknown to Paul Sweezy.[34]

Sweezy's finest critic, Nicholas Georgescu-Roegen, made two concluding remarks in a paper published in 1960: first, in his view, the original Marxist scheme of expanded reproduction could not be cast into 'a mathematical correct model'. If one took into account all the elements of capitalist dynamics as considered by Marx (and Bauer and Sweezy), one ended up with no less than ten unknown functions (including their first derivatives, as already specified by Bauer and Sweezy). The second difficulty is related to the confusion between stocks and flows, variables and their increments in time pertinent to these early efforts to construct a dynamic model in the Marxist tradition. Moreover, the proof for the inevitability of crisis (and even more so with respect to an alleged breakdown) is unconvincing, as a capitalist economy can grow at a decreasing rate for a very long time, perhaps even infinitely. The strongest critical counterargument by Georgescu-Roegen, however, is geared to the principal aim of all such efforts: to predict the future of capitalism. In his view, this is simply too complicated for mathematics. When it comes to the problem of capitalism's change, its evolution or mutation into another form in historical time, 'mathematics proves to be too rigid and hence too simple a tool for handling it' (Georgescu-Roegen 1960, p. 415). Rosa Luxemburg tried to explain a historical phenomenon, imperialism in its heyday, and failed to bridge the gap between Marx's general analysis of capitalism and historical changes in the real world of markets, states and capitalisms. Neither her critics nor her followers were to fare much better. The biggest problem for them

[34]There is a whole array of unpublished theoretical and empirical works on the crisis by Marxist economists that were stimulated by the Great Crisis of the 1930s, among them the doctoral dissertation by Richard Löwenthal of 1935, still unpublished, and a large study on the crisis by Louis B. Boudin, written in 1937, and still unpublished as well. For details see my introduction to Bauer (2015).

was disentangling the maze of theoretical problems that had become mixed up since the times of Tugan-Baranowsky and Kautsky: the problems of an analysis of capital accumulation, the problems of an explanation of the general conditions of cyclical crises and the problems of an analysis of the long-term, secular development of capitalism as a world system – towards a state of enduring stagnation. Marx's great project still remains unfinished today, although thanks to the debate triggered by Rosa Luxemburg's ill-fated revision of Marx we have a better understanding of some of the peculiar features of capitalist dynamics.

An Unexpected Result: Rosa Luxemburg and the (Post-)Keynesians

The first English translation of Rosa Luxemburg's *The Accumulation of Capital* was published after World War II, in 1951, with an introduction written by Joan Robinson, by that time already a well-known figure of 'Left' Keynesianism (Robinson 2003 (1951)). A few years later, Joan Robinson was to publish her own magnum opus with the same title as Rosa Luxemburg, *The Accumulation of Capital* (Robinson 1958). In this later book, Robinson tried to do for the Keynesians what Rosa Luxemburg had tried to do for the Marxists in 1913: to combine an analysis of effective demand with an analysis of the overall development of capitalism as a whole in the long run. Robinson viewed Luxemburg's effort to establish a better version of Marx's unfinished modelling of the accumulation process as a pioneer's work. Her praise notwithstanding, she raised the same objections that had already been raised by Rosa Luxemburg's various Marxist critics, particularly Otto Bauer. Unfortunately, she was unaware of the Luxemburg debate as it had unfolded from 1913 onwards. Had she known this body of Marxist scholarship, she would have been aware of the reasonably well-advanced level of dynamic analysis that had already been attained by Marxist economists, more or less at the same time as Keynes was struggling with the same problems.[35]

[35] Otto Bauer was, of course, well aware of Keynes' work and made several references to it in his book on the great crisis.

Joan Robinson's perception, and perhaps even her awareness of Luxemburg's book, was due to the influence of Michał Kalecki, whom she had first met in 1936.[36] Kalecki, though lacking formal training as an economist, had long been fascinated by the problem of the business cycle – or, as Marxists would have it, the theory of crisis. As a young socialist, he had become acquainted with the Marxist debates on imperialism and world crisis, and was familiar with Luxemburg's work. Trying to understand the causes of the great world economic and financial crisis as it had unfolded after 1929, Kalecki started to work on a general theory of the capitalist business cycle since the early 1930s (Kalecki (1939); Toporowski 2013). Searching for the key determinants of this cyclical movement he ran into earlier efforts to deal with the 'laws of motion' of the capital accumulation process, such as those advanced by both Tugan-Baranowsky and Rosa Luxemburg. While accepting her basic idea about the importance of aggregate demand and its increase for a sustainable rate of capital accumulation, he rejected her solution to the problem: that capitalist economies could only overcome insufficient aggregate demand by forcing the creation of new markets and new consumer demand in non-capitalist regions of the world. Accordingly, he did not share her perspective that the exhaustion of such newly created markets in non-capitalist territories would usher in the final critical phase of capitalist development on a world scale. Governments in capitalist countries had more choices than that, and some of them were clearly linked to imperialist policies – such as the growth of the arms sector and increased public spending to buy arms and build armies and navies. Rosa Luxemburg herself had devoted a whole chapter of her book to the economic effects of 'militarism', that is increased military spending, although she did not attempt to spell out the consequences of this new development for the process of capital accumulation at large. In the context of her analysis, this failure to analyse public sector demand and increased military expenditure by the government in particular is explicable. Unlike at least some of her critics, Luxemburg did not envisage the possibilities of credit and debt finance. Kalecki, well versed in monetary analysis, could easily imagine external export markets and debt-financed domestic government spending as alternatives and functional equivalents (Kalecki 1971).

[36] For the relationship between Robinson and Kalecki see Asimakopoulos (1989).

The link between Rosa Luxemburg and Michał Kalecki has rarely been discussed, tending to be avoided by Marxists. The exception that confirms the rule was provided by the work of the late Tadeusz Kowalik who devoted a whole book to the topic (see Toporowski's chapter in this volume). It is a great book, explaining in much detail how Rosa Luxemburg, had she allowed herself to be enlightened by her critics, and how some later Marxists, allowing themselves to be enlightened by the Luxemburg debate, might have rethought and reformulated the basic ideas of *Accumulation of Capital* and saved them from oblivion (Kowalik 2014).

The Legacy of Rosa Luxemburg

Except for the polemics it provoked, Rosa Luxemburg's great book was soon forgotten. When confronted with serious criticism, she refused to engage in a strictly theoretical debate geared at solving the analytical problems that Marx had left unsolved. Nonetheless, and despite the repetition of older arguments, some analytical progress was made, although it went largely unrecognised by the majority of Marxists of the time (Turban 1980). Thus, she deserves credit for opening up new vistas of Marx's theory of accumulation and crisis by attacking it boldly and exposing some of its defects. The fruits, however, were only reaped after a long and winding detour into a series of debates which were more often than not determined by petty political preoccupations. The Luxemburg debate suffered – as do so many debates around the unsettled questions of Marx's critique of political economy – from the vice of over-politicisation.

Her theory of imperialism, ill-founded in economic analysis and stricken by inconsistencies as it was, had the strongest impact. Some of this was due to the popularity of any theory that would allow to restore and maintain the old 'Marxist' idea of a causal link or 'trigger effect' between great economic crises and political revolutions. When the Third International established the existence of a 'general crisis' of capitalism as its official doctrine in the late 1920s, 'Luxemburgism' was created as a new deviation, associated with all sorts of dangerous thoughts. Even the leading economist of the Comintern, Eugen Varga, was repeatedly accused of 'Luxemburgist' thinking by his adversaries. In the guise of 'Luxemburgism', Rosa Luxemburg's economic and political thought became completely distorted, and the official reading of her work was dominated by enumerations of her alleged 'mistakes'.

Good Leninists, however, believing in the value of Lenin's pamphlet on imperialism as part of the official gospel, could not dismiss her completely. After all, Rosa Luxemburg had tried to show that imperialism was inherent in the very fabric of capitalism and could not be regarded as a variety of policies which the great powers might or might not pursue. Imperialism, invading and pervading non-capitalist territories, was fundamental, a 'law'-like feature of capitalist development. Even if Marxists disagreed on the details, Luxemburg's approach had an undisputable merit; mainly in political terms, as it drew attention to the colonial world outside of the heartlands of a few advanced capitalist countries. If these regions of the world were vital for the viability of capitalism as a world system, as Luxemburg had maintained, then it was worth the while of the socialist and communist movements in those heartlands to engage in and support struggles there – even if Luxemburg was wrong in theoretical terms.

On the other hand, however, Luxemburg's analysis made little contribution to the understanding of the transformations of the capitalist world economy triggered and/or accelerated by World War I and the Great Crisis of the 1930s (Krätke 2010). Most Marxists, including her most capable critics, were caught in the spatial metaphor of the 'non-capitalist' areas or regions. They did not take into account the possibilities of further capitalist expansion that lay in the transformation of those areas of everyday life and the economy at large in the capitalist countries that were not yet fully subdued by and integrated into the logic of capitalist production, exchange, consumption and accumulation. Eduard Bernstein had told them so as early as 1899, insisting upon the vast possibilities of an intensive capitalist development of all parts of the capitalist world economy instead of a spatial expansion by means of colonialism (Bernstein 1899, p. 168f). But who would listen to Eduard Bernstein, anyway?

Bibliography

Alexander, W. (1932). *Kampf um Marx. Entwicklung und Kritik der Akkumulationstheorie*. Potsdam: Alfred Protte Verlag.

Asimakopoulos, A. (1988–9). Kalecki and Robinson: An "outsider's" influence. *Journal of Post-Keynesian Economics, 11*(2), 261–278..

Bauer, O. (1904). Marx' Theorie der Wirtschaftskrisen. *Die Neue Zeit, XXIII*(1), 133–138, 164–175.

Bauer, O. (1906). Mathematische Formeln gegen Tugan-Baranowsky. *Die Neue Zeit, XXV*(1), 822–823.

Bauer, O. (1911). Marx-Literatur. *Der Kampf, IV*, 237–238.

Bauer, H. (1927, January). Der Imperialismus, *Der Kampf*, 7–13.

Bauer, H. (1929, June). Ein neuer Zusammenbruchstheoretikers, *Der Kampf*, 270–280.

Bauer, O. [1907] (1975). Die Nationalitätenfrage und die Sozialdemokratie. In *Otto Bauer Werkausgabe, Volume 1*. Vienna: Europaverlag.

Bauer, O. [1936] (1976). Zwischen zwei Weltkriegen?. In *Otto Bauer Werkausgabe, Volume 4*. Vienna: Europaverlag.

Bauer, P. [1913] (1979). Die Akkumulation des Kapitals. In *Otto Bauer Werkausgabe, Volume 7*. Vienna: Europaverlag.

Bauer, O. (2015). In M. Krätke (Ed.), *Die größte Krise der kapitalistischen Weltwirtschaft*. Hamburg: VSA.

Benedikt, O. (1929). Die Akkumulation des Kapitals bei wachsender organischer Zusammensetzung des Kapitals. *Unter dem Banner des Marxismus, 6*, 869–911.

Bernstein, E. [1899] (1993). *The preconditions of socialism*. Cambridge: Cambridge University Press.

Boudin, L. (1907a). *The theoretical system of Karl Marx in the light of recent criticism*. Chicago: Charles H. Kerr & Co..

Boudin, L. (1907b). Mathematische Formeln gegen Karl Marx. *Die Neue Zeit, XXV*(1), 524–535, 557–567, 603–610.

Braunthal, A. (1927). *Die Entwicklungstendenzen der kapitalistischen Wirtschaft*. Berlin: E. Laubsche Verlagsbuchhandlung.

Braunthal, A. (1929). Der Zusammenbruch der Zusammenbruchstheorie. *Die Gesellschaft, 5*, 289–304.

Braunthal, A. (1933). Marx, der Entdecker der ökonomischen Dynamik. *Der Kampf, 25*, 122–130.

Bukharin, N. [1926] (1997). *Imperialism and the accumulation of capital*. London: Allen Lane and Penguin.

Cunow, H. (1899). Zur Zusammenbruchstheorie. *Die Neue Zeit, XVII*(1), 356–364, 396–403, 426–430.

Danielson, N. (1893). *Our post-reform economy*. St Petersburg: A. Benke.

Day, R., & Gaido, D. (Eds.) (2011). *Witnesses to permanent revolution. The documentary record*. Chicago: Haymarket Books.

Day, R., & Gaido, D. (Eds.) (2012). *Discovering imperialism: Social democracy to World War I*. Chicago: Haymarket Books.

Domar, E. [1948] (1957). The problem of capital accumulation. In *Essays in the theory of economic growth* (pp. 109–128). New York: Oxford University Press.

Eckstein, G. (1913). Rosa Luxemburg, Die Akkumulation des Kapitals. Eine Besprechung. *Vorwärts, 40*(16).

Georgescu-Roegen, N. [1960] (1967). Mathematical proofs of the breakdown of capitalism. In *Analytical economics*. Cambridge: Harvard University Press.

Grossmann, H. (1929). *Das Akkumulations- und Zusammenbruchsgesetz des kapitalistischen Systems*. Leipzig: C.L. Hirschfeld.

Hilferding, R. [1910] (1981). *Finance capital*. London: Routledge & Kegan.

Howard, M. C., & King, J. E. (1989). *A history of Marxian economics. Volume I, 1883–1929*. Basingstoke/London: Macmillan.

Kalecki, M. (1939). *Essays in the theory of economic fluctuations*. London: George Allen and Unwin.

Kalecki, M. (1971). The problem of effective demand with Tugan-Baranowsky and Rosa Luxemburg. In *Selected essays on the dynamics of the capitalist economy* (pp. 146–155). Cambridge: Cambridge University Press.

Kautsky, K. (1902). Krisentheorien. *Die Neue Zeit, XX*(2), 37–47, 76–81, 110–118, 133–143.

King, J. E. (1986). Otto Bauer's accumulation of capital (1913). *History of Political Economy, 18*(1), 87–110.

Kowalik, T. (2014). *Rosa Luxemburg: Theory of accumulation and imperialism*. Basingstoke: Palgrave.

Krätke, M. (2005). Marx' Tableaux économiques und Engels' Redaktion, presentation at the International Symposium on Capital, Volume II, Kyoto University.

Krätke, M. (2008). The "Grundrisse" as a research manuscript. RRIPE Research Papers. Amsterdam: University of Amsterdam.

Krätke, M. (2010). Rosa Luxemburg und die Analyse des gegenwärtigen Kapitalismus. In I. Narihiko (Ed.), *Rosa Luxemburg. Ökonomische und historisch-politische Aspekte ihres Werkes* (pp. 130–174). Berlin: Dietz Verlag.

Krätke, M. R. (2015). *Towards a global history of Marxist crisis theories, lecture cycle*. Sendai: Tohoku University.

Laschitza, A. (2000). *Rosa Luxemburg. Im Lebensrausch, trotz alledem. Eine Biographie*. Berlin: Aufbau Taschenbuch Verlag.

Lenin, V.I. (1985). Pometki na Kapitale in *Leninskij Sbornik*, T. XL (Moscow), pp. 105–173.

Luxemburg, R. [1903] (1970). Karl Marx. In *Gesammelte Werke, Volume 1–2*. Berlin: Dietz Verlag.

Luxemburg, R. [1913a] (2003). *The accumulation of capital*. London/New York: Routledge.

Luxemburg, R. [1913b] (2015). The accumulation of capital. A contribution to economic theory of imperialism. In *The complete works of Rosa Luxemburg. Volume II: Economic writings 2* (pp. 7–344). London: Verso.

Luxemburg, R. [1915] (2015). The accumulation of capital, or, what the epigones have made out of Marx's theory – An anti-critique. In *The complete works of Rosa Luxemburg. Volume II: Economic writings 2* (pp. 345–450). London: Verso.

Luxemburg, Rosa [1925] (2013). Introduction to political economy. In *The complete works of Rosa Luxemburg. Volume I: Economic writings 1* (pp. 89–300). London: Verso.

Mandel, E. (1978). Introduction. In *K. Marx Capital, Volume II*. London: Penguin Books.

Marchlewski, J. (1913, January 24–25). Eine marxistische Untersuchung über den Imperialismus, *Münchener Post*.

Mehring, F. (1913, January 16–18). Rosa Luxemburg: Die Akkumulation des Kapitals. *Leipziger Volkszeitung*.

Mehring, F. [1918] (1974). *Karl Marx. Geschichte seines Lebens*. Berlin: Dietz Verlag.

Pannekoek, A. (1910). Herrn Tugan-Baranowskys Marx-Kritik. *Die Neue Zeit, XXVIII*(1), 772–783.

Pannekoek, A. (1913, January 24–25, 29–30). Rosa Luxemburg: Die Akkumulation des Kapitals. *Bremer Bürgerzeitung*.

Pannekoek, A. (1934). Die Zusammenbruchstheorie des Kapitalismus. *Rätekorrespondenz. Theoretisches und Diskussionsorgan für die Rätebewegung, 1*.

Robinson, J. (1958). *The accumulation of capital*. London: Macmillan and Co.

Robinson, J. [1951] (2003). Introduction. In R. Luxemburg (Ed.), *The accumulation of capital*. London/New York: Routledge.

Rosdolsky, R. [1969] (1992). *The making of Marx's capital*. London: Pluto.

Schippel, M. (1913). Das Grundgeheimnis des Imperialismus. *Sozialistische Monatshefte, 19*(3), 147–152.

Schmidt, C. (1901). Zur Theorie der Handelskrisen und der Überproduktion. *Sozialistische Monatshefte, 5*(2), 669–682.

Schmidt, C. (1915). Rosa Luxemburg: Die Akkumulation des Kapitals. *Archiv für Sozialwissenschaft und Socialpolitik, 39*, 256–261.

Sternberg, F. (1926). *Der Imperialismus*. Berlin: Malik Verlag.

Sternberg, F. (1929). *Der Imperialismus und seine Kritiker*. Berlin: Soziologische Verlagsanstalt.

Sternberg, F. (1930). *Eine Umwälzung der Wissenschaft? Kritik des Buches von Henryk Grossmann: Das Akkumulations- und Zusammenbruchsgesetz des kapitalistischen Systems*. Berlin: R.L. Prager.

Sweezy, P. (1942). *The theory of capitalist development*. New York: Oxford University Press.

Sweezy, P. (1953). Reply to my critics. In *The present as history* (pp. 352–362). New York: Monthly Review Press.

Toporowski, J. (2013). *Michał Kalecki: An intellectual biography, Volume 1*. London: Palgrave/Macmillan.

Tugan-Baranowsky, M. (1901). *Studien zur Theorie und Geschichte der Handelskrisen in England*. Jena: G. Fischer.

Tugan-Baranowsky, M. (1905). *Die theoretischen Grundlagen des Marxismus*. Leipzig: Duncker und Humblot.

Turban, M. (1980). *Marxsche Reproduktionsschemata und Wirtschaftstheorie*. Berlin: Duncker und Humblot.

Von Charasoff, G. (1910). *Das System des Marxismus*. Berlin: Bondy.

Wolff, S. (1915). Accumulatie en crisis. *De Nieuwe Tijd, 20*, 6–22, 353–372, 469–480.

6

Tadeusz Kowalik's Interpretation of Accumulation

Jan Toporowski

Introduction

In 1971, Tadeusz Kowalik's *Rosa Luksemburg Teoria Akumulacji i Imperializmu* was published in Poland by the small independent publisher Ossolineum. Reception of Kowalik's interpretation of Rosa Luxemburg was not confined to the Polish-speaking world, as Italian and Spanish translations of the book appeared later in the 1970s. Nevertheless, on the whole, the book did not reach a broader audience until many years later. The original edition was reprinted in Poland by the publishing house Książka i Prasa in 2012 and, two years later, an English translation (by Hanna Szymborska and the author of the present chapter) was published by Palgrave Macmillan.

J. Toporowski (✉)
Economics Department, School of Oriental and African Studies, University of London, London, UK

J. Dellheim, F.O. Wolf (eds.), *Rosa Luxemburg: A Permanent Challenge for Political Economy*, DOI 10.1057/978-1-137-60108-7_6

The book was and remains the most important monograph devoted to Rosa Luxemburg's *The Accumulation of Capital*. Tadeusz Kowalik reconstructs Luxemburg's attempt to correct Marx's analysis of capitalist reproduction, but in dealing with the criticisms her work provoked and the many weaknesses contained in her arguments also reveals the link in Luxemburg's analysis between Marx's schemes of capitalist reproduction (as outlined in Volume II of *Capital*) and mid-20th-century macroeconomics. His book therefore puts forward Rosa Luxemburg's major theoretical work as the foundation for a critique of 20th-century political economy.

As Kowalik shows, Luxemburg's attempt was not entirely theoretically consistent or successful. Nevertheless, it represented the first crack in the widespread underconsumptionist interpretation of Marx, the notion that capitalist depression and crisis arise because workers are not paid the full value of their labour. This interpretation, embodied most famously in Paul Sweezy's widely respected *The Theory of Capitalist Development* (1942), is revived every time capitalist countries fall into depression, such as during the crisis of the 1970s (Howard and King, 1992) or the more recent preoccupation with the 'wage share' prevalent among radical economists today (Onaran and Galanis 2012; see also the conclusion below). Although Luxemburg was widely regarded as an underconsumptionist (indeed, Sweezy memorably referred to her as 'the queen of underconsumptionists' (1942, p. 171)), Tadeusz Kowalik's book presents a much more complex picture based on the theory developed by his second mentor, Michał Kalecki, whose business cycle analysis ironed out the inconsistencies in Luxemburg's theory (see Toporowski 2013a).

Tadeusz Kowalik

To the extent that Tadeusz Kowalik (1926–2012) is known outside of Poland, it is as the last surviving co-author of Michał Kalecki, an advisor to *Solidarność* during its key role in bringing down the Polish Communist regime in the 1980s, and subsequently as a fierce critic of the capitalist system established in its wake. Kowalik was born on 19 November 1926 in the village of Kajetanówka, outside the city of Lublin in eastern Poland –

traditionally the poorer, more backward part of the country. In 1951, he completed his undergraduate studies in law at Warsaw University and went on to write a doctoral thesis on the work of the pioneering Polish Marxist sociologist and economist Ludwik Krzywicki (1859–1941) under the supervision of Poland's other great Marxist economist, Oskar Lange. On completion of his doctorate, Kowalik commenced work on his *habilitacja*, the post-doctoral thesis that Polish academics must complete before securing academic advancement. The subject of his thesis was the economic theories of Rosa Luxemburg. He had already taken over the political economy course at the Party school from Lange. Traces of those lectures (and also those of Lange) may be found in his later book on Luxemburg. His thesis was approved in 1963. Various articles from it were published, including one in the *Festschrift* for Kalecki (Kowalik 1964b).

Tadeusz Kowalik's book is both a guide to Rosa Luxemburg's great work, and also an explanation of its background in the debates concerning the future of Russian capitalism conducted by the Narodniks and the 'Legal Marxists', of whom Mikhail Tugan-Baranowski[1] was the most notable. In the course of writing the book, Tadeusz Kowalik incorporated key figures of mid-20th-century political economy into his analysis in a strikingly original way. Not only does he illuminate the structure of said political economy, but he also integrates it into central questions of Rosa Luxemburg's analysis of capitalist accumulation and their derivation from Marx's original work.

He proceeds from the Russian Narodniks' explanation as to why, in their view, the limited markets found in Russia at the end of the 19th century made further capitalist development impossible. This led to Tugan-Baranowski's response, his famous rejection of the underconsumptionist argument on the grounds that capitalism can continue producing machines for the sake of production irrespective of the state of consumer demand. But there was much more to Tugan-Baranowski's analysis than just his observation that capitalism can stabilise itself by producing more means of production. Almost by stealth, Tugan-Baranowski became a

[1] Translator's note: Luxemburg (and others) spells the name Tugan-Baranovsky, not Baranowski, as the present author does.

central and deeply ambiguous figure in 20th-century political economy. This was not because of his solution to an abstract problem of capitalist accumulation, but rather due to his study of English banking crises (Tugan-Baranowski 1901). Despite never appearing in English, it became a key text on the business cycle and was an important influence on British exponents of monetary business cycle theory, among them John Maynard Keynes and Denis Robertson.[2]

Kowalik located the roots of 20th-century political economy in the discussions of Marx's schemes of capitalist reproduction contained in Volumes II and III of *Capital.* Marx's critique of Say's Law revealed that capitalist reproduction or growth cannot take place in a stable or crisis-free manner. The question of external markets thus opens the door for Keynesian political economy, constructed around demand deficiency and the notion of the state as an external market.

Marx's Unfinished Work

Tadeusz Kowalik proceeded from the same discovery that surprised Rosa Luxemburg in Marx's drafts for the second and third volumes of *Capital*, edited and published by Engels. As is well known, Marx's political economy is based on a theory of value that shows how value is created. Volume II of *Capital* was supposed to show how value is realised, hence the subtitle 'The Process of the Circulation of Capital'. This 'process' is what we now call the circular flow of income, which represents the income flows that Marx described in the reproduction schemes laid out in this volume (Marx 1885). However, he was not satisfied with the draft he had written and intended to revise it. Specifically, Marx did not complete his exposition of expanded reproduction – although the volume does include a simple reproduction scheme, in the absence of any increase in production or of the stock of capital (Marx 1885, Chapters XX and XXI). The question of the conditions for the realisation of surplus value would later be

[2] '… I find myself in strong sympathy with the school of writers – Tugan Baranovski, Hull, Spiethoff and Schumpeter – of which Tugan-Baranovski was the first and the most original …' (Keynes, 1971, pp. 89–90).

taken up by Rosa Luxemburg in her *Accumulation of Capital*. In his book on Luxemburg's theory, Tadeusz Kowalik shows that Kalecki's theory of the business cycle is in effect the solution to the value realisation problem that had eluded both Marx and Luxemburg (see Appendix of Kowalik 2014).

A radical change had occurred in the functioning of the capitalist economy since the publication of *Capital*: namely, the emergence and proliferation of markets for long-term debt and shares in capitalist enterprises established by legislation from the 1860s onwards, which enabled the establishment of joint stock companies in the advanced capitalist countries. This change transformed capitalism from its 'classic' mid-19th-century form, in which capitalist enterprises were owned and controlled by individual capitalists and their more or less active partners, into its modern, 20th-century form dominated by large joint stock companies (Kindleberger, 1993, Chap. 11). Engels tried to incorporate this shift into Marx's *Capital* with a short chapter on the stock market that he added to Volume III of *Capital* (Engels 1894, pp. 1027–47), but he restricted himself to a superficial condemnation of financial speculation.

This change in the capitalist economy had two significant consequences for the stability of the system. Firstly, large capitalist enterprises with access to capital (long-term debt and equity) markets were able to 'fund' their long-term industrial assets through the issuing of bonds or equity, which reduced their vulnerability to credit shortages. The second major change affecting the expansion of long-term finance was the rise of monopoly capital. Companies could now expand far more expeditiously by buying their competitors' long-term debts or shares, rather than entering into the precarious business of outcompeting them. The trusts and monopolies that dominated the end of the 19th century were the creation of capital markets, rather than the result of either 'natural' monopolies or increasing returns to scale. For Rudolf Hilferding, this link with capital markets forms the essence of monopoly capital. Hence his term for it: 'finance capital'. In *Finance Capital*, Hilferding first advanced an explanation of the rise of capitalist instability, caused by the interplay between monopolistic and competitive segments of the capitalist economy (Hilferding 1981, Chapter 20). This theme was later studied systematically by Michał Kalecki, who believed he was addressing Rosa

Luxemburg's and Mikhail Tugan-Baranovski's respective explanations of the conditions under which value is realised in the capitalist economy, but who was really engaging in a critique of Hilferding's conclusion that cartelisation stabilises capitalism (Kalecki 1990, 1991).

Luxemburg did not mention Hilferding in her original book, but he features prominently in her response to critics in *Anti-Critique*, where she denounces him vigorously for ignoring the possibility of general overproduction. In Luxemburg's view, Hilferding's decision to ignore this possibility brought him into agreement with that 'wretched fellow' Jean-Baptiste Say, an early (and perhaps the most notorious) proponent of the theory that overproduction is impossible as long as market prices are flexible (Luxemburg (1915/2015), p. 375). Kowalik nevertheless noted that the export of capital is a common component of both of their theories of imperialism (Kowalik 2014, pp. 156–7). In the second half of the 20th century, analysis of monopoly capital came to be associated with Paul Sweezy (see, in particular, Magdoff and Sweezy, 1987).

At the heart of these attempts to complete Marx's work is the analysis of how value is realised, and how the failure to realise value is central to capitalism's periodic inability to achieve the economic dynamism that distinguishes capitalism from previous modes of production, and is supposedly capitalism's greatest contribution to civilisation. For most Marxists, the failure to realise value is inherent in the relationship between capitalists and workers and the process of capitalist production itself, in which workers produce more value than for which they are paid. This leads to an 'underconsumptionist' view of insufficient demand in the economy: since workers spend their incomes but are paid less than the full value of their labour, demand remains insufficient to ensure full employment and economic growth. A Marxist view of this theory was advanced by Eugen Varga (1935) and the aforementioned Paul Sweezy (1942) in the middle of the 20th century. Maurice Dobb (1937) was unusual among Marxists in rejecting underconsumptionism and its implied solution to deficient demand: higher wages (pp. 111–16).

It is this 'mainstream' Marxist view that Kalecki challenges with his theory of the business cycle, in which he demonstrates, on the basis of Marx's reproduction schemes, that the average rate of profit in a capitalist economy (and hence output and employment) is determined by the level of investment rather than by the level of consumption (Kalecki 1939, pp. 45–6). The link between this 'Keynesian' view and Marx's reproduction schemes lay in the work of Rosa Luxemburg. Kalecki concludes that:

> In her *Akkumulation des Kapitals* she stressed the point that, if capitalists are saving, their profits can be 'realized' only if a corresponding amount is spent by them on investment. She, however, considered impossible the persistence of net investment (at least in the long run) in a closed capitalist economy; thus, according to her, it is only the existence of exports to the non-capitalist countries which allows for the expansion of a capitalist system. The theory cannot be accepted as a whole, but the necessity of covering the 'gap of saving' by home investment or exports was outlined by her perhaps more clearly than anywhere else before the publication of Mr. Keynes's *General Theory*. (Kalecki 1939, pp. 45–6)

Kowalik takes on this interpretation of Luxemburg's analysis. He therefore advances more than just an explanation of Luxemburg's critique of contemporary Marxists who argued that Marx's work in Volume I of *Capital*, supplemented by the remaining volumes of *Capital* and *Theories of Surplus Value*, was complete – thus rendering irrelevant the inconsistencies in Volumes II and III that Marx intended to revise. Kowalik also shows that Luxemburg was not an underconsumptionist; rather, implicit in her analysis is the possibility that realisation problems are caused by insufficient investment or the insufficient accumulation of capital. This accumulation of capital is then the solution that Kalecki (and, albeit unwittingly, Keynes) provided to Marx's uncompleted analysis of how value is realised.

Inspired by his discussions with Kowalik, Kalecki further developed this point in his 1967 paper on Rosa Luxemburg and Tugan-Baranowski (Kalecki 1980). Tadeusz Kowalik worked with Kalecki on his last paper on the 'Crucial Reform' of capitalism, placing the 'Keynesian Revolution' in the context of debates around capitalist reproduction (Kowalik and Kalecki 1980). Kowalik returned to Kalecki's pioneering work in 20th-century macroeconomics and the foundations of that work in an analysis of capitalist production as a whole throughout his career, as found in the controversies surrounding Rosa Luxemburg's *Accumulation of Capital*. Most importantly, it is through Kalecki's business cycle theory that Keynesian ideas are linked to late-19th-century debates on capitalist reproduction. This is obvious in the biographical essay on Kalecki that Kowalik wrote soon after receiving his *habilitacja* (1964a), and continues into his last essays on Rosa Luxemburg (2009).[3] Nevertheless, Tadeusz Kowalik's reconstruction of capitalist political economy around the Marxian schemes of reproduction led him, in the second part of his book on Luxemburg, to reject the idea that Kalecki was a 'precursor' of Keynes. Rather, Keynes saw in an imperfect way what Kalecki had realised much more clearly on the basis of Marxist discussions around the work of Rosa Luxemburg.

Conclusion: Accumulation and the Critique of Political Economy Today

Rosa Luxemburg: Theory of Accumulation and Imperialism cannot be regarded as Tadeusz Kowalik's final word on the subject of Rosa Luxemburg and the controversies surrounding her work. In the 1990s he had planned a new introduction to a new Polish edition of this book, but no trace of that introduction has been found and the book was not republished until after his death in 2012.

In at least one respect, Tadeusz Kowalik may have intended to revise his book. In 1966, Paul Baran and Paul Sweezy had published *Monopoly Capital: An Essay on the Economic and Social Order*. This work marked a shift away from the underconsumptionism of Sweezy's 1942 book, recognising the key role played by business investment and gov-

[3] Some scope of Michał Kalecki's influence on Tadeusz Kowalik's thinking on Rosa Luxemburg is provided by the paper Kowalik contributed to the Kalecki *Festschrift*, entitled 'R. Luxemburg's Theory of Accumulation and Imperialism (An Attempted Interpretation)'. Kowalik refers to this paper in this book as containing the essential conclusions of his *habilitacja* thesis (see note 17 at the end of the Introduction). But in the earlier paper, he merely states that Kalecki resolved problems in Rosa Luxemburg's analysis, while the paper itself makes much more of Oskar Lange's criticisms of Luxemburg's theory. By the time that Kowalik's book was published in 1971, Kalecki received a much more central role as the link between the Marxian political economy of Luxemburg, Tugan-Baranowski, Hilferding, and others and mid-20th-century Keynesian political economy, while Lange is reduced to expressing his view that realisation problems are purely monetary phenomena (see note 15 at the end of Chapter 4). A full list of Tadeusz Kowalik's publications is given at the end of Bellofiore et al. 2014.

ernment expenditure in the realisation of profit along similar lines to those originally put forward by Kalecki (Baran and Sweezy, 1966; see also Toporowski, 2013b). A Polish translation appeared soon afterwards and would have been available to Tadeusz Kowalik well before his book was published in 1971. However, Kowalik did not note this change in Sweezy's view in the version that came out in 1971, nor in the version that was being prepared for publication in Poland at the time of his death. This change is highlighted here in fairness to Sweezy.

During the writing of his book Tadeusz Kowalik was unaware that important financial and monetary aspects of the analyses of Tugan-Baranowski and Rosa Luxemburg also anticipated the work of Hyman Minsky. As Kowalik shows, Tugan-Baranowski advances pro-cyclical shifts in bank liquidity as a cause of financial crisis and instability. In the case of Rosa Luxemburg, her analysis of the role of international banks in creating markets for the export of capital leading to debt crises in what we would now call emerging market countries foreshadowed the international debt crises of the 1980s onwards (see Toporowski 2009). Minsky himself, when trying to understand value relations in a capitalist economy in *Stabilizing an Unstable Economy* (1986), lays out a two-sector model of capitalist production that is, at least in its essentials, the same as the system of capitalist reproduction put forward in Volume II of *Capital*. That same system was the analytical foundation of the contribution by both Tugan-Baranowski and Rosa Luxemburg.

Minsky remained a relatively isolated figure during his lifetime, distanced from both Marxists and Keynesians alike. With the distinguished exception of Paul Sweezy and his followers, Marxist political economy in the second half of the 20th century rejected Keynesianism, citing its lack of a theory of production and value. This critique thus essentialises the theory of value as *the* distinctive feature of Marxian political economy. An increasingly narrow focus on the law of value as the analytical core of Marxism has largely excluded considerations of the conditions for the realisation of value from Marxian political economy. While analyses from the 'regulationist' and 'social structure of accumulation' schools of Marxist theory have incorporated the state as the organ determining the conditions for the realisation of value, Marxists in general have not followed up on the work of Rosa Luxemburg and Rudolf Hilferding to analyse the conditions for the realisation of value that emerge directly from capitalist relations of production – that is, the accumulation of capital as such and the financing thereof. Instead, a retrogression to a political economy of capitalism that would have been familiar to Ricardian socialists such as Charles Hall and John Bray, who argued that value can only be realised through consumption, has become increasingly common. Key factors in the 2007 crisis are interpreted not so much as problems of production (which were supposedly eliminated by the weakening of organised labour from the 1980s onwards), but as a combination of neoliberalism, deregulation and speculation. In the absence of any broader analysis of the conditions for the realisation of value, most Marxists have joined the post-Keynesian wage-led growth theorists in asserting the underconsumptionist conclusion that if capitalism does indeed suffer from a problem of value realisation, then it arises because workers are not paid the full value of their labour.

Bibliography

Baran, P., & Sweezy, P. (1966). *Monopoly capital: An essay on the economic and social order*. New York: Monthly Review Press.

Bellofiore, R., Karwowski, E., & Toporowski, J. (Eds.) (2014). *The legacy of Rosa Luxemburg, Oskar Lange and Michał Kalecki. Volume 1 of essays in honour of Tadeusz Kowalik*. Basingstoke: Palgrave.

Dobb, M. (1937). *Political economy and capitalism. Some essays in economic tradition*. London: George Routledge and Sons.

Dymski, G. (2014). "Crucial reform" in post-war socialism and capitalism. In R. Bellofiore, E. Karwowski, & J. Toporowski (Eds.), *Economic crisis and political economy. Volume 2 of essays in honour of Tadeusz Kowalik* (pp. 42–61). Basingstoke: Palgrave.

Engels, F. [1894] (1991). Supplement and Addendum to Volume 3 of Capital. In: Marx, Capital, III., London 1981: Penguin, pp. 1027–1047.

Hilferding, R. (1981). *Finance capital: A study of the latest phase of capitalist development*. London: Routledge and Kegan Paul.

Howard, M. C., & King, J. E. (1992). *A history of Marxian economics. Volume I: 1929–1990*. Houndmills/Basingstoke/Hampshire/London: Macmillan.

Kalecki, M. (1939). *Essays in the theory of economic fluctuations*. London: George Allen and Unwin.

Kalecki, M. (1980). Zagadnienie realizacji u Tugana-Baranowskiego i Róży Luksemburg. In M. Kalecki (Ed.), *Dzieła tom 2: Kapitalizm Dynamika Gospodarcza*. Warsaw: Państwowe Wydawnictwo Ekonomiczne.

Kalecki, M. (1990). The influence of cartelization on the business cycle. In J. Osiatyński (Ed.), *Michał Kalecki collected works, Volume I: Capitalism: Business cycles and full employment*. Oxford: The Clarendon Press.

Kalecki, M. (1991). The problem of effective demand with Tugan-Baranovsky and Rosa Luxemburg. In J. Osiatyński (Ed.), *Michał Kalecki collected works, Volume II: Capitalism: economic dynamics*. Oxford: The Clarendon Press.

Keynes, J.M., (1971). A Treatise on Money Volume 2 The Applied Theory of Money Basingstoke: Macmillan for the Royal Economic Society.

King, J. (2014). Whatever happened to the "Crucial reform"? In E. Karwowski, R. Bellofiore & J. Toporowski (Eds.), *Economic crisis and political economy, Volume 2 of essays in honour of Tadeusz Kowalik* (pp. 29–41). Basingstoke: Palgrave.

Kindleberger, C. P. (1993). *A financial history of Western Europe*. New York: Oxford University Press.

Kowalik, T. (1964a). Biography of Michał Kalecki. In *Problems of economic dynamics and planning. Essays in honour of Michał Kalecki*. Warsaw: Państwowe Wydawnictwo Naukowe.

Kowalik, T. (1964b). R. Luxemburg's theory of accumulation and imperialism. In *Problems of economic dynamics and planning. Essays in honour of Michał Kalecki*. Warsaw: PWN-Polish Scientific Publishers.

Kowalik, T. (2009). Luxemburg's and Kalecki's theories and visions of capitalist dynamics. In R. Bellofiore (Ed.), *Rosa Luxemburg and the critique of political economy* (pp. 81–91). London: Routledge.

Kowalik, T. (2014). *Rosa Luxemburg: Theory of accumulation and imperialism*. Basingstoke: Palgrave.

Kowalik, T., & Kalecki, M. (1980). Uwagi o "reformie przełomowej". In M. Kalecki (Ed.), *Dzieła tom 2: Kapitalizm Dynamika Gospodarcza*. Warsaw: Państwowe Wydawnictwo Ekonomiczne.

Luxemburg, R. [1915] (2015). The accumulation of capital – An anti-critique. In *The complete works of Rosa Luxemburg, Volume II: Economic writings 2*. London and New York: Verso.

Magdoff, H., & Sweezy, P. (1987). *Stagnation and the financial explosion*. New York: Monthly Review Press.

Marx, K. [1885] (1992). *Capital. A critique of political economy, volume II*. New York: Penguin Books.
Marx, K. [1894] (1991). *Capital. A critique of political economy, volume III*. New York: Penguin Books.
Minsky, H. (1986). *Stabilizing an unstable economy*. New Haven: Yale University Press.
Onaran, O., & Galanis, G. (2012). *Is aggregate demand wage-led or profit-led? National and global effects*. Geneva: International Labour Office.
Sweezy, P. (1942). *The theory of capitalist development. Principles of Marxian political economy*. New York: Oxford University Press.
Toporowski, J. (2009). Rosa Luxemburg and finance. In R. Bellofiore (Ed.), *Rosa Luxemburg and the critique of political economy* (pp. 81–91). London: Routledge.
Toporowski, J. (2013a). *Michał Kalecki: An intellectual biography. Volume 1: Rendezvous in Cambridge, 1899–1939*. London: Palgrave.
Toporowski, J. (2013b). Tadeusz Kowalik and the accumulation of capital. *Monthly Review, 64*, 33–44.
Tugan-Baranowskii, M. (1901). *Studien zur Theorie und Geschichte der Handelskrisen in England*. Jena: G. Fischer.
Varga, E. (1935). *The great crisis and its political consequences: Economics and politics 1928–1934*. London: Modern Books.

7

Luxemburg and the Balance of Power in the 21st Century

Hanna K. Szymborska

Introduction

The following chapter discusses the relevance of Rosa Luxemburg's *Accumulation of Capital* in understanding the shift in the contemporary balance of power, rooted in the transformation of financial sectors since the second half of the 20th century. It argues that deepening social disparities served as a precondition for the establishment of finance-led capitalism, which can be interpreted as parallel to Rosa Luxemburg's theory of the necessity of non-capitalist accumulation for the development of capitalism. The following section outlines the problem of emerging power imbalances in society since the 1980s. The chapter then links these events to concepts derived from Marx and Luxemburg to show that their insights are indispensable in understanding the rationale behind the shifting distribution of power and the crisis of the late 2000s.

H.K. Szymborska (✉)
University of Leeds, LS2 9JT, United Kingdom

J. Dellheim, F.O. Wolf (eds.), *Rosa Luxemburg: A Permanent Challenge for Political Economy*, DOI 10.1057/978-1-137-60108-7_7

The Historical Institutional Conditions of Financial Exploitation at the Outset of the 21st Century

Much ink has been spilled over the formation of modern capitalism characterised by the penetration of financial sector dynamics into the real economy. On the heterodox and radical edges of economics, these changes have been described as 'financialisation', or the rise of 'finance-dominated capitalism' (cf. Epstein 2005; Palley 2007; Hein 2009; Lapavitsas 2009; Van Treeck 2009; Kus 2012; Fine 2013a; Lin and Tomaskovic-Devey 2013; Sawyer 2013; Van Arnum and Naples 2013). Finance's increased economic and political power over the real economic sector has manifested itself in a multitude of dimensions (cf. Fine 2011) and can be defined in a variety of ways. We understand the assumption of economic power by financial sectors as the ability to concentrate material gains (in terms of both national income and accumulated wealth) among the wealthiest financial investors while dispersing losses associated with financial crises to the rest of the society – particularly to those with the least resources to protect themselves from economic vulnerability. Political power is seen as the influence of finance over policymaking. We focus specifically on high-income economies and much of our analysis is applicable primarily to the USA, which represents the most advanced articulation of 'finance-dominated' capitalism. For analytical purposes, we distinguish between 'financialisation processes' and the 'financialisation thesis', treating the former as a series of historical developments in both financial and non-financial sectors, while the latter is an emerging economic argument establishing a causal negative influence of 'financialisation processes' on the economy. In this section we trace the historical conditions and the institutional transformations associated with financialisation processes in order to describe the channels through which the financial sector has assumed its dominant role in modern capitalist dynamics. With the help of literature on the financialisation thesis, we then outline how these processes have laid the ideological groundwork for financial exploitation of the working classes.

Financialisation processes' penetration of and growing influence on the dynamics of the real economy (that is, those sectors producing non-financial goods and services) has manifested itself in the changing functions that finance fulfils in society. This is closely linked to the political and economic situation of the 1970s, flowing from the breakdown of the Bretton Woods system. Macroeconomic instability in that period, coupled with stagflation and high interest rates, undercut deposits as the main source of bank profits, forcing non-financial firms to increasingly turn to savings outlets and money market funds for financing (Dymski 2009, p. 157). An increasing number of large non-financial companies entered financial markets to raise capital. Consequently, the size of financial profits (broadly defined as capital gains and proceeds from interest and dividend payments) has expanded rapidly over the past few decades. In the USA, financial profits have become the dominant source of raising and accumulating capital not only within but also outside of financial sectors, surpassing the relative importance of trade and production revenue (Krippner 2005, pp. 174–5).

Shifting sources of financing led to a transformation of the business model adopted by non-financial firms. Corporate behaviour shifted towards shareholder value maximisation, aiming to alleviate the 'agency costs' of asymmetric information by aligning the interests of managers with those of shareholders (and thus financial markets) via various remuneration schemes, such as bonuses and stock options. Financial expansion at the firm level has thus occurred at the expense of real investment, as firms' business orientation has shifted from long- to short-term profitability. Consequently, non-financial firms became active players in financial markets in order to boost short-run revenues, as required by new corporate strategies.

The prospect of higher returns through financial investment spurred innovation in, and proliferation of, financial instruments. Coupled with the increased participation of non-financial firms in financial markets, stock market trading relative to GDP expanded rapidly in a number of high-income countries. Consequently, an increasing volume of financial obligations – primarily debt – were transformed into financial securities in a process called 'securitisation'. This created networks of contracts not only between debtors and creditors, but also between creditors and financial investors (Pollin and Heintz 2013, p. 113). Mortgages became one of the most heavily securitised instruments, forming a component of collateralised debt obligations (CDOs) which combined financial instruments of varying levels of risk. Moreover, the establishment of derivatives and credit swaps allowed investors to bet against possible default, leading to a transformation of traditional lending relations based on intermediation towards the 'originate and redistribute' model, in which default risk becomes 'originated' by creditors and then spread across the financial system through securitisation. The actors of this new lending model were not only conventional banks transformed into highly consolidated 'megabanks' as a result of intense merger activity, but also non-bank intermediaries who functioned in a way similar to formal sector banks but outside of central bank jurisdiction when obtaining liquidity (Pollin and Heintz 2013, p. 115). Due to securitisation and a greater reliance of non-financial firms on financial markets for credit, banking profitability grew rapidly as fees incurred from security underwriting became the main source of bank revenue, overtaking interest payments (Lapavitsas 2009, p. 126). Simultaneously, however, bank performance became more vulnerable to economic shocks, falling sharply during crises.

The proliferation of financial instruments and the changing role of banks from being intermediaries to becoming active underwriters under the new banking model would not have been possible without changes in policy to facilitate such a shift. Initiated by Federal Reserve chair Paul Volcker and US President Ronald Reagan in the 1980s as well as Prime Minister Margaret Thatcher in the UK, this new policy agenda aimed to remove the existing regulations on financial sector activity. The repeal of the Glass–Steagall Act through the Gramm–Leach–Bliley Act in 1999 allowed commercial banks in the USA to engage in financial investment activities for the first time since 1933 (Pollin and Heintz 2013, p. 49). Coupled with the low interest rates adopted by the Federal Reserve, security trading was increasingly financed through leverage, as financial assets were bought with future profits.

These policy changes cannot be viewed in isolation from the transformation of mainstream economic scholarship underpinning said changes. The 'financialisation' of academic practice, rooted in a firm belief in the efficiency of markets and their ability to optimally allocate resources without external intervention (cf. DeMartino 2011), gathered pace following the oil crisis of the 1970s, challenging Keynesian post-war policies while placing greater emphasis on mathematical methods over an analysis of political economy. Buoyed by the support of economic scholarship and policy, securitisation (and, in turn, bank profits) rose to historically unprecedented levels while financial capital (profits from financial activity and investment in financial assets) became globally mobile as a result of the liberalisation of exchange rate and capital account regulations. Consequently, though financialisation processes remain most advanced in the Anglo-American economies, they have become interdependent across the high-income world, escaping both national and international regulation.

Financial deregulation coincided with measures promoting labour market liberalisation – eroding minimum wages, unemployment benefits and unionisation rights – in the name of greater labour allocation efficiency. This led to an increase in unemployment rates across the high-income world and shifted national income away from wages and towards profits. As a consequence thereof, labour income has stagnated and become more vulnerable to economic shocks. Work intensity as well as job insecurity has increased, which is also linked to the aforementioned shifts in employer objectives away from long-term investment (which, in contrast to short-run shareholder value maximisation, promotes nurturing the labour force in order to enhance long term output).

Responsibility for the provision of pensions, housing and public goods such as health care was simultaneously delegated to a large extent from the state to the private sector. Faced with stagnant wages, the working class was forced to seek external financing in the form of borrowing in order to pay for basic consumption, as well as to keep up with rising expectations (cf. Cynamon and Fazzari 2008). This greater demand for consumer credit was matched by financial intermediaries' need for new customers as their corporate clients increasingly turned to financial markets to raise capital (cf. Dymski 2009). Banks expanded their lending to households partly to compensate for diminishing deposits from non-financial firms and partly to generate more underlying assets for CDOs in order to keep pace with the rapidly growing demand for securitised instruments among financial investors.

The pressing need to satisfy demand for securitised assets pushed financial intermediaries to exploit lax financial regulation and engage in predatory lending practices by offering 'subprime' mortgages to vulnerable social groups that had previously been excluded from access to credit. Housing usually constituted the required collateral for subprime loans. Households targeted by predatory lenders were allowed to take out a number of loans against their house, thereby extracting home equity to finance consumption needs and compensate for stagnant wage levels. During the 'good times' of the 2000s, this created an illusion of greater prosperity for those previously excluded from credit. However, this prosperity was based entirely on inflated housing values. As soon as prices plummeted at the outset of the downturn, widespread predatory lending practices triggered a wave of foreclosures, evictions and unsustainable levels of debt for mortgage holders, spreading the burden of the crisis unequally between different race and gender groups (Dymski et al. 2013).

This scenario, coupled with the weakening of trade unions and the transfer of income away from workers towards investors as a result of shareholder value maximisation and labour market liberalisation, has caused intra-national economic inequality to increase at the aggregate level (Van Arnum and Naples 2013, p. 1166). Available data suggest that disparities in income have risen as a greater income share is captured by the upper echelons of society, evidenced by the more rapid growth of wealth at the top (as opposed to bottom) end of the income spectrum in a number of countries (Bell and Van Reenen 2010; Zalewski and Whalen 2010; Kus 2012; Saez and Zucman 2014). Piketty (2014) suggests that this disparity is due to rates of return on capital being persistently higher than rates of economic growth overall.

Increased income inequality, coupled with the exponentially growing demand for securitised assets, has been reflected in a massive expansion of bank and non-bank intermediaries in the private sector. As a result, business cycles have become more prone to asset price inflation and financial booms, fuelling the rise and dramatic collapse of debt-financed consumption dictated by asset price movements (Palley 2007, p. 24). These processes have made crises more frequent, acute and widespread. It is in this context of growing economic volatility and deepening social inequality that heterodox and radical economists have sought to understand the dynamics and aftermath of financialisation processes. The emergent financialisation thesis argues that the aforementioned changes in the intermediation model, the heightened importance of private credit as a source of financing for non-financial firms and workers alike, along with financial deregulation contribute significantly to relatively slower real economic growth, falling real investment and more pronounced economic volatility. Pollin and Heintz (2013) indicate that financial innovation in the USA was one of the key factors behind the 2007–8 financial crisis, contributing to greater risk and hence instability of the financial sector (p. 117). Orhangazi (2007) shows that real investment in the USA has suffered due to shareholder value maximisation and greater reliance on the external financing of production among non-financial firms. Securitisation and globalisation of financial services caused the crisis spread globally to non-financial sectors, inducing negative GDP growth across the high-income world. Problems associated with financial innovation in the USA were a causal factor behind the sovereign crises experienced by some Eurozone countries since 2009. Varoufakis (2013) argues that credit default swaps owned by foreign investors were at the heart of mounting sovereign debt in Greece, Spain, Ireland, Italy and Portugal (pp. 203–5).

In this chapter we interpret finance's ability to influence real economic outcomes as an assumption of economic and political power by the financial sectors. We focus on the particular role it has played in gaining control over the incomes and economic vulnerabilities of the working class. Financialisation emerges as a powerful instrument for redistributing gains from financial development and costs of volatility through securitisation, financial deregulation, predatory lending, a greater reliance on finance as a source of funding, and policies intended to erode labour market protection and reduce overall government spending. The expanding role of financial markets in economic policy and decision-making observed since the 1980s is a highly complex phenomenon, redistributing gains from financial development towards the richest and spreading losses incurred from financial volatility across the rest of the society. Arguably, the ultimate achievement of the financialisation process has been to create a culture and norms of its own, becoming an integral part of modern capitalism by aligning the interests of society with those of financial investors (Lapavitsas 2009; Fine 2013b; Arestis et al. 2013; Arestis et al. 2014). It may also affect human psychology itself, indicated by society's quiet acceptance of greater concentrations of profits in the financial sector and the shared burden of greater economic volatility fed by the promises of 'trickle-down' economics. It is in this context that understanding the specific nature and dynamics of the redistribution of economic and political power induced by financialisation processes is so crucial.

The Contribution of Marx and Luxemburg's Critique

We argue that the insights of Karl Marx, as well as the arguments put forward by Rosa Luxemburg in her critique of *Capital*, are indispensable to understanding the persistence of the aforementioned power imbalances in society and their role in the recent economic crisis in high-income countries. In *The Accumulation of Capital*, Luxemburg argues that monetisation of surplus value can only occur through the exploitation of markets external to capitalism or by military action, realised in colonialist and imperialist expansion (cf. Luxemburg 1913). Despite a number of inconsistencies, Luxemburg's thesis contained in the third part of her magnum opus, 'The Historical Conditions of Accumulation', initiated a critique of the approach to Marx's *Capital* which links the crisis of capitalism to underconsumption rooted in inadequate wages – an argument found in modern literature placing rising functional inequality at the core of the crisis (Toporowski 2014, p. viii; cf. Van Treeck and Sturn 2012; Mian and Sufi 2013).

Marx's analysis of credit creation by banks sees them as pooling savings and surplus value (for example, from some workers or a group of productive capitalists) in order to lend to other productive capitalists (Argitis et al. 2014, p. 13). Importantly, credit is used not only to finance fixed investment, but also to fuel speculation. Marx considers credit created in the bank lending process to be fictitious capital because its circulation occurs independently of real capital accumulation. Increases in fictitious capital raise the volatility of capitalist reproduction as the inability to sell enough commodities, sudden halts in lending as interest rates rise and asset prices collapse, as well as pressures stemming from greater demand for funds needed to cover outstanding payments result in economic crisis (Argitis et al. 2014, p. 16).

While Marx emphasises the sources of money underpinning the realisation of surplus value, Luxemburg highlights that the actual problem of realisation lies in the sources of demand needed to extract surplus value. In her most famous critique of Marx she notes that capitalism does not exist in isolation, but in fact requires the presence of 'non-capitalist strata' – that is, areas not yet subject to the laws of capital accumulation – in order to realise produced surplus value (cf. Kowalik 2014). It is only through extending investment into areas previously excluded from capital accumulation that the problem of insufficient demand can be solved and surplus value monetised.

These insights are crucial to grasp the dramatic shift in economic and political power towards the financial sector described in the previous section. Mainstream economics regards securitisation and financial deregulation as necessary to alleviate informational asymmetries in credit markets, thereby enhancing the efficient allocation of resources and combating adverse selection and moral hazard on the part of borrowers (cf. Dymski 2005; Dymski et al. 2013, p. 125). The financial sector is thus seen as a socially neutral entity. The Marxist perspective challenges this notion by highlighting the social underpinnings of financial institutions and processes. It acknowledges the existence of unevenly distributed economic power and its influence on financial sector outcomes. It illuminates the historical and institutional conditions behind the massive expansion of financial capital generated in the process of securitisation and transformed financial intermediation, and highlights the active role played by banks in the creation and circulation of financial capital. By emphasising that circulation occurs largely independently of the accumulation of productive capital, Marx's analysis sheds light on the limits of financial capital expansion as such.

Utilising the analytical lens provided by Luxemburg, we can take our analysis a step further by recognising the dependence of financial capital's rise on the existence of persistent imbalances in society. Luxemburg's theory of the necessity of non-capitalist strata helps us to interpret the emergence and deepening of social divisions in terms of income and wealth as necessary preconditions for the development of financial capitalism over the past decades, as well as the crisis beginning in 2007. However, rather than imagining non-capitalist strata as lower-income countries in line with Luxemburg's original argument, we consider these strata to be the sections of the working class previously excluded from access to credit, who were then incorporated into the financial system via exploitative predatory lending. The financially excluded are most often the precariously employed, as well as racial minorities and women – all of whom are the most vulnerable to the dire consequences of default (cf. Dymski 2009; Hernandez 2009; Dymski et al. 2013). By creating the conditions that necessitate debt-financed consumption, financial investors were able to exploit the most vulnerable sections of the working class to satisfy their demand for lucrative financial assets. It thus becomes clear that the rapid growth of the financial sector relative to the rest of the economy and ballooning bank profits would not have been possible without the exploitation of economic sectors previously reliant on other forms of consumption financing (such as wages or public provision) via the extension of private credit. Through asset securitisation and changes in the bank intermediation model, personal incomes and workers' consumption became the precondition for the extraction of surplus value created by the financialisation process. A deepening of social inequalities and the 'colonisation' of those sections of the working class previously exempt from the rules of financial capital accumulation was instrumental to this purpose.

This reinterpretation of Rosa Luxemburg's argument regarding the necessity of non-capitalist strata for the development of capitalism and its application to the contemporary problem of increasing financial exploitation of vulnerable workers demonstrates that finance-led capitalism depends on the existence of social groups which are persistently disadvantaged in wealth and income relative to the top owners of financial wealth. Previously excluded from credit, these groups had to be forcefully included in the financial system via predatory lending practices characterised by higher interest rates and harsh, non-renegotiable penalties in the case of non-payment in order to satisfy the growing demand for securitised financial assets. Given simultaneous wage stagnation and growing insecurity in employment, individual consumption and the provision of public services resulting from financialisation, these sections of the working class have been effectively abandoned by the state and exploited by the financial sector for the sake of surplus value realisation.

Furthermore, our reinterpretation of Luxemburg's thesis highlights the paradoxical nature of this relationship. The crisis of 2007 that originated in the US financial sector and subsequently spread to other sectors and countries exposed the limits of financial exploitation of workers. Securitisation and predatory lending are reminiscent of Rosa Luxemburg's theory of imperialism, namely, that capitalism's violent creation of markets, in which natural economies are coercively commoditised, ultimately leads to an acute paradox of capitalist development as the non-capitalist strata required for capitalist growth gradually disappear, thus drawing capitalism into further crisis. This exploitation can be seen more clearly in the way that securitisation encouraged individual loans to be bundled and sold back and forth between financial institutions, essentially making debt forgiveness at the level of origination impossible. This has placed an unequal burden on highly leveraged households, often located at the bottom end of the income spectrum. Once the crisis materialised in the financial sector, a lack of adequate buffers in the form of income or accumulated wealth forced many into default, which then undercut spending in the economy as a whole and turned the financial crisis into a full-blown economic storm. In this way, exploitation of vulnerable workers by the financial sector planted the seeds for its own demise as it endogenously fuelled greater economic instability through speculative asset price bubbles based on lending to the most vulnerable. The onset of the crisis in 2007 can be thus seen as the moment when the exploitative capabilities of the financial sectors were exhausted.

Remarkable in the case of finance-led capitalism is the strong link between economic power related to ownership of income and wealth and political power as such, understood as the ability to influence policymaking. The period associated with the dominance of finance has not seen a reduction in the power of the state, but has in fact shifted it from policy solutions benefiting workers towards privatisation and measures such as bank bailouts and austerity, which favour the interests of the financial sector and further exacerbate income inequality (cf. Fine 2013a). It subsequently provided fertile ground for the extraction of profits from workers and low-income households by financial capital. Lack of any pronounced policy changes in recent years suggests that the political power of finance has not diminished in the aftermath of the crisis. There is thus a real danger that the financial exploitation of the working class will become a structural feature of capitalism in the years to come. This is because economic instability at the household level accompanied by sluggish wages growth has profound long-term consequences for the income prospects of future generations (cf. Dymski et al. 2013, p. 140; McKnight and Karagiannaki 2013). As long as this uneven balance of power persists with absent policy responses restricting the unconditional expansion of the financial sectors, the financial institutions of modern capitalism will be able to adjust, escaping internal contradictions in the short term. This could create a spiral of ever-deepening social disparities accompanied by short spurts of economic growth based on the exploitation of the most vulnerable sections of society, followed by pronounced crises concentrated among the working class. It is in this context that we must revisit Rosa Luxemburg's ideas, drawing lessons from her determination to fight for economic prosperity for all based on fairness rather than exploitation.

Conclusion

This chapter argues that the extension of credit and the subjection of low-income and highly leveraged groups to the laws of securitised finance can be reinterpreted through the lens of Rosa Luxemburg's thesis on the necessity of non-capitalist strata for the expansion and development of capitalism. Social inequalities, exploited and deepened by the workings of 'financialising' capitalism, created the conditions for the boom of the 2000s. Subjected to tremendous strain, the contradictions of the emergent system pushed finance-led capitalism into both financial and real crises, as is consistent with Luxemburg's theory. However, despite the ongoing crisis, modern capitalism remains largely unchallenged. The 2007 financial crisis turned out to be more of a missed opportunity than a wake-up call for mass social action against socio-economic injustice and financial exploitation, generating only a few, isolated social movements in response. This stands in sharp contrast to Rosa Luxemburg's own time. Inspired by Luxemburg's theories, it is more necessary than ever to draw lessons from her determination and ceaseless striving to fight for an alternative system based on fairness and equality, in order to successfully challenge the systemic exploitation of workers by finance that we have seen in recent decades.

Acknowledgments The author wishes to acknowledge Dr Judith Dellheim from the Rosa Luxemburg Foundation for her kind support and cooperation as well as Prof. Gary Dymski (University of Leeds), Prof. Giuseppe Fontana (University of Leeds) and Prof. Jan Toporowski (SOAS, University of London) for their advice and comments on the draft of this chapter.

Bibliography

Arestis, P., Charles, A., & Fontana, G. (2013). Financialization, the great recession, and the stratification of the US labor market. *Feminist Economics, 19*(3), 152–180.

Arestis, P., Charles, A., & Fontana, G. (2014). Identity economics meets financialisation: Gender, race and occupational stratification in the US labour market. *Cambridge Journal of Economics, 38*, 1471–1491.

Argitis, G., Evans, T., Michell, J., & Toporowski, J. (2014). Finance and crisis: Marxian, institutionalist and circuitist approaches. FESSUD Working Paper 39.

Bell, B., & Van Reenen, J. (2010). Bankers' pay and extreme wage inequality in the UK. Centre for economic performance special papers, 21.

Cynamon, B. Z., & Fazzari, S. M. (2008). Household debt in the consumer age: Source of growth – Risk of collapse. *Capitalism and Society, 3*(2), 1–30.

DeMartino, G. F. (2011). *The economist's oath: On the need for and content of professional economic ethics*. Oxford: Oxford University Press.

Dymski, G. A. (2005). Financial globalization, social exclusion and financial crisis. *International Review of Applied Economics, 19*(4), 439–457.

Dymski, G. A. (2009). Racial exclusion and the political economy of the subprime crisis. *Historical Materialism, 17*, 149–179.

Dymski, G. A., Hernandez, J., & Mohanty, L. (2013). Race, gender, power, and the US subprime mortgage and foreclosure crisis: A meso analysis. *Feminist Economics, 19*(3), 124–151.

Epstein, G. A. (Ed.) (2005). *Financialization and the world economy*. Cheltenham: Edward Elgar.
Fine, B. (2011). Financialisation on the rebound? http://eprints.soas.ac.uk/12102/1/dumenil.pdf.
Fine, B. (2013a). Financialisation from a Marxist perspective. *International Journal of Political Economy, 42*(4), 47–66.
Fine, B. (2013b). Towards a material culture of financialisation. FESSUD Working Paper Series, 15.
Hein, E. (2009). A (post-)Keynesian perspective on "financialisation", *Studies*, 1 (Düsseldorf: Macroeconomic Policy Institute, Hans Böckler Foundation).
Hernandez, J. (2009). Redlining revisited: Mortgage lending patterns in Sacramento 1930–2004. *International Journal of Urban and Regional Research, 33*(2), 291–313.
Kowalik, T. (2014). *Rosa Luxemburg. Theory of accumulation and imperialism*. Basingstoke: Palgrave Macmillan, vii-xiv.
Krippner, G. (2005). The financialization of the American economy. *Socio-Economic Review, 3*, 173–208.
Kus, B. (2012). Financialisation and income inequality in OECD nations: 1995–2007. *The Economic and Social Review, 43*(4), 477–495.
Kowalik, T. (2014). *Rosa Luxemburg. Theory of accumulation and imperialism*. Basingstoke: Palgrave Macmillan, vii–xiv
Lapavitsas, C. (2009). Financialised capitalism: Crisis and financial expropriation. *Historical Materialism, 17*(2), 114–148.
Lin, K. H., & Tomaskovic-Devey, D. (2013). Financialization and U.S. Income inequality, 1970–2008. *American Journal of Sociology, 118*(5), 1284–1329.
Luxemburg, R. (2015) [1913]. The accumulation of capital. A contribution to the economic theory of imperialism. In *Rosa Luxemburg. Complete works, Volume 2*. pp. 7–344. London and New York: Verso.
McKnight, A., & Karagiannak, E. (2013). The wealth effect: How parental wealth and own asset-holdings predict future advantage. In J. Hills, F. Bastagli, F. Cowell, H. Glennerster, E. Karagiannaki, & A. McKnight (Eds.), *Wealth in the UK: Distribution, accumulation, and policy*. Oxford: Oxford University Press.
Mian, A., & Sufi, A. (2013). *House of debt*. Chicago: University of Chicago Press.
Orhangazi, O. (2007). Financialization and capital accumulation in the non-financial corporate sector: A theoretical and empirical investigation of the US

Economy: 1973–2003. Political Economy Research Institute University of Massachusetts Amherst Working Paper, 149.
Palley, T.I. (2007). Financialization: What it is and why it matters. The Levy Economics Institute Working Paper, 525.
Piketty, T. (2014). *Capital in the twenty-first century*. Harvard: Harvard University Press.
Pollin, R. and Heintz, J. (2013). Study of U.S. financial system. FESSUD studies in financial systems, 10.
Saez, E., & Zucman, G. (2014). Wealth inequality in the United States since 1913: Evidence from capitalized income tax data. NBER Working Paper, 20625.
Sawyer, M. (2013). What is financialisation? *International Journal of Political Economy, 42*(4), 5–18.
Toporowski, J. (2014). 'Preface' in T. Kowalik (2014).
Van Arnum, B. M., & Naples, M. I. (2013). Financialization and income inequality in the United States 1967–2010. *American Journal of Economics and Sociology, 72*(5), 1158–1182.
Van Treeck, T. (2009). A synthetic stock-flow consistent macroeconomic model of financialisation. *Cambridge Journal of Economics, 33*, 467–493.
Van Treeck, T., & Sturn, S . (2012). Income inequality as a cause of the great recession? A survey of current debates. *Conditions of work and employment series*, 39. Geneva: International Labour Office.
Varoufakis, Y. (2013). *The global minotaur: America, Europe and the future of the global economy* (2nd ed.). London: Zed Books.
Zalewski, D. A., & Whalen, C. J. (2010). Financialization and income inequality: A post-Keynesian institutionalist analysis. *Journal of Economic Issues, 44*(3), 757–777.

8

A Feminist Approach to Primitive Accumulation

Tove Soiland

Introduction

Since the outset of the millennium, Marxist theory has witnessed a revitalisation of approaches which, drawing on Rosa Luxemburg, productively utilise the continuing existence of forms of primitive accumulation to analyse post-Fordist accumulation regimes.[1] Echoing many of his colleagues, David Harvey states that Marxist theory today is obliged to explain the remarkable stability of the capitalist mode of production 'in the face of multiple crises and reorganizations' (2003, p. 87). Marx agreed with bourgeois economics that forms of primitive accumulation

The original version of this chapter was revised.
An erratum to this chapter can be found at DOI 10.1057/978-1-137-60108-7_12

[1] For the English-speaking world, see Perlmann (2000), Harvey (2003), De Angelis (2007), Federici (2010), Ezquerra (2014) and the discussion about the Commons (see, for example, The Commoner http://www.commoner.org.uk/); for the German-speaking world, see Zeller (2004), who speaks of an economy of dispossession, Dörre (2009, 2012), who speaks of a 'new *Landnahme*', as well as Backhouse et al. (2013).

T. Soiland (✉)
Rothstrassse 9, Zürich, CH-8057, Switzerland

J. Dellheim, F.O. Wolf (eds.), *Rosa Luxemburg: A Permanent Challenge for Political Economy*, DOI 10.1057/978-1-137-60108-7_8

were only significant in the beginning of capitalism, during the replacement of feudal modes of production. Following the conclusion of this process, capital accumulation takes place exclusively within what he referred to as 'expanded reproduction'.[2] Today's debate around a 'new *Landnahme*' assumes that these persisting forms of primitive accumulation contribute much more significantly than previously thought to the survival of capitalism.[3] According to Harvey, forms of 'accumulation by dispossession' have replaced the accumulation of surplus value in terms of their relevance to overall capital accumulation since the mid-1970s (Harvey 2003, pp. 137ff).

This is important because it shifts the attention of Marxist theory to other forms of exploitation beyond the exploitation of traditional wage labour, which reflects, in turn, a broader historical shift: while the traditional subject of working-class politics, the blue-collar worker in western capitalist societies experienced extensive integration into the capitalist system on the basis of social partnership during the Fordist era, by '68 (at the latest) new political subjects and struggles had entered the world stage. From '68 onwards, the new social movements insisted on a global perspective that shifted its focus to other actors and forms of exploitation than just the exploitation of wage labour performed by relatively affluent workers. In this sense, the theorem of ongoing forms of primitive accumulation is important not only for the theorisation of the forms of oppression and exploitation which diverge from the classical Marxist topics mentioned here. Rather, the concept itself has most likely acquired its modern meaning precisely because of said movements. The theorem of an ongoing *Landnahme* can thus be considered the essential theorem of social movements which sought to embed their struggles within a global

[2] 'Expanded reproduction' denotes the generation and subsequent re-investment of surplus value, that is, the contractually legitimised form of accumulation, cf. Marx (1978, pp. 418–599). Marx's concept of reproduction must be distinguished from that which was so essential for developing feminist theory. When Marx uses the term, he is thinking of the reproduction of the totality of capitalist relations, of which the reproduction of the labour force is only one partial aspect.

[3] Various terms are common. In the English-speaking world, Perlmann (2000) speaks of a history of primitive accumulation, Harvey (2003) of an 'accumulation by dispossession' and De Angelis (2007, p. 135) of 'enclosures'as 'continuous characteristic of "capital logic"'. The term "new *Landnahme*" coined by Klaus Dörre cannot be accurately translated into English because of the implied metaphorical connotation (2012, p. 664).

perspective from the very beginning. At the same time, it represents an attempt to bridge the dichotomy between traditional Marxist theory and the theory of imperialism as such (Harvey, 2001, p. 263).[4]

What seems largely forgotten in the current international discussion over forms of ongoing primitive accumulation in highly developed societies is that a previous feminist reception of Rosa Luxemburg had already occurred at the end of the 1970s. Feminist theoreticians engaging in the housework debate of the time, most notably development sociologists Maria Mies, Claudia von Werlhof and Veronica Bennholdt-Thomsen, argued that labour performed in the domestic sphere – unpaid and mostly by women – is subjected to such a form of primitive accumulation in the sense that the household produces the most important element of capitalist production – the labour commodity – essentially free of charge.[5] By highlighting unpaid female labour, they addressed a form of exploitation that takes place outside of exploitation for surplus value and is not confined to the capitalist centres, but rather represents a form of exploitation beyond wage labour that is continuously brought forth by capitalism itself.

This chapter argues that this feminist reception of Rosa Luxemburg puts forward an interpretation of Rosa Luxemburg's elaboration of the Marxist theory of accumulation that not only anticipates today's discussion of contemporary forms of dispossession,[6] but also theorises the latter rather differently. Through its focus on a specific aspect of Luxemburg's deliberations, this feminist reception analysed ongoing processes of

[4] It should be added that Mandel (1972, p. 43) and the developmental sociology that drew on his ideas always assumed the ongoing existence of primitive accumulation in its theory of geographically unequal development (dependency theory).

[5] *The Commoner* (15) special issue on 'Care Work and the Commons' returns to this older debate. The issue also features some important texts from that time.

[6] At this point, I cannot definitely say whether this is also an anticipation of Harvey's reflections. Comprehensive clarification would be required to determine how exactly Harvey's concept of 'spatio-temporal fix', developed since the 1970s, is linked to his 'accumulation by dispossession', introduced in 2003 to explain the endurance of forms of primitive accumulation in our times. It seems to me, however, that the early concept of spatio-temporal fix (see Harvey 2001, 1982) is closer to Marx's model of 'expanded reproduction' than to what lies at the heart of the discussion (to which Harvey has contributed greatly since the early 2000s) about contemporary forms of dispossession: the basic assumption that forms of dispossession must be understood as distinct forms of accumulation not arising from wage labour, forms that are absolutely vital for capital accumulation today (Harvey, 2003, p. 137). At least in *Space of Capital*, in which his older texts from the 1970s are collected, Harvey speaks of expropriation only in relation to primitive accumulation.

Landnahme as an articulation between distinct modes of production (see Mies, 2007). In hindsight, this reception also provides a valuable instrumentarium for the analysis of post-Fordist accumulation regimes, although they differ from Fordist regimes in that (inter alia) a significant share of this unpaid labour once performed by women has meanwhile been converted into forms of wage labour – albeit without effecting a general improvement in the status of women or an end to their overexploitation as such.

As is widely known, Rosa Luxemburg did not consider herself a feminist. She was a determined revolutionary and thus focused her theoretical writings on questions of political economy. A century after her analyses, in a world that has seen many changes, and in which the possibility of proletarian revolution seems to have receded into the remote distance, and a neoliberal project has been established based on a mixture of violent implementation and hegemonic consent, the question of capitalism's sweeping mechanisms of integration presents itself in a new way. It is precisely with view to this question that Luxemburg's theoretical analyses provide an instrumentarium for analysing the intangibility of certain forms of exploitation in the reproductive sphere, which presumably contribute significantly to the integrative capacity of capitalist modes of production today. Even though Rosa Luxemburg may not have drawn this connection herself, the question as to what is currently taking place within the sphere of reproduction in the capitalist metropoles is of utmost importance for the questions she raised. After all, we know today (not least thanks to the seminal work of the aforementioned sociologists from Bielefeld) that international political economy and the question of reproduction so central to a feminist approach are far more closely related than Rosa Luxemburg could have known in her time. Accordingly, we do not have to choose between the feminist and political economic perspective, but rather can pursue both.

This chapter begins from Silvia Federici's claim that we are currently witnessing a 'restructuring of the (re)production of labor-power in the global economy' (Federici 2010), which must be understood as a form of primitive accumulation, a process which may be among the most important forms of accumulation by dispossession that are so characteristic of neoliberalism today. Neoliberalism is not merely the privatisation of the railways or of the air we breathe. It also stands for, and indeed may consist primarily of, an all-out incursion into the ways in which people around the world are forced to reproduce themselves. In this sense an analysis thereof must bring into focus and theoretically conceptualise the specific forms of primitive accumulation operating in the sphere of reproduction.

This chapter therefore pursues two concrete objectives: to begin with, I seek to expand today's discussion on accumulation by dispossession by incorporating this important aspect affecting women and their work environments, so as to draw attention to an issue that has so far been excluded from the discussion, yet is of tremendous importance with regard to the forms of exploitation specific to women: The ongoing parallel existence of different modes of production and their respective articulation even in advanced capitalist societies. In this sense, the deliberations presented here focus on dynamics which originate in the advanced western capitalist societies themselves. On the other hand, and directly related to the aforementioned objective, we must also address and update the housework debate of the 1970s for it to apply to post-Fordist conditions. This requires taking into consideration the fact that since the 1970s a share of the unpaid household labour traditionally performed by women has meanwhile assumed the form of wage labour. In order to do so, I will draw on some considerations rooted in feminist economics, the true accomplishment of which is the analysis of paid as well as unpaid care work and their interrelationship through the establishment of the concept of the care economy, thereby allowing us to illustrate this sector's relation to the larger economic process both in terms of economic dynamics as well as its actual scale (Madörin 2006, pp. 286–93, 2014, p. 180f, 2013, p. 89f).

The Early Reception of Rosa Luxemburg by the Bielefeld Sociologists

The Bielefeld sociologists'[7] most significant accomplishment was to apply Rosa Luxemburg's claim that capitalism remains dependent on 'noncapitalist forms of production' (Luxemburg 1913, p. 265) even at an advanced

[7] Mies (2007, p. 268) notes that the expression 'Bielefeld approach' is misleading because the advocates of this approach could not find employment in Bielefeld, on account of, among other things,

stage to largely unpaid reproductive labour, thus anticipating that which is today described by the theorem of a *New Landnahme*. These theoreticians were able to utilise the idea of 'ongoing primitive accumulation' (Mies 2014, p. 216)[8] to conceptualise the respective relevance of non-capitalist modes of production which persist under capitalist conditions to capital accumulation. Their hypothesis was that unpaid housework represented a field of exploitative relations thus far neglected by critical economic theory, thereby not only contributing to the persistence of hierarchisation between men and women, but also representing the actual, unrecognised base of the conceptual 'iceberg' (Mies 2014, p. 225) upon which the exploitation of 'normal' wage labour rests in the first place. They postulated that this normal form of exploitation was actually based on top of another form of exploitation, reaching much further in its dimensions.

In this description, the Bielefeld sociologists based themselves on Rosa Luxemburg's argument that capitalism, even in full bloom, resorts to forms of accumulation in which not the contract[9] but 'violence, fraud, oppression, and plunder' are the dominant forms of appropriation (1913, p. 329). Luxemburg thereby contradicted Marx's assumption that 'primitive' forms of accumulation (1913, p. 446) – what he referred to as '*ursprüngliche* (literally 'original') *Akkumulation*' (Marx 1876, p. 873) – could only be found in the early stages of the capitalist mode of production, and that violence thus played a role as a means of accumulation only in the genesis of capitalism, as its 'midwife', so to speak (Marx 1876, p. 916). Against the backdrop of World War I, Luxemburg concluded that Europe's colonies, along with the predominant forms of violent exploitation associated with them, had to be considered in terms of their *economic function* for the capitalist mode of accumulation. Her criticism was that although Marx addressed the 'looting of the colonial countries by European capital', he 'merely treated from the point of view

---

these basic assumptions they proceeded from. I nevertheless use this term because it has come to be accepted and used internationally.

[8] In *Patriarchy and Accumulation on a World Scale* (1986), Mies speaks of 'ongoing primitive accumulation', cf. Mies (1986, p. 145).

[9] 'Here, on the level of form, it is peace, property, and equality that prevail, and it required the acute dialectic of a scientific analysis to expose the way in which, during the process of accumulation, the right of property turns into the appropriation of alien property, commodity exchange turns into exploitation, and equality turns into class domination' (Luxemburg, 1913, p. 329).

of so-called "primitive accumulation"' (Luxemburg 1913, p. 262): 'In Marx's account, the processes specified here merely illustrate the genesis of capital, the moment that it comes into the world – they constitute the birth pangs as the capitalist mode of production emerges from the womb of feudal society. As soon as Marx begins his theoretical analysis of the process of capital (of production as well as circulation), he constantly returns to his presupposition of the universal and exclusive dominance of capitalist production' (Luxemburg 1913, p. 262). In contrast to this, Rosa Luxemburg insists on an understanding of colonialism as an expression of the fact that 'violence [...] has been a constant method of capital accumulation as a historical process, not merely during its emergence, but also to the present day' (1913, p. 267). It is in this context that she formulates her famous hypothesis of an ongoing primitive accumulation: 'This is no longer a question of original accumulation: this is a process that continues to this day. Each new colonial expansion is accompanied by capital's relentless war on the social and economic interrelations of the indigenous inhabitants and by the violent looting of their means of production and their labor-power' (Luxemburg 1913, p. 267).

Rosa Luxemburg modifies Marx's theoretical analysis of the capital process in one crucial aspect, namely that it is by no means necessary for capitalism to produce all the components of capital accumulation by itself (that is, under capitalist conditions) – a view that Marx shared with bourgeois economics[10]:

> The aspiration to restrict capitalism to 'peaceful competition,' i.e. to commodity exchange proper as it occurs between capitalist producing countries, rests on the doctrinaire delusion that the accumulation of capital could manage without the productive forces and demand of the more primitive social formations. (Luxemburg 1913, p. 267)

When Luxemburg remarks in this context 'that, even in its full maturity, capitalism depends in all of its relations on the simultaneous exis-

[10] It is important to note that Luxemburg's criticism of Marx concerned an economic problem, as she challenged his basic assumption of the 'absolute dominance of the capitalist mode of production': 'On closer inspection, the schema of expanded reproduction itself points beyond itself to relations lying beyond capitalist production and accumulation' (Luxemburg 1913, pp. 252–3).

tence of noncapitalist strata and societies' (1913, p. 262), this leads her to her decisive expansion of Marxian accumulation theory: 'Accumulation is not merely an internal relation between the branches of the capitalist economy – it is above all a relation between capital and its noncapitalist milieu [...]' (1913, p. 303). She specifies this in more detail in the following:

> While it is true that capitalism lives from noncapitalist formations, it is more precise to say that it lives from their ruin; in other words, while this noncapitalist milieu is indispensable for capitalist accumulation, providing its fertile soil, accumulation in fact proceeds at the expense of this milieu, and is constantly devouring it. Historically speaking, the accumulation of capital is a process of metabolism occurring between capitalist and precapitalist modes of production. The accumulation of capital cannot proceed without these precapitalist modes of production, and yet accumulation consists in this regard precisely in the latter being gradually swallowed up and assimilated by capital. Accordingly, capital accumulation can no more exist without noncapitalist formations, than these are able to exist alongside it. It is only in the constant and progressive erosion of these noncapitalist formations that the very conditions of the existence of capital accumulation are given. (1913, p. 302)

It was this exterior–interior dialectic and the emphasis on the paramount significance of relations 'beyond capitalist production and accumulation' (1913, p. 253) it implies that inspired today's discussion of 'new *Landnahmen*', that is, primitive forms of accumulation. David Harvey, one of the main initiators of this debate, on the one hand shares Luxemburg's view that the capitalist system requires an 'exterior' in order to stabilise itself. However, he criticises the breakdown thesis implicit in her argument, i.e. Luxemburg's prediction that capitalism would sooner or later run out of 'exteriors', and thus out of foreign markets, once the constant *Landnahmen* exhausted all available 'land' (2003, p. 137). But reducing Luxemburg's hypotheses to the question of foreign markets is incorrect. It is true that Luxemburg explicitly rejects the consideration of non-capitalist strata simply in terms of 'realization of surplus value', that is, foreign markets, as she repeatedly emphasises that the 'material elements' (Luxemburg 1913, p. 255) of production may also come from this milieu and can thus be acquired by capital far below their actual value or even stolen.[11] Although Luxemburg does address 'noncapitalist social strata as a market in which to realize its surplus value' (1913, p. 265), she nevertheless stresses that capitalism requires these 'noncapitalist forms of production' 'as a source for its means of production and as a reservoir of labor-power for its wage system' (1913, p. 265), by specifying: 'The accumulation process of capital is tied to noncapitalist forms of production in all of its value relations and material relations […]' (1913, p. 262). By doing so she outlined the interconnection between internal and external spaces which underlies Harvey's theory: 'The external market, from the point of view of capital, is the noncapitalist social environment, which absorbs its products and supplies it with elements of production and labor-power' (1913, pp. 263–4).

It is this form of subsumption targeting the subsistence resources of a different mode of production – referred to by Luxemburg as the 'noncapitalist social environment' (1913, p. 446) – that inspired the Bielefeld sociologists in the late 1970s to conceive of domestic labour in western capitalist societies as such a 'subsistence production' (Bennholdt-Thomsen 1981; Mies 1983) in Luxemburg's sense. Long before Harvey argued that 'colonies' are not necessarily geographical exteriors, they conceptualised household production as just such an 'exterior' of the capitalist mode of production, moreover one that is not only located within it, but indeed one that the former permanently creates anew: household production is not a geographically external colony, but instead, as Maria Mies formulates in her specification of the 'interior-exterior dialectic', an 'internal colony' which can be subsequently reconquered by capital (Mies 1986, p. 110, 1983, p. 117) Thus, by the early 1980s the Bielefeld sociologists formulated the concept guiding today's discussion[12] that capitalism constantly creates non-capitalist 'islands' within its own interior which it can then reconquer at a later point, namely in the form of subsistence

[11] Compare, for example, Luxemburg (1913, p. 262): 'This relation of dependence is not exhausted by the bare question of the market for the "excess product," as the problem was posed by Sismondi and the later critics and skeptics of capitalist accumulation.' Or: '[T]he realization of surplus value […] is a priori bound up with noncapitalist producers and consumers' (Luxemburg, 1913, p. 263).

[12] Cf. Feministische Autorinnengruppe (2013).

production that permanently expands as a consequence of the capitalist mode of production.

In hindsight, Mies illustrates what she and her colleagues tried to grasp theoretically with the image of an 'underwater economy' in which wage labour and thus the normal form of exploitation is only the 'tip of the iceberg' resting on an invisible base of unpaid subsistence labour exposed to very different forms of expropriation (Mies 2014, p. 226). The Bielefeld sociologists thereby claim that a form of exploitation exists which far exceeds the scope of wage labour and that at the same time represents the central hypothesis in today's discussion of 'accumulation by dispossession' (Bennholdt-Thomsen 1981, p. 38; Mies 2014, pp. 209ff). They saw it as a misconception of the contemporary Left to proceed from the notion that an advancing capitalism would eventually integrate everyone into normal relations of employment and thus into the 'normal' form of exploitation. In contrast, they claimed that the former's advance would lead to a situation in which a growing share of the population reproduces itself largely outside of wage-labour relations.

By coining the term of the 'housewifisation of wage labour' in this context, they also anticipated in a way today's discussion of precarisation. This expression, used for the first time by Claudia von Werlhof (1988; German 1983, originally in 81-2), describes a type of wage labour which neither serves to ensure one's existence in terms of organisation nor remuneration – work is presented, like that of the housewife, as simply a source of 'additional earnings', although it factually is not. At the time, the Bielefeldians already associated this term with a tendency of globalisation affecting not just women, but rather inaugurating the transition from standard employment relations (which were really only 'normal' during the brief period of Fordism anyway) to deregulated forms of wage labour for everyone. They predicted that over the course of globalisation all wage-earners, men included, would sooner or later be affected by 'housewifisation' (Mies 2014, pp. 218ff). However – and this is the point I would like to address here – they linked this analysis to the question of how people nevertheless reproduce themselves, as it were, 'below' society's replacement level. Mies and Bennholdt-Thomsen found the term 'subsistence production' adequate to answer this question. To them, this implied an economy of survival, which is precisely not an anti-capitalist island, but rather is constantly subsumed by the interests of capital (Bennholdt-Thomsen 1981, p. 31f; Mies 1983, p. 117).[13] Labour in the reproductive sphere is *production*, but one that hardly appears as such and can therefore be silently conquered, since labour in this area – at least as long as people continue to try to survive – seems to be available at no cost, just like 'air and water'. Mies therefore emphasises that 'housewife-ization means the externalization, or ex-territorialization of costs which otherwise would have to be covered by the capitalists' (Mies 1986, p. 110). In today's precarisation debate it would thus be crucial to recognise that it is often not primarily the precarised person him- or herself who bears the brunt of precarisation, but rather those who nevertheless and for the time to come maintain the former's reproduction, often via a complex combination of paid and unpaid labour.

In order to grasp this phenomenon, Bennhold-Thomsen as early as in the 1980s had coined the term 'marginal mass' (1981, p. 43). 'Mass' in this sense implies that today a majority (in the advanced capitalisms such as the one we live in) is compelled to function in such a way. 'Marginal' signifies that they are forced to lead a 'marginal existence', yet one which then becomes 'normality'. With respect to the issue of dispossession in the reproductive sphere that is the subject of this chapter, it is essential to note that Bennholdt-Thomsen does not speak primarily of this marginal mass insofar as it depresses wages – the 'reserve army mechanism' which Marx assumes and to which Dörre also refers (Dörre 2015). For Bennholdt-Thomsen the significance of the 'marginal mass' lies rather in the fact that from the vantage point of capital it reproduces itself at no cost, but is nevertheless available when needed. As a result, although the members of this mass are undoubtedly wage-labourers, their reproduction

[13] This is a central point, as the Bielefeld sociologists are often equated with the 'subsistence perspective' which some of its proponents adopted at a later point and in which subsistence was conceived of as a strategy for overcoming the capitalist mode of production. In their earlier writings, however, the term 'subsistence production' is clearly used exclusively to denote an economy of survival (and its associated overexploitation) generated by capitalism itself. In this regard, the concept is indeed applicable to contemporary forms of precarised lifeforms in the metropolises of capitalism. For examples of a current application of the Bielefeld approach see, for example, Hürtgen (2015, pp. 59–62).

costs are not paid for by capital in any way – an aspect that Marx did not foresee.[14] Bennholdt-Thomsen remarks on this:

> The fact that part of the population provides the necessary subsistence labour without generating costs for capital enormously heightens the possibility of appropriation surplus labour for capital. [...] The marginal mass is not outside or at the margins, but rather represents an integral component of the capitalist system.
>
> Bennholdt-Thomsen therefore labels this subordinating integration 'marginal subsumption'. 'Marginal subsumption' means 'that only a minimal share of the work necessary for their reproduction appears as costs for the capital side', that is, 'reproduction is ultimately left to [the workers] themselves', precisely because they are in part wage-labourers. (Bennholdt-Thomsen 1981, p. 44)

It was the claim that capital has the possibility to extraterritorialise costs that linked the Bielefeld sociologists to Rosa Luxemburg. At the same time, they expanded her thesis of ongoing primitive accumulation with the concept of 'subsistence production'. With Luxemburg's help they placed the interrelationship between paid employment and unpaid reproductive labour at the heart of their own analysis of capital accumulation, thereby developing an understanding of the core function of domestic labour for a process of 'housewifisation' so characteristic of the late capitalist accumulation regime. Since the time of their writing, however, this very sphere – that of unpaid household work – has undergone decisive changes, namely that a share of this work has indeed been converted into wage labour. In other words, though the discussion at the time did address the housewifisation of wage labour, what it did not address (and what was certainly not as virulent as today) is that today the paid care sector itself has become the preferred site of 'housewife-ised' relations of employment.

To understand what is essentially a duplication of the problematic raised by the Bielefeld sociologists, I would like to return to some reflec-

[14] Marx assumed that the wage would have to encompass all the goods needed to reproduce workers and their families. This is how he determines the value of the labour commodity. Marx thus left untheorised the fact that many workers do not engage in waged activities without interruption but nevertheless reproduce themselves during these in between periods. What is central to reproduction understood in this way is the labour performed by family networks.

tions rooted in feminist economics. For it is no coincidence that the latter begins to form in the late 1980s, as the term 'care economy' is developed, unlike in the housework debate (in whose tradition feminist economy only partly stands anyway),[15] to combine paid and unpaid labour.[16] The term 'care' also reflects an historical shift. It enables feminist economics to offer a partial explanation of why the conversion of previously unpaid housework performed by women to the wage-labour form, once demanded by parts of the women's movement as a strategy of emancipation, is not effective in every case, in the sense that it does not always lead to the improvement of women's position in society. In contrast to the previous housework debate, which emerged in response to an era in which paid care work did not yet exhibit the scale nor carry the same importance for the national economy as it does today, feminist economics assumes that it is the waged form of care work which under certain conditions brings new dynamics into play which inevitably result in the care sector remaining a low-wage sector.

An Historically New Situation for Capitalism: The Expansion of Low Value-Added Sectors and the Productivity Dilemma

A few thoughts on economic theory are necessary to better understand why of all things the care sector is currently subject to far-reaching precarisation. To begin with, let us turn to a consideration taken from the regulation school, which emerged in Paris in the mid-1970s and sought

[15] In the form of the publication *Feminist Economics*, founded in 1996. On the partial continuity between the older housework debate and feminist economics of the late 1980s cf. Cağlar (2009, pp. 230–35). It is important to note, however, that feminist economics possesses a distinct theoretical background, as it evolved out of a dispute with neoclassical economics and partly follows the institutional approach. On this, cf. Heck (2010, pp. 45–63).

[16] On this point cf. S. Donath's expression 'the other economy', which concerns 'the direct production and maintenance of human beings' (2001, p. 115). On this, compare the appraisal by Madörin (2014, p. 179f). In reference to Madörin, the care economy encompasses the daily provisions humans require, which means, among other things, that production and 'consumption' cannot be separated (2007, p. 142f, 2006, pp. 277–86). The paid care work sector includes education, health, social services.

to theoretically conceptualise the historic sea change in the mode of accumulation that we know today as the transition from Fordism to post-Fordism.[17] The regulation school assumes that we cannot speak of an ahistorical capitalism as such; we must distinguish between different historical forms of capitalist modes of production which differ according to respective accumulation regimes. Essentially, an accumulation regime denotes the historically specific mode in which private profits are realised. From a feminist perspective, one could add with reference to Silke Chorus that these different accumulation regimes are each accompanied by respective, specifically corresponding historical 'modes of reproduction'.[18]

In order to understand the impact the crisis of Fordism had on the reproductive sector, we must take a look back in economic history to find the reasons that allowed restructuring to appear necessary from the perspective of capital valorisation in the first place. Which were the changes, in response to what? In other words, in the eyes of capital owners, what were the economic reasons that exerted pressure on the Fordist mode of production and apparently also necessitated new modes of reproduction?

Historically speaking – that is, since the beginnings of industrialisation – capitalism has attained profits through productivity increases. For the most part, this also represents the reason why the capitalist mode of production was able to raise the standard of living for the majority of the population. Productivity increases essentially mean that production per time unit is increased quantitatively through technical innovations or the rationalisation of work processes. Consequently, the Fordist phase of prosperity, the economic boom following World War II, can largely be attributed to the fact that as a result of Taylorist work process innovation and other technical innovations, basic necessities became cheaper and cheaper. The associated expansion of production volume represented the starting point for that historical compromise between capital and labour that characterised Fordism: rising profit rates allowed employers to pay high wages which, in turn, enabled the working classes to actually pur-

[17] Cf. Hirsch and Roth (1986, pp. 10–45) and Hirsch (1995, pp. 75–100).

[18] On the expansion of the regulation school cf. the important works by Silke Chorus (2007a, 2011, p. 393f, 2007, pp. 44–100, 2013, pp. 60–99).

chase the products produced, thus securing further demand (Dörre 2015, pp. 32–6). In this context, the expression of the 'thorough capitalisation of lifeworlds' (Hirsch and Roth 1986, pp. 50ff) has been used, meaning that more and more basic goods were produced within the framework of the capitalist mode of production and no longer outside of it – for example, through forms of subsistence economy.

This historical equation collapsed during the crisis of Fordism in the mid-1970s. One major cause of this development was that productivity increases had been declining since the 1960s and resulted in falling profit rates, which could primarily be attributed to the fact that the intensification of work through the Taylorisation of work processes was reaching its limits (Hirsch and Roth 1986, pp. 78–82). Neoliberal structural adjustment programmes therefore initially started here, as employers sought to restore productivity increases and thus profits through other means. These means included a general reduction of the wage level, a breaking of the power of trade unions (see Boltanski and Chiapello 2007) and (as quid pro quo, so to speak) the introduction of new forms of work organisation based less on hierarchy and more on self-organisation (Dörre 2015, pp. 46–51). Besides outsourcing production to low-wage countries, however, new management practices also included forms of work intensification (Boltanski and Chiapello 2007, pp. 142–6), as market risks were 'passed on' directly to the workforce through 'market-centred' forms of direction implemented by employers intended to achieve a consolidation of the principle of competition (Dörre 2015, p. 43f). However, it was not until the breakthrough of the IT revolution at the end of the 1980s that considerable productivity increases (innovations in actual production) became possible. Moreover, for the first time since the stagnation beginning in the 1960s, labour productivity increased as well (Hirsch 1995, p. 88f).

What is central for our concern here is that restructuring also involved, in the first instance, an abandonment of the male breadwinner model. From the perspective of private capital valorisation this represented an economic necessity. It was reinforced by demands of the women's movement which rejected the model as paternalistic, criticised the reduction of female economic activities to a housewife existence and demanded free access to the labour market for women.

One effect of this increase in gainful female economic activity which was both desired and imposed by force was that part of the labour women had previously performed without pay now assumed the form of wage labour. This aspect is so pivotal because it introduced an entirely new dynamic to the equation: the enormous expansion of paid care work and thus the emergence of a significant care sector means that today the share of wage labour that is growing is of little interest to capital owners as far as generating profits through an increase in productivity is concerned. The possibility of productivity increases exists only to a very limited extent in all activities within the care sector: children do not grow and develop faster as a result of technical innovation and nor is it possible to force the alphabet down their throat any quicker; similarly, neither the care of the sick nor assisted living for the elderly can be performed substantially more efficiently through such means. What is true for the goods of commodity production and of the service sector more generally, as feminist economist Mascha Madörin tirelessly points out, does not apply to services in the care sector due to the internal logic of person-oriented services (Madörin 2006, pp. 291–93, 2007, pp. 148–53, 2011, pp. 57–63). Even though we can observe attempts to make these areas more profitable, the prospect of quick profits is rather slim due to the inherent nature of these kinds of services not generating a technically produced commodity, but instead an element of intersubjectivity or a personal relationship (Madörin 2007, p. 153f).[19]

In retrospect we can therefore safely say that the Fordist model of the male breadwinner plus housewife successfully excluded these so-called low value-added activities[20] from the area of production and wage labour, as Silke Chorus notes correctly (2007a, pp. 49, 54, 57f). The Fordist mode of production was a phase of prosperity precisely because production rested largely on *industrial* production enjoying the blessings of productivity increases for quite some time. Seen from this angle, how-

[19] Wherever profits are nevertheless extracted from person-oriented services, such as in privatised nursing services or hospitals, this is only possible by way of the exertion of massive downward pressure on wages, often leading to wages so low they are below the level necessary for care workers' own reproduction. Cf., for example, Chorus (2013, pp. 199–235).

[20] In economics, low value-added denotes any work that cannot be produced faster through productivity increases. Almost all person-oriented services are thus low value-added.

ever, the problem that neoliberal restructuring was supposed to solve has instead been further aggravated by this 'solution': the expansion of that sector which displays very few opportunities for productivity increases exacerbates macroeconomically the very problem of declining profit rates out of which the crisis of Fordism emerged in the first place. Chorus speaks, therefore, of a 'double productivity dilemma' (2007b, pp. 209ff, 2007a, pp. 64–8) in this context.

We thus find ourselves in a completely novel situation as far as the capitalist mode of production is concerned: the share of those types of labour through which private capital valorisation can generate profits is shrinking continuously in relation to those in which conditions are not conducive to valorisation. Linda McDowell and Mascha Madörin calculate for England and Switzerland that the present-day share of the latter type of labour amounts to roughly 30 per cent of the total gross domestic product (Madörin 2007, p. 146f; McDowell 2009, p. 37). This tendency is further aggravated by the fact that care work in advanced western societies, alongside finance and general services, is the sector exhibiting the highest growth rates – assuming it does not become the *only* remaining growth sector following the financial crisis.[21] Government restructuring of the care sector occurring as part of overall restructuring of the welfare state, oftentimes enforced by the employer side, should therefore be understood not least as a response to this aforementioned profitability dilemma. In this sense, it is no coincidence that contemporary neoliberal measures intervene primarily in this area, in the low value-added area of person-oriented services. The care sector has thus become a highly charged economic battleground, as it has the greatest relevance to private profit interests.[22]

It is precisely here, in this sector where primarily women are economically active, that the golden rule of the historical class compromise –

[21] This development can be observed both in the rather conservative care regime in Switzerland (Madörin 2010, p. 100f, 2007, p. 159) and in the largely neoliberalised care regime in the UK (McDowell, 2009, pp. 36–8). Unfortunately, I have no prepared figures available for other countries; impressive figures on the relation of employment in the care sector to the rest of the economy for the New York metropolitan area are also available in Chorus (2013, pp. 199–211).

[22] The low rate of value added in this sector, which was previously left to state-run welfare for precisely this reason, would require a continuous increase in the public spending ration due to the economic dynamic illustrated. On this, cf. Madörin (2011, p. 57, 2010).

rising profits coupled with decent wages – can no longer apply. What we lack today is not mobile phones or refrigerators the production costs of which can be lowered by way of productivity increases. What we lack is the time and money more generally required to care for and assist those who for whatever reason cannot care for themselves, as well as for the care of children, which is by no means ensured by the (ideally full-time) school system. We lack the necessary time because increasingly all employable adults, grandparents included, who used to assume these functions are involved in some kind of gainful economic activity which not only requires them to be available to their employer around the clock, but is also tied to flexibilisation requirements incompatible with most reproductive duties. Yet we also lack the money required to purchase all these (relatively) expensive services on the market,[23] as we no longer have time to perform them ourselves. In contrast to the Fordist era, then, today's scarcity lies not so much in the realm of basic daily consumer goods, but in that of services which only to a very limited extent can be made more profitable or cheaper by means of productivity increases. This leads to completely new struggles over redistribution and, as Silvia Federici correctly points out, to new class relations (2010, p. 2, 2012, p. 22).

The economic dynamic described here represents a phenomenon which, as liberal economist William Baumol had identified as early as the 1960s, necessarily appears in all advanced capitalist societies (Baumol 2012, pp. xvii–xix).[24] What Baumol calls 'diverging productivities' (Baumol 2012, p. 21; compare Madörin 2011, p. 57) between high-value added and low value-added sectors do not automatically pose a problem as such, but most certainly become a problem in the

[23] It should be emphasised that this means a *relative* cost increase for these services in relation to the goods from commodity production as a result of technical innovation. Cf. on this Madörin (2007, p. 150f).

[24] This raises the question as to whether the crisis of over-accumulation Harvey addresses (2003, p. 110f) is perhaps rooted in this problem of diverging productivity, insofar as the problem identified by Baumol is an expression of the fact that an ever increasing share of GDP is low value-added and thus hardly conducive to private profit interests and investment opportunities: what is referred to as 'expanded reproduction' in Marxism cannot or can hardly expand into profitable investment opportunities, due to its expansion in advanced western capitalist societies occurring primarily in the person-oriented service sector.

context of private capital valorisation interests. How this problem makes itself felt, and what consequences it entails for individual men and women and for gender relations as a whole, is determined largely by the political solutions designed to come to grips with this problem. As we know, the current solution is rather business-friendly. The private sector so far seems to have successfully avoided taking on any of the costs entailed by the 'double productivity dilemma'. Instead, it seeks to avoid taking any responsibility for the (in relative terms) ever-increasing reproductive costs whatsoever. It does so by demanding that these services be subordinated to the logic of a market economy. Wherever this is not possible and the state continues to provide these low value-added services, the private sector exerts immense pressure on the state to cut costs, effectively leading to the same outcome: in either case massive downward pressure is exerted on wages in this sector, resulting in relations of reproduction which, as Linda McDowell notes, in parts more resemble early capitalist exploitation than a Fordist social partnership (McDowell 2009, p. 37).

On the whole, we can no longer assume the existence of a general contradiction or conflict of interest between capital and labour, as was the case in Marx's time. In today's capitalism, not all wage-earners are subjected to such downward pressures. Instead, it is mostly those involved in some way or another in paid and unpaid reproduction work, that is, those working in the care sector, who have to confront them. Seen from this angle, the new contradiction of our time can be located between the high-value added and the low value-added sectors of the economy and the respective groups of workers involved in them. At the same time, however, we must remember that women – as Madörin calculates for the Swiss case[25] – spend about four-fifths of their entire working life in the care sector when paid and unpaid activities are counted together. The question as to *what* exactly happens in this sector is thus absolutely central to their position in society. This, in turn, depends on what kind of welfare state compromise is or is not resorted to in response to this 'twofold productivity dilemma'.

[25] This can be assumed valid in terms of scale for the EU member states as well, cf. Madörin (2007, p. 146, 2010, pp. 106–8).

A New Form of *Landnahme*: Targeted Integration into Wage Labour

Naturally, capital has always sought to keep reproduction costs as low as possible. While it was historically able to lower the costs of reproduction by producing the goods of basic consumption at an ever lower cost through technical innovation, this is precisely what is impossible today because an increasing share of reproduction costs consist of person-oriented services which become increasingly expensive in relation to the goods of commodity production (Baumol 2012, pp. 25–32).[26] When Marxists say that capital exhibits the tendency to lower the costs of reproduction, they mean those goods needed for daily basic consumption – which do indeed become cheaper as productivity increases. They do not, however, account for the labour that is required to prepare and process these goods. Nor do they, as a result, see that care work is not reduced by productivity increases nor that this central difference must be taken into consideration if one is to understand how capital lowers the costs of reproduction today: namely, by no longer remunerating households for the time dedicated to care work while at the same time withholding certain wage components that would in fact enable them to purchase these services on the market independently. If the costs of such services increase and thereby assume an ever greater portion of the household budget, then really this should find expression in generally rising wages – which, as we know, is not the case.

As a result, we can identify an externalisation of a part of reproduction costs away from wage components. What is more, then, is that states are pressured into withdrawing their investments in social and individual reproduction, for example over the course of financial crisis-induced

[26] The same applies to the possibility of relocating 'production': while this is unproblematic for industrially produced goods, allowing the West to benefit enormously from the dramatic differences in wages worldwide, most person-oriented services cannot be moved to a low-wage country. There is, however, the phenomenon of care migration, both westwards and vice versa, meaning that people in need of care are moved to nursing homes in a low-wage country specifically established for this purpose.

spending deficits and subsequent structural adjustment measures.[27] In combination, what we find is a form of dispossession and thus of primitive accumulation, primarily targeting the resources of reproduction.[28]

If we consider the welfare state reforms implemented in most western societies over the past thirty years in this light, it becomes clear that the reforms oriented towards the adult worker model and individual responsibility for securing one's livelihood were designed to reduce the share of reproduction costs as a component of total wage costs. In this sense, the adult worker model represents an ideological cloak for a novel form of *Landnahme* that externalises reproduction costs onto private households under the pretext of emancipation. This is the reason why Federici speaks in terms of a globally occurring 'restructuring of the (re-)production of labour power' (2010, pp. 1, 12): the way in which people reproduce themselves is currently subjected to far-reaching changes which, dictated largely by external conditions, ultimately drain households of resources required for their own reproduction in the form of time and money. What must not be forgotten, however, is that this is a process, which occurs mostly silently and thus remains rather imperceptible to those affected – a kind of secret structural adjustment programme for which no official documentation seems to exist.

At this point, it may be useful to again draw a comparison to the current discussion about new *Landnahmen* being conducted in international Marxist contexts. Both David Harvey and the feminist discussion proceed from the assumption that *Landnahmen* must not necessarily be directed at a geographical exterior because capitalism, in a dialectical way, ceaselessly produces this exterior within its own interior anew. David Harvey lists mergers, debt peonage, the looting of pension funds, biopiracy, the commodification of the natural world and the privatisation of the commons such as water, energy, communication and transport, collective landownership and social institutions as examples of such contemporary *Landnahmen* which do not concern a geographical 'exterior', but instead one that has been fabricated within its interior (2003, p. 147).

[27] Federici speaks of a 'disinvestment by the state in the reproduction of the work-force' in this context (2010, 2012, p. 77f).

[28] Ezquerra shows this very clearly in the case of Spain, speaking of the 'New Enclosure of the Reproductive Commons' (2014, p. 1).

At the heart of Harvey's interest in these new forms of primitive accumulation, which he terms 'accumulation by dispossession' (2003, p. 145), is his postulation of a tendency towards over-accumulation inherent in advanced capitalisms. Crises of over-accumulation essentially mean that capital has exhausted profitable investment opportunities. One response to over-accumulation may be that capital in search of investment opportunities is invested in public infrastructural goods and thereby absorbed, only to be reconquered at a later point. Another way is to respond with targeted devaluations, which occur mostly during financial crises: for example, in order to fill a barren government treasury, a railway is sold off cheaply to investors who are then able to generate higher profits than the state could as they are granted limited performance liability and are not obligated to charge socially sustainable prices. When assets are sold far under their market value, over-accumulated capital is then able to realise profits from them. If capital was obliged to purchase these goods at their actual value, there simply would not be any profit to be realised. In the same way, existing capital stock and labour power can also be devalued in a targeted manner. State-decreed austerity programmes over the course of financial crises, for example, cause such devaluations at the local level through the credit policies of international financial institutions. These regional crises are coordinated to the degree that no total collapse results from them. Harvey regards these crises as 'a primary means by which capitalism perpetually creates its own 'other' in order to feed upon it' (2003, p. 137).

Forms of accumulation by dispossession thus represent the means with which to react to crises of over-accumulation which, according to Harvey, have taken centre stage in the overall goings-on related to capitalist crisis – at least since the crisis of Fordism. Financial capital and credit institutions operating under the protection of governments, above all in the USA (and, for the Eurozone, Germany), in Harvey's words constitute the 'umbilical cord that ties together accumulation by dispossession and expanded reproduction' (Harvey 2003, p. 137).

If we then refer back to forms of dispossession affecting households and thus the sphere of reproduction, one difference becomes evident: while such dispossessions and devaluations often assume spectacular forms (during financial crises, for example) and linger in the public consciousness (as illustrated by public debates over the commons), *Landnahme* in the sphere of reproduction occurs rather tacitly and therefore remains largely hidden. This mode of *Landnahme* moreover appears all the more impalpable because of its specific integration into the world of waged employment. While Marx could still assume that although exploitation occurs in wage labour, wages paid would nevertheless have to correspond to the value of the commodity of labour power (that is, covering the elementary costs of its reproduction), this is no longer the case with today's paid care work. Since the care sector as a low value-added sector within the capitalist mode of production must inevitably remain a low-wage sector (in light of the aforementioned reflections taken from economic theory), the people working in this sector, primarily women, remain largely dependent on unpaid labour for their own reproduction. What emerges from this is a complex web of precarised paid care work and unpaid care work: people, mostly women, who work in the care sector below their level of reproduction, must often provide for both themselves and their children – as they are frequently the heads of single-income households[29] – via unpaid reproductive labour, which is, in turn, performed by other women, exposing them to the same mechanism: Because they are only partially available to the labour market, they are also predestined to work in the precarised care sector, which accordingly provides an income insufficient to secure their existence, compelling them to rely on the unpaid labour of other women. It is a never-ending cycle. Thus, the conversion of unpaid labour previously performed by women into wage labour under capitalist conditions has the paradoxical effect that the demand for unpaid labour also rises, yet nobody is available to perform said unpaid labour under the adult worker model.[30]

The reproductive sphere is thus subjected to a *Landnahme*, or exposed to forms of dispossession, in terms of both paid and unpaid care work. In this process both forms interfere with one another in a complex interrelationship. As a result, 'accumulation by dispossession' in the area of reproduction takes on a specific form that contradicts the dominant

[29] Ezquerra (2014, p. 7) also emphasises this point in the case of Spain.

[30] Federici (2010) correctly emphasises that Marx's productivist bias led him to overlook the fact that growth in productivity is always accompanied by an increase in poverty of a certain part of the population.

assumption in the current discussion about a New *Landnahme*, namely that an 'ongoing primitive accumulation' entails forms of dispossession outside of the wage form.

However, this is precisely the aspect for which Rosa Luxemburg's analysis of the capitalist mode of production as one that 'depends in all of its relations on the simultaneous existence of noncapitalist strata and societies' (Luxemburg 1913, p. 262) turns out to be so useful. When she states that 'the movement of capitalist accumulation requires an environment of non-capitalist social formations, that it is in a constant process of metabolism with the latter as it proceeds, and that it can only exist for as long as it finds itself within this milieu' (1913, p. 263), she underlines that this relation is an *articulation* of distinct modes of production. In her insistence that the capitalist mode of production both appropriates 'noncapitalist means of production' (1913, p. 262) and also utilises these non-capitalist strata as a 'reservoir of labor-power' (1913, p. 265), she not only emphasises that this articulation represents a distinct form of *Landnahme*, but also provides important clues as to how this articulation could be theoretically conceptualised in the first place – namely, as a form of subsumption in which the subsistence production of a given mode of production is subsumed under the capitalist mode of production as a whole. Although Rosa Luxemburg does not use the term subsistence production herself (at least not in the well-known older translations), her wording clearly indicates that she has the subsistence resources of what she called 'noncapitalist forms of production' in mind. In this sense, we could say that she ultimately suggests a subsumption of the subsistence production of 'non-capitalist strata' (1913, p. 262) under the capitalist mode of production (Bennholdt-Thomsen 1981, p. 38).

The Articulation of Modes of Production: Luxemburg and the Analysis of Neoliberal Restructuring of Individual and Social Reproduction

It is this aspect of an articulation between distinct modes of production that renders Luxemburg's work so fruitful for a feminist standpoint, which is, by definition, one 'from the viewpoint of social reproduction'

(Federici 2010, p. 9). It was this notion of an articulation of distinct modes of production that prompted the Bielefeld sociologists to arrive at the conclusion (which is still relevant today) that the expansion of capitalism and the associated proliferation of the wage form is inevitably accompanied by an expansion of subsistence production as early as they did.[31] This aspect is particularly valid for the most important change in reproduction since the crisis of Fordism, namely that a share of the unpaid housework previously performed by women was converted into wage labour. Contrary to what could have been expected and what the women's movement at the time had indeed hoped for,[32] this change did not lead to any significant reduction in unpaid work performed in households (Chorus 2007b, p. 208). Thus, in the words of Geneviève Fraisse, 'servitude' remains 'a puzzle for the emancipation of women' (Fraisse 2009, p. 14). At least as far as reproduction is concerned, it seems that capitalism not only creates its own 'exterior', but also has a great interest in preserving this exterior in order to continue to live off its resources. The concept of articulation captures this aspect far more precisely than that of *Landnahme* or even dispossession: in order to serve as a constant supplier of hidden resources, the 'exterior' need not be expropriated but – on the contrary – preserved.

Using Bennholdt-Thomsen's concept of the 'marginal mass' we can describe this resource transfer in the sense that the advance of the capitalist mode of production brings about a situation in which people are increasingly forced to reproduce themselves outside of wage labour relations. The rise in precarious wage labour observed in the advanced capitalisms lives integrally off the resources of subsistence production. We must note, however, that each type of precarised wage labour taps into reproductive labour resources – and thus 'surplus labour' situated outside wage labour, which flows back into the latter in the form of surplus labour – in a specific manner.

---

[31] Hürtgen (2015, pp. 59ff) also analyses this for western post-Fordist societies, likewise with reference to the Bielefeld sociologists.

[32] This was by no means undisputed, however; cf. *Frauen in der Offensive* ('Women on the Offensive') (1974) which called this strategy into question with the slogan 'Wage Labour Won't Set You Free' (*Lohnarbeit macht nicht frei*).

> 'The basic common feature of all subsistence production within the capitalist mode of production', Bennholdt-Thomsen writes, 'lies in the fact that capital precisely does not assume responsibility for the labour time required for the reproduction of labour power and families'. 'This surplus labour distinguishes itself from that surplus labour in the context of wage labour in that it is expended in a work process not directly controlled by capital [...].' (Bennholdt-Thomsen 1981, p. 34f)

Therefore, the crucial aspect in Bennholdt-Thomsen's 'marginal subsumption' is not the question of a conversion from unpaid to paid labour as such,[33] but the very preservation of unpaid labour required by the post-Fordist accumulation regime – or, more precisely, the interrelation of paid and unpaid care work constitutive of post-Fordism which *together* subsidise 'normal' wage labour. Correspondingly, Madörin calculates for Switzerland that paid and unpaid care work combined account for about two-thirds of GDP when GDP is expanded to encompass unpaid labour,[34] which means that these two-thirds of economic activity are essentially the foundation on which the actual remainder of GDP – as calculated – is based (Madörin 2007, p. 147).

The notion of a subsumption or articulation of another mode of production is in a certain sense further elaborated by feminist economics, introducing the term of the care economy to deliberately encompass paid and unpaid care work in one and the same expression. The term care economy takes the latter's central feature – of serving the 'production and reproduction of the material conditions of life' (Madörin 2011, p. 59) – and conceptualises it as a distinct mode of production, which nevertheless – within capitalist relations – is subsumed under the remaining wage labour. The emphasis on this interference between the two forms of care – which has led Susan Donath to describe the care sector as 'the other economy' (2001) – is what allows such an analysis to go beyond the common critique of neoliberalism, whose one-sided focus on wage

[33] Cf. on this also Ezquerra (2014, p. 7) who argues that the question of *Landnahme* in the area of reproduction cannot be reduced to the commodification of care work, as the unpaid care sector remains central as a possible site of hidden cost absorption.

[34] For Switzerland, expanded GDP has been determined by the Federal Statistical Office through time budget surveys of private households since the year 2000. These figures exist for most EU countries; for Germany cf. Schaffer and Stahmer (2006).

labour principally associates privatisation with a mere dismantling of welfare state standards in the sphere of wage labour (Dörre 2015, pp. 62–6, 2013, pp. 102–5; Dörre and Haubner 2012, pp. 80–90). Privatisation, however, always involves a strategy of restructuring reproductive labour and does not take place simply in one or the other area (that is, of paid or unpaid work) respectively, but rather sets them in a certain relation to one another. Canadian political scientist Janine Brodie therefore believes that privatisation always entails a double process (1994, p. 56, 1997, pp. 235–7), in that the conversion to a commodity form is inevitably accompanied by a privatisation of social costs.

In consequence, for Brodie privatisation entails two distinct, yet nevertheless interrelated strategies of governing: either subordination to the commodity form – the transformation of public into purchasable private goods – or the shifting of responsibility from public to private, from collective to individual (see Brodie 2004, p. 23).

This double aspect of privatisation, that is to say the fact that the relocation of previously public services and goods to the 'private sector' is complemented by its flipside, the externalisation of costs to the 'private sphere' (Brodie 2004, p. 23) and thus by a kind of restructuring that always targets the resources of household reproduction, allows us to address a widespread misunderstanding in the reception of the Bielefeld approach: it is important to distinguish between on the one hand the 'subsistence perspective', which some of the authors (Mies 2014) later adopted, and 'subsistence production' on the other. While the former can be accused of presenting a rather simplistic notion of the possibilities for overcoming existing social relations, specifically by proposing a return to local, community-oriented production (Federici 2012), the theorem of subsistence production is a consistent theoretical instrumentarium for the analysis of the expanding form of another mode of production under capitalist conditions which is not pre-capitalist, but rather represents a specific outcome of capitalist *Landnahmen*.[35] In this sense, the Bielefeld

[35] Correspondingly, Bennholdt-Thomsen criticises the Marxist disregard of this mode of production and the failure to recognise its significance for capital accumulation (1981, p. 38):'Even though it appears to be dealing with it, the actual analysis of subsistence production is evaded by banning its relations of production from the capitalist mode of production by definition, depicting them as pre-capitalist or non-capitalist.'

sociologists must be credited with the achievement of having generated interest in the specificity of household modes of production, which constitutes the precondition for an understanding of how households, as individual units of subsistence production, can provide resources which enter into capital circuits without appearing as such.

The focus on the more spectacular forms of dispossession that characterises the current discussion around new *Landnahmen* thereby partially obscures this impalpable and therefore silently occurring resource transfer. The latter is not simply robbery, but rather a form of articulation between distinct modes of production which the Left has yet to theorise adequately. Neoliberalism is more than just the privatisation of the commons. Instead, it seems to cultivate a 'metabolism' (Luxemburg 1913, p. 302) with a carefully cultivated exterior from which it takes what it needs and to which it passes on what it does not. Consequently, privatisation also affects the supposedly private, created by capitalism for the sole purpose of feeding off it – more or less silently, or at least undisturbed by any theoretical scrutiny from the Left. Even today, then, this resource drain on households and on the care sector as a whole takes place largely undetected by Left theorisation and the scandalous nature of neoliberal restructuring is not fully detected.

Conclusion

Rosa Luxemburg's thought proves useful for a feminist approach precisely because she shared the objective of theoretically accommodating and thereby rendering visible the forms of exploitation previously neglected by Marxist theory formation and thus once invisible. Even though she sought to comprehend the relevance of the most brutal forms of colonial warfare to capitalist accumulation, and we (at least in the western centres of capitalist production) are no longer confronted with this kind of violence, there is nevertheless an ongoing silent war which, similar to the colonial wars of Luxemburg's time, does not affect the main political actors. It can still be argued, however, that both cases turn on the same topic: the extraction of means of subsistence from a majority of the population in order to subordinate it to the self-valorisation of value.

In any case, Rosa Luxemburg's deliberations offer a reading of ongoing primitive accumulation that, by applying the concept of an articulation between distinct modes of production, allows us to account theoretically for the expansion of the care sector as well as the altered conditions of domestic labour in the post-Fordist accumulation regime. The concept of articulation is so crucial because it allows us to conceive of reproduction in both its paid and unpaid forms as a distinct mode of production that is subsumed under another mode of production. This is the only way to take into account the internal logic of the care sector, which otherwise has no corresponding model within the Marxist tradition. Traditional Marxism possesses no concept of the interrelation of paid and unpaid work typical of the care sector.

It is the remarkable achievement of the Bielefeld sociologists to have recognised the relevance of such forms of exploitation as early as the end of the 1970s. The question as to whether their adaptation of Rosa Luxemburg's imperialism theory to a 'softer' topic such as reproductive labour was correct or not, or, on the contrary, whether it was through this that they recognised how the area of reproductive labour becomes a central battleground as capitalism advances in the first place, will have to be answered elsewhere.

Bibliography

Backhouse, M., Gerlach, O., Kalmring, S., & Nowak, A. (Eds.) (2013). *Die globale Einhegung – Krise ursprünglicher Akkumulation und Landnahmen im Kapitalismus*. Münster: Westfälisches Dampfboot.

Baumol, W. J. (2012). *The cost disease. Why computers get cheaper and health care doesn't*. New Haven and London: Yale University Press.

Bennholdt-Thomsen, V. (1981). Subsistenzproduktion und erweiterte Reproduktion. Ein Beitrag zur Produktionsweisendiskussion. In H. G. Backhaus et al. (Eds.), *Gesellschaft: Beiträge zur Marxschen Theorie 14* (pp. 30–51). Frankfurt am Main: Suhrlamp.

Boltanski, L., & Chiapello, E. (2007). *The new spirit of capitalism*. London and New York: Verso.

Brodie, J. (1994). Shifting the boundaries: Gender and the politics of restructuring. In I. Bakker (Ed.), *The strategic silence. Gender and economic policy* (pp. 46–60). London: Zed Books.
Brodie, J. (1997). Meso-discourses, state forms and the gendering of liberal-democratic citizenship. *Citizenship Studies, 1*(2), 223–242.
Brodie, J. (2004). Die Re-Formierung des Geschlechterverhältnisses. Neoliberalismus und die Regulierung des Sozialen. *Widerspruch, 46*(24), 1, 19–32.
Cağlar, G. (2009). Transnationale Wissensnetzwerke und Geschlechterpolitik im Feld der internationalen Wirtschafts- und Handelspolitik. In G. Cağlar (Ed.), *Gender and economics. Feministische Kritik der politischen Ökonomie* (pp. 278–303.). Wiesbaden: VS.
Chorus, S. (2007a). *Ökonomie und Geschlecht? Regulationstheorie und Geschlechterverhältnisse im Fordimus und Postfordismus*. Saarbrücken: VDM Verlag.
Chorus, S. (2007b). Who cares? Kapitalismus, Geschlechterverhältnisse und Frauenarbeit. Regulationstheoretische Sehkorrekturen. *Feministische Studien. Zeitschrift für interdisziplinäre Frauen- und Geschlechterforschung, 25*(2), 202–216.
Chorus, S. (2011). Care-Seiten in der politischen Ökonomie'. *In Das Argument (Care – eine feministische Kritik der politischen Ökonomie), 53*(3), 392–401.
Chorus, S. (2013). *Care-Ökonomie im Postfordismus. Perspektiven einer integralen Ökonomietheorie*. Münster: Westfälisches Dampfboot.
De Angelis, M. (2007). *The beginning of history. Value strugles and global capital.* London: Pluto Press.
Donath, S. (2001). The other economy. A suggestion for a distinctively feminist economics. *Feminist Economics, 6*(1), 115–123.
Dörre, K. (2009). Die neue Landnahme. Dynamiken und Grenzen des Finanzmarktkapitalismus. In K.Dörre, St. Lessenich, H. Rosa: Soziologie, Kapitalismus, Kritik (pp21–86). Frankfurt/M: Suhrkamp.
Dörre, K. (2012). 'Landnahme'. *Historisch-kritisches Wörterbuch des Marxismus, 8*(1), 644–688.
Dörre, K. (2013). Landnahme und die Grenzen sozialer Reproduktion. Zur gesellschaftstheoretischen Bedeutung Rosa Luxemburgs. In I. Schmidt (Ed.), *Rosa Luxemburgs ‚Akkumulation des Kapitals'. Die Aktualität von ökonomischer Theorie, Imperialismuserklärung und Klassenanalyse* (pp. 82–116.). Hamburg: VSA.
Dörre, K. (2015). The new Landnahme: Dynamics and limits of financial market capitalism. In K. Dörre, S. Lessenich, & H. Rosa (Eds.), *Sociology, capitalism critique* (pp. 11–66). London and New York: Verso.

Dörre, K., & Haubner, T. (2012). Landnahme Durch Bewährungsproben – Ein Konzept für die Arbeitssoziologie. In K. Dörre, D. Sauer, & V. Wittke (Eds.), *Kapitalismustheorie und Arbeit. Neue Ansätze soziologischer Kritik*. Frankfurt am Main: Campus Verlag, pp. 63–108.

Ezquerra, S. (2014). Spain, economic crisis, and the new enclosure of the reproductive commons. *Montly Review, 65*(11).

Federici, S. (2010). The reproduction of labour-power in the global economy, Marxist theory and the unfinished feminist revolution, Reading for Jan. 27, 2009, UC Santa Cruz seminar. *The crisis of social reproduction and feminist struggle*. https://caringlabor.wordpress.com/2010/10/25/silvia-federici-the-reproduction-of-labour-power-in-the-global-economy-marxist-theory-and-the-unfinished-feminist-revolution/. Last accessed 4 Feb 2015.

Federici, S. (2012). Der Feminismus und die Politik der Commons. In S. Federici (Ed.), *Der Aufstand aus der Küche. Reproduktionsarbeit im globalen Kapitalismus und die unvollendete feministische Revolution* (pp. 87–105). Münster: Westfälisches Dampfboot.

Feministische Autorinnengruppe (2013). Das Theorem der neuen Landnahme: eine feministische Rückeroberung. In H. Baumann, I. Bischel, et al. (Eds.), *Care statt Crash. Sorgeökonomie und die Überwindung des Kapitalismus. Denknetz Jahrbuch 2013* (pp. 99–118). Zürich: Denknetz.

Fraisse, G. (2009). *Service ou servitude. Essay sur les femmes toutes maines*. Paris: Editions Le Bord de l'eau.

Frauen in der Offensive (1974). *Lohn für Hausarbeit oder: Auch Berufstätigkeit macht nicht frei*. München: Trikont Verlag.

Hürtgen, S. (2015). Das Konzept der strukturellen Heterogenität und die Analyse fragmentierter Wachstumsgesellschaften in Europa. University of Jena, unpublished manuscript.

Harvey, D. [1982] (1999) *The limits to capital*. Oxford: Basil Blackwell.

Harvey, D. (2001). *Spaces of capital: Towards a critical geography*. New York: Routledge.

Harvey, D. (2003). *The new imperialism*. Oxford: Oxford University Press.

Heck, S. (2010). Von ‚Reproduktion'zu ‚Care'. Analysen feministischer Ökonomie, 1960s to 1990s. University of Hannover, unpublished Master's thesis.

Hirsch, J. (1995). *Der nationale Wettbewerbsstaat. Staat, Demokratie und Politik im globalen Kapitalismus*. Berlin and Amsterdam: ID Verlag.

Hirsch, J., & Roth, R. (1986). *Das neue Gesicht des Kapitalismus. Vom Fordismus zum Postfordismus*. Hamburg: VSA.

Luxemburg, R. [1913] (2015). The accumulation of capital: A contribution to the economic theory of imperialism. In *The complete works of Rosa Luxemburg, volume II, economic writings 2.* pp. 7–344. London: Verso.

Madörin, M. (2006). Plädoyer für eine eigenständige Theorie der Care-Ökonomie. In T. Niechoj & M. Tullney (Eds.), *Geschlechterverhältnisse in der Ökonomie* (pp. 277–297). Marburg: Metropolis.

Madörin, M. (2007). Neoliberalismus und die Reorganisation der Care-Ökonomie. Eine Forschungsskizze. In Denknetz (Ed.), *Zur politischen Ökonomie der Schweiz. Eine Annäherung. Jahrbuch 2007* (pp. 141–162). Zürich: Denknetz.

Madörin, M. (2010). Care-Ökonomie – eine Herausforderung für die Wirtschaftswissenschaften. In C. Bauhardt & G. Cağlar (Eds.), *Gender and Economics. Feministische Kritik der politischen Ökonomie* (pp. 81–103). Wiesbaden: VS Verlag.

Madörin, M. (2011). Das Auseinanderdriften der Arbeitsproduktivitäten: Eine feministische Sicht. In Denknetz (Ed.), *Gesellschaftliche Produktivität jenseits der Warenform. Jahrbuch 2011* (pp. 56–70). Zürich: Denkwerk.

Madörin, M. (2014). Kommentar zu Donaths Artikel aus der Sicht einer feministischen Politökonomin. In I. Bischel, U. Knobloch, et al. (Eds.), *Kritik des kritischen Denkens. Denknetz Jahrbuch 2014* (pp. 178–187). Zürich: Denknetz.

Madörin, M., & Soiland, T. interview(2013). Care Ökonomie? Offene Fragen und politische Implikationen. In H. Baumann, I. Bischel, et al. (Eds.), *Care statt Crash. Sorgeökonomie und die Überwindung des Kapitalismus. Denknetz Jahrbuch 2013* (pp. 84–98). Zürich: Denknetz.

Mandel, E. (1972). *Late capitalism.* London: Humanities Press.

Marx, K. (1867). *Capital. A critique of political economy, volume I.* London: Penguin.

Marx, K. (1885). *Capital. A critique of political economy, volume II.* London: Penguin.

McDowell, L. (2009). The rise of the service economy. In *Working bodies. Interactive service employment and workplace identities* (pp. 25–48). Malden and Oxford: Wiley-Blackwell.

Mies, M. (1983). Subsistenzproduktion, Hausfrauisierung, Kolonisierung. *Beiträge zur feministischen Theorie und Praxis, 9–10*(6), 115–124.

Mies, M. (1986). *Patriarchy and accumulation on a world scale. Women in the international division of labour.* London: Zed Books.

Mies, M. (2007). Patriarchy and accumulation on a world scale – revisited. *Journal of Green Economics, 1*(3–4), 268–275.

Mies, M. (2014). Housewifisation – Globalisation – Subsistence-perspective. In M. Linden and K.H. Roth, *Beyond Marx*. pp. 209–239. Leiden: Brill.

Perlmann, M. (2000). *The invention of capitalism: Classical political economy and the secret history of primitive accumulation*. Durham: Duke University Press.

Schaffer, A., & Stahmer, C. (2006). Erweitertes Gender-BIP – Eine geschlechtsspezifische Analyse des traditionellen Bruttoinlandproduktes und die Haushaltsproduktion in Deutschland. *Jahrbücher für Nationalökonomie und Statistik, 226*(3), 308–328.

The Commoner. (2012). "Care Work" and the Commons, 15. http://www.commoner.org.uk/wp-content/uploads/2012/01/commoner_issue-15.pdf.

Von Werlhof, C. (1988). The proletarian is dead: Long live the housewife!. In von Werlhof, C. von and M. Mies, V. Bennholdt-Thomsen (eds), Women. The last colony. pp. 168–181 London: Zed Books.

Zeller, C. (Ed.) (2004). *Die globale Enteignungsökonomie*. Münster: Westfälisches Dampfboot.

9

Limits to Landnahme. Growth Dilemma as Challenge

Klaus Dörre

People have not only been speaking, but actively complaining about capitalism for quite some time now. Complaining–the original form of social critique–is widespread in everyday consciousness, to the extent that it even reaches the ears of economic elites. Correspondingly, the founder of the World Economic Forum in Davos, Klaus Schwab, spoke of a planet suffering from 'burnout syndrome', only to conclude that 'capitalism in its current form does not fit the world around us.' (BBC, 24 January 2012)[1] of such arguments are even being heard among economic elites,

The original version of this chapter was revised.
An erratum to this chapter can be found at DOI 10.1057/978-1-137-60108-7_12

[1] The Allensbach polling institute confronted a representative population sample starting at 16 years of age with the question: 'Recently, someone said: "capitalism, in its current form; no longer fits the world around us." Do you agree with that or do you disagree?' While 48 per cent agreed with the statement, only 18 per cent disagreed, and 34 per cent indicated they were undecided (Allensbach Archiv IfD-Umfrage 10,086).

K. Dörre (✉)
Friedrich-Schiller-Universität Jena
Institut für Soziologie
Lehrstuhl für Arbeits-, Industrie- und Wirtschaftssoziologie, Jena, Germany

J. Dellheim, F.O. Wolf (eds.), *Rosa Luxemburg: A Permanent Challenge for Political Economy*, DOI 10.1057/978-1-137-60108-7_9

then capitalism seems to be in bad shape indeed. Voices predicting a slow withering away of the capitalist social formation are also growing within the social sciences (Wallerstein et al. 2013). Yet while the debate about an imminent end to capitalism has been established in the mainstream of the social sciences (cf. Streeck 2014), the financialised version of this social formation continues to dictate social reality, at least in the old capitalist centres and despite the global crisis of 2008–9. Phrases such as the 'Strange Non-Death of Neo-Liberalism' (Crouch 2011) or the 'Triumph of failed Ideas' (Lehndorff 2012) suggest a mantra of 'keep calm and carry on'. The world stumbles from one crisis to the next, yet the political future apparently belongs to radical free-market recipes from pre-crisis times.

Predictions of decay to the left, continuity or even radicalisation of market fundamentalism to the right–how does this fit together? Is capitalism really coming to an end? Is it making way for, as some have suggested (Collins 2013), a post-capitalist exploitation society? Is there any possibility for a neo-social democratic-regulated variant (Mann 2014)? Or are we indeed entering a window of opportunity for a transformation towards a democratic, egalitarian community? The following chapter grapples with these questions. It proceeds from the assumption that global capitalism is in a structural crisis, an economic-ecological double or 'pincer grip crisis' (Sakar 2010). Nevertheless, this social formation will not die off in the foreseeable future. Capitalism, as runs the second hypothesis, does not come to an end by itself, but it can certainly be overcome. I will substantiate this view in five steps. Starting with the question as to what capitalism actually is (1), I will then turn to the expansive dynamic of capitalist *Landnahmen* (2, 3), before finally discussing the question of whether the capitalist mode of (re-)production can be overcome and how this can be realised (4, 5).

What Is Capitalism?

As long as contemporary sociology had not completely given up on 'thinking big', it was content to spell out capitalism in the plural. Surely, there can be no doubt that different varieties of capitalism exist and that diverging institutional systems influence the basic rules according to which distinct capitalisms function. However, there is a 'astonishingly resilient elemental kernel' (Vogl 2014, p. 95) that can be identified throughout all varieties of capitalism. Capitalism is not confined to the sub-system of the economy. It is not a homogenous system, but rather 'a particular way of organizing the relationship between economic processes, social order, and technologies of government in accordance with the mechanisms of capital reproduction' (Vogl 2014, p. 96). Understood in this sense, capitalism represents a social formation. Even though Karl Marx (1867) only rarely used this term,[2] he is widely seen as the father of social-scientific analysis of capitalism. Classical sociological theories of capitalism, however, have emerged largely only after and in analysis of Marx. According to Dobb (1946, pp. 1–13), three basic definitions of capitalism can be identified.

The first definition, and the one perhaps most commonly used in sociology, comes from Werner Sombart. According to Sombart, capitalism depicts a certain economic disposition combining the entrepreneur and adventurer with the calculating, rational 'bourgeois spirit'. This economic mindset creates its own organisations and subjects (Sombart 1928, p. 25). Max Weber formulated this thought slightly differently: in his view, we can speak of capitalism if the fulfilment of the needs of a group of people is founded on rational enterprise: 'Where capitalistic acquisition is rationally pursued, the corresponding action is adjusted to calculations in terms of capital' (Weber 1930, p. xxxii). An enterprise can be said to be capitalist if its profitability is managed by calculative balances and accounting. According to Weber's definition, a capitalist mindset already existed in antiquity; it was only the modern nation state, however, which allowed for a consolidation of capitalism in its modern-occidental variant (Weber 1921, p. 901). Capitalism in its modern form becomes a 'fateful force'; 'in a wholly capitalistic order of society, an individual capitalistic enterprise which did not take advantage of its opportunities for profit-making would be doomed to extinction' (Weber 1930, p. xxxi).

A second definition describes capitalism as a trade system, money economy or 'organization of production for a distant market' (Dobb

[2] Marx actually spoke of the capital relation or of the capitalist mode of production.

1946, p. 6). This definition stems to a large extent from the German historical school's theory of development. According to this definition, the expansion of market relations increases the distance a commodity travels from producer to consumer. It is only this spatio-temporal expansion of market socialisation that paves the way for an economic system in which the drive for profits becomes the prime motivator of a certain class of actors. Capitalism is in this view an 'economy of exchange' (Arthur Nußbaum 1925, compare Pirenne 1947), the guiding principle of which is the unrestrained pursuit of profit. The emergence of capitalism is consequently associated with the development of merchant or mercantile capitalism in the 12th century. Here we find parallels to Fernand Braudel's definition of capitalism (Braudel 1984; Annales School) and to world-systems theory (Wallerstein 1984). In their view, the capitalist money economy emerges in the northern Italian city states during the 16th century. Braudel distinguishes systematically between market economy and capitalism. Capitalism signifies the exploitation of market society through networks of social power. The sphere of market economy, small-scale entrepreneurship and trades is not really capitalist production in the proper sense. Accordingly, capitalism–the sphere of large fortunes, capitals and enterprises–can never pervade society entirely, for there is 'a dialectic still very much alive between capitalism on the one hand, and its antithesis, the "non-capitalism" of the lower level on the other. It is sometimes said that big business tolerates small firms [...] The truth is that they need the small firms' (Braudel 1984, p. 630 f.). Capitalism requires a hierarchy of social spaces and modes of production, and 'it takes up a position at the top of the hierarchy, whether or not this was created by itself' (Braudel 1984, p. 65).

The Annales School and world-systems theory address a third definition which has emerged from Marxian theory. For Marx, neither the pursuit of profit and calculative behaviour nor the emergence of long-distance trade, the credit system or certain classes of merchants and financiers represent sufficient preconditions for identifying capitalist socialisation: 'Capitalism could be regarded as being present as soon as the acts of production and of retail sale came to be separated in space and time by the intervention of a wholesale merchant who advanced money for the purchase of wares with the object of subsequent sale at a profit' (Dobb 1946, p. 6). Capitalism can be identified by the emergence of an economic mode in which, as runs the basic rule of capitalist production, accumulated money (M) is invested in commodities (C) with the aim of generating more money (M')–or M-C-M'–and the processes required for this aim (production, circulation, consumption) are continuously reproduced on an expanding scale. The transformation of labour power and natural resources into capital which is then fed back into the economic cycle with the aim of profit maximisation, that is to say, the increase of the capital to be re-invested, is what characterises the capitalist social formation. Only with the onset of the Industrial Revolution does capitalism begin to reproduce itself largely on its own foundations.[3] Its emergence requires the division of society into classes of capitalists and wage labourers, respectively. Even though the capitalist mode of production generalises the exchange of equivalents on commodity markets, it nevertheless rests on the exploitation of wage-earners by the class of owners of the means of production, who appropriate the surplus value generated. Class struggle, conceived of as the constant battle to reconcile conflicting interests, competitive relationships and conflicts among diverging groups and individuals with the objective of valorisation, represents one of the main driving forces of capitalist development.

In the following, I will draw on the Marxian concept of capitalism. That said, it can only be sensibly applied today by integrating some central components of the other two aforementioned definitions of capitalism. There are some contemporary sociological conceptions which claim to do so by addressing and combining the elements of classical definitions of capitalism in different ways (Fulcher 2004; Wright 2010). Boltanski and Chiapello's minimal definition of capitalism (2003, 2007), with which I generally agree, thus contains three characterising indicators: in reference to Marx (a), the necessity of unrestricted capital accumulation in a monetary form which gradually detaches itself from material-substantial wealth and thus becomes a kind of a perpetuum mobile; as a new element (b), a system of competition in which each actor is constantly challenged by the actions of other actors and a situation of permanent restlessness is created, making '[s]elf-preservation [...] a very strong motivation for

[3] Theories of capitalist Landnahme (as I would espouse) challenge this notion and point out the necessity of periodic stimulation of the accumulation process by applying instruments of extra-economic state power.

capitalists–[…] a never-ending catalyst for the accumulation process' and, based on Weber and Sombart (c), an ideology 'that justifies people's commitments to capitalism, and which renders this commitment attractive' (Boltanski and Chiapello 2005, p. 241).

At the same time though, the 'spirit of capitalism' is not simply a circumstance of an ideological 'superstructure' determined by the material 'base' of capitalist socialisation. Rather, this 'spirit' imposes limits on the accumulation process, as it allows, for example, for differentiation between legitimate and illegitimate profits (Boltanski and Chiapello 2005, p. 292). The formula (or basic rule) of M-C-M' is thus the essence of an 'absurd system' (Boltanski and Chiapello 2005, p. 290) which subjects the activity of both capitalists and wage-earners to an abstract purpose that is separate from their actual life activity. For the mass of both wage-earners as well as small business owners, tradesmen, peasants, welfare recipients and their families, then, the rule of C-M-C′ essentially applies. These groups work in order to perhaps improve their life conditions at some point. The transformation of absurdity into subjective meaning is the magic of the respective 'spirit of capitalism', or, more precisely: the institutions, practices and social conflicts from which this hegemonic spirit forms. The actual hegemonic capitalist spirit that varies and modifies the basic rules of capitalism and adjusts them to specific conditions represents the means through which capitalist principles intrude upon areas in society that actually follow quite different principles of rationality. A capitalist society can only be identified at the point where 'capitalist principles exhibit a certain dominance' and tend to 'proliferate into other spheres beyond the economy' and influence even non-capitalist relations (Kocka 2013, p. 12). Capitalist development thus implies the expansion of a capitalist social order–which as such varies–to previously non-capitalist sectors and milieus.

How Does Capitalism Develop? Schumpeter and Polanyi

This raises the question of the driving forces of capitalist development. Just as the general characteristics of capitalism are the subject of controversies in the social sciences, so are its historical transformations. Marx contended that the generalisation of wage labour and the resulting social polarisation would create the social preconditions for a revolutionary overthrow of capitalism. This hope did not materialise as such–even though there have been attempts at socialist transformation and societal formation which at one point covered half the globe. That said, even advanced capitalism has undergone several transformations in which the institutions, modes of production and life forms of capitalist societies have witnessed qualitative changes.

Most authors in the social sciences distinguish between two major transformations: (a) the transition from early, 'anarchic' market capitalism to organised capitalism at the end of the 19th and early 20th century which led to a differentiation of different developmental paths (The New Deal in the USA, fascism in continental Europe, Industrial Democracy in Sweden) following the World Economic Crisis of 1929–1932, and (b) the transformation of organised capitalism into a revitalised market capitalism which began in the 1970s (Fulcher 2004, pp. 57–125) and escalated during the crisis of 2008–09. Over the course of these transformations, sociological theories of capitalism have in turn changed as well.

The first metamorphosis of capitalism was the subject of at least two significant theoretical innovations. The first came from Joseph Schumpeter, who interpreted the capitalist dynamic as a constant process of creative destruction. Schumpeter places the creative labour of a businessman, as a special 'leader' (*Führergestalt*), at the heart of this theory. The entrepreneur does not invent the new, but he facilitates its breakthrough. His (or her) social milieu is constituted by middle classes eager to advance socially and whose members take their chances at points of decline in a production cycle, take entrepreneurial risks, market new inventions and thereby engender permanent structural change. The result is an ever increasing multiplicity of products, increasingly sophisticated product differentiation and permanently improving product quality. Schumpeter thus points to a condition of capitalist dynamic which Marx left underexposed: innovation processes require breathing room for creative activity (which includes implicit knowledge). If these spaces are curtailed too much, the innovation dynamic may be weakened. Schumpeter therefore feared that organised capitalism with its tendencies of bureaucratisation would undermine the innovative tendencies of enterprises and ultimately cause the (undesired) triumph of socialism (Schumpeter, [1912] 1934, [1942] 1943).

While Schumpeter considers the creative destruction driven by market competition to be the agent of capitalist development, Karl Polanyi implies an opposing emphasis. In his *Great Transformation* (Polanyi 1944) Polanyi describes the first metamorphosis of capitalism as a double movement: the social embedding of markets triggers a preservation of quite dysfunctional regulatory systems as a response, whose violent destruction then leads to social catastrophe, to fascism and war. Polanyi's real discovery was the particular character of labour, land and money, which he describes–more precisely than Marx–as fictitious commodities. According to Polanyi, labour is 'only another word for the forms of life of common people' which meant 'that the development of the market system would be accompanied by a change in the organization of society itself. All along the line, human society had become an accessory of the economic system' (Polanyi 1944, p. 79). Labour is a commodity which, similar to land and money, can only be bought and sold on markets with the aid of a fiction: 'the alleged commodity "labor power" cannot be shoved about, used indiscriminately, or even left unused, without affecting also the human individual who happens to be the bearer of this peculiar commodity. In disposing of them one would, incidentally, dispose of the moral entity "man" attached to that tag' (Polanyi 1944, p. 76).

What Schumpeter considers to be an incentive for innovation, namely the unleashing of market competition, Polanyi describes as a 'satanic mill'; a pure market economy would simply destroy society. What is interesting is that both basic motives, innovation and critique of the market, resurface in the theorems that analyse the second capitalist transformation. At the beginning of this second transformation it appeared as if 'capitalism' was losing the status of key category in sociological analysis of society. The ecological social conflict, differentiated inequalities and new social movements had to be processed by the social sciences equally as much as the subsequent collapse of state-socialist societies. Instead of a crisis of capitalism, social scientists now referred to a crisis (Offe 1984, p.7) or even an end of the work (or work-centred) society (Gorz 1985, p.53). The 'problems of "overweight"' began to outweigh those of 'hunger' (Beck 1992, p. 20), and the 'colonization of the lifeworld'

(Habermas 1987, p. 322) represented a feature not only of capitalism, but of modernity as such. While previously state-socialism and–at least in continental Europe–social (or welfare) capitalism had confronted each other in a fierce competition between the respective social systems, now diverging national models of capitalism competed for advantages in the process of globalisation (Albert 1993). Theories which only partially grasped reality such as (neo-)corporatism, (neo-)institutionalism, or the regulation school inquired about convergence and divergence between capitalist institutions and arrived at heterogeneous answers.

Capitalist Dynamic as Ongoing Landnahme

An alternative to these partial theories, which focus above all on the social reality of welfare-state capitalisms, are (neo-)Marxist and feminist approaches which interpret the capitalist dynamic as ongoing primitive accumulation or–as I would call it–an ongoing *Landnahme*. The category of *Landnahme* is crucial to theories that analyse and criticise capitalism as an expansive system. What unites such theories is the notion that capitalist societies do not reproduce exclusively from within. Capital accumulation remains continually tied to 'noncapitalist strata and societies' (Luxemburg [1913] 2015: p. 253, 262). Capitalist development thus occurs as a complex internal-external movement. It always involves the internalisation of the external, the occupation of a non-capitalist or non-market(-like) other. Capitalism in its purest form–generalised exchange of commodities and a two-class social system–as Marx himself used for his reproduction schemes (Marx [1885] (1992), pp. 486–564), cannot survive. Or at least, such a capitalism does not exist (and never has existed) anywhere. Instead there is constant exchange which areas that are directly subsumed by exploitation purposes cultivate with those social sectors that are not yet (fully) commodified.

In the final analysis, every spurt of capitalist growth can be interpreted as *Landnahme* (Lutz 1984, p. 213). In contrast to argumentation based on linear subsumption or modernisation theory, the *Landnahme* concept in the form we favour emphasises the contradictoriness and asynchrony of such processes. *Landnahmen* come at a price, for the commodification of non-capitalist milieus cannot be implemented entirely. Market relations are always associated with other forms of exchange and social interaction.

To put it more precisely: every *Landnahme* is accompanied by specific respective forms of 'land surrender' which manifest themselves as thrusts of de-commodification (either by detaching from or becoming excluded from market relations and processes of valorisation) (Dörre 2015, p. 30). As time passes, *Landnahmen* undermine their own socio-economic preconditions, making each one historically specific. Once a specific exterior has been consumed, a non-capitalist Other can be actively manufactured into new shapes and forms (Dörre 2015, p. 257; Harvey 2003, p. 140).[4] This is why *Landnahmen* may result in minor or even major crises of capitalist accumulation, but no automatism of breakdown is inherent in the crisis cycles.

This fundamental idea, which was almost forgotten for quite some time, has experienced a surprising renaissance in discussions on globalisation and financial market capitalism. It is already being ascribed the status–perhaps somewhat prematurely–similar to that which regulation theory had assumed in the context of the analysis of Fordism (Backhouse et al. 2013, p. 11; Bischoff and Lieber 2013, pp. 158–75). Attempts to analyse capitalist development as '"land-grabbing" by the market' (Streeck 2014, p. 25) or 'accumulation by dispossession' (Harvey 2003, pp. 137ff.), however, concentrate primarily on the finance-capitalist modus operandi of the state and the economy, whereas changes not only within waged labour but especially in reproductive activities are left under- or unconsidered. Feminist researchers (Federici 2012; Aulenbacher 2013, pp. 105–26; Feministische Autorinnengruppe 2013, pp. 99–118) have criticised this weak point, as they consider the withdrawal of resources for social reproduction to be central to the new *Landnahme*.

[4] By using the term in this way, we distance ourselves from definitions of Landnahme in which the concept signifies primarily an occupation of land, that is to say, physical land and resources (Exner et al. 2011, Mahnkopf 2013) or specific practices of the agribusiness (Land Grabbing, Liberti 2013). Criticism that the concept of Landnahme 'does not fit modern capitalism too well' because 'commodification', 'marketization' or 'thorough capitalisation' of all social relations is more important for capitalist development than 'spatial expansion or the colonisation of new territories' (Krätke 2013, p. 60; similar: Peter 2011, p. 151f.), on the other hand, is pushing at an open door. Landnahme always means the commodification or at least subjection of a non-capitalist Other.

The *Landnahme* concept I propose shares the assumption of an *ongoing primitive accumulation of capital.* In his engagement with contemporary interpretations, Marx denoted the transition to industrial capitalism as 'so-called primitive accumulation' (Marx 1867, pp. 873–94). Primitive accumulation means the social formation of wage workers free in the double sense, free from any means of production as well as free from being owned by anyone else, forced to sell their labour power in order to survive. The protracted 'setting free' of labour forces and the simultaneous emergence of a class of capital owners represented the basic precondition for the capitalist mode of production. At least in pre-industrial England, which Marx analysed as the most important case in this process, it rested on the violent appropriation of property, the destruction of traditional forms of production and life and on a disciplining of labour forces built on extra-economic coercion (Kößler 2013, pp. 18–37). Yet while Marx considered violence and extra-economic coercion to be transitional phenomena which would become a thing of the past as people grew accustomed to the capitalist mode of production, Rosa Luxemburg and, building on her insight, authors as diverse as Hannah Arendt, Maria Mies, Burkard Lutz or, more recently, David Harvey have demonstrated the necessity of ongoing primitive accumulation. The decisive aspect in this is not the open violence of primitive accumulation. The Fordist *Landnahme* of the traditional artisanal sector in the welfare-state capitalisms took place largely peacefully. Nevertheless, this *Landnahme*, in terms of its consequences for the traditional sector, its modes of production and life, can 'by all means be seen in analogy to the "external Landnahme" of imperialism' (Lutz 1984, p. 213).

What is central to the topic at hand is that extra-economic, political impulses were needed in order to occupy the traditional sector. The labour forces of this sector (but not only this sector), their qualifications, social identities and life forms had to be adapted to the new Fordist mode of production. Such adaptations, however–and this is a blind spot in many *Landnahme*-based analyses (Haller and Chorus 2013, pp. 64–72)–each involve a change in the forms of social reproduction and care work. As Marx concentrated on the value form of labour and its significance for the production of surplus value, he indeed failed to consider the characteristics of care work as corresponding to wage labour. As a result, the productive function of emotional dedication and attention, as is typical for care work which serves the production of the labour force (Haller and Chorus 2013, p. 66), was completely overlooked by Marx. Such limitations can be overcome, however, if the concept of an ongoing primitive accumulation is expanded to apply to reproductive activities. These activities can be regarded as an exterior of capitalist accumulation (Dörre and Haubner 2012, pp. 67–90) which–to a certain extent–can become the object of an internal *Landnahme*.

The internal-external dialectic of processes of *Landnahme* implies that a capitalist formation encompasses various modes of production, forms of life and reproduction, each of which must be specifically hierarchised and institutionalised. This includes *a parallel existence of internal capitalist as well as external non-capitalist markets*, a thought systematised by Luxemburg. For her, external markets are by not necessarily markets outside of national borders, while internal markets are not equated exclusively with national relations of exchange. Rather, internal and external markets co-coexist within national societies, remaining in a constant process of exchange.[5] For Luxemburg, capitalist development dynamic is thus based on an interlinkage of different modes of socialisation and market relations. Within the sphere of internal markets, which are structured (at least at the level of formal contract relations) by the rationality of the exchange of equivalents, capitalist societies reproduce largely of their own accord. At the same time, however, they remain, both inside as well outside of national societies, dependent on non-commodified or not yet fully commodified regions, milieus, groups, activities, and ways of life, that is to say, on external markets. At best, the principle of the exchange of equivalents applies to this external with limitations. Here, arbitrariness up to downright violence–as well as subtler forms of extra-economic disciplining–generally render the relations of exchange rather asymmetric. External markets are subjected to relations of dominance, meaning they do not imply relationships between free

[5] 'From the standpoint of capitalist production, the internal market is the capitalist market, this production is itself the purchaser of its own products and the supplier of its own elements of production. The external market, from the point of view of capital, is the noncapitalist social environment, which absorbs its products and supplies it with elements of production and labor-power.' (Luxemburg [1913] 2015, pp. 263–4.

and equal contract partners even on the level of formal contracts; here exchange is always unequal.

The relations between internal and external markets are (3) structured by an expansive dynamic which can be described as the 'structural requirement of growth' (Jackson 2009, p. 121) of capitalist accumulation and reproduction. Only by assimilating non-capitalised labour power and land does capital acquire 'a power of expansion that permits it to augment the elements of its accumulation beyond the limits apparently fixed by its own magnitude' (Luxemburg, [1913] 2015, pp. 256–7). Luxemburg only partially and unsystematically works out the reasons for capital's expansive drive. She correctly notes the micro-economic compulsion to rationalise resulting from competition as one of the main drivers of expansionism. In an anarchic capitalist economy, businesses are constantly forced to increase labour productivity in order to raise output per capital unit. In the process, and not least because it also increases the material output as well as the tendency of falling commodity prices, the increase of labour productivity exacerbates, macro-economically speaking, the realisation problem. This concerns the already mentioned impossibility of selling the capitalised additional surplus value for a profit on internal capitalist markets. According to Luxemburg, the capitalist mode of production therefore 'does not merely generate the drive to endless expansion of reproduction through the hunger for surplus value of the capitalist, but it also transforms this expansion into a veritable law of necessity, an economic condition of existence for the individual capitalist' (Luxemburg [1913] 2015, p. 14).

The compulsion to increase labour productivity and expanded reproduction does not, however, affect all sectors equally. In trades and small-scale commodity production it is mostly other rationalities that are dominant. Luxemburg explicitly rejects the notion that 'the history of the middle-size capitalist establishments proceeds rectilinearly in the direction of their progressive disappearance' (Luxemburg ([1900] 1986). Instead, she assumes that small capitals which oscillate between a tendency of rise and fall would assume 'the role of pioneers of technical change' (Luxemburg ([1900] 1986). Luxemburg thus moves towards an understanding of capitalism that systematically distinguishes between market economy and capitalism. Capitalism unfolds above the market economy structured by small-scale businesses (Braudel 1984, p. 36), it develops within a hierarchy of social spaces and modes of production and it 'takes up a position at the top of the hierarchy, whether or not this was created by itself' (Braudel 1984, p. 65).

The expansive access the capitalist mode or production has to valorisable resources therefore does not necessarily imply that the entire existent labour power reserves are integrated into commodity production equally. From the perspective of the individual capitalist's interest in valorisation, it can appear quite reasonable to utilise segments of individual labour capacity as a gratuitous resource, or in the form of unfree labour. One reason for this is the variety of possibilities to increase labour productivity, another is the chance of obtaining additional profits through the use of precarious, socially devalued work. Rosa Luxemburg analysed this with reference to the 'the systematic, planned destruction and annihilation of any noncapitalist social formation that it encounters' enforced by French colonial politics in France's Arabian colonies (Luxemburg, [1913] 2015, p. 267), as well as to the introduction of 'forced wage labor', an instrument of Spanish colonial policies applied to exploit the indigenous population in the American and Caribbean colonies (Luxemburg [1925] 2013, p. 211). In contrast to Marxist orthodoxy, Luxemburg thus established a 'wholly original approach to the evolution of social formations' which 'breaks with linear evolutionism, positivist "progressivism"' (Löwy 2011).

The dependence of capital accumulation on internal and external markets structures not only the interrelations between wage labour and other activities, but simultaneously implies a limited plurality of relations of exploitation. For a long time now, the term exploitation has been almost completely absent in sociological literature. Its use therefore demands an explanation. In its general use, the category of exploitation signifies a causal relationship between the 'good fortune of the strong [...] and the misery of the weak' (Boltanski and Chiapello 2003, p. 360). According to Dubet, one does not need to agree with 'the Marxist notion of value and surplus value in order to understand the power of the feeling of being exploited in the industrial society', for it was 'the very experience of exploitation that made possible the success of Marxist interpretations of the relations of production, even when the former, in a strict sense, were not even capitalist' (Dubet 2008, p. 119).

The authors associated with the Bielefeldian 'housewifisation approach' in their expansion of Luxemburg's accumulation theory argued quite similarly: 'Exploitation means to loot, to appropriate something by violent means, something that was not produced by one's own labour, to take something without giving something of equal value in return' (Mies 1983, p. 120). By reference to the violence involved in relations of exploitation, an aspect that (surely) applies to subsistence work, Mies thereby claims a universal validity and fundamental relevance of a mechanism that is *un*specific to any social formation and which precisely does *not* correspond to the principle of capitalist exchange of equivalents. Exploitation in its basic form, located, so to speak, in front of the exploitation found in surplus value production, is regarded as fraud carried out by the already-powerful, as 'robbery'. Marxist theory, by contrast, seeks to explain why exploitation is possible in spite of the labour market's (formal) principle of contractual legal equality. In a capitalist enterprise, this principle can be realised and at the same time covertly violated because wage-earners receive the equivalent of their labour power and not that of the value product they produce. While Luxemburg argues that class struggle is necessary to even enforce the exchange of equivalents on the labour market, this exchange relation can, and neither Marx nor Luxemburg could have foreseen this, be 'pacified' (Habermas 1987, p. 352); exploitation can be attenuated through an improvement in the living standards of the exploited and reframed subjectively so as to be perceived as 'just'–because legitimate–inequality.

The institutionalisation of workers' power in the welfare state (Arbeitskreis Strategic Unionism 2013, pp. 345–375), in labour law and in collective bargaining has a market-forming effect, as it at least formally asserts the principle of the exchange of equivalents. I propose terming this case the *primary* form of exploitation, as it is exclusive to the capitalist formation. From this capitalism-generated *primary* exploitation we can then distinguish between mechanisms of *secondary* exploitation that are not specifically capitalist in nature. While relations of primary exploitation are commonly established via formal or informal contractual relations which evoke the principle of the exchange of equivalents (labour power in return for a fair pay) and therefore ideally function without recourse to extra-economic disciplining, forms of secondary exploitation create relations of equivalence of a different type. Secondary exploitation occurs when symbolic-cultural mechanisms of disciplining, or those sanctioned by the state or politically, are applied in order to preserve internal-external differences with the aim of pushing the living standard of social groups markedly below the general welfare state-secured level of wages or reproductive resources–for example, by means of racism or sexism–or in order to create the possibility to partake of activities inside as well as outside the sphere of waged employment as unpaid gratuitous resource.

If the external parameters and the inter-societal balance of forces allow for it, an intensification of secondary exploitation is a potential option for economic and political elites to react to stagnations in capital accumulation. In this sense, mechanisms of primary and secondary exploitation are not independent of one another. The exchange of equivalents within the sphere of surplus production and its institutional guarantees constitute the standard from which those exchange relations deviate that are based on extra-economic dominance and have their own trajectory independent of capitalism (racism, sexism), and which to some extent occur outside the capitalist enterprise and sphere of production. If, say, societal dependency on non- or only hardly rationalisable person-oriented services and care activities in the reproductive process increases, extra-economic mechanisms of disciplining can be employed in order to keep the price of this activity low or to continue to provide demand with a free resource. These forms of secondary exploitation do not exhaust themselves in methods of absolute surplus value production (by means of prolongation of the work day or deterioration of working conditions (Marx, in [1867] 1967: pp. 283–428), if only for the fact that the corresponding activities of surplus value production are often only indirectly subsumed, at best.

This leads me to a final thought concerning the 're-conquest of land'. Both exploitation and alienation are expressed by experiences of injustice. They engender a 'raw material' (Kluge and Negt 2014) of problem awareness that drives individuals and groups to obstinate responses. Precisely because capitalist subjection of labour capacities can never be totally realised, attempts at occupation create frictions that may provoke counter-movements, struggles for the 're-conquest of land'. The 'surrender of land' becomes a goal more or less consciously pursued by collective social actors. Rosa Luxemburg's political sociology referred to counter-movements of the Marxian type, to socialist workers' movements. Yet she ascribes significantly more importance to experience, spontaneity and democratic freedom of expression within these movements than the Marxist orthodoxy and especially the Leninism of her time. The recognition of the intrinsic value of non-capitalist modes of production and life forms moreover implies an approximation of a plural understanding of social antagonisms and anti-capitalist movements. If a pure capitalism does not exist, then neither can the counter-movements be reduced to organised socialist or unionised workers' movements. Instead, Luxemburg considers spontaneous mass movements and thus non-class-specific movements of the Polanyian type which resist the 'maelstrom' of levelling market power (Silver 2003, p. 22) to be important social actors.

Why Should and Must Capitalism be Overcome?

What reasons may motivate social movements and collective actors to not only fight against capitalism but actually search for ways to overcome it? To me, there are mainly two–capitalism's intrinsic socio-economic crisis dynamic (4.1) and the 'carrying on' of permanent economic growth with the associated ecological dangers and socially destructive consequences.

The Crisis Dynamic

Economic crises are part and parcel of the modus operandi of capitalist *Landnahmen*, they function as the 'irrational rationalisers of an always unstable capitalism' (Harvey 2011, p. 71). Crises are virtually indispensable for the stimulation of growth, as they cause capital devaluation and encourage innovation. This is equally true for the numerous minor and major economic turbulences that preceded the global recession of 2008–9. A crisis management underwritten (in sharp contrast to the ideological superelevation of the free market) by massive state intervention ensured time and again that the state stepped in to rescue investment funds and banking institutions from bankruptcy. Systematic state intervention facilitated the privatisation of profits and the socialisation of losses. This 'irrational rationalisation', however, led to the development of a 'systemic "moral hazard"' (Harvey 2011, p. 10) in the case of several important financial market actors and in turn fed into the accumulation of crisis potential in the financial sector as a whole. Investors, bankers, and hedge fund managers all operated under the impression that they could act at almost no risk to themselves whatsoever, which of course encouraged their inclination toward practices of high-risk speculation even further. From the perspective of investment banks and their executive employees, equipped with unique insider knowledge (and thus essentially uncontrollable) as they were, it appeared absolutely rational when confronted with the prospect of high returns to take just about any risk imaginable. After all, they knew that it would be others who had to cover the incurred losses in the case of failure, not them or their institutions. State-funded rescue packages in turn prevented market adjustments and seemed to render institutional innovation unnecessary, thereby blocking the crisis mechanism's function of economic cleansing and rectification. The potential for economic crisis was allowed to expand and deepen until finally the flapping of a butterfly's wings was enough to trigger an explosion within the non-linear financial system that would come to shake the whole world.

How are capitalist *Landnahmen* related to economic crises? Let us take a closer look at this causal mechanism. Capitalist dynamic is mainly a result of the capacity of social actors to turn seemingly absolute boundaries to accumulation into surmountable barriers–a process in which production moves in 'contradictions which are constantly overcome but just as constantly posited' (Marx 1986, p. 337). Crises are conceivable in any and all of the stages of capital flow (production, circulation, consumption). Their roots may lie in insufficient seed capital for capital-intensive innovations, labour force shortages, sectoral disproportionalities, resource scarcity, ecological imbalances, rapid technological changes, workers' resistance, under-consumption, or in the monetary and financial system. Every crisis is unique and cannot be adequately extrapolated from some abstract logic of capital nor from a universal imperative of escalation found within modern societies, but must instead be empirically investigated, if its origins and trajectory are to be revealed. There is, however, one basic problematic of capital accumulation which is revealed in some way or another in every crisis. In reference to Rosa Luxemburg, David Harvey has termed this basic problematic the '*capital surplus absorption problem*' (Harvey 2010, p. 94). To put it in simple terms: an economy that grows during a period of production must create markets capable of absorbing the extra surplus value during the subsequent period–a task only possible through market-expanding investments. Therefore, the rule of thumb reads: 3 per cent growth requires 3 per cent additional investment (Harvey 2010, p. 95). The higher a given society's level of wealth and the greater its economic growth, the more difficult it becomes to acquire and develop new markets. This *capital surplus absorption problem* represents the central socio-economic driving force of capitalist *Landnahmen*. It explains why the process of capital accumulation requires and demands the ability to 'mobilise world labour power without restriction' so as to 'utilise all productive forces of the globe' (Luxemburg [1913] 2015, p. xiii)–at least to the extent possible within the confines of surplus value production.

As Harvey and others have correctly observed, Luxemburg underestimated important stabilisation mechanisms of capitalist accumulation. This includes the functions of credit as well as the significance of process and product innovation in particular. If, in a capitalist economy, no other viable alternative solutions exist, then money is applied as medium of exchange in order to bridge the gap between yesterday's surplus product and today's re-investment(s). Should capital owners hoard their assets instead of directly re-investing them, then money creation on the part of the banks and deficit spending by the state are the most important means of countering the lack of solvent demand. Moreover, credit stimulates investment, and (in the event of successful implementation) even leads to market expansion.

These two methods of resolving the *capital surplus absorption problematic* are so vital to the maintenance of the capitalist dynamic that special networks or configurations of relations and institutions are relied upon to ensure their smooth operation. Harvey names two institutional configurations: the state-finance nexus and the state-corporate nexus. The list of self-stabilising factors would remain incomplete, however, should we fail to add a state-labour-reproduction nexus to the two 'central nervous systems' of capitalist accumulation. This institutional mesh regulates labour relations but is also the space in which labour capacities are developed, qualified, nurtured and looked after, so as to ensure the proper functioning of social reproduction as a whole. The way in which said networks are institutionalised indicates a particular variety of capitalism, while at the same time also pointing to distinct crisis types.

It is necessary to distinguish, in a systematic way, between (minor) cyclical economic crises that arise every seven to eight years as well as other disruptions to capital flows from a type of crisis that affects the entire ensemble of social regulations and the (re-)productive structures of society as a whole. *Major* crises can last for a long time, as the aforementioned actor-institution networks are no longer able to fulfil their economic regulatory function without new institutional configurations taking their place. In any case, 'major crises' result from the increasing incompatibility of accumulation regimes and modes of regulation. Thus they are always also crises of production models, the welfare state, social rules and, if existent, of democratic institutions. They ultimately lead to an old, crisis-ridden modus operandi of capitalist *Landnahmen* being replaced by a new one, a process in which the state and politics are particularly challenged to act as central structure-forming force(s). Equipped with such a heuristic, we can now determine a bit more precisely what is special about the sustained socio-economic crises.

The New Depression of 1973–4 was interpreted by the dominant capitalist actors of the time as the result of an overall profit squeeze. Wage earners' power institutionalised in the developed welfare states appeared to be the main obstacle to accumulation and market expansion. The deregulation of labour markets, wage differentials, tax cuts for businesses and top earners, privatisation of public enterprises and the expropriation of social goods and the commons, or, in short: a new *Landnahme* of the social, aimed to transform these seemingly absolute barriers to growth into surmountable hurdles. The state-finance nexus assumed the leadership role in this process, attempting to effect changes in the state-labour-reproduction nexus. From the elite's perspective this operation has been hugely successful: both the organised labour movement as well as the institutions designed to restrict market power more generally were weakened to such a degree that the fruits of credit-driven growth could be reaped by the already-privileged.

The erosion of trade union power, the political representation of wage earners and welfare-state institutions also created a new barrier to further accumulation in the form of structurally deficient solvent demand incurred by wage stagnation and decline. Money which could not be profitably invested in the productive economy was instead diverted to high-risk investments in the financial sector. Furthermore, and particularly in the Anglo-Saxon capitalisms, the issuing of mortgage loans to low-income groups was intended to compensate for stagnant wage levels. This linking of the credit system to members of the wage-earning classes led directly to the catastrophe of 2008/09, as the crisis began in the financial sector. In the construction sector, the credit institutions influenced both supply (loans to construction firms) and demand (mortgage loans to homeowners), which inevitably lead to a loss of control. The underlying problem, however, was and remains 'excessive capitalist empowerment vis-a-vis labour' (Harvey 2011, p. 118.) as well as a devaluation of reproductive activities and a general weakening of social rules which are actually prerequisites for functioning markets. Thus, the fundamental economic problem of the early 1970s has been effectively reversed. Triggered by a profit squeeze, the new *Landnahme* has, by eliminating a specific barrier to capitalist accumulation, created a new one, i.e. structurally insolvent demand, which in turn has evoked the threat of deflation (price slump as driving force of economic recession) in the Eurozone and which, moreover, holds within it the seed of a new financial crisis.

This is the case especially as the upward re-distribution continues. Finance-capitalist *Landnahme* implies that the increasing wealth of a minority of society carries the poverty and precarity of much larger groups in its wake. To put it more bluntly, there exists a causal relationship between the concentration of wealth in the hands of a few and the precarisation of the conditions of work and life for broad layers of the population. The capital-owning class factions are not only growing in numbers, but their wealth is moreover increasing in relation to all other major social groups (Piketty 2014). This trend is particularly pronounced in the Anglo-Saxon capitalisms, above all in the USA. Here, the top one per cent owns 35 per cent of all private assets nationally. The top tenth of the one per cent earns that which about 90 per cent of earners make in one year in just one and a half days, and the top 20 per cent earn (after tax) more than the remaining 80 per cent combined (Stiglitz 2013, p. 24). But the once relatively egalitarian 'German capitalism' has also taken big steps toward a similar level of inequality. According to recent calculations, the top per cent of households owns 32 per cent of assets (Vermeulen 2014). The increase in class-specific inequalities additionally accentuates the capital surplus absorption problem. The concentration of wealth in the hands of a few means that the appropriated surplus is more difficult to reinvest, as capitalist consumption is of course bounded by physical limits at some point. At the same time, the accumulation of money as a universal form of wealth fosters the accumulation of social power which can then be used politically to push the implementation and preservation of privileges in tax law. This distributive imbalance reduces the scope for productive state consumption, thus obstructing further public investment. While privately-held surplus capital is concentrated in the financial sector due to a lack of profitable investment opportunities in the so-called real economy, the state–particularly at the local and regional levels–lacks the necessary funds to implement urgently-needed ecological and social infrastructural investment. The relative destruction of Fordist social capitalism seems to have shaken the social foundation of investment activity to a degree that this essential stabiliser of the capitalist dynamic's ability to fulfil its systemic function has been substantially impaired.

The consequences of the crisis-inducing dynamic presently affect mainly those who become the object of a forced secondary exploitation–precarised groups, the new service proletariat, women in segments of politically devalued care work and above all the populations of the countries of the Global South. Even in advanced capitalisms the integration into the labour market occurs mainly via the expansion of precarious employment. In Germany, a society of precarious full-time employment has emerged in which a decreasing volume of paid working hours is asymmetrically shared between a record number of economically active people. The 'German job miracle' rests on a reduction of unemployment at the cost of protected full-time employment as well as through the expansion of 'undignified' (Castel 2011, p. 63)–because precarious–(wage) labour (Dörre et al. 2013). The situation is far worse in the European crisis-ridden European countries. Take, for example, the case of Greece: as a result of the global financial and fiscal crisis, the country has gone through a six-year period of economic contraction. As a consequence thereof, unemployment rose from 7.7 per cent (2008) to 27.1 per cent (2013), while youth unemployment rose from 22.1 per cent to 59.1 per cent in the same period. In 2010 and 2011 alone, the average income dropped by a total of 8 per cent, wage cuts in the public sector have reached 20 per cent–in extreme cases even 50 per cent. The proportion of jobs not subject to social security or insurance contributions has climbed to 36 per cent. Pension cuts vary between 14 and 48 per cent; homelessness, which increasingly affects even the educated middle classes, is currently 45 per cent above pre-crisis levels. Even the suicide rate is hitting record highs: following an increase of 25 per cent in 2009–2010, it rose again by 40 per cent in the following year (Markantonatou 2014, pp. 217–228). And yet, despite all of the sacrifices the Greek people have been forced to make, the country's public debt has increased from 120 per cent of the GDP in 2010 to 175 per cent in 2013; in 2015 it will likely approach 200 per cent. Behind these figures lies the transition to a type of society previously unknown in continental Europe. Greece, along with other crisis-ridden states, has become a precarious society of capitalist slump. Of the most contracting economies worldwide, Greece is ranked third, only topped by Sudan and South Sudan. We are talking about a European society which, following a 13-year growth period, is now marked by economic and social regression. Given that roughly three million people have dropped out of the collective social security systems, many of the most basic social provisions can now only be guaranteed through various forms of self-help. Doctors add extra hours to their official work day to treat patients who cannot afford or are not entitled to regular medical provisions free of charge. Material scarcity promotes subsistence production, while networks of barter exchange secure basic provisions for the utterly destitute, and informal social networks offer shelter to families who can no longer afford their rent in the form of crowded apartments or camp sites. Societies are now emerging in the heart of the Eurozone which display informal structures that were for a long time only known in the Global South. Economic contraction and the expropriation of social goods and the commons create conditions in which not only gainful employment, but indeed more or less *all* basic social institutions have become unstable. If we were to include social status insecurity and private indebtedness in this list, we could confidently state that a *majority* of people in these societies live under precarious conditions. Here, governance amounts to maximising insecurities while granting the bare minimum of social security required to avoid the threat of social unrest and revolt, or at least keep them under control (Lorey 2015, p. 2).

The Metabolic Rift

The social polarisation throughout the capitalist world economy is dramatic for the very reason that it is accompanied by a problematic of the 'keep calm and carry on'. A vital aspect of an understanding of the ongoing crisis is the evolution of society's relation to the natural world. Finance-capitalist *Landnahme* implies that land, water, oceans, forests, clean air, and even properties of the human body itself are gradually subjected to the principle of competition. The commodification of nature, which really began with the emergence of capitalism itself, produces barriers to accumulation for which the term 'crisis' is not quite an adequate description, even though it is used in this context (Foster et al. 2010, p. 399). Whereas crisis entails a condition that can (at least theoretically) be dealt with and overcome, the creation of global ecological dangers represents a continuous and ongoing process. The beginning of permanent and accelerated interventions into the labour-mediated metabolism (Foster et al. 2010, p. 402) of humanity and the earth coincided with primitive accumulation, the enclosures and the associated transformation of communal land into private property. Industrialisation and the systemic compulsion towards permanent economic growth triggered a kind of expansionism that negates the absolute limits inherent in any metabolism. One pivotal reason for this is the specific form of the capital surplus absorption problem as formulated in what is referred to as the Lauderdale Paradox. The Lauderdale Paradox posits that private assets in the form of land and natural resources can only be expanded through the elimination or destruction of public assets. This way a lack of X is actively created, where X is something that was once abundantly available as part of the commons, such as water, land, and clean air (Foster et al. 2010, p. 432).

This form of primitive accumulation persists and can be observed to this day. An end to these sorts of *Landnahmen* is nowhere in sight, at least not for the foreseeable future. Emissions trading is a striking example of how our very biosphere is being enclosed (through the creation of ownership titles) and assigned a monetary value. So far, the scarcity of natural resources has only been felt indirectly as far as purchasing prices are concerned, and becomes visible as a driver of economic crisis only in a mediated way, such as is the case with petrol prices.

Reaching (at least, so it seems) 'peak oil'–that is to say, the point of maximum possible output of crude oil–has simply resulted in an increase in high-risk exploration and exploitation (fracking) of previously unprofitable reserves, also known as "so-called 'unconventional oil'". Shortages, which are not expressed in price levels, are not taken into account during the accumulation process unless other regulations necessitate it–for these costs are usually externalised and passed on to the wider community (*Gemeinschaft*) as a whole. One fundamental problem of this externalisation mechanism is that it renders the over-stepping of the limits of natural systems invisible over long stretches of time and exempts it from economic calculations.

The ongoing commodification of the human as well as non-human natural world and the externalisation of the associated ecological risks, along with accelerated extraction of raw materials and pollutant emissions, is resulting in the over-stepping of planetary limits (Rockström et al. 2009, pp. 472–475). When measured by pre-industrial standards and the 'tipping points' based on them, we have already crossed the 'red line' of irreversible damage as far as climate change, biodiversity and the nitrogen cycle is concerned. Acidification of the oceans, lack of ozone, fresh water consumption, land use and atmospheric aerosol loading are all rapidly approaching the limits of planetary tolerance. The main polluters are the growth-driven capitalisms of the global North, even though the larger emerging economies such as China are quickly catching up in this race. At present, a quarter of the earth's population–mainly from the Global North–consumes three quarters of its resources and produces three quarters of waste and emissions. If the Global South is ever to have even a *chance* at development, then ecological re-orientation must begin in the historical capitalist centres. The term 'crisis' is appropriate to describe this predicament insofar as phenomena such as climate change are not subjected to any kind of linear principle of escalation; rather, complex feedback effects ensure that human-influenced natural systems can reach a point at which they are irreversibly destabilised.

This destabilisation, however, does not imply that ecological catastrophes necessarily or automatically bring about a 'final' crisis of capitalism. There are 'endless predictive uncertainties' with regard to the complex interactions between humans and the natural world (Foster et al. 2010, p. 425). Standard values and climate tipping points are dependent upon shared knowledge and definitions; they are also sites of struggle concerning interpretation, political negotiations and social conflicts. What seems safe to assume, though, is that the time frame in which fundamental changes must be implemented in order to allow for a globally sustainable metabolism of the earth cannot be extended indefinitely. The method of overcoming economic crises which has been taken for granted since the Industrial Revolution, namely the generation of economic growth through utilisation of fossil energy sources, has now become a primary driving force of ecological destruction. Essentially, the world has been living beyond its means since the 1970s–and not only in terms of the impact on the climate, but also with view to the actual consumption of finite resources. The ecological footprint, which measures resource consumption in comparison to the planet's overall carrying capacity, represents an important indicator of this. Even before the turn of the millennium, human resource consumption was about 20 per cent above the sustainability limit. The crisis years of 1980–83 were the last time that resource consumption had approached the sustainability boundary. It has risen to such an extent since then that we are now approaching the limits of long-term economic growth, at least in the advanced capitalisms.

Given this historically novel accumulation and mutual interleaving of economic, ecological and social dislocations, it seems appropriate to describe the current constellation as an economic-ecological double crisis or 'pincer-grip crisis'. Neither ecological nor economic crises can be traced back to *one* sole cause or origin. The term double crisis depicts mainly a spatial and temporal synchronisation of highly diverse flashpoints and causes of crisis. What makes the current crisis constellation a true historical novelty, however, is that the growth dilemma of the advanced capitalisms is being exposed in a qualitatively new way. The tried and true, unquestioned method of overcoming economic crises as described above is currently (and necessarily) leading to an accumulation of ecological dangers. This is the reason why the capitalisms of the Global North in particular are confronted with the historic decision, essentially between two alternatives: 'One is to make growth sustainable; the other is to make de-growth stable' (Jackson 2009, p. 128; Dörre 2012a). Within existing finance-capitalist dominated societies–supposedly–neither one nor the other is possible. The expansive dynamic intrinsic to all varieties of capitalism drives the system 'towards one of two states: expansion or collapse' (Jackson 2009, p. 64). That is why it makes absolute sense to work on the overcoming of capitalism.

Can Capitalism be Overcome?

Is there a realistic chance of overcoming capitalism? Incidentally, I believe so. However, there is no automatism of capitalism's collapse, and even its supersession does not necessarily have to lead to a better society.

What Should be Done?

Whether or not this process is to continue is decided in the tests of new competitive capitalism. In the long term, three different development paths seem plausible. One possibility is the emergence of an order of exploitation which is no longer based on the compulsion to permanent economic growth. Such a transformation becomes probable should economic growth fail to materialise over a longer period of time, redistribution from top to bottom be blocked and capitalist *Landnahmen* be forced to draw on already existing substance. In such a scenario, that which remains latent throughout ongoing primitive accumulation may become dominant. A finance-capitalist oligarchy deploys its wealth in order to maintain an order of exploitation primarily by means of extra-economic coercion and violence, that is to say, through the enforcement of secondary exploitation.

Projects intended to open up new markets for capital, as are currently being advanced in the form of the proposed TTIP and CETA free trade agreements, can only be implemented to the detriment of competing economic and geopolitical interests. This tension will manifest itself in inter-state rivalries over mineral deposits, scarce resources and spheres of influence. Such a development is tremendously dangerous, as it may reinforce what is already presenting itself as a renewed confrontation between East and West (Ukraine), ethnic nationalism consuming and destroying entire countries (Yugoslavia), the right-wing populist 'tsunami' in Europe (for example, Marine Le Pen and the Front National), or, in a totally different form, as organised terrorism motivated by religious fundamentalism (Islamic State), as an anti-democratic and indeed civilisation-threatening logic of conflict. As Hannah Arendt illustrates in her analysis of totalitarianism, a worst case scenario is possible in which surplus capital can merge with the supposedly redundant sectors of society to give an impetus to an expansive capitalist spirit which gradually detaches itself from socio-economic interests completely, so as to fully commit itself to the accumulation of political power; a force that operates according to the territorial principle and which can only be implemented through violently drawing and re-drawing of territorial boundaries. In today's capitalist centres, however, it tends to be the relatively secured groups of wage earners who practice exclusive solidarity (Dörre et al. 2013, pp. 222–28), by which they dissociate themselves from the top, but also from 'below' and from the 'Other'. These groups demand zones of protection and demarcations which, should the need arise, may have to be enforced by an authoritarian state in an authoritarian capitalism. Resembling its imperialist predecessors, such a capitalist state would also base itself on the accumulation of political power. Yet the unlimited accumulation of power permanently 'needs more material to devour in its never-ending process', as it is insatiable, and even 'the last victorious Commonwealth cannot proceed to "annex the planets", it can only proceed to destroy itself' (Arendt 1962, pp. 146–147).

Green capitalism: a possible alternative to these apocalyptic visions are neo-Schumpeterian or neo-Keynesian projects of technology- and efficiency-based green capitalist *Landnahmen*. Such projects have already been put forth in the form of the digitalisation of industrial production (industry 4.0), the credo of 'smart growth', or assorted variants of a Global Deal or Green New Deal.[6] There can hardly be any doubt that technological and organisational innovations such as, for example, the transition to renewable energy sources as well as the improvement of overall energy efficiency and efficacy are urgently needed if civilisation is to respond to the coming ecological threats adequately. Thus, it would be a mistake to outright reject strategies which rely on 'green' growth, such as the Green New Deal, as some currents within the growth-critical movements do. For as we have learned from European climate policy (utterly insufficient as it is), even moderate ecological reforms only become a viable political option when a substantial degree of social pressure is present. From the perspective of the emerging economies of the Global South, moreover, they represent 'a stepping stone towards more fundamental options in the longer term' (Pillay 2014, p. 162). Any sustainability strategy worthy of the name, however, would be heavily reliant on state intervention, movements of civil society, democratic control of financial markets, public ownership, a revaluation of reproductive labour, a new-found balance between the Global North and South, egalitarianism and reduced overall consumption. The question is, would a society that exhibited all these features still be a capitalist society?

Ultimately, we simply cannot escape the fact that a social system which relies on an inscribed growth imperative will at some point collide with the reproductive capacities of a planet whose resources are finite. The abandonment of the growth illusion may be easier for us once we realise that, as Joseph Schumpeter so brilliantly analysed, creative destruction has long become the creative *preservation* of indefensible and unsustainable social relations. Growth capitalism has become a kind of treadmill that continues to function only because more and more people are forced to expend more and more energy just to avoid falling off the belt. Anyone who is serious about sustainability goals has to mount a fundamental challenge to this treadmill itself. This will only be possible if the rest of society, meaning everyone and everything beyond the interests of pri-

[6] Cf. Inter alia.: Brynjolfson and McAffe 2014; Fücks 2013; Stern 2007; Müller and Niebert 2012.

vate profit, exert their influence regarding the questions of the 'what', the 'how', and the 'what for' of production and reproduction.

Democratic and socialist post growth society: a perspective of transformation with this aim requires not only reforms, but also necessitates a break with growth capitalism and a search for viable alternatives. Such a perspective can only emerge from a comprehensive critique of alienation and exploitation that combines radical democratisation and 'substantive equality' (Foster et al. 2010, p. 61) into an ecologically sustainable project of emancipation. Sustainable is that which 'stands fast, which bears up, which is long term, resilient. And that means: immune to ecological, economic or social breakdown'. Sustainability is above all rooted in the 'basic human need for security' (Grober 2012, p. 16)–an insight that can hardly be reconciled with a system incapable of distinguishing improvement from destruction or progress from wastefulness.

The only task that remains for sociology, at least for now, may very well be the designation of certain coordinates which could serve as points of orientation for social forces seeking to transform the current system. The *first coordinate* is a conscious social rejection of the imperative of permanent economic growth. An ethically-inspired critique of growth which attacks the greedy materialism of the lower classes (because the argument concerning 'the fair distribution of an assumed yield from human performance' is allegedly really only about 'the appropriation of the spoils that, from an ecological perspective, should have never been created in the first place' (Paech 2012, p. 35; similar: Rosa 2013)) presents the goal of transformation in a rather problematic way. Such variants of critique are likely to drive even those wage earners already critical of the consumerism of capitalist life into the counter-revolutionary camp. A left critique of growth that is socially blind and neglects the pressing issue of equality is hardly distinguishable from an intelligent neo-conservatism which utilises ecological crises as justification for declining prosperity and inequality (Miegel 2010).

To protect against neo-conservative or racist usurpation of our argument, we require a *second coordinate*–namely, a culture of 'substantive equality'. Finance-capitalist *Landnahme* implies that the increasing wealth of a growing yet nevertheless comparatively tiny minority of society carries the poverty, misery and precarity of much larger groups in its wake. Contrary to the widely-asserted claim that the collapse of the financial markets has primarily affected the owners of large fortunes, it has in fact been the poorest of the poor–disproportionately female (Karamessini and Rubbery 2013)–who have been hit the hardest by the effects of the crisis. In Mexico, Ecuador or Haiti, where entire sections of the population depend on remittances from overseas relatives, the laying off of construction workers or dock workers can lead to widespread malnutrition and even starvation. For this reason alone, an ethically motivated critique of growth cannot dismiss questions of distribution, even if the latter, similarly to projects fighting global poverty, exhibit few system-transforming qualities, if any at all. Equally important is how the production of class-specific inequalities in their interconnections to axes of gender and ethnicity repeatedly function to amplify and intensify ecological crises. Ecological threats are generally concentrated in the poorest countries. A climate-induced sea level rise will initially pose a problem for countries lacking the financial resources to develop protective measures for their populations. Extreme weather, which is expected to increase in both frequency and intensity, will wreak havoc in the slums of the world's megacities. Moreover, the increased strain on natural systems, which is largely a product of Western consumption patterns, is also distributed unequally. As a general rule, it is safe to say that the higher the income, the bigger the ecological footprint.[7]

What is more, benchmarks toward ecological sustainability are far more difficult to meet in countries with more pronounced class-specific inequalities. Inequality fosters positional consumption–driven not least by the fear of losing touch with or decoupling from social norms, or missing an opportunity for upward social advancement. The desire to distinguish oneself from others, as well as the activities of the advertising industry as a whole, and above all the unequally distributed decision-making powers as far as investment, products and production methods are concerned mean that consumers do not really have much choice in

[7] According to a Canadian study, the top tenth of salaried workers have an ecological footprint that is nine times as high in transportation and four times as high in consumption as that of the bottom tenth. Cf. J. B. Foster et al. 2010, p. 390.

how they live their lives. If they could, they would soon realise that a large portion of a society's energy consumption occurs in the productive sector, the lion's share of emissions with a climatic effect are produced by private companies and waste is also mostly amassed by industry. For these reasons, the notion of extensive consumer sovereignty is just as implausible as the assumption that ecological destruction could be countered primarily through conscious consumption.

The corrective of 'substantive equality' implies the opposite of levelling down; it does, however, entail much more than the concept of an equality of social status as linked to the national welfare state. A culture of 'substantive equality' seeks–and this is the *third coordinate*–a radical democratisation of decision-making in production, meaningful labour and social reproduction. Democratisation represents the only remaining possibility to concentrate and cohere a multiplicity of social identities. What is needed is an 'insurgent democracy' (Abensour 2011, pp. 47–72) articulating an explicit challenge to capitalist elites. Such a democracy can no longer be understood simply as a political category but must be re-defined as an economic one as well. In a comprehensive sense, it has to prove itself as the social motor or 'driving mechanism' of the economy (Meiksins Wood 1995, p. 290). Simultaneously, democratisation must be linked to a redistribution of resources from the high-productivity to the low-productivity sectors. The latter would imply seeking a break with the capitalist principle of replacing human labour power with machines. Societies that were to conduct a revaluation of care work and care workers within a framework of a comprehensive democratisation strategy would become modern post-growth societies, as they would only grow socially, and thus more slowly, due to the relative resistance of person-oriented services as care work to rationalisation. Labour productivity would only be increased gradually and not at the expense of living labour and social reproduction. Economic growth would no longer be an end in itself, but merely a consciously applied means that serves the purpose of creating work that satisfies real human needs. Such a prospect of transformation, which aims at a transition to selective, socially and ecologically sustainable growth, ultimately transcends–or at least points to the necessity of transcending–capitalism.

Who Can Overcome Capitalism?

Will protagonists capable of driving such a transformation forward emerge? From a sociological perspective, this question cannot be answered with any certainty. What is possible, however, is to spell out the construction principle of such antagonisms. If relations of power and exploitation are being investigated, a systematic distinction must be made between labour power and labour capacity. Wage labour, unpaid care work, pro-active, self-directed labour, and activities exclusively conducted in pursuit of individual self-realisation all represent distinct respective labour capacities. These must be linked to one another and coordinated through navigational labour (*Steuerungsarbeit*) (Kluge and Negt 2014). Individuals are hardly able to fundamentally correct the imbalance of labour capacities produced by flexible production modes and life forms. That is why those compulsions that contemporary capitalism produces especially in the export sector and via flexible time regimes, encompass not only paid employment but gradually come to occupy all other labour capacities and activity potentials, as well.

A loss of control due to such an occupation occurs socially, sector by sector, organisationally as well as individually, every time material and time resources necessary for balancing out the different labour capacities are withdrawn. In this context, Negt and Kluge speak of a 'balance imperialism' that operates via the 'withdrawal of coordinating energies' (Negt and Kluge 2014). The requirements of flexible production and reproduction necessitate that more and more activity is expended for coordinating one's different life areas and activities. What arises from this is an exploitation problematic entailing more than just the appropriation of unpaid work time within the capitalist production process. The compulsions generated within flexible production modes and the corresponding time regimes prey on and privatise unpaid 'navigational' labour which needs to be performed individually and on an ever greater scale as institutionally secured social coordination that would allow for a more long-term life planning gradually falls to the wayside.

This is where the 'sting' of a contemporary critique of capitalism, so to speak, would have to start from. Even and especially among those still relatively protected groups (core workforces) in prospering export sectors, the pursuit of a good life subjectively entails a critique of growth in competition-driven capitalism. Many respondents consider the ecological crisis to be a result of the 'always more and never enough' which they know from the workplace, but also from other areas of life. A principle of competition which has taken on a life of its own is identified as the main driving force whose destructive impact is felt in different contexts. This expansive principle of competition is known from workplace routine and is described and criticised in various ways.

One characteristic experience is that every 'victory' in the game of competition is only temporary. As soon as a competitive advantage has been achieved, the company already announces the subsequent rationalisation programme. Once more, the company needs to improve its competitive position, and once more this means that work must be completed even more quickly and efficiently. The insatiability of competition is not only felt in workplaces or the world of work as such, but in the view of many respondents it has long since begun to penetrate all spheres of society and is even encroaching on the lives of children and adolescents. Society seems to have become an accumulation of individual contests in which the principle of competition is insatiable. It permanently produces winners and losers. It takes effect in more or less all social spaces of experience and restricts the quality of life, even in the eyes of executive managers, to an almost unbearable extent. This principled critique of competition represents a bridge between individual experience and subjective images of society. Additionally, this cognitive bridge mediates between experiences in the 'small world' of the workplace, the private world of the family, and the attitudes towards the 'outer world of society' (compare Dörre et al. 2014, pp. 543–554). This bridge could be the link to a mosaic left (Urban 2013) which, as Étienne Balibar (2012) analogously states, defines democracy less in terms of its institutions and more by its–above all oppositional–actors, by its social movements, by the general willingness to engage in protest and resistance. The remaining hope for a social transformation that transcends capitalism may be based on the circumstance that a new fundamental democratic consensus is emerging that is decisively shaped from below and must be mediated by social movements and protests. Such a basic consensus, and in this I agree with Raul Zelik

(2011), must combine viable alternatives and reforms from above with elements of a systemic rupture.

There are points of connection for elements of an anti-capitalist transformation in contemporary societies. Even today's capitalist economies cannot exist in a 'pure' form. As shown not least by the Greek example, they remain dependent on 'land surrender' and thus on the functionality of sectors which neither operate according to growth imperatives nor pursue a profit motive. Therefore, the valorisation of increasingly flexible productive labour depends in the stricter sense on an ever greater volume of–paid–nurturing, nursing, educating, assisting, and caring activities. These activities, often the domain of female workforces, represent a sphere of overexploitation and discrimination. This could be countered through the implementation of an economy of plural labour capacities that includes care work as an activity of equal value. In the present we can already see that health, care, education and nursing are increasingly becoming fields of social conflict. Labour conflicts are female-dominated, they resonate among the precariously employed and by encompassing child care workers, doctors or nursing staff in hospitals they involve groups whose professional ethics for a long time were rather antithetical to strike action. A professional ethics that rejects the principle of competition may in fact become the most important source of critique of precarious employment conditions as well as of the deterioration of care services (compare Kutlu 2013, pp. 226ff.).

It will be the social sectors, if any, that could grow (slowly, that is) in the advanced capitalisms. Appreciation and improved remuneration for some of these activities, funding via taxes and redistributive policies, new forms of ownership such as cooperative service providers, innovative interlinking of public and private, democratisation of service work through codetermination by producers and clients, gender-neutral reductions in working hours, and time to work on democracy are only some of the key issues for a transformatory perspective that prioritises the question of meaningful work. Such a transformation could not do without the public control of key sectors in society (energy, finance). It would have to turn the large, market-dominating corporations into that which they implicitly are already–public institutions whose activities ought to be subject to the democratic collective will. This would be a neo-socialist perspective which, as Erik Olin Wright argues (2010), would more generally entail the strengthening of social power vís-a-vís economic or state power and thus an expansion of democracy. Political actors who abstain from the discussion about such a radical social transformation place their own political future at risk.

The prospects for a neo-socialist society beyond growth imperatives and the *diktat* of competition may not look particularly good at the moment. In order to even aim for such a society though, there is one thing that is utterly necessary among the fragmented Left: the never-ending tendency towards sectarianism and the proclamation of eternal truths needs to end. Socialist politics can take place in many social fields. It can start from a critique of destructive lifestyles just as well as from conflicts over wages or practical assistance to refugees from the Global South. It is possible from the opposition as well as from the government bench. What is crucial is that it is conceived of as the undertaking of a transformative process that aims to transcend. Behind the demands for higher pay, say, by striking nursery nurses in Germany, lies the desire for appreciation and social recognition of their activities. This desire ultimately aspires to a fundamental reshaping of society, its reproductive sector and the latter's funding. To realise this goal is not only important and just for the women and migrants working in this sector, but also matches the best interests of the parents and children involved.

Bibliography

Abensour, M. (2011). *Democracy against the State. Marx and the Machiavellian moment.* Cambridge: Polity Press.

Albert, M. (1993). *Capitalism against capitalism.* London: Whurr.

Allensbach Archiv IfD-Umfrage 10,086 1986.

Arbeitskreis Strategic Unionism (2013): Jenaer Machtressourcenansatz 2.0. In: S. Schmalz & K. Dörre (Eds.): *Comeback der Gewerkschaften? Machtressourcen, innovative Praktiken, internationale Perspektiven* (pp. 345–375). Frankfurt am Main/New York: Campus.

Arendt, H. (1962). *The origins of totalitarianism.* Cleveland and New York: World Publishing Company.

Aulenbacher, B. (2013). Ökonomie und Sorgearbeit. Herrschaftslogiken, Arbeitsteilungen und Grenzziehungen im Gegenwartskapitalismus. In E. Appelt, B. Aulenbacher, & A. Wetterer (Eds.), *Gesellschaft–Feministische Krisendiagnosen* (pp. 105–126). Münster: Westfälisches Dampfboot.

Backhouse, M., Gerlach, O., Kalmring, S., & Nowak, A. (Eds.) (2013). *Die globale Einhegung–Krise, ursprüngliche Akkumulation und Landnahmen im Kapitalismus*. Münster: Westfälisches Dampfboot.

Balibar, É. (2012). *Gleichfreiheit: Politische Essays*. Berlin: Suhrkamp.

Beck, U. (1992). *Risk society. Towards a new modernity*. London: SAGE.

Bischoff, J., & Lieber, C. (2013). *Die "große Transformation" des 21. Jahrhunderts. Politische Ökonomie des Überflusses vs. Marktversagen*. Hamburg: VSA.

Boltanski, L., & Chiapello, È. (2003). *Der neue Geist des Kapitalismus*. Konstanz: UVK.

Boltanski, L., & Chiapello, È. (2005). The role of criticism in the dynamics of capitalism: social criticism versus artistic criticism. In M. Miller (Ed.), *Worlds of capitalism. Economic performance, governance and economic change in the era of globalization* (pp. 237–266). London/New York: Routledge.

Boltanski, L., & Chiapello, È. (2007). *The new spirit of capitalism*. London: Verso.

Braudel, F. (1984). *Civilization and capitalism, 15th-18th century, Volume III: The perspective of the world*. London: Collins.

Brynjolfson, E., & McAffe, A. (2014). *The second machine age. Work, Progress, and prosperity in a time of brilliant technologies*. New York: W.W. Norton.

Castel, R. (2011). *Die Krise der Arbeit. Neue Unsicherheiten und die Zukunft des Individuums*. Hamburg: Hamburger Edition.

Crouch, C. (2011). *The strange non-death of neoliberalism*. Cambridge/Malden: Polity Press.

Dobb, M. [1946] (1950). *Studies in the development of capitalism*. London: Routledge/Kegan Paul.

Dörre, K. (2012a). Landnahme, das Wachstumsdilemma und die "Achsen der Ungleichheit". *Berliner Journal für Soziologie, 22*(1), 101–128.

Dörre, K., & Haubner, T. (2012). Landnahme durch Bewährungsproben–Ein Konzept für die Arbeitssoziologie. In K. Dörre, D. Sauer, & V. Wittke (Eds.), *Kapitalismustheorie und Arbeit. Neue Ansätze soziologischer Kritik* (pp. 63–106). Frankfurt am Main/New York: Campus.

Dörre, K., Happ, A., & Matuschek, I. (Eds.) (2013). *Das Gesellschaftsbild der LohnarbeiterInnen. Soziologische Untersuchungen in ost- und westdeutschen Industriebetrieben*. Hamburg: VSA.

Dörre, K., Holst, H., & Matuschek, I. (2014). Zwischen Firmenbewusstsein und Wachstumskritik. Empirische Befunde aus einem Industriebetrieb. *WSI-Mitteilungen, 67*(7), 543–550.

Dörre, K., Rosa, H., & Lessenich, S. (2015). *Sociology, Capitalism, Critique.* London/New York: Verso.

Dubet, F. (2008). *Ungerechtigkeiten. Zum subjektiven Ungerechtigkeitsempfinden am Arbeitsplatz.* Hamburg: Hamburger Edition.

Exner, A., Fleissner, P., Kranzl, L., & Zittel, W. (Eds.). (2011). *Kämpfe um Land. Gutes Leben im post-fossilen Zeitalter.* Wien: Mandelbaum.

Federici, S. (2012). *Revolution at point zero. Housework, Reproduction and feminist struggle.* San Francisco: PM Press.

Feministische Autorinnengruppe. (2013). Das Theorem der neuen Landnahme. In H. Baumann, I. Bischel, M. Gemperle, U. Knobloch, B. Ringger, & H. Schatz (Eds.). *Care statt Crash. Sorgeökonomie und die Überwindung des Kapitalismus* (pp. 99–118) (8th ed.). Zürich.

Foster, J. B., Clark, B., & York, R. (2010). *The ecological rift. Capitalism's war on the earth.* New York: Monthly Review Press.

Fücks, R. (2013). *Smart growth: The green revolution.* Berlin: Heinrich-Böll-Stiftung.

Fulcher, F. (2004). *Capitalism. A very short introduction.* Oxford: Oxford University Press.

Gorz, A. (1985). *Wege ins Paradies.* Berlin: Rotpunkt.

Grober, U. (2012). *Sustainability. A cultural history.* Totnes (UK): Green Books.

Habermas, J. (1987). *Theory of communicative action, Volume 2.* Boston: Beacon Press.

Haller, L. Y. and Chorus, S. (2013). Care, Wert und der Wohlfahrtsstaat. Plädoyer für die Berücksichtigung des Staates als zentraler Akteur der politischen Ökonomie. In *Denknetz Jahrbuch 2013. Care statt Cash*, pp. 65–74.

Harvey, D. (2003). *The new imperialism.* Oxford / New York: Oxford University Press.

Harvey, D. (2010). *The Enigma of capital and the crisis of capitalism.* London: Profile Books.

Harvey, D. (2011). *Marx' »Kapital« lesen. Ein Begleiter für Fortgeschrittene und Einsteiger.* Hamburg: VSA.

Jackson, T. (2009). *Prosperity without growth. Economics for a finite Planet.* London/New York: Earthscan.

Karamessini, M., & Rubbery, J. (Eds.) (2013). *Women and austerity. The economic crisis and the future for gender equality.* London/New York: Routledge.

Kocka, J. (2013). *Geschichte des Kapitalismus.* Munich: C.H. Beck.

Kößler, R. (2013). Prozesse der Trennung–Gewalt im Ursprung und fortgesetztes Prozessieren des Kapital. In Backhouse et al. (Eds.), *Die globale Einhegung–Krise, ursprüngliche Akkumulation und Landnahmen im Kapitalismus* (pp. 20–39). Münster: Westfälisches Dampfboot.

Krätke, M. (2013). 150 Jahre Diskursgeschichte der SPD-Linken. Die Aktualität der Rosa Luxemburg. *SPW. Zeitschrift für sozialistische Politik und Wirtschaft* 5(198), 54–58.

Kutlu, Y. (2013). Partizipative Streikführung: Der Erzieherinnenstreik. In S. Schmalz & K. Dörre (Eds.), *Comeback der Gewerkschaften? Machtressourcen, innovative Praktiken, internationale Perspektiven* (pp. 226–242). Frankfurt am Main/New York: Campus.

Lehndorff, S. (Ed.) (2012). *A triumph of failed ideas. European models of capitalism in the crisis.* Brussels: ETUI.

Löwy, M. (2011). *Western Imperialism against Primitive Communism. A new reading of Rosa Luxemburg's economic writings.* Moscow: Ms.

Lorey, I. (2015). *State of insecurity. Government of the precarious.* London/New York: Verso.

Lutz, B. (1984). *Der kurze Traum immerwährender Prosperität. Eine Neuinterpretation der industriell-kapitalistischen Entwicklung im Europa des 20. Jahrhunderts.* Frankfurt am Main/New York: Campus.

Luxemburg, R. ([1900] 1986). *Reform or revolution, Part 1, chapter 2, The adaptation of capitalism.* London: Militant Publication.

Luxemburg, R. [1913] (2015). The accumulation of capital. In *The complete works of Rosa Luxemburg: Volume II, Economic writings 2.* pp.7–344. London: Verso.

Luxemburg, R. (2013). Introduction to national economy. In *The complete works of Rosa Luxemburg, volume I, Economic writings 1.* pp. 89–300. London: Verso.

Mahnkopf, B. (2013). *"Peak Capitalism"? Wachstumsgrenzen als Grenzen des Kapitalismus. Folgen der sozial-ökologischen Krise für die Dynamik des historischen Kapitalismus.* Working Paper der DFG-KollegforscherInnengruppe Postwachstumsgesellschaft, 02/2013, Jena.

Mann, M. (2014). Das Ende ist vielleicht nah - aber für wen? In I. Wallerstein, R. Collins, M. Mann, G. Derluguian, & C. Calhoun (Eds.), *Stirbt der Kapitalismus? Fünf Szenarien für das 21. Jahrhundert* (pp. 89–122). Frankfurt am Main/New York: Campus.

Markantonatou, M. (2014). Die Entwicklung der Arbeit, die Automatik der Sparpolitik und die Krise in Griechenland. In K. Dörre, K. Jürgens, & I. Matuschek (Eds.), *Arbeit in Europa* (pp. 217–228). Frankfurt am Main/ New York: Campus.

Marx, K. [1867] (1976). *Capital. A critique of political economy, Volume I.* New York: Penguin Books.

Marx, K. [1885] (1992). *Capital. A critique of political economy, Volume II.* New York: Penguin Books.

Marx, K. (1986). Economic Manuscripts of 1857–58. *Marx Engels complete works, Volume 28.* New York: International Publishers.

Meiksins Wood, E. (1995). *Democracy against capitalism. Renewing historical materialism.* Cambridge: Cambridge University Press.

Miegel, M. (2010). *Exit. Wohlstand ohne Wachstum.* Berlin: List Verlag.

Mies, M. (1983). Subsistenzproduktion, Hausfrauisierung, Kolonisierung. In *Beiträge zur feministischen Theorie und Praxis, 9 and 10, Zukunft der Frauenarbeit.* pp. 115–124.

Müller, M., & Niebert, K. (2012). *Epochenwechsel. Plädoyer für einen grünen New Deal.* München: oekom Verlag.

Nußbaum, A. (1925). *Das Geld in Theorie und Praxis des deutschen und ausländischen Rechts.* Tübingen: Mohr.

Kluge, A., & Negt, O. (2014). *History and obstinacy.* Cambridge: MIT Press.

Offe, C. (1984). *Arbeitsgesellschaft. Strukturprobleme und Zukunftsperspektiven.* Frankfurt am Main: Campus.

Paech, N. (2012). *Liberation from excess: The road to a post-growth economy.* Munich: oekom.

Peter, L. (2011). Kapitalismus und soziologische Kritik. Symposium zu: Klaus Dörre / Stephan Lessenich & Hartmut Rosa: Soziologie – Kapitalismus – Kritik, Frankfurt: Suhrkamp 2009. *Soziologische Revue, 34*(2), 129–152.

Picketty, T. (2014). *Capital in the twenty-first century.* Cambridge: Cambridge University Press.

Pirenne, H. (1947). *Sozial- und Wirtschaftsgeschichte Europas im Mittelalter.* Bern: Francke.

Pillay, D. (2014). Marx and the eco-logic of Fossil capitalism. In M. Williams & V. Satgar (Eds.), *Marxisms in the 21st century: Crisis, Critique & struggle* (pp. 143–165). Johannesburg: Wits University Press.

Polanyi, K. [1944] (2001). *The great transformation.* Boston: Beacon Press.

Rosa, H. (2013). Klassenkampf und Steigerungsspiel: Eine unheilvolle Allianz. Marx' beschleunigungstheoretische Krisendiagnose. In R. Jaeggi & D. Loick

(Eds.), *Nach Marx. Philosophie, Kritik, Praxis* (pp. 394–411). Berlin: Suhrkamp.

Rockström, J., Steffen, W., Noone, K., et al. (2009). A safe operating space for humanity. *Nature, 461*, 472–475.

Sakar, S. (2009). *Die Krisen des Kapitalismus. Eine andere Studie der politischen Ökonomie*. Köln/Mainz: Initiative Ökosozialismus.

Schmitter, P. C. (1996). Sektoren im modernen Kapitalismus. Steuerungsformen und ihre Performanzunterschiede. In P. Kenis & V. Schneider (Eds.), *Organisation und Netzwerk. Institutionelle Steuerung in Wirtschaft und Politik* (pp. 313–355). Frankfurt am Main: Campus.

Schumpeter, J. A. [1912] (1934). *The theory of economic development. An inquiry into profits, Capital, Credit, Interest, and the business cycle.* Harvard: Harvard University Press.

Schumpeter, J. A. (1942). *(1943): Capitalism, Socialism and democracy*. London/New York: Routledge.

Silver, B. (2003). *Forces of labor. Workers' movements and globalization since 1870.* Cambridge: Cambridge University Press.

Sombart, W. (1928). *Der moderne Kapitalismus. Band 1.* Leipzig: Duncker und Humblot.

Stern, N. (2007). *The economics of climate change. The Stern review*. Cambridge: Cambridge University Press.

Stiglitz, J. (2012). *Der Preis der Ungleichheit. Wie die Spaltung der Gesellschaft unsere Zukunft bedroht*. München: Siedler.

Stiglitz, J. (2013). *The price of inequality. How today's divided society endangers our future*. New York/London: W.W. Norton.

Streeck, W. (2014). How capitalism will end. In *New Left Review*, 87, May-Jun, pp. 35-64.

Urban, H. J. (2013). Gewerkschaftsstrategien in der Krise: Zur Handlungsfähigkeit der Gewerkschaften im Gegenwartskapitalismus. In S. Schmalz & K. Dörre (Eds.), *Comeback der Gewerkschaften? Machtressourcen, innovative Praktiken, internationale Perspektiven* (pp. 269–289). Frankfurt am Main/New York: Campus.

Vermeulen, P. (2014). How fat is the top tail of the wealth distribution?. In *EZB working papers series, No 1692*, July.

Vogl, J. (2014). *The spectre of capital.* Stanford, CA: Stanford University Press.

Wallerstein, I. (1984). *Der historische Kapitalismus*. Berlin: Argument.

Wallerstein, I., Collins, R., Mann, M., Derluguian, G., & Calhoun, G. (Eds.) (2013). *Does capitalism have a future?* Oxford: Oxford University Press.

Weber, M. [1921] (1978). *Economy and society. An outline of interpretive sociology.* Berkeley: University of California Press.
Weber, M. [1930] (2005). *The protestant ethic and the spirit of capitalism.* London: Routledge.
Wright, E. O. (2010). *Envisioning Real Utopias.* London: Verso.
Zelik, R. (2011). *Nach dem Kapitalismus. Perspektiven der Emanzipation oder: Das Projekt Communismus anders denken.* Hamburg: VSA.

10

A Critical Reception of *Accumulation of Capital*

Michael Brie

The Actuality of Rosa Luxemburg in the Midst of Capitalist Crisis

The unfettering of neoliberal financial market capitalism and its crises had one not particularly surprising side-effect: a renewed intellectual turn to the works of Rosa Luxemburg. The organic crisis of Fordism a few decades earlier had also triggered a similar wave of renewed attention to Rosa Luxemburg's writings. Indeed, capitalist crises and Left reorientation(s) have always proven to be her strong suit. This renewed turn has featured reference not only to her awareness of the power of social movements, but also to her theory of accumulation.[1] This is only logical. After all, such crises are crises of the deep structure of capital-dominated

The original version of this chapter was revised.
An erratum to this chapter can be found at DOI 10.1057/978-1-137-60108-7_12

[1] An overview of the current discussion and important relevant approaches can be found in Backhouse et al. (2013a) as well as in Schmidt et al. (2013b).

M. Brie (✉)
Institute for Critical Social Analysis of the Rosa Luxemburg Foundation, Berlin, Germany

J. Dellheim, F.O. Wolf (eds.), *Rosa Luxemburg: A Permanent Challenge for Political Economy*, DOI 10.1057/978-1-137-60108-7_10

accumulation and social reproduction, in the course of which both are subject to change (on the four current projects of social reconfiguration, see Candeias 2014). As will be shown below, a renewed and altered analysis of capitalist accumulation and the processes of strategic orientation of the Left mutually necessitate each another.

Furthermore, Rosa Luxemburg was one of the first to question the basic Marxian notion of capitalist accumulation—with far-reaching theoretical implications. She took aspects Marx had consciously left unexamined in *Capital*—including the non-capitalist strata, the colonies, and all that appeared as an 'exterior' to capital and wage labour—and assigned them a systematic position within the Marxist theoretical orbit. She quite literally opened the eyes of many to that which had been sidelined and marginalised, and thus aided in the exploration of new strategic possibilities.

The Marxian Concept of Capitalist Accumulation and Its Strategic Implications

Karl Marx's *Capital*, in all its manuscripts and preparatory drafts, amounts, essentially, to a depiction of the basic structures of capitalist accumulation with one specific objective in mind: to substantiate the possibility of socialist transformation from the innermost centre of this accumulation, from what he saw as the developing relation between capital and wage labour within the industrialised production process. In order to understand the modifications Rosa Luxemburg and others made to the Marxian concept, I will first briefly reconstruct the latter's basic argumentative structure. In this endeavour I will pay special attention to one extremely narrow, yet crucial segment: the depiction contained in the first volume of *Capital*, or rather, an even narrower aspect of this already narrow segment. As is so often the case with receptions of the classics, this will not do the complexity of Marxist thought justice.

Karl Marx takes as his point of departure societies 'in which the capitalist mode of production prevails' (Marx 1867, p. 125). In such societies, wealth appears as an 'an immense collection of commodities'. Provided an exchange of equivalents and absent robbery, fraud, slavery, and so forth, this is only possible if a commodity exists whose use is more valuable than its worth as such, or as Marx writes: 'In order to extract value out of the consumption of a commodity, our friend the money-owner must be lucky enough to find within the sphere of circulation, on the market, a commodity whose use-value possesses the peculiar property of being a source of value, whose actual consumption is therefore an objectification [*Vergegenständlichung*] of labour, hence a creation of value. The possessor of money does find such a special commodity on the market: the capacity for labour [Arbeitsvermögen], in other words labour-power [Arbeitskraft]' (Marx 1867, p. 270). While Smith and Ricardo (in exemplary bourgeois style) follow John Locke in placing the activities of the capital owners—who invest, organise, realise surplus value and thereby drive society forward in line with their own agenda—at the centre of their analysis, Marx demonstrates that this accumulation of capital is possible 'only when the owner of the means of production and subsistence finds the free worker available, on the market, as the seller of his own labour-power. And this one historical pre-condition comprises a world's history' (Marx 1867, p. 274).

For Marx, the socialisation of labour and production occurs within a double antagonism. On the one hand, the systematic planning found in an individual enterprise contrasts with the competition and anarchy of the overall economic process. One of the consequences is that: 'Capitalist production, therefore, develops technology, and the combining together of various processes into a social whole, only by sapping the original sources of all wealth—the soil and the labourer' (Marx, op. cit., pp. 507–8). Major crises repeatedly disrupt the reproduction process anew. On the other hand, as he observes, productivity is driven—to the extent of the development of the relative surplus value and the subordination of labour to capital—particularly by the development of constant capital (machinery), while the labour of individual workers is simultaneously deskilled and he or she is degraded to an appendage of said machinery, trained to perform suboperations and function as a mere natural force. This aims mainly at breaking the resistance of skilled workers. The protest of workers is therefore often specifically directed against this ongoing deskilling of labour.

According to Marx, 'a historical tendency of capitalist accumulation' (Marx 1867, p. 929) emerges from these processes, which he summarises as follows: 'Along with the constant decrease in the number of capitalist magnates, who usurp and monopolize all the advantages of this process of transformation, the mass of misery, oppression, slavery, degradation and exploitation grows; but with this there also grows the revolt of the working class, a class constantly increasing in numbers, and trained, united and organized by the very mechanism of the capitalist process of production. The monopoly of capital becomes a fetter upon the mode of production which has flourished alongside and under it. The centralization of the means of production and the socialization of labour reach a point at which they become incompatible with their capitalist integument. This integument is burst asunder. The knell of capitalist private property sounds. The expropriators are expropriated' (Marx 1867, p. 929). This is, of course, not a statement of fact but rather a hypothesis and prediction, and should be understood as such. Marx was convinced that his theory of accumulation provided the socialist project with a strictly scientific foundation. This is why here, where he depicts the 'historical tendency of capitalist accumulation', he also refers to the *Communist Manifesto* and the statements made there together with co-author Friedrich Engels.

In summary, we can state that, for Marx, capitalist accumulation represents the process of expanded reproduction of the relation between capital and labour as a relation of power, based on the separation of workers from the means of production and ensuing pressure on them to sell their labour power. Marx envisions a field of struggle between capital and labour over aspects such as wages, working hours, work organisation, the introduction and scale of machinery, working conditions, and so on. Contradictions within the various factions of the working class as well as competition between capitalists mediate this field. State actors intervene in order to, firstly, ensure that the process of capital accumulation runs smoothly and at the same time to, secondly, regulate the conditions under which it takes place. According to Marx, this reality is what makes the conquest of state power by the working class a precondition of its own emancipation.

In the introduction to their remarkable *Beyond Marx*, Marcel van der Linden and Karl Heinz Roth summarise central points of criticism of

Marx's *Capital* which get to the very core of his theory of accumulation: according to them Marx, firstly, 'neglected studying the working class in favour of studying capital' (Linden/Roth 2014, p. 9). Secondly, his work was supposedly 'in the thrall of' objectivism: 'Subjects that resist these laws never feature in this view of history, except as Don Quixotes' (Linden/Roth 2014, p. 11). And, thirdly, his analysis privileges wage-earners, free in the double sense, 'vis-à-vis other segments' (Linden/Roth 2014, p. 12). Furthermore, they fourthly highlight Marx's 'methodological nationalism' (Linden/Roth 2014, p. 13) and, fifthly, a kind of 'Eurocentrism' (Linden/Roth 2014, p. 14). Upon this analytical foundation, they conclude: 'It is our main hypothesis that these five limitations of radical theory discussed here need to be overcome if theory is to provide useful orientation in the years to come.' (Linden/Roth 2014, p. 15).

However, beginning with Rosa Luxemburg, repeated attempts have been made to break open these 'limitations' at the heart of the Marxian theory of accumulation. They do not represent 'errors', however; rather they were intended by Marx, as part of his decision to follow a process of high methodological reflection. The discrepancy between his research and his representation thereof is thus deliberate. Marx sought to substantiate the possibility of universal emancipation and the role of the working class in it through an analysis of the innermost (and thus limited) core of the capitalism of his time, from the processes that engender such an incredibly expansive dynamic in production and transportation, the tremendous gravitational pull and expansive thrust of the capitalist mode of production. To him, capitalist accumulation represented the core of this system. Marx then went about rigorously trimming down all the material he had studied in great depth by applying Occam's razor, in order to demonstrate intrascientifically the fundamental tendencies he believed to point beyond capitalism using as few variables as he deemed necessary *and* sufficient as possible. He wanted to explain a lot with a little, and this rationale must not be overlooked in retrospect (Fig. 10.1).

However, his theoretical 'abstractions' also contained their own political rationality: they corresponded, at least to a significant extent, to the

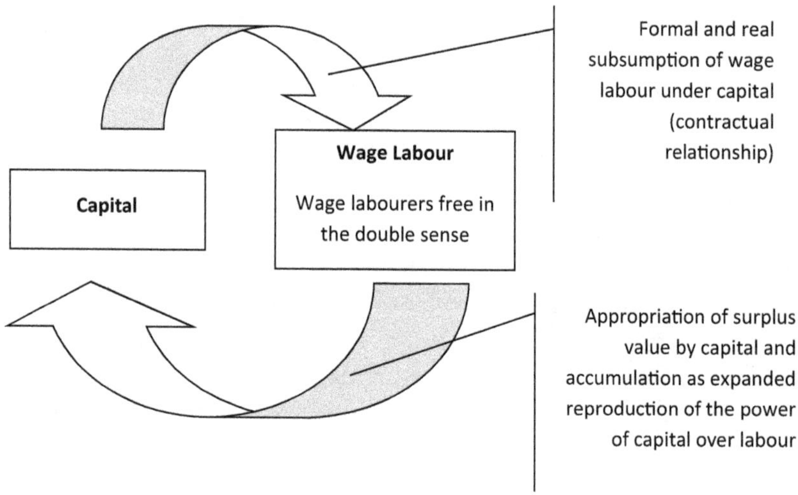

Fig. 10.1 Capital accumulation in Marx

actual social and political movements of the second half of the 19th century. They were 'real abstractions' (*Realabstraktionen*). Had Marx's assumptions—that the industrial proletariat with all its possibilities and limitations (as a special class) has both the interest and the will to initiate a socialist transformation and to allow it to flow into a reshaping of the entire mode of production and way of life, leading to universal emancipation—been correct, then (and only then) would Marx's 'real abstractions' have continued to be valid. This (somewhat narrow) particular would have embodied the universal. With regard to the subsequent evolution of Marx's accumulation theorem, however, it became clear that the objection raised by Occam's contemporary, Walter Chatton, did indeed apply: 'If three things are not enough to make a sound statement about something, then a fourth must be added, and so on.' For a modern substantiation of a political strategy within capitalism that simultaneously exceeds it, the double transformation (Klein 2013, pp. 13 ff.) consisting of the variables chosen by Marx have proven to be too few indeed. Rosa Luxemburg was the first to take an initial but nevertheless significant step forward in the elaboration of this approach.

Rosa Luxemburg's Reformulation of the Law of Capitalist Accumulation and Its Implications for the Revolutionary Workers' Movement

The period following 1890 was an era of relative calm in the centre of the capitalist world-system, accompanied by the definitive partitioning of the world into colonial domains, the explosion of overall wealth and the meagre, but growing access of the working classes in the capitalist centres to this wealth, the expansion (or at least anticipated expansion) of parliamentary democracy, and the crisis of liberalism. The predominance of the propertied bourgeoisie in England was replaced by the rule of financial and industrial oligopolies acting in close alliance with the imperialist states (on the paradoxes of this period, see Hobsbawm 1989, p. 9f.). While some metropolises witnessed the development of a war of position between capital and labour, conflicts were erupting more fiercely on the periphery—firstly, between the imperialist states themselves; secondly, between these states and the emerging anti-colonial movements; and, thirdly, with the Russian Revolution of 1905, within the weakest of these imperial states. The socialist movements required a new strategy and theory. For some, a number of central assumptions of Marxian theory of capital accumulation appeared disproven (see Bernstein 1993, who initiated his revisions in 1896, right after Engels' death). To others, Marxian political economy appeared to require further elaboration.

Marxist analyses of societies in which the capitalist mode of production was dominant published during this time were all influenced to some extent by Rudolf Hilferding's formidable study of financial capital which was published in 1910 (Hilferding 1981). All leading theoreticians of the Second International, from Kautsky (1911, 1914) to Bucharin (1969) or Lenin (1917), made explicit reference to him. They proceeded from the development of credit and stock companies already observed by Marx, as well as from the centralisation he predicted and extrapolated to the point 'when the entire social capital was united in the hands of either a single capitalist or a single capitalist company' (Marx 1867, p. 779). It is worth noting that Rosa Luxemburg's approach to capitalist accumulation deviates from this discourse. She recognises the significance of major banks and large corporations and cartels, but in contrast to many of the aforementioned theoreticians, she does not see in this centralisation and concentration socialist precursors which need only to be reversed to the benefit of workers, but instead emphasises the destructive impact they have on colonial or semi-colonial economies, as well as on small-holding production. She analyses in great detail re-distribution in favour of the monopolistic organisations as mediated by the state. Her positive point of reference is not the major organisations of capital or the state, but, on the one hand, forms of worker self-organisation and, on the other, the pre-capitalist communities upon which she repeatedly draws to illustrate the possibility of a non-capitalist economic and non-ownership-related social order (see especially in Luxemburg 1974). It is the use (or rather abuse) and destruction of the latter by the societies of the capitalist centres which she places at the heart of her analysis.

As Christel Neusüß (1985, p. 306) noted, Rosa Luxemburg's main point of concern is the reproduction of the totality of society. She begins her work on the accumulation of capital by reflecting upon the maintenance of society as a whole (that is to say, not only of the relation between capital and labour), and immediately includes the cultural sphere in these reflections. According to her, it is always civilisations that 'reproduce', not merely technological and economic relations. She writes: 'In the first instance, the regular repetition of production is the general precondition and foundation of regular consumption, and is thus a prerequisite of human civilization in each of its historical forms. In this sense, the concept of reproduction contains a historical moment, one that is defined by the history of civilization'. (Luxemburg 2015, p. 7).

Rosa Luxemburg believed capitalism's increasing propensity for crisis was rooted in the fact 'that the movement of capitalist accumulation requires an environment of noncapitalist social formations, that it is in a constant process of metabolism with the latter as it proceeds, and that it can only exist for as long as it finds itself within this milieu' (Luxemburg 2015, p. 263). In her view, this was the 'solution as defined by Marx's theory', but regardless is a fundamentally different take on capital accumulation from that which Marx presented in the first volume of *Capital.* According to Luxemburg, Marx had only considered 'one aspect' of this accumulation, that is, the one occurring between capital and labour in 'the process that occurs at the point of production of surplus value'. 'The other dimension of capital accumulation', she writes, 'consists in a process that takes place between capital and noncapitalist forms of production' (Luxemburg 2015, p. 329). Yet she considered this side of capital accumulation to be as finite as our Planet Earth, which even in her day could already be circumnavigated in far less than eighty days.

To Luxemburg, capital accumulation is above all a destruction of non-capitalist civilisations, in the latter of which she identifies those traits she considers absent in capitalism—production for immediate needs and direct resolution of communal issues. The model is the 'economic organization of the communist rural commune' (Luxemburg 2015, p. 265). She finds justification for the necessary dependence of capital accumulation on non-capitalist milieus in the hypothesis that continuously increasing surplus value cannot be realised under the conditions of equivalent exchange and in the fact that it cannot be consumed by capitalists themselves, because surplus value is ultimately something that has been generated through the exchange of equal values. In her view, the Marxian reproduction schemes contained in the second volume of *Capital* failed to convincingly explain where the additional demand for the additionally created value should come from. What was essentially required were 'third parties' (Luxemburg 2015, p. 252). She established that '*at the very least*, the surplus value that is to be capitalized and the corresponding part of the capitalist mass of products cannot possibly be realized within the capitalist sphere, and must therefore at all costs find purchasers outside this sphere' of capitalist circulation—in the 'the surrounding noncapitalist world' (op. cit., p. 259). In contrast to all previous modes of production, capitalism necessarily displaces all non-capitalist forms, while simultaneously depending on them for its very existence; capitalism is thus a form of economy that at 'the same time as it tends to become the universal form, it is smashed to smithereens by its intrinsic inability to be a universal form of production' (Luxemburg 2015, p. 341). This leads to a momentous expansion of the Marxian account of accumulation (see chart 2).

In her periodisation Luxemburg states that capital expands in its present militaristic form and, in doing so, destroys—both internally as well as externally—the very purchasing power it requires for the realisation of surplus value. She arrives at a rather brilliant conclusion: 'The more violently capital uses militarism to exterminate noncapitalist strata both at home and abroad, and to worsen living standards for all strata of workers, the more the day-to-day history of capital accumulation on the world stage is transformed into a continuous series of political and social catastrophes and convulsions, which, together with the periodic economic cataclysms in the form of crises, will make it impossible for accumulation to continue, and will turn the rebellion of the international working class against the rule of capital into a necessity, even before the latter has come up against its natural, selfcreated economic constraints.' (Luxemburg 2015, p. 341) (Fig. 10.2).

Her strategic conclusions for the socialist workers' movement include: the necessity of a consistent and determined engagement with imperialism, militarism and colonialism; unequivocal solidarity with peoples enslaved and dispossessed by capitalism; the further development of workers' offensive capacities (general strikes, a full-scale struggle for universal suffrage and social reforms); the cultivation of independent learning processes as a precondition for struggle; but also the seizure of political and economic power by the workers' movement. Luxemburg wants a socialism not *for* the workers, but *by* the workers. 'The essence of social-

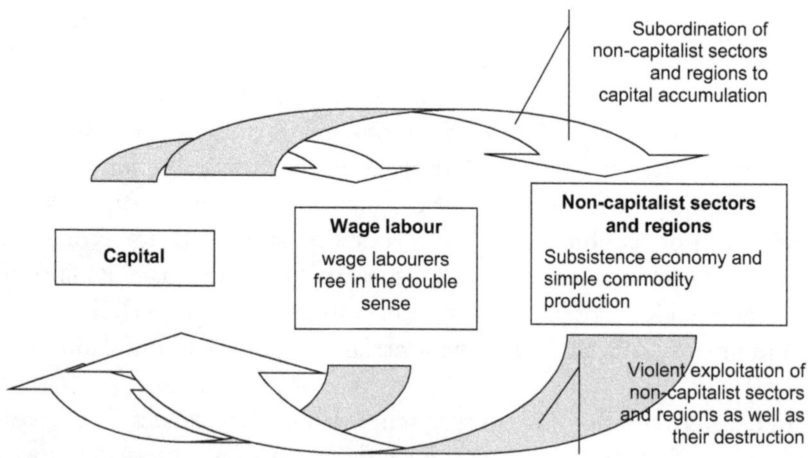

Fig. 10.2 Capital accumulation in Luxemburg

ist society consists in the fact that the great laboring mass ceases to be a dominated mass, but rather, makes the entire political and economic life its own life and gives that life a conscious, free, and autonomous direction' (Luxemburg 1918). This is moreover one of the reasons behind her comprehensive study of pre-capitalist economic forms. For Luxemburg, socialism is 'inherently a universal one and simultaneously a harmonious system in itself, since it is oriented not to accumulation, but to the satisfaction of the vital needs of laboring humanity itself through the development of all of the world's productive powers' (Luxemburg 1913, p. 342), as the final lines of *Accumulation of Capital* explain. According to her vision, a new society that supersedes capitalism will witness the re-emergence of pre-capitalist economic forms: production based on actual needs, transparency of immediate social relationships, democratic self-determination by producers and direct democracy (one of many examples is the depiction of the Germanic or Peruvian 'mark community'[2] in Luxemburg (1974, p. 127); for a more systematic approach cf. Löwy 2013). For Luxemburg, her reconceptualisation of Marx's theory of accumulation and her argument for a new strategy of workers' independent organisation—and be it in response to the dominance of bureaucratised structures within the movement—represented two components of a unified whole.

The Theory of Accumulation in 'Third World' Marxism

World War II was followed by a global stalemate between the USA and the Soviet Union. The socio-political structures of this bipolar world order appeared static and ossified. As a consequence, the dissolution of this historic standstill only seemed possible from the so-called margins—that is, from the 'Third World' and out of conflicts traditional Marxism had conceived of as 'secondary contradictions' next to the 'primary con-

[2] Translator's note: A footnote on the same page explains: 'The *Mark* was an ancient Germanic communal form of village organization that survived in modified form into modern times. Luxemburg subsequently uses the term more universally, applying to what she saw as similar forms in various societies around the world.'

tradiction' between capital and labour. At this point in history, emancipatory forces found themselves in a phase of strategic reorientation. The aforementioned developments have served as the backdrop for a wave of positive receptions of Luxemburgian accumulation theory since the 1970s. This was true, firstly, for Marxist-inspired left theoreticians in the Third World looking for a scientific point of reference for the argument that the post-colonial world may possibly serve as the centre of future revolutions, of which they of course found more in Luxemburg than in Marx. As Samir Amin (1974, p. 61) writes: 'It was Rosa Luxemburg's great merit to have seen the relations between the center and the periphery depend on the mechanisms of primitive accumulation, because what is involved is not the economic mechanisms characteristic of the internal functioning of the capitalist mode of production, but relations between this mode of production and formations that differ from it.' Strategic reorientation was once again linked to a renewal of the theory of accumulation.

By the 1970s, however, the non-European countries were no longer colonies with a mode of production characterised primarily by subsistence agriculture and the limited development of industrial capitalist wage labour, but rather had become independent countries of the Third World conducting intensive industrialisation efforts. Enterprises oriented toward the world market grew continuously while subsistence agriculture and informal sectors were restructured and sometimes even expanded. Yet it appeared that the 'mechanism' of equal exchange identified by Samir Amin as the predominant form in the centres had failed to materialise. Inequality deepened and Ricardo's theory of comparative advantage contradicted the reality of solidifying comparative disadvantages of the Third World in international trade. Processes of socialisation were not fostering harmonisation, but rather represented mutually contradicting dynamics of development in centre and periphery, respectively—two distinct faces of one world. Samir Amin attributed this to the fact that the accumulated developmental advantages of the countries of the capitalist centres enabled them to produce goods upon which the developing countries relied or were in high demand among these countries' upper and middle classes, and which cannot be produced in the technically less advanced countries. According to Amin, the terms of trade for developing countries would therefore always tend to become less favourable (Amin 1974, pp. 70ff.). In contrast to Marx's assumption, surplus value arises not only from so-called equal exchange, but also 'unequal exchange, transferring surplus from peripheral to core zones' (Amin et al. 1982, p. 9). This also includes the transfer from '"semiproletarian" extended households' (Wallerstein 1982, p. 21) which lowers wage costs in the immediately capitalist sectors of the periphery. The always merely '*partial* freedom of the factors of production, the *partial* realization of the law of value' (Amin et al. 1982, p. 24), is conceived of by Wallerstein and other theoreticians of this persuasion not as an obstacle for but, on the contrary, a precondition of the functioning of global capital accumulation. These in turn stand in deep contradiction to an ever-increasing 'fuller realization' of this very law of value—very much in the spirit of Rosa Luxemburg's argumentation. Wallerstein concludes: 'The two asymptotes of geographical expansion and commodification have reached the level where they have begun to act as structural constraints on the survival of capitalism' (Amin et al. 1982, p. 25).

It is in this context that Samir Amin develops the concept of a dominant mode of production. While Luxemburg had analysed the permanent coexistence of the capitalist mode of production and other, non-capitalist modes of economic activity as a functioning whole under the dominance of capital accumulation, Amin now generalised this notion: 'Dominance should not, under any circumstances, be reduced to the statistical predominance of one form of economic activity. The concept of domination is very precise and includes: (1) domination by the fundamental law of the dominant mode, which determines the conditions of reproduction of the entire formation (thus, for example, the law of capitalist accumulation determines both the conditions of reproduction of capitalist society, and all the complex relations between its various parts, including a capitalist industrial economy and a peasant economy); (2) the consequent transfer of a portion of the surplus generated in the dominated modes to the dominant mode (thus, for example, the transformation of a portion of rent into profit); (3) the political supremacy of the dominant class in the dominant mode, the other dominant class being, at best, reduced to the status of allies; (4) the supremacy of the ideology of the dominant mode' (Amin 1977, p. 39).

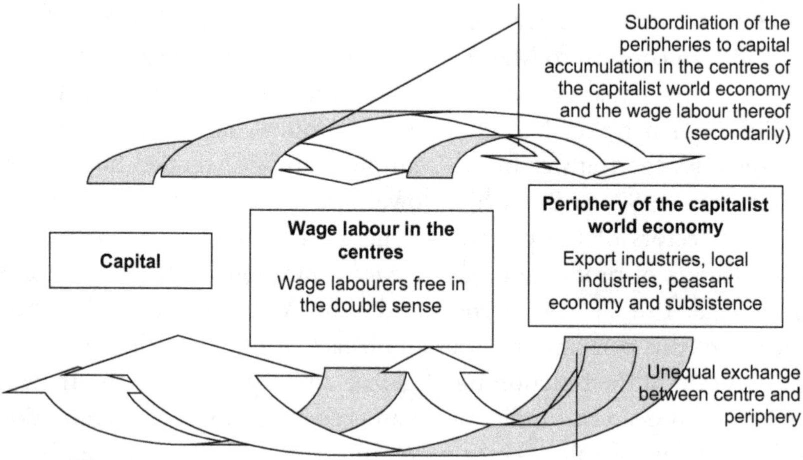

Fig. 10.3 Capital accumulation in Amin, inter alia

Each subordinate mode of production assumes a specific function within the overarching whole. Their relative independence and particularity is merely functional with respect to this dominance (Fig. 10.3). A thorough capitalisation in the sense of *immediate* transformation into capitalist wage labour would undermine this functionality. The heterogeneity of modes of production within capitalist societies is therefore continuously generated anew. Even the state-socialist countries were affected by this tendency. Thus, in contrast to what Marx and Luxemburg had thought, there exists no tendency towards a steadily progressing homogenisation (see Arrighi 1990, p. 64).[3] The result is a pluralisation of forces critical of capitalism, or as Wallerstein wrote in the late 1980s: 'In a very short space of time then, essentially since the 1960s, where previously we had three main varieties of antisystemic movements in the world-system—Social-Democrats largely in the West, Communists largely in the East, and nationalists largely in the third world—we suddenly had six varieties. In addition to the '"old" three, we now have the "new social movements" largely in the West, the "anti-bureaucratic" movements largely in the East, and the "anti-Westernizing" movements largely in the South' (Wallerstein 1990, p. 43).

[3] With view to the newly emerging middle classes, but also to tradesmen and peasants, Bernstein had pointed out this problem at a fairly early stage (Bernstein 1993).

The reinterpretation of capitalist accumulation by the Marxist and oftentimes Maoist-inspired socialists of the Third World was closely linked to a new vision of what constituted the main lines of conflict of the 1960s and 1970s. As Samir Amin summarises:

> The current crisis reminds us forcefully of the chief characteristics of the capitalist system in its imperialist phase—the transfer of the contradictions of the capitalist mode of production from its dominant imperialist centers to its dominated periphery: the revolutionary and socialist potential of the struggle for national liberation; the social-democratic ideological domination of the working classes in the centers. (Amin 1977, p. 14)

It was no longer the industrial working class in the centres of the capitalist world economy that seemed like the transformative force that would defeat capitalism, but rather the peasants and semi-industrial classes and strata—possibly in alliance with nationalist forces—who could initiate such a change. The perspective was thus no longer one of catching up to the West through 'modernisation', but of separate paths of independent modes of development and forms of socialisation which would connect much more directly to pre- and non-capitalist modes of production and ways of life.

The Feminist Reception of Rosa Luxemburg

During this same period (the 1960s–70s) conflicts came to the fore within the highly developed centres which could not be directly explained by the relation between capital and labour but may nevertheless be considered to be linked to capitalism and its mode of accumulation. It was in this context that the German women's movement rediscovered Rosa Luxemburg's work in political economy. Here as well, the task at hand was that of strategic reorientation—this time from the fight for a transformation of gender relations and the emancipation of women to one for the transformation of capital-dominated societies as a whole.

One quite representative example of the West German feminist reception of Rosa Luxemburg's political economic work is the collection of texts by Claudia von Werlhof, Maria Mies and Veronika Bennholdt-Thomsen, published under the title *Frauen, die letzte Kolonie. Zur Hausfrauisierung der Arbeit* (*Women: the Last Colony: On the 'Housewifisation' of Work*) in 1983. Some time later, Werlhof would write the following: 'Rosa Luxemburg, who paradoxically was unaware that she had written on the issue of women's rights in *Accumulation of Capital*, anticipated today's discussion to a remarkable degree' (Werlhof 1991, p. 40f.).

> Maria Mies made the connection to Luxemburg explicit, writing: 'The recent discussion of the modes of production and on "ongoing primitive accumulation" and the reanalysis of Rosa Luxemburg's work (1913) on capital accumulation, have gone a long way to explain the relationship between subsistence reproduction and capital accumulation. According to Rosa Luxemburg, capitalist penetration means both the destruction and the preservation of subsistence economies, or to use her expression, of natural economies. Her argument is that capital accumulation, i.e. the reproduction of capital, is not possible without the existence is non-capitalist strata and regions.' (Mies 1988, p. 43).

In this feminist reception, the Luxemburgian position is taken up, deconstructed, transformed and radicalised at the same time. A critique of capitalism from the feminist perspective would consider it reasonable 'to posit not the wage worker but instead the housewife as paradigm of exploitation under capitalism' (Werlhof et al. 1988, p. 85). According to her, it is the housewives in western industrialised countries as well as the 'non-wage workers', women and peasants in the post-colonial dependent states who perform the bulk of the labour within this kind of capitalism. That is why 'capitalist penetration does not mean the transformation of all non-capitalist subsistence production into capitalist production units and of the use-value producers into "free" wage labourers' (Mies 1988, p. 44).

As Claudia Neusüß objects to Marx: 'Capital's own economy, the measurement of "wealth" by "value", by working hours, practically excludes anything that it treats uneconomically, that it wastes and plunders. Yet by describing this distinct economy while at the same time largely ignoring that which is excluded, the critique loses a decisive sting. And I contend that it was the limited male-dominated pattern which blurred the view' (Neusüß 1985, p. 233).

A radical shift of perspective vis-à-vis Marx was undertaken, in which Marx's paradigm represented both paragon and antithesis. According to this view, for Marx the 'bottom' had meant the proletariat, the non-estate of bourgeois society, since 1843. This was 'a class with radical chains', ensnared in a sphere 'which cannot emancipate itself without emancipating itself from all other spheres of society and thereby emancipating all other spheres of society' (Marx 1844, p. 186). Indeed, that is why Marx turned to the critique of political economy in the first place. To Marx, the analysis contained in *Wage Labour and Capital* represented the theoretical basis of emancipation. Claudia von Werlhof, however, asks whether this bottom sits on top of another, much deeper 'bottom'. She focuses on aspects Marxists had hitherto taken for granted and failed to systematically integrate into politico-economic analysis—on the type of labour that creates and maintains human labour power itself.

She draws the following conclusion: 'If we have understood housework, then we have understood everything [...] The women's question is the most general—not the most specific—of all social questions, because it contains all the others and, in contrast to all other questions, it leaves no one out. This is neither feminist conceit nor arrogance, but is inherent in the functioning or our society itself. For, historically, our society has to date created a unique situation, namely one in which the women are always 'the ones below'. But only from below—at the bottom—can the whole be seen as a whole' (Werlhof 1988a, p. 168).

This perspective has implications for the understanding of bourgeois-capitalist society as well. It is neither a society of the free and equal nor a society of classes whose members manage their relations to one another on the basis of a formally equal contract (the wage labour contract); the most important site is not the factory and certainly not the parliament, but instead the home, its kitchen, its nurseries and its bedrooms. Werlhof writes:

> The proletarian is apparently free, equal, fraternal and so on; the housewife is not. In reality she is doubly fettered since, first of all, she may not choose or change the place, type of work or her particular job freely, she is bound: to the house/apartment, the husband and the children; secondly, neither is she free from all means of production, so it cannot be said that she merely

> possesses her labour power, as, in a certain sense, does the proletarian. What she does have, and no man has, and which is treated as a means of production is her child-bearing capacity; also she 'has' the husband as 'bread-winner'. (Werlhof 1988a, p. 175)

It is precisely wage labour that she does *not* consider to be the basis of modern capitalism; wage labour is seen as a particular and endangered outlier. The historical tendency, according to her, is one not of 'proletarisation' but rather of 'housewifisation'. She writes: 'not only is the wage labour relationship not being universalized, but it has been on the retreat for some time, both quantitatively and qualitatively, and at an accelerating pace [...] a push back into nature—"feminization", "domestication", "housewifization", "marginalization"—is taking place' (Werlhof 1988b, p. 109).

> From this position, Veronika Bennholdt-Thomsen expands the Marxist concept of labour: 'If we include in the Marxist definition of labour belly, breast and gender aside from arms and legs, hands and head, then the decisive distinction for the determination of our own human nature, which is the ability to conceive and give birth, becomes visible. Men and women experience themselves differently in the metabolism with nature. A woman sees herself as an immediate part of nature, as she produces new life and nurtures it with her own body. The male relation to nature is an exchange much more mediated through hands and head' (Bennholdt-Thomsen 1988b, p. 200).

And given that the 'production of humans', as opposed to the production of things, is at the heart of domestic labour, the future belongs to it—quite literally (see Werlhof 1988a, p. 178). The naturalisation of social critique through its association with 'femininity' is rather conspicuous.

In terms of political economy, the relationship between subsistence agriculture and the production of life as the two most fundamental activities in every economy (see Mies 1988, p. 86) on the one hand, and capital on the other hand, is defined as appropriation of unpaid labour in the form of a double income—'women's income' and 'colonial income' (see Werlhof 1988b, p. 154) (Fig. 10.3). What results is not the disappearance of subsistence agriculture, but rather its transformation.

Subsistence agriculture assumes modern forms (Bennholdt-Thomsen 1988b, p. 202). Areas that Rosa Luxemburg had still assumed to be a (relevant) exterior of capital accumulation in the strict sense are virtually created anew while being directly or indirectly subordinated to capital accumulation in the process.

The same holds true for the production of life as such: 'The conclusion from what that depicted is both general and specific: the separation of subsistence production from the remaining social production must be understood as a cornerstone of class contradictions in capitalism. Subsistence production is the area in which human life is produced and labour capacity is produced and reproduced—that the work performed here and the people active in this area at the same time receive very little appreciation can only be described as perversion—which is, in turn, the basis for the alienation of the contemporary social formation' (Bennholdt-Thomsen 1988a, p. 59).

One aspect that remains peripheral in this analysis is the permeation and refinement of subsistence production through the dominance of capital, a process that far exceeds mere underappreciation of this production.

According to this view, what Marxism considered the primary relation of bourgeois society—that of capital and wage labour and its reproduction through capitalist accumulation—becomes a secondary relation of exploitation. The relationship between capitalist forms of subsistence and domestic economy now appears as 'necessary foundation and the "permanent underground" of modern society' (Werlhof 1991, p. 90f.).

According to Werlhof, one is only able to understand 'capitalism as totality', if conditions 'which have thus far been regarded as extra-economic, even "natural" and thereby trans-historic, only because they were not situated within a wage labour relation' are included in the analysis: 'in particular, for example, women's work, giving birth and child-rearing, the satisfaction of men's needs for food, sexuality, attention' (Werlhof 1991, p. 43f.).

The conclusion Claudia von Werlhof, Maria Mies and Veronika Bennholdt-Thomsen drew from this new understanding of capitalist accumulation inspired by Rosa Luxemburg was the necessity of revealing the hidden and suppressed foundation of this society—meaning the subsistence and domestic labour commonly performed by women. In

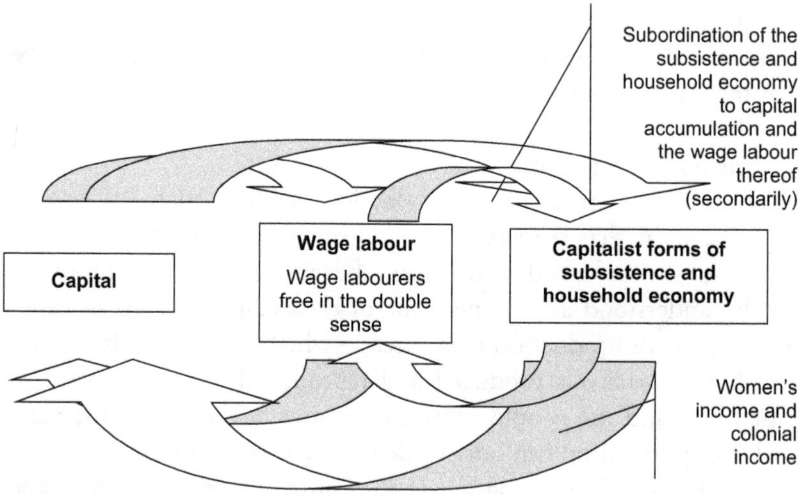

Fig. 10.4 Capital accumulation according to Werlhof, Mies and Bennholdt-Thomsen

their view there was a 'division both between and within social "classes"' (Werlhof 1991, p. 91) that could no longer be ignored. Both service and industrial workers have 'an interest in the exploitation of peasant producers through so-called "unequal exchange"', commodity production seeks 'subsidisation through subsistence production' and 'men, finally, be they workers or peasants, must have an interest in appropriating their wives' housework including by means of applying direct force in the sense of the typical method of primitive accumulation' (Werlhof 1991, p. 92). The outcome of this debate is a reformulated understanding of accumulation under capitalist conditions (Fig. 10.4).

Proceeding from the interests of those at the bottom of society, particularly of women and those who generally perform subsistence and domestic labour, the unification of all struggles against the totality of relations of exploitation becomes the goal:

> The task at hand is the abolishment of conditions in which one part can declare itself human at the cost of the subordination of the other part: generally, men at the cost of women, society at the cost of nature, the

> industrial nations at the cost of the peoples they have conquered. In this, these distinct relations are connected to one another in terms of content and structure. Any strategy for the overcoming of one of these conditions therefore must include that of the others, too. (Werlhof et al. 1988, p. 139)

The Contemporary Reception of Luxemburg's *Theory of Accumulation*—A Brief Overview

The crisis of the Fordist accumulation regime and the implementation of the financial market-driven accumulation regime (see Klein 2008; Candeias 2009; Bischoff 2009; Haug 2012; Busch and Land 2013, among others) brought about a new, enlarged audience for the Luxemburgian theory of accumulation. This took place against the backdrop of rejuvenated strategic debate and discussion on the Left, which also called for a redefinition of the theoretical points of reference within the Marxist accumulation theory. In the following, I will briefly introduce six different approaches which reformulated Marx's accumulation theory.

First: Accumulation by Dispossession

David Harvey's analysis of the 'new imperialism' proceeds from the hypothesis that over-accumulated finance capital is reinvested through repeated waves of dispossession: 'What accumulation by dispossession does is to release a set of assets (including labour power) at very low (and in some instances zero) cost. Overaccumulated capital can seize hold of such assets and immediately turn them to profitable use' (Harvey 2003, p. 149). These 'waves' include the privatisation of public services and incursions by capital into the post-Soviet sphere and China, but also the devalorisation of capital and labour (see also the distinction between five different types of this dispossession presented by Zeller 2004, p. 11). According to Harvey, the primary means of this accumulation by dispossession was financialisation, reinforced by a renewed display of imperial power. Harvey follows Marx in viewing the initial separation of producers from the means of production as a 'necessary though ugly stage through which the social order had to go in order to arrive at a state where both capitalism and some alternative socialism might be possible' (Harvey 2003, p. 163).

Harvey associates the two different types of accumulation—that of expanded reproduction based on the complete separation of producers from the means of production on the one hand, and accumulation by dispossession on the other hand—with two distinct types of struggle. Struggles around the expanded reproduction of the relation of capital and wage labour represent the domain of the traditional workers' movement, which was able to force through the establishment of democratic welfare states in the highly developed countries. These struggles were centred around industrial disputes (op. cit., p. 170). Feminism, the environmentalist movement, and the struggle for urban and rural spaces were supposedly seen as irrelevant. Yet during the same period, capital shifted its focus from accumulation through expanded reproduction to accumulation by dispossession. Harvey draws the following conclusion: 'Luxemburg's formulation stands as extremely helpful. Capital accumulation indeed has a dual character. But the two aspects of expanded reproduction and accumulation by dispossession are organically linked, dialectically intertwined. It therefore follows that the struggles within the field of expanded reproduction (that the traditional left placed so much emphasis upon) have to be seen in a dialectical relation with the struggles against accumulation by dispossession that the social movements coalescing within the anti- and alternative globalization movements are primarily focusing upon. If the current period has seen a shift in emphasis from accumulation through expanded reproduction to accumulation through dispossession, and if the latter lies at the heart of imperialist practices, then it follows that the balance of interest within the anti- and alternative globalization movement must acknowledge accumulation by dispossession as the primary contradiction to be confronted. But it ought never to do so by ignoring the dialectical relation to struggles in the field of expanded reproduction.' (op. cit., pp. 176–7).

Second: Accumulation Through *Landnahme* and Colonisation

In reference to Burkart Lutz's analysis of the 'internal *Landnahme*' in agriculture, skilled labour and the service sector after World War II in particular, and of their transformation into modern sectors of valorisation (Lutz 1984, pp. 62ff.), Klaus Dörre raises the *Landnahme* theorem to the status of a universal law of capitalist societies. According to Dörre, capitalism is unable to 'reproduce from within' and must therefore occur in 'socio-spatial or physical-material' dimensions, 'sectorally as well as field-specific, within the medium of time', and encompasses 'different modes of production, social groups, life forms and even personality structures' (Dörre 2013a, p. 113; see also 2011, 2013b). The basic postulate of the *Landnahme* theorem is that a 'pure capitalism' is impossible and that there are certain, absolute limits to the commodification and generalisation of the commodity form. Therefore, one must 'systematically take an *exterior* of capitalist market societies into account' (Dörre 2013a, p. 113) at all times.

Ingo Schmidt highlights some tendencies of a dependent industrialisation and the creation of new consumer markets in the South as a form of neo-colonial rule post-1945, paying particular attention to the 'colonisation of lifeworlds' in the North: 'The penetration of private households with mass-produced appliances and entertainment electronics replaced much economic activity that had previously been done outside the circuits of capital accumulation. The colonization, or commodification, of household production ranged from cooking and washing to canning and sewing. Sprawling cultural industries similarly colonized leisure time and also contributed to post-World War II prosperity' (Schmidt 2014).

The *Landnahme* and colonisation theorem remains one-sided as long as countervailing processes are not also taken into consideration at all times: it emphasises the subordination, colonisation or even dissolution of non-capital-based areas of society, yet it does not address the creation of such areas throughout the history of bourgeois-capitalist societies, let alone at the height of the neoliberal onslaught. Important insights from the feminist debates of the 1960s and 1970s have been lost.[4] The leading actors of this type of capitalism are more than eager to integrate the social, democratic, as well as ecological and libertarian 'land' (so to speak) gained by counter-movements and class compromises directly into processes of valorisation. The 'exterior' that Klaus Dörre speaks of is thus above all a historically cultivated 'interior' of capital-dominated societies whose ability to reproduce depends on their capacity to functionally combine a plurality of forms of socialisation *and* to subordinate them. As Ingo Schmidt illustrates with regard to post-war capitalism in Western Europe: 'The expansion of the public sector and social security contributed to the de-commodification of labour power. [...] While the welfare state and the unions reduced the pressure on individuals to sell their labour power, capital was able to extend its hold over labour power within the production process, thus limiting autonomous spaces for action of workers inside the workplace' (Schmidt 2013a, p. 150). Even in the midst of today's crisis, tendencies toward declining levels of social security and a re-commodification of the labour force go hand in hand with the tendencies of an expansion of the welfare state (education, care work). In the process, wage-earners and the new self-employed are segregated into two oppositional groups.

Third: Accumulation Through Valorisation

The new *Landnahme* and market radicalisation can also be seen as an attempt to resolve the problems of capital's problems of accumulation through repeated waves of valorisation (*Inwertsetzung*). This was addressed at an early stage in the German debate by Elmar Altvater (1992; see also more recently 2013) and Mohssen Massarrat (1993). Christoph Görg taps into this argument to vehemently oppose the overemphasis on the purely parasitic character of capitalism as mere robbery and naked dispossession. The 'nature of capitalist accumulation today' cannot be located 'in the fraudulent absorption of surplus value by capital funds etc.' (Görg

[4] It is quite interesting how little the connection between the feminist discussion of the 1970s and the 1980s is acknowledged in the current debate, while the reference to Latin America remains largely intact.

2004a, p. 724). The point of departure is commonly 'the problematic assumption of an exhaustion of the capitalist innovation dynamic', while it is precisely the 'expansion of capitalist valorisation opportunities' that can be observed (Görg 2004a, p. 725). Görg uses the term 'valorisation' (*Inwertsetzung*) to describe these processes. According to him, new resources are subsumed under capitalist relations of production: 'What is central, then, is the social form, the value or capital form, in which these resources are transferred while at the same time destroying other social relations—violently or legally' (Görg 2004a, p. 727). Monetisation alone is not sufficient to characterise valorisation. What is decisive is 'the actual inclusion of objects or social processes into the process of capital accumulation' (Görg 2004b, p. 1501). But this process is itself marked by a deep ambivalence, as it is shaped by various mutually oppositional forces, which also identify opportunities in at least a partial monetisation (see also the case studies in Backhouse 2013; Fatheuer 2013).

This inclusion encompasses the valorisation of hitherto state-run public services, infrastructure, knowledge, genetic and other natural resources (see Brand and Görg 2003). Christoph Görg therefore aims at a counter-movement in the sense of the 'defense of society' (Foucault) in order to reduce 'the centrality of wage labour for individual reproduction' and 'structural competition between precarised workers' (Görg 2004a, p. 730). He proposes a guaranteed minimum income (for a critical take on this, see Dellheim 2007), the institutionalisation of 'cosmopolitan solidarity' and the concept of a 'social policy as social infrastructure', concluding: 'This is perhaps not truly subversive, let alone revolutionary—but it would chip away at the foundations of neoliberal domination, at least a little' (Görg 2004a, p. 730).

Fourth: Accumulation by Capitalisation of the Future

In his contribution 'Das Außen des Kapitals' (The Exterior of Capital), Frank Engster shifts the attention from the space of accumulation to its temporal dimension. He points out that capitalism is all about the 'additional labour time of profit' (Engster 2014, p. 4). According to him, the logic of valorisation is the 'temporal relationship with the *self* that living labour time enters into with its own past as accumulated by capital' (Engster 2014, p. 8).

In his view, it is capitalism's civilising mission to reduce necessary labour time (by increasing relative surplus value) (Engster 2014, p. 10). After this mission reached its limits with the exhaustion of Fordism, he believes only those forms remain which include '1. Uncompensated appropriation outside the principle of equivalence, 2. Redistribution and wealth transfers, and 3. Valorisation or even 4. The creation of ficticious money and wealth' (Engster 2014, 12). The form of fictitious money and wealth creation can be understood as a 'second original accumulation'. It is the 'production of claims vis-à-vis future (surplus) labour time' (Engster 2014, p. 19). He adds:

> Granted, the anticipation of future valorisation via forms of ficticious capital has been a feature of the capitalist mode of production since its beginning and was in effect long before the second accumulation began. But these anticipations were deduced from current valorisation and always overtaken by it. In this sense they remained secondary to valorisation and thus passive. [...] Since the second origin of accumulation and its anticipation of future profits, however, a veritable disproportion in relation to this valorisation has emerged, a kind of "capitalisation of the future", as if accumulation were living above its means, above the valorising relationship of labour and capital. (Engster 2014, p. 19–20).

Here, ficticious capital assumes an active role in directing accumulation. Two reservations should be noted: first of all, capital valorisation is per se oriented towards the future. Any granting of credit within the movement of M-C-M' means anticipating and staking claim to future profits, but whether this prospect comes to fruition or not always remains an unknown. Moreover, the control of accumulation through future expectations concerning ficticious capital is nothing new. Engster's 'second primitive accumulation' may well turn out to be another new wave of over-accumulation. To me, claiming that capital's 'historical mission' of reducing the amount of necessary labour has been completed, thereby implying a definite limit to capitalist accumulation, seems at odds with the amount of necessary labour still being performed today. A transition to an ecologically sustainable social model will require all sorts of labour.

Even the comprehensive automation of production expected to occur over the coming decades will require large investments. Furthermore, society will have to decide what kinds of work are actually 'necessary' in the first place. In the highly developed countries this is more so the case than ever. The limits of capitalism do not exist 'as such', but rather are heavily contested.

Fifth: The Emergence of a New 'Exterior'

De Angelis raises the question as to whether in the conflicts around current tendencies of capital accumulation in 'the myriad of communities struggles taking place around the world for water, electricity, land, access to social wealth, life and dignity' an 'exterior' perhaps emerges from the 'interior' in the form of 'a social space created by virtue of creating relational patterns that are other than and incompatible with the relational practices of capital' (De Angelis 2006, p. 1). According to him, this is '*our* outside that is the realm of value practices outside those of capital and, indeed, clashing with it' (loc. cit.). It then results in a detritus (a decay product), 'a space in which the problematic of social reproduction is uniquely in the hands of the dispossessed, and dramatically depends on the effectiveness, organisational reach and communal constitution of their struggles and ability to reclaim and constitute commons' (loc. cit.). Alternatives can (and thus will) only arise from such struggles. Yet how could they simultaneously threaten capitalism and create new forms of an Other connected to the self-preservation of individuals, their communities, and their value systems? He adds: 'But this is a big, too big of a question, for which I do not have an answer' (op. cit., p. 10). The question as to how alternative communal practices could be comprehensively produced and stably reproduced under the conditions of financial market capitalism remains unanswered. The Other, the new non-capitalist exterior, could then remain a mere ephemeral moment of precarious aspirations, struggles and unstable relationships.

Silvia Federici makes a similar argument but goes beyond De Angelis, as she assumes a decidedly feminist standpoint: 'shaped by the struggle against sexual discrimination and over reproductive work' (Federici 2011,

p. 2). She correctly calls attention to the fact that even from a perspective committed to the preservation of the capitalist system, total privatisation and commodification of the world is not only unrealistic, but also undesirable (Federici 2011, 3). So far, the Left has not seriously posed the question 'of how to bring together the many proliferating commons that are being defended, developed, and fought for, so that they can form a cohesive whole and provide a foundation for a new mode of production' (Federici 2011, p. 4). She identifies the basis for truly alternative commoning in the way in which we produce ourselves as a 'common subject' (Federici 2011, p. 6); according to her, this begins with the 'effort to collectivize reproductive labor', the 'communalization of housework' (Federici 2011, p. 7). In her view, the task is to create 'collective forms of living' (loc. cit.): 'If the house is the *oikos* on which the economy is built, then it is women, historically the house workers and house prisoners, who must take the initiative to reclaim the house as a center of collective life, one traversed by multiple people and forms of cooperation, providing safety without isolation and fixation, allowing for the sharing and circulation of community possessions, and, above all, providing the foundation for collective forms of reproduction' (Federici 2011, p. 8). A twofold problem must be solved: 'to undo the gendered architecture of our lives and to reconstruct our homes and lives as commons' (Federici 2011, 9).

The question is what this actually means in practical terms. How can the achievements of the universalised production of wealth be preserved, which are the flipside of capitalist accumulation? Is it possible that an unfolding commons economy and peer-to-peer exchange are sufficient to provide the necessary socialisation capacities? Or is this path always only a makeshift solution in times of despair, or just a niche of a negligible number of groups continuously subject to enclosure? These and similar approaches are driven by the conviction that it is possible to create areas within the dominance of capital accumulation which correspond to completely different criteria and largely to elude the functionalisation generated by valorisation imperatives. They represent strategies of expanding the non-capitalist interstices, or interstitial strategies (see Wright 2010, pp. 321–337).

Sixth: New Struggles of the Marxian or Polanyian Type

In this discussion an analytical distinction was made between struggles associated directly with the capital–wage labour relation on the one hand, and struggles against the capitalist 'expansion into non-capitalist milieus' (Schmidt 2014) on the other. While the struggles within the capital–wage labour relation are considered struggles of the 'Marx type', the latter are of the Polanyi type. In elaborating this notion, Ingo Schmidt refers to Beverly Silver, who wrote, albeit with a slightly different understanding of such a distinction: 'By Polanyi-type labor unrest, we mean the backlash resistances to the spread of a global self-regulating market, particularly by working classes that are being unmade by global economic transformations as well as by those workers who had benefited from established social compacts that are being abandoned from above. And by Marx-type labor unrest, we mean the struggles of newly emerging working classes that are successively made and strengthened as an unintended outcome of the development of historical capitalism, even as old working classes are being unmade' (Silver 2003, p. 20). While workers in struggles of the Marx type assert their power in production and on the market, struggles of the Polanyi type instead aim at the limitation of these markets. According to Silver, people here resist to 'the disruption of established ways of life and livelihood' (Silver 2003, p. 106).

Michael Burawoy also makes a similar distinction, albeit reformulated: he postulates that the 'conventional Marxist claim that production provide the foundation of opposition to capitalism' is 'no longer tenable: in part because production is the locus of the organisation of consent to capitalism, and in part because in the face of the global production of surplus populations, exploitation is rapidly becoming a sought-after privilege of the few. Exploitation continues to figure centrally in the dynamics of accumulation, but not in the experience of subjugated populations. In the Marxian analysis the experience of the market appears as "the fetishism of commodities", a camouflage for the hidden abode of production, but it is much more than that, shaping multiple dimensions of human

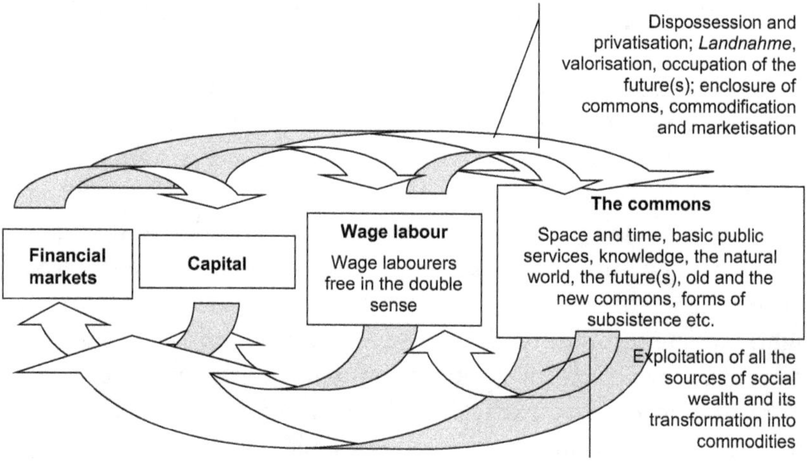

Fig. 10.5 Capital accumulation in financial capitalism (the current debate)

existence' (Burawoy 2013, p. 37).[5] In his view, the market represents 'a fundamental prop of human existence' in capitalism, as Polanyi quite rightly recognised (Burawoy 2013, p. 37). As much as these struggles originate in capitalist production and the relation between wage labour and capital (in the Marxian form), they nevertheless manifest in contradiction to a generalisation of the markets and the danger to humanity, nature and society arising from such a generalisation—that is, in a Polanyian form. In terms of strategy, an emphasis on Polanyi type struggles means concentrating on the defense, expansion and participatory-democratic composition of commons in the broadest sense. They turn out to be the actual foundation of a solidary society of the free and equal (Brie 2012b).

The Luxemburgian opening up of Marx's accumulation theorem has reached a new level of breadth and diversity in the current debate (Fig. 10.5). The insights from the discussion of the 1960s and 1970s by theoreticians from the Third World and by feminists, from analyses of cul-

[5] It should be noted that these statements do not really acknowledge the reality of workplaces as embattled sites (see e.g. Detje et al. 2013; Dörre et al. 2013). Besides, as the Frankfurt School was not the first to point out, consumer markets in particular represent spaces where the consent of the actively passivated is manufactured.

tural transformations within the periphery of the New Left as well as from the field of political ecology have been taken up and integrated. From this perspective, the current struggles over the right to the city, fair trade, housing availability, energy, food security, water and clean air, climate justice, control over one's own body, over collectively produced and shared knowledge and so on no longer appear as secondary contradictions, but rather as part of one and the same primary contradiction between the tendencies of capital accumulation and the great majority's aspirations to reproduce and develop, as long as the latter reflect the vision of a society 'in which everyone enjoys socially equal access to the basic preconditions of a self-determined life, that is, the basic goods of freedom' (Klein 2003, p. 122). The basis for these aspirations are the new as well as the old commons.

The development of the Marxian accumulation theory discussed here as an example of the reception of Rosa Luxemburg's work, *firstly*, exhibits an increasing complexity. More and more processes are attributed to a second primitive accumulation, *Landnahme* or wave of expropriation. Yet if this is the case, then we must also factor in the interdependence, mutual correspondence and functionality of capital accumulation and the diversity of social reproduction in our analysis. This interrelation must be included. It is not only the central capitalist valorisation sectors that depend on other sectors, but vice versa as well. One of the—subordinate (!)—implications of the dominance of capital valorisation over these sectors is that capital valorisation must occur in a way that promotes or at least tolerates these sectors.

Secondly, it ought to be pointed out that capital accumulation cannot be reduced exclusively to its disintegrative-destructive aspects. It represents and creates interrelations of socialisation, it is part of the creation of producers' new forms of relation and mediation vis-à-vis the conditions of social production and reproduction, the division of labour and cooperation. Manifold forms of appropriation are mediated through capital accumulation, albeit on very unequal terms and under the primacy of capital valorisation. As Kalmring illustrates, the tendency of subsumption intersects with the tendency of insubordination: 'The reorganisation of relations of division is not a project that capital pushes through by itself, but rather is a struggle between classes against the backdrop of asymmetrical relations of gender and other differences, the outcome of which remains relatively open' (Kalmring 2013, p. 106). He would only have to add that the relations of separation are actually relations of a specific (capitalist) linkage of the separated. One group of wage-earners has experienced a reintegration of work activities. Rigid Taylorisation and detailed workplace supervision are accompanied by tendencies toward teamwork and autonomous work organisation. The original unity between producers and the conditions of production has been irreversibly dissolved, and can only be re-established in a mediated form.

Thirdly, the dominance of capital accumulation over other forms of reproduction is accompanied by numerous forms of oppression, disenfranchisement and manipulation. However, its dominance cannot be reduced to this alone, and does not ultimately gain its power from these characteristics, but rather from its capacity to unfetter the driving forces of wealth production. Capitalism converts many of its most fierce critics into believers at the very moment they exercise political or economic power and depend on the expanded reproduction of resources. Market sociologist Neil Fligstein succinctly expresses the cause of this conversion when he writes: 'Market society has produced more income, wealth, goods, and services than any other form of human social organization' (quoted in Schimank 2011, p. 7). Above all, market-economic social orders have proven to be superior forms of innovation (for the author's own position see Brie 2010).

Fourthly, Boltanski and Chiapello draw attention the fact that capitalist accumulation in the late 1960s and early 1970s was confronted with three separate challenges in the workplace: 'Three sets of demands, associated with three different social groups […] attracted particular attention from socioeconomists of work: the refusal of work by the *young*, the strikes and crisis of *semi- and unskilled workers*; finally, demands which, especially among *cadres*, express a need for autonomy, a demand for greater participation in control of the firm or, in its most radical forms, for self-management' (Boltanski and Chiapello 2007, p. 174). The 'new spirit of capitalism' successfully integrated these demands by utilising flexibilisation, the further division of the working classes, network and project forms of work organisation, the expansion of precarious employment and tightened rules of conditionality for social welfare provisions and more in combination with new incentives and threats. The negative freedoms of important social groups were increased, while increased autonomy, self-determined cooperation and self-exploitation converged to the point that the traditional separation of work and private life vanished for significant parts of the workforce. The plurality of realistic life plans and the alteration of them over the course of an individual life has increased notably. The participation of women in gainful employment has risen considerably. The mobility and interconnectivity of these middle classes has exploded, while the pressure on these same groups to self-valorise and self-assert in the competitive game has increased. Other groups, by contrast, have faced a neo-fordist division of labour, social extortion, state-directed compulsion to work, and informalisation of employment. New freedoms and new inequalities, new opportunities and new barriers have merged in such a way that the flexibilisation and dynamisation of capitalist accumulation, high-tech development, expansion of global, simple mass labour on one side, and the formation of new underclasses, particularly in the service sector, on the other, go hand in hand.

From a Theory of Accumulation to a Theory of Social Reproduction Under the Primacy of Capital Valorisation

Rosa Luxemburg's *Accumulation of Capital* remains fully within the orbit of Marx's question as to how capitalist accumulation can be explained based on the law of exchange of equal values between independent owners of goods in the first place: 'The conversion of money into capital has to be developed on the basis of the immanent laws of the exchange of commodities, in such a way that the starting-point is the exchange of equivalents' (Marx 1867, p. 268). However, accumulation neither takes place solely as the appropriation of wage labour (Marx), nor is it explained by supplementing exchange with existing non-capitalist sectors according to the principle of equivalence (Luxemburg) alone, and surely it cannot be reduced to dispossession, *Landnahme*, or the exploitation of completely unpaid (female) domestic labour. It is more accurate to say that capital accumulation represents a particular concentration of economic power through which the overall process of social reproduction in all of its diversity and heterogeneity, its spatio-temporal rhythm, its social structures of class, gender, ethnicity, citizenship, age, and physical and mental state is specifically shaped. The actors in control of capital accumulation successfully compel other actors (states, regions, diverse social groups) to depend on them more than they depend on these other actors. It is a question of subordination, or subsumption (on the use of this term see also Fraser 2014, p. 12).

In his manuscript from 1863 to 1867, Marx summarises the results of his depiction as the subsumption of labour under capital. One could also say that irrespective of the theoretical explanation Marx provides on the basis of the labour theory of value, he still supplies a depiction which contains many aspects worth revisiting today: capital valorisation is primarily a specific subordination or subsumption of labour, production, distribution and exchange as well as consumption of temporal and spatial reproductive interrelationship, of politics and culture, of the military and the police—in short: of the entire society—under the rule of capital. This subsumption does not dissolve the autonomy of the different areas, tendencies, and institutions, but in fact requires it. Indeed, it may even contribute to such autonomy (albeit not automatically), or at least tolerate it to a certain extent. Polanyi's 'double movement' (Polanyi 1944) represents one possible manifestation of such a reproductive interrelationship.

Using the concepts of systems theory developed by Bob Jessop it is possible to formulate the interrelation of capital accumulation's overall influence on the totality of social reproduction and its individual processes. He uses the term ecological dominance adopted by Niklas Luhmann to illustrate the subsumption of all subsystems and the interrelationship of social reproduction contexts under capital accumulation. Even assuming the autonomy of individual subsystems, some of these systems are still more equal than others. According to Jessop, this is the case if 'one system in a self-organising ecology of self-organising systems imprints its developmental logic on other systems' operations more than any of the latter can impose their respective logics on that system' (Jessop 2008, p. 7). Such an approach allows us to acknowledge the autonomy of individual areas of social reproduction, taking seriously each specific life-worlds' spaces and institutional logics, addressing the desires, interests, and potentials for action, taking into consideration the plurality of forms of cooperation and contestation, while at the same time not ignoring the dominance of capital. On the contrary: this is precisely how the latter makes itself felt in its respective specific manifestations throughout the individual areas.

Accumulation, it could be argued, should no longer be understood as a one-sided process of exploitation, dispossession, *Landnahme* or colonisation. Each of these processes also entails its opposite. Dominance relies not only on coercion, but also on cooperation; it encounters autonomy and resistance. A living theory which does justice to actual struggles and does not reduce subalterns to mere victims (however well-intentioned) must, in my view, conceptualise the accumulation of capital in its contradictory nature of exploitation of wage labour and self-assertion within wage labour, of dispossession and appropriation, *Landnahme* and 'land reclamation', colonisation and obstinate development—always under the dominance of capital valorisation, yet nevertheless open for attempts at a reversal of relations of domination in the form of concrete pilot projects towards a solidary social transformation. Capital accumulation can thus be conceived of as the subsumption of social reproduction processes within the interrelationship of the dominance of capital valorisation and the counter-tendencies which emerge from commoning, from attempts to make solidarity the foundation for organising the social conditions of production and life (Brie and Klein 2007) (Fig. 10.6).

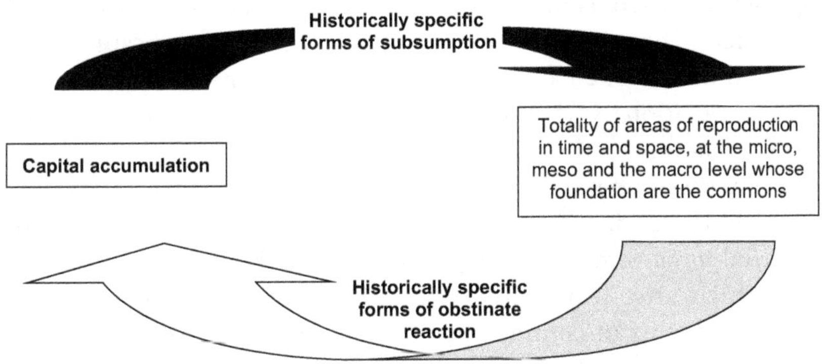

Fig. 10.6 Subsumption of social reproduction under capital accumulation

The increasingly all-encompassing subordination of social reproduction to capital accumulation exhibits an unintended side-effect which had already triggered the double movement in the 19th century: to the extent that the entire social reproduction process became subordinated to the needs of capital accumulation, the requirements of social reproduction—which are also always the claims of certain social groups—had to be accommodated in an equally comprehensive manner, albeit selectively and under the premise of the dominance of capital accumulation. Waves of increased capital dominance provoked waves of struggles, of reforms (often from above), of individual groups' niche strategies seeking to push the former back. Moreover, these counter-waves may then exhibit tendencies towards a solidary, participatory society (see Reißig 2009, pp. 141ff.) shaped by a new social and economic order. It is an open-ended process of searching, at the heart of which lies the struggle for social and ecological standards, for a democratisation of financial policy and alternative local and regional development (for more on this, see Dellheim et al. 2012, pp. 159–230). Whether and under which conditions the relation of dominance could be overturned and a transformation *within* capitalism could become a social transformation *beyond* capitalism that is more than just a mere tendency comprising counter-tendencies, projects, subsystem logics and individual praxes, remains unanswered.

As the now century-long debate has demonstrated, the central conflict in capital-dominated societies is not that between capital and wage labour. There is not the one conflict, but rather a whole bundle of conflicts. They originate in the contradiction between capital accumulation on the one hand and the life expectations of major sections of the population as well as requirements for social reproduction (not least in relation to the terrestrial environment) on the other. More precisely: these are conflicts arising from the tensions between capital accumulation and: (1) the requirements of the reproduction of the terrestrial environment (the Gaiasphere); (2) the needs and expectations which arise from people's collective-individual lifeworlds; (3) the requirements of complex institutions in society (state, law, security, etc.); as well as, finally, (4) the values and orientations within the public-cultural sphere (for more on this see Brie 2014b). These conflicts manifest themselves in the mark left on the entire metabolism of people and nature throughout the reproduction of capital oligarchies, concentrated in the sectors of finance and high-tech industries on one side, and in the energy sector, transport sector, agribusiness and the military-industrial complex on the other (see Dellheim et al. 2012, pp. 69ff.).

One could also describe it as the contradiction between capital accumulation and the requirements of reproduction of the communist foundations of any complex society (the modern commons) as well as the corresponding horizon of human rights (again, for more elaboration, see Brie 2012a). An understanding of the extremely complex contradictory nature of the interrelations between a social reproduction subsumed under capital valorisation, which have been rendered considerably more comprehensible in the more recent discussion, offers the possibility of accounting for actual forms of cooperation, conflict and protest, and of conceiving of and practising transformation in a double sense—both within capitalism and beyond capitalism (Klein 2014). This opens up new strategic horizons for a Left that is simultaneously plural and mutually supportive in its diversity.

***

It has been a long way from Rosa Luxemburg's brilliant *Accumulation of Capital* to more recent attempts at a better understanding of capital accumulation and at laying out a theoretically consistent foundation for counter-hegemonic struggles (Brand 2011). Her discovery that capital valorisation never occurs in its pure form, never exists by itself, but rather depends on a multiplicity of modes of social reproduction and is embedded into these while at the same time dominating them, is pivotal to an understanding of today's bourgeois-capitalist societies and critical to the formulation of a contemporary transformational and thereby truly revolutionary politics.

Acknowledgments I would like to thank Judith Dellheim and Ingo Schmidt as well as the colleagues from the Jena Post-Growth College for important suggestions and comments during work on this manuscript.

Bibliography

Altvater, E. (1992). *Der Preis des Wohlstands oder Umweltplünderung und neue Welt(un)ordnung*. Münster: Westfälisches Dampfboot.

Altvater, E. (2013). Wachstum, Globalisierung. Anthropozän. Steigerungsformen einer zerstörerischen Wirtschaftsweise. *Emanzipation, 3*(1), 71–88.

Amin, S. (1974). *Accumulation on a world scale. A critique of the theory of underdevelopment*. New York: Monthly Review Press.

Amin, S. (1977). *Imperialism and unequal development*. Hassocks: Harvester Press.

Amin, S., Arrighi, G., Frank, G., Wallerstein, I. (1982). Introduction: Common premises In Dynamics of global crisis. pp. 7–10 New York: Monthly Review Press.

Arrighi, G. (1990). Marxist Century—American Century: The making and remaking of the world labor. In S. Amin, G. Arrighi, G., G. Frank, & I. Wallerstein (Eds.), *Transforming the revolution. Social movements and the world-system* (pp. 54–95). New York: Monthly Review Press.

Backhouse, M. (2013). Grüne Landnahmen in Brasilien. Das Beispiel der Palmöl-Expansion im Amazonasbecken. In M. Backhouse, O. Gerlach, S. Kalmring, A. Nowak, & Andreas (Eds.), *Die globale Einhegung—Krise, ursprüngliche Akkumulation und Landnahmen im Kapitalismus* (pp. 263–283). Münster: Westfälisches Dampfboot.

Bennholdt-Thomsen, V. (1988a). Die stumme Auflehnung der Bauersfrauen. Bericht aus einem Dorf im Süden Mexikos. In *Frauen, die letzte Kolonie. Zur Hausfrauisierung der Arbeit* (pp. 47–61). Reinbek bei Hamburg: Rowohlt Taschenbuch.

Bennholdt-Thomsen, V. (1988b). Zur Bestimmung der geschlechtlichen Arbeitsteilung im Kapitalismus. In *Frauen, die letzte Kolonie. Zur Hausfrauisierung der Arbeit* (pp. 194–202). Reinbek bei Hamburg: Rowohlt Taschenbuch.

Bernstein, E. (1993). *The preconditions of socialism*. Cambridge: Cambridge University Press.

Bischoff, J. (2009). *Jahrhundertkrise des Kapitalismus. Abstieg in die Depression oder Übergang in eine andere Ökonomie?* Hamburg: VSA.

Boltanski, L., & Chiapello, E. (2007). *The new spirit of capitalism*. London and New York: Verso.

Brand, U. (2011). *Post-Neoliberalismus? Aktuelle Konflikte und gegenhegemoniale Strategien*. Hamburg: VSA.

Brand, U., & Görg, C. (2003). *Postfordistische Naturverhältnisse. Konflikte um genetische Ressourcen und die Internationalisierung des Staates*. Münster: Westfälisches Dampfboot.

Brie, M. (2010). Solidarische Gesellschaftstransformation—Skizze über eine (noch) unmögliche Möglichkeit. In H. Müller (Ed.), *Von der Systemkritik zur gesellschaftlichen Transformation* (pp. 12–56). Norderstedt: Books on Demand.

Brie, M. (2012a). Die kommunistischen Fundamente und der menschenrechtliche Horizont in der kapitalistischen Moderne—Die Experimente des Robert Owen. In M. Brie & M. Candeias (Eds.), *Transformation im Kapitalismus und darüber hinaus. Beiträge zur Ersten Transformationskonferenz des Instituts für Gesellschaftsanalyse der Rosa-Luxemburg-Stiftung* (pp. 101–118). Berlin: Rosa-Luxemburg-Stiftung.

Brie, M. (2012b). Making the common good of humanity concrete—For a life in solidarity. In B. Daiber & F. Houtart (Eds.), *A post-capitalist paradigm. The common good of humanity* (pp. 133–158). Brussels: Rosa-Luxemburg-Stiftung.

Brie, M. (Ed.) (2014a). *Futuring. Perspektiven der Transformation im Kapitalismus über ihn hinaus*. Münster: Westfälisches Dampfboot.

Brie, M. (2014b). Transformationen des Reichtums – Reichtum der Transformationen. Eine Vier-in-Einem-Perspektive. In M. Brie (Ed.), *Futuring. Transformation im Kapitalismus über ihn hinaus* (pp. 194–241). Münster: Westfälisches Dampfboot.

Brie, M., & Klein, D. (2007). *Elementare Fragen neu bedenken. Kapitalismus, Sozialismus, Eigentum und Wege der Veränderung*. Berlin: Rosa-Luxembug-Stiftung.

Bukharin, N. (1972). *Imperialism and world economy*. London: Martin Lawrence Limited.

Burawoy, M. (2013). Marxism after Polanyi. In M. Williams & V. Satgar (Eds.), *Marxisms in the 21st century. Crisis, critique & struggle* (pp. 34–52). Johannesburg: WITS University Press.

Busch, U., & Land, R. (2013). *Teilhabekapitalismus. Aufstieg und Niedergang eines Regimes wirtschaftlicher Entwicklung am Fall Deutschland 1950 bis 2010*. Norderstedt: Books on Demand.

Candeias, M. (2009). *Neoliberalismus. Hochtechnologie. Hegemonie. Zweite, erweiterte und überarbeitete Auflage*. Berlin/Hamburg: Argument.

Candeias, M. (2014). "Wenn das Alte stirbt ..." – Organische Krise bei Antonio Gramsci. In M. Brie (Ed.), *"Wenn das Alter stirbt..." Die organische Krise des Finanzmarktkapitalismus. Zweite Transformationskonferenz der Rosa-Luxemburg-Stiftung, Manuskripte Neue Folge Rosa-Luxemburg-Stiftung* (pp. 14–28). Berlin: Rosa Luxemburg Stiftung.

Dellheim, J. (2007). *Bedarfsorientierte Soziale Grundsicherung versus Bedingungsloses Grundeinkommen*. Berlin: Rosa Luxemburg Stiftung.

Dellheim, J., Brangsch, L., Wolf, F. O., Spangenberg, J. (2012). *Den Krisen entkommen. Sozialökologische Transformation*. Berlin: Dietz.

Detje, R., Menz, W., Nies, S., Sauer, D. (2013). *Krisenerfahrungen und politische Orientierungen: Der Blick von unten auf Betrieb, Gewerkschaft und Staat*. Hamburg: VSA.

De Angelis, M. (2006). *Enclosure, Commons, and the "Outside"*. Retrieved February 5, 2014, from http://ccs.ukzn.ac.za/files/De%20Angelis%20 Enclosures%20and%20the%20outside.pdf.

De Angelis, M. (2014). *Enclosure, commons, and the „outside'*. http://ccs.ukzn.ac.za/files/De%20Angelis%20Enclosures%20and%20the%20outside.pdf. Date accessed 5 Feb 2014.

Dörre, K. (2011). Landnahme und die Grenzen kapitalistischer Dynamik. Eine Ideenskizze. *Initial, 22*(4), 56–72.

Dörre, K. (2013a). Landnahme. Triebkräfte, Wirkungen und Grenzen kapitalistischer Wachstumsdynamik. In M. Backhouse, O. Gerlach, S. Kalmring, & A. Nowak (Eds.), *Die globale Einhegung—Krise, ursprüngliche Akkumulation und Landnahmen im Kapitalismus* (pp. 112–140). Münster: Westfälisches Dampfboot.

Dörre, K. (2013b). Landnahme und Grenzen sozialer Reproduktion. Zur gesellschaftstheoretischen Bedeutung Rosa Luxemburgs. In I. Schmidt (Ed.), *Rosa Luxemburgs „Akkumulation des Kapitals". Die Aktualität von ökonomischer Theorie, Imperialismuserklärung und Klassenanalyse* (pp. 82–116). Hamburg: VSA.

Dörre, K., Happ, A., Matuschek, I. (2013). Das Unbehagen am Kapitalismus und die Lohnarbeiterinnen. In Dörre, K., A. Happ, I. Matuschek (eds), Das Gesellschaftsbild der LohnarbeiterInnen. Soziologische Untersuchungen in ost- und westdeutschen Industriebetrieben. pp. 9–28. Hamburg: VSA.

Engster, F. (2014). Das Außen des Kapitals. Landnahme als Produktion zusätzlicher Arbeitszeit und die Krise relativer Mehrwertproduktion. http://kapacc.blog.rosalux.de/files/2014/01/Engster-RLS-Workshop-2014.pdf.

Fatheuer, T. (2013). Eine neue grüne Inwertsetzungsstrategie für Amazonien: REDD—Erwartungen, Ambivalenzen, Kontroversen. In M. Backhouse, O. Gerlach, S. Kalmring, & A. Nowak (Eds.), *Die globale Einhegung—Krise, ursprüngliche Akkumulation und Landnahmen im Kapitalismus* (pp. 284–301). Münster: Westfälisches Dampfboot.

Federici, S. (2011). Feminism and the politics of the commons. *The Commoner*. http://www.commoner.org.uk/?p=113. Last accessed 17 Feb 2014.

Fraser, N. (2014). Can society be commodities all the way down? Post-Polanyian reflections on capitalist crisis. *Economy and Society, 43*(4), 1–18.
Görg, C. (2004a). Enteignung oder Inwertsetzung? Zur Aktualität der "ursprünglichen Akkumulation". *Das Argument, 257*, 721–731.
Görg, C. (2004b). Inwertsetzung. *Historisch-kritisches Wörterbuch des Marxismus, 6*(II), 1501–1506.
Harvey, D. (2003). *The new imperialism*. Oxford; New York: Oxford University Press.
Haug, W. F. (2012). *Hightech-Kapitalismus in der großen Krise*. Hamburg: Argument Verlag.
Hilferding, R. (1981). *Finance capital*. London: Routledge & Kegan Paul.
Hobsbawm, E. (1989). *The age of empire, 1875–1914*. New York: Vintage.
Jessop, B. (2008). Zur Relevanz von Luhmanns Systemtheorie und von Laclau und Mouffes Diskursanalyse für die Weiterentwicklung der marxistischen Staatstheorie. In J. Hirsch, J. Kannankulam and, & J. Wissel (Eds.), *Der Staat der Bürgerlichen Gesellschaft. Zum Staatsverständnis von Karl Marx* (pp. 157–179). Baden-Baden: Nomos.
Kalmring, S. (2013). Die Krise als Labor gesellschaftlicher Entwicklungen. Fortgesetzte ursprüngliche Akkumulation und die großen Krisen der Kapitalakkumulation. In M. Backhouse, O. Gerlach, S. Kalmring, & A. Nowak (Eds.), *Die globale Einhegung—Krise, ursprüngliche Akkumulation und Landnahmen im Kapitalismus* (pp. 72–111). Münster: Westfälisches Dampfboot.
Kautsky, K. (1911). Finanzkapital und Krisen. *Die Neue Zeit*, pp. 29, 22–25, 764–772, 797–804, 874–883.
Kautsky, K. (1914). Der Imperialismus. *Die Neue Zeit, 32*(2), 908–922.
Klein, D. (Ed.) (2003). *Leben statt gelebt zu werden. Selbstbestimmung und soziale Sicherheit. Zukunftsbericht der Rosa-Luxemburg-Stiftung*. Berlin: Dietz.
Klein, D. (2008). *Krisenkapitalismus. Wohin es geht, wenn es so weitergeht*. Berlin: Dietz.
Klein, D. (2013). *Das Morgen tanzt im Heute. Transformation im Kapitalismus und über ihn hinaus*. Hamburg: VSA.
Klein, D. (2014). 'Doppelte Transformation'. In M. Brie (Ed.), *Futuring. Transformation im Kapitalismus über ihn hinaus* (pp. 101–125). Münster: Westfälisches Dampfboot.
Lenin, V. I. (1917). *Imperialism, the highest stage of capitalism*. In *Selected works* (pp. 667–766). Moscow: Progress Publishers.
Linden, M. van der, & Roth, K. H. (Eds.). (2014). *Beyond Marx. Theorising the Global Labour Relations of the Twenty-First Century*. Leiden; Boston: Brill.
Löwy, M. (2013). Westlicher Imperialismus gegen Urkommunismus. Eine neue

Lesart von Rosa Luxemburgs ökonomischen Schriften. In I. Schmidt (Ed.), *Rosa Luxemburgs "Akkumulation des Kapitals". Die Aktualität von ökonomischer Theorie, Imperialismuserklärung und Klassenanalyse* (pp. 53–62). Hamburg: VSA.

Lutz, B. (1984). *Der kurze Traum immerwährender Prosperität. Eine Neuinterpretation der industriell-kapitalistitschen Entwicklung im Europa des 20. Jahrhunderts*. Frankfurt am Main: Campus.

Luxemburg, R. (1913, 1974). Die Akkumulation des Kapitals. Ein Beitrag zur ökonomischen Erklärung des Imperialismus. In *Gesammelte Werke, Bd. 5* (pp. 5–411). Berlin: Dietz. Retrieved from http://www.marxists.org/deutsch/archiv/luxemburg/1913/akkkap/index.htm.

Luxemburg, R. (1918). *What does the Spartacus League want?*. http://marxism.halkcephesi.net/Rosa%20Luxemburg/1918/12/14.htm.

Luxemburg, R. (2013). Introduction to political economy. In *The complete works of Rosa Luxemburg, volume I: Economic writings 1* (pp. 89–300). London/New York: Verso.

Luxemburg, R. (2015). The accumulation of capital. A contribution to the economic theory of imperialism. In *The complete works of Rosa Luxemburg, volume II: Economic writings 2* (pp. 3–344). London/New York: Verso.

Marx, K. [1844] (1975). *Contribution to the critique of Hegel's philosophy of law* in *Marx-Engels collected works, Volume 3* (pp. 3–130). New York: International Publishers.

Marx, K. [1867] (1982). *Capital. A critique of political economy, volume I.* New York: Penguin Books.

Massarat, M. (1993). *Endlichkeit der Natur und Überfluß in der Marktökonomie. Schritte zum Gleichgewicht.* Marburg: Metropolis.

Mies, M. (1988). Capitalist development and subsistence production: Rural women in India. In C. von Werlhof, M. Mies, & V. Bennholdt-Thomsen (Eds.), *Women, the last colony*. London: Zed Books.

Neusüß, C. (1985). *Die Kopfgeburten der Arbeiterbewegung oder die Genossin Luxemburg bringt alles durcheinander*. Hamburg: Rasch und Röhring.

Polanyi, K. (1944). *The great transformation*. New York: Farrar & Rinehart.

Reißig, R. (2009). *Gesellschafts-Transformation im 21. Jahrhundert. Ein neues Konzept sozialen Wandels*. Wiesbaden: VS.

Schimank, U. (2011). Wohlfahrtsgesellschaften als funktionaler Antagonismus von Kapitalismus und Demokratie: Ein immer labilerer Mechanismus? in MPIfG Working Paper, 2.

Schmidt, I. (2013a). 'Geschichte und Sozialismus'. In I. Schmidt (Ed.), *Rosa Luxemburgs "Akkumulation des Kapitals". Die Aktualität von ökonomischer Theorie, Imperialismuserklärung und Klassenanalyse* (pp. 138–165). Hamburg: VSA.

Schmidt, I. (Ed.) (2013b). *Rosa Luxemburgs "Akkumulation des Kapitals". Die Aktualität von ökonomischer Theorie, Imperialismuserklärung und Klassenanalyse*. Hamburg: VSA.

Schmidt, I. (2014). Rosa Luxemburg: Economics for a new socialist project. *New Politics, XV*(1). http://newpol.org/content/rosa-luxemburg-economics-%E2%80%A8for-new-socialist-project. Last accessed 30 July 2014.

Silver, B. J. (2003). *Forces of labor. Workers' movements and globalization since 1870*. Cambridge/New York: Cambridge University Press.

von Werlhof, C. (1988a). The proletarian is dead: Long live the housewife! In C. von Werlhof, M. Mies, & V. Bennholdt-Thomsen (Eds.), *Women, the last colony* (pp. 168–181). London: Zed Books.

von Werlhof, C. (1988b). On the concept of nature and society in capitalism. In C. von Werlhof, M. Mies, & V. Bennholdt-Thomsen (Eds.), *Women, the last colony* (pp. 96–112). London: Zed Books.

von Werlhof, C. (1991). *Was haben die Hühner mit dem Dollar zu tun? Frauen und Ökonomie*. Munich: Frauenoffensive.

von Werlhof, C., Mies, M., & Bennholdt-Thomsen, V. (1988a). Frauen, die letzte Kolonie. In *Zur Hausfrauisierung der Arbeit*. Reinbek bei Hamburg: Rowohlt Taschenbuch.

von Werlhof, C., Mies, M., & Bennholdt-Thomsen, V. (1988b). *Women, the last colony*. London: ZedBooks.

Wallerstein, I. (1982). Crisis as transition. In *Dynamics ofglobal crisis* (pp. 11–54). New York: Monthly Review Press.

Wallerstein, I. (1990). Antisystemic movements: History and dilemmas. In S. Amin, G. Arrighi, G. Gunder, & I. Wallerstein (Eds.), *Transforming the revolution. Social movements and the world-system* (pp. 13–53). New York: Monthly Review Press.

Wright, E. (2010). *Envisioning real utopias*. London and New York: Verso.

Zeller, C. (2004). Die globale Enteignungsökonomie. In C. Zeller (Ed.), *Die globale Enteignungsökonomie* (pp. 9–20). Münster: Westfälisches Dampfboot.

11

From 'Accumulation of Capital' to Solidarity Based Ways of Life

Judith Dellheim

Introduction

The following deliberations are motivated by a desire to understand the contemporary weakness of emancipatory-solidary forces. If we are to overcome this weakness, we must initially identify in what it consists. After all, the coming years will turn on the question as to whether there will only be 'change in order for things to remain as they are, that is, for the existing power relations to be able to reproduce themselves, or if something more important will change, raising the possibility of overcoming core social relations of domination' (Wolf 2012, p. 7). This forces us to ask ourselves why it is that the rulers have grown stronger throughout their management of the crisis they caused, and why the Left remains largely on the defensive. This in turn poses the question as to why the Left is more or less unable to convince people to develop the

J. Dellheim (✉)
Rosa-Luxemburg-Stiftung, Berlin, Germany

J. Dellheim, F.O. Wolf (eds.), *Rosa Luxemburg: A Permanent Challenge for Political Economy*, DOI 10.1057/978-1-137-60108-7_11

desire to live a self-determined, ecologically sustainable life in dignity and solidarity with one another, and not least to stand up and fight for this aim. Our society's way of life tends to paralyse and to corrupt individuals. The coercive mechanisms of the capitalist mode of production appear either tolerable or insurmountable. Given this state of affairs, we must also inquire, once again, about these coercive mechanisms and how they are fetishised. This would confirm Pierre Bourdieu's claim that 'nothing is more urgent than to make a social history of the Marxist tradition'. According to Bourdieu, this is necessary 'in order to resituate modes of thought of expression, which have been fixed and fetishized by the forgetting of history, in the historical context of their production and successive use' (Bourdieu 1993, p. 50).

It was Karl Marx who discovered both the nature and the specious characters of capital accumulation, as well as the 'silent compulsion' (Marx 1867a, p. 899) that binds the wage labourer to the capitalist exploiting him or her, and who pointed out that this compulsion also occurs 'outside the production process' (Marx 1867a, p. 717). Building on Marx's work, Rosa Luxemburg showed how capital in a highly concentrated and centralised form had given rise to imperialism – a combination of capital's 'dull compulsion' in the interior and the violence of gunboats and machine guns in the exterior. Both maintained that the laws of economics do not stipulate an end to the capitalist mode of production as such. Only people who wish to live in a different way – and workers in particular – can fight for an end to the dominance of capital accumulation and introduce a new mode of socialisation.[1]

The direction and the way in which socialisation develops depends primarily on social actors, the balance of forces between them, as well as the balance of forces in society as a whole. Social development is determined by who can mobilise which sources of accumulation: the mobilisation and utilisation of sources of accumulation by specific actors affects productive, economic and social structures, social relations, the social

[1] Translator's note: The term 'socialisation' (in German: *Vergesellschaftung*) is to be understood in a Weberian sense; that is, as the process of integration of individuals into society as a whole and of situating individual activities in social relations.

actors themselves, and the natural resources that serve as the basis of life itself. New infrastructural megaprojects and new plans for liberalisation, privatisation and free trade attest to the extraordinary dynamic of contemporary conflicts over sources of accumulation. The ruling classes have once again begun an offensive with the intent of forestalling any and all social alternatives.

Proceeding from these considerations, this chapter aims to substantiate the following hypothesis: the rulers' offensive could by all means be disrupted and halted by emancipatory-solidary actors, *if* the latter were able to motivate and activate people to struggle for a good life for all. In such an endeavour, central themes necessarily include questions of housing, living environment and mobility, as well as social security. Any corresponding political strategy must be based on a discussion of finance capital's sources of accumulation and suggest potential paths of political action. A counter-offensive could possibly succeed if actors were to self-critically transform their own lifestyles and political culture. Such a counter-offensive could then pave the way for a more general social-ecological transformation.

Accumulation and way of life are directly related to one another. In 1947 Henri Lefèbvre explained why socialist theory and politics must address the advance of modernity/capital accumulation and its corresponding fetishisms in people's everyday lives (Lefèbvre 1991). Lefèbvre's *Critique of Everyday Life* marks the point of departure for Paul Langley in his book *The Everyday Life of Global Finance. Saving and Borrowing in Anglo-America* (2010). In it he shows how neoliberal policies were applied to transform saving and borrowing and shift the latter's focus to housing and pensions. Langley, however, locates his financial analysis in everyday life, in the sphere of circulation. A critical reading of his book may be helpful in developing a more profound understanding of the coercive mechanisms analysed by Marx and Luxemburg, as well as in devising strategies for socialist politics to engage in a debate about the method of political economy. In this sense, this chapter seeks to demonstrate that a political economy which aims to strengthen emancipatory-solidary actors must take up the legacy of Marx and Luxemburg and address relations of socialisation, capital accumulation and everyday social life.

Learning How to Search from Marx and Luxemburg

Almost 150 years after the publication of Karl Marx's *Capital* and more than 100 years after Luxemburg's *The Accumulation of Capital*, their vision of a society of the free and equal seems beyond reach. This forces us to address once more, beginning with Marx and Luxemburg, the developmental capacity of the capitalist mode of production. This in turn raises the question of the potentials and limitations of socialisation through capital accumulation, that is, the mobilisation and combination of accumulation sources resulting from exploitation. What matters most in this context are the fetishisations engendered by the capitalist mode of production which allow its internal interrelationships to appear as objective laws of nature.

Marx's point of departure for an analysis of these forms of fetishisation is the realisation that the development of productive forces and of private property increasingly separates individuals from the community, that in this process individuals as well as the community as a whole change while remaining connected in an altered way. To the extent that this separation progresses, individuals experience both increasing freedom and increasing alienation – they enjoy greater degrees of personal freedom, but are trapped in impersonal dependencies and unable to fully comprehend nor shape their relationships with others. Yet these social relationships do indeed function; particularly when a labour product produced by a more or less isolated producer must be regarded as useful by others in order for this producer's labour to be rewarded, in turn enabling him or her to acquire the products of others. If the movement of goods and money expands, it appears as the creation of an overpowering force endowed with a will of its own, determining all individual destinies.

'Men' [and, we would add today, women], equipped with consciousness, are able to deal with their 'social existence' (Marx 1859, p. 425), with the social relationships that assert themselves and with their fetishisations. In order to do so, men must comprehend processes of socialisation in which the overall context, mediated through competition, manifests itself. In this, Marx outlines the following tendency: 'The development of modern industry, therefore, cuts from under its feet the very foundation on which the bourgeoisie produces and appropriates products. What the bourgeoisie, therefore, produces, above all, is its own gravediggers' (Marx and Engels 1848, p. 48). The bourgeoisie draws 'all, even the most barbarian, nations into civilisation' (Marx and Engels 1848, p. 40). 'The bourgeoisie has through its exploitation of the world market given a cosmopolitan character to production and consumption in every country' (Marx and Engels 1848, p. 39) and has created new desires. The scientifically-founded idea of and hope for the 'association, in which the free development of each is the condition for the free development of all' (Marx and Engels 1848, p. 60), culminates in the exhortation: 'Working men of all countries, unite!' (Marx and Engels 1848, p. 74). This challenge pertains to 'action in the present' (Balibar 2007, p. 21).

In his 'Contribution to the Critique of Political Economy', Marx explains how people who produce use-values for exchange based on a division of labour always also dedicate a certain share of their labour to the creation of a social relationship, that is, socialised, abstract labour. Because workers possess neither the means of production nor the goods produced, they do not receive an equivalent of the abstract labour they perform, realised in commodities and carried out within a social context. The capitalist appropriates the unpaid additional labour, the surplus value, in the form of entrepreneurial profit. Capital accumulation, then, means using this profit to expand production. It drives the division of labour throughout society and the socialisation of labour forward. In the process, it reproduces and reinforces capital-based power relations. These were originally a result of 'the process which divorces the worker from the ownership of the conditions of his own labour; it is a process which operates two transformations, whereby the social means of subsistence and production are turned into capital, and the immediate producers are turned into wage-labourers' (Marx 1867a, p. 874). This is what is termed 'so-called primitive accumulation'.[2] The sources of this

[2]Translator's note: There is a minor controversy surrounding the common English translation of Luxemburg's 'Ursprüngliche Akkumulation'. Since the literal translation would be 'original accumulation', this version can frequently be found in English texts on Luxemburg, including Harvey. However, we have decided to use the commonly accepted translation of 'primitive accumulation' throughout this book.

accumulation included the colonial system, state debts, taxes and protectionism. Moreover, they fuelled further capital accumulation. The latter 'not only maintains this separation [between the means of production and those who work with them, J.D.], but reproduces it on a constantly extending scale' (Marx 1867a, p. 874). The illusion is created that capitalists give workers an advance to pay for their livelihood while at the same time providing the means of production. In reality, however, all these means were generated by the previous unpaid labour of wage earners (Marx 1867a, pp. 508–516).

Viewed in terms of class relations 'the further socialization of labour and the further transformation of the soil and other means of production into socially exploited and therefore communal means of production takes on a new form. What is now to be expropriated is not the self-employed worker, but the capitalist who exploits a large number of workers' (Marx 1867a, p. 928).

The logical limit of capital accumulation is the destruction of the labour force and/or the natural conditions of social life. This is the point at which the accumulation of capital comes to an end. However, there is no certainty whatsoever that the expropriation of the expropriators will be the outcome of this development, as that would only be possible through the action of people who desire to live a self-determined and solidary life and who empower themselves to attain this goal. Moreover, a vastly different tendency stands in the way of this occurring: 'The advance of capitalist production develops a working class which by education, tradition and habit looks upon the requirements of that mode of production as self-evident natural laws. The organisation of the capitalist process of production, once it is fully developed, breaks down all resistance. The constant generation of a relative surplus population keeps the law of the supply and demand of labour, and therefore wages, within narrow limits which correspond to capital's valorisation requirements. The silent compulsion of economic relations sets the seal on the domination of the capitalist over the worker' (Marx 1867a, p. 899). The 'silent compulsion' becomes even more difficult for workers to recognise when the production and reproduction of capital accumulation is mediated by expanding credit relations, that is, interest-bearing capital and fictitious capital. This complicates an engagement with practical constraints. Capital owners, industrial and financial capitalists form cooperations and establish corporations in order to profitably realise major projects both domestically and abroad. In order to mobilise the necessary sources of accumulation, they collect assets and incomes from broad sections of society – including from workers. Exploitation is thereby socialised, and all those providing credit to groups of capitalists (among them, again, workers) gain an interest in renewed exploitation as they enter into partnerships with the functionaries of capital accumulation. Ties between workers and capitalists thus develop not only within the production process, but also outside of it.

While capitalists are generally interested in incorporating an ever larger part of the population into the mobilisation of sources of accumulation for the production of surplus value, simultaneous redistribution also occurs, because: firstly, wages can be curtailed if they circulate partly in the form of stocks; secondly, circulating claims to future profits are always linked to speculation in which one side wins and the other loses out; thirdly, crises occur, the consequences of which are passed onto the weak by the strong; and, fourthly, the mobilisation of a required minimum amount of capital for military armaments, war and colonial policies amounts to targeted redistribution carried out by the state.

It becomes obvious that: (1) cooperation between the capital owner organising surplus labour in the production of goods on one side, and the capital owner organising surplus labour in the form of interest-bearing capital in the mobilisation and movement of monetary capital on the other side, requires the collaboration of state actors; (2) the 'dull compulsion' of capital relations becomes even greater once wage-earners are integrated into the capitalist mode of production via a developed financial system; (3) the 'dull compulsion' expands even further as this financial system increasingly permeates areas of workers' everyday lives and society as a whole; (4) in this process the cooperation of capital thus grows to encompass ever more capital elites; (5) the result of ongoing socialisation of labour and exploitation is that socially heterogeneous groups of society enter into contradictory partnerships with capitalists and capital elites.

What, then, is even possible in the face of so much impenetrability and forced relations? Again and again, it appears as if one group of wage-earners benefits at the cost of other groups of wage-earners. The fact that wage-earners represent the vast majority of the population is only one side of the coin. As Marx emphasises, 'numbers weigh only in the balance, if united by combination and led by knowledge. Past experience has shown how disregard of that bond of brotherhood which ought to exist between the workmen of different countries, and incite them to stand firmly by each other in all their struggles for emancipation, will be chastised by the common discomfiture of their incoherent efforts' (Marx 1864, p. 12).

Rosa Luxemburg was always committed to the liberating revolution, to the 'bonds of brotherhood', and thus engaged with both the 'dull compulsion' as well as with its 'sharp' counterpart, the compulsion flanked by guns. She called on her comrades to join in a collective search for a democratic development of socialist politics. This is why she analysed international capital accumulation and the imperialist politics of the capitalist oligarchies.

If capitalist accumulation in its 'pure' form characteristic of highly developed countries like England had been Marx's primary focus, Luxemburg was more interested in the conditions and consequences that the imperialist era entailed for the labour movement. It was against this backdrop that she studied the role of the colonies in the realisation of surplus value and thus in the protection of solvent demand and accumulation sources.

For Luxemburg, capital accumulation reaches its limit when there are no longer any non-capitalist actors able to buy products from capitalist production. According to her argument, surplus value can no longer be realised in this case: 'Capitalism is the first form of economy with propagandistic power; [...] Thus, at the same time as it tends to become the universal form, it is smashed to smithereens by its intrinsic inability to be a universal form of production' (Luxemburg 1913, p. 341). She concludes, while at the same time explaining the expansionist drive of capital seeking profit maximisation:

> 'In its drive to appropriate these productive forces for the purposes of exploitation, capital ransacks the whole planet, procuring means of production from every crevice of the Earth, snatching up or acquiring them from civilizations of all stages and all forms of society. [...] for the productive employment of realized surplus value, it is necessary for capital to dispose ever more fully over the whole globe in order to have available to it a

quantitatively and qualitatively unrestricted range of means of production' (Luxemburg 1913, p. 258).

It means a global mobilisation of accumulation sources by capitalist oligarchies.

This points to questions of the expansion of capital relations and the relationship between the modern class of wage-earners and those majorities of the world population who live in pre-modern modes of production: does the working class permit the capitalist raid to occur, does it accept the combination of economic and military forms of coercion? Does it partake in the 'competitive struggle over the unspoiled remainder of the noncapitalist world environment' (Luxemburg 1913, p. 325)? Does this propel them to participate in national wars against one another, to brutally repress the local population in conquered territories? And reversely: how do workers become willing and able to change their material needs and ways of life so as to put an end to, to abolish, to overcome violence against one another, violence against the wage-earners of other countries, violence against socially weaker populations across the globe, violence against nature? How can people living in pre-capitalist modes of production, given the introduction and continuation of socialist development, participate in actual socialisation in the industrial centres? These questions were carefully evaded by revisionism. At the same time, they represent a criticism of the 'reductionism' of the impoverished orthodox reception of Marx (Brie 2015).

Utilising the example of the so-called 'War of Secession' (1861–1865) between the northern and the southern states of the USA over the course of future social development, Luxemburg demonstrates how social conflicts, the search for sources of accumulation and international balances of power intersect. This war was not least a struggle over the model of society best suited to the United States, and, ostensibly, over the enslavement of the black population. It resulted in, among other things, an enormous national deficit, which raised the question of new sources of capital accumulation. High taxes and protective tariffs facilitated the rapid development of infrastructure and mechanised industry. Particularly acute, however, was the rapid increase in the exploitation of wage-earners. The economic importance of the stock exchange and tax privileges for large fortunes were on the rise. All this was accompanied by a shift in the sociopolitical balance of forces in favour of industrial and financial capitalists.

'This shift in U.S. fiscal policy marked the beginning of flagrant parliamentary corruption and the undisguised and unscrupulous use of elections, legislation, and the press as the instruments of the naked financial interests of large capitals. [...] the Yankee liberator of African Americans indulged in orgies of mercenary speculation on the Stock Exchange; in Congress, he endowed himself with public lands, and enriched himself through duties and taxes, through monopolies, fraudulent share-issues, and the theft of public assets' (Luxemburg 1913, p. 289).

Individual and social life was commercialised and provided growing spaces for capital accumulation. 'Now [the small- and medium scale farmer] always needed money – in great quantities – in order to pay his taxes, and he soon found that he needed to sell everything that he produced in order to acquire everything that he needed in turn from manufacturers in the form of commodities' (Luxemburg 1913, p. 290). Many farmers had no choice but to take on mortgages and pay horrendous interest rates. Countless indebted farmers lost their land. Ergo:

'[H]aving been driven from the land in the U.K., the peasant was first pushed to the eastern United States, and then westward, where he was once again transformed into a petty commodity producer on the ruins of the American Indian economy. Suffering ruin yet again in the west, he was driven northward. Railways led the way, and ruin followed in their tracks – in this movement, capital was both engine driver and executioner bringing up the rear' (Luxemburg 1913, p. 297).

Yet the 'executioner' brings about not 'only' the railways and mechanised industry, but also 'financial agriculture' and thereby mechanised labour in agriculture. It socialises and, in the guise of capital oligarchies, organises an 'economic metabolism' (Luxemburg 1913, p. 323), the destruction of pre-capitalist modes of production, or rather their incorporation into capital circuits, their exploitation and use as sources of accumulation. Luxemburg's depiction reveals that internationally accumulating capital has a specific national, transnational and international history, and in particular a 'history of accumulation' (cf. Luxemburg 1913, p. 327). This includes free trade, debt, bonds, protective tariffs, colonial policies, state contracts, the development of cartels and corporations, state guarantees, laws, a politics of 'spheres of interest' (Luxemburg 1913, p. 329), militarisation and war.

A political economy that seeks to explain capital accumulation in its complexity and its social interdependencies, to reveal, criticise and fight the fetishisation of advances and interest, of omnipotent markets and impotent politics, must overcome the isolated points of view engendered by this mode of production and develop a specific 'cosmopolitical gaze': any thinking must proceed from humanity and the world economy, even though the former does not really constitute a subject as such. This would mean looking, on the one side, at those who live from their labour and those performing unpaid labour for others, as well as at those whose hard-earned resources are taken from them. On the other side are those who exploit and rob the former. Furthermore, such an analysis would have to examine the relations the exploited and robbed enter into with those who exploit and rob with the aim of living off the labour of others. This also means analysing the diverse gender relations involved at all times.

Of particular interest for such an analysis are the possibilities for solidarisation among wage-earners themselves, as well as between wage-earners, others depending on their labour, and those who perform unpaid labour for others or whose resources are taken from them. The social position of these groups must be strengthened, especially that of the weakest among them. Their common political interest must emerge from their own self-activity. What cannot be ignored, however, is that the solidarisation strived for implies that many in the global industrial regions will have to forego some of their privileges. This means that majorities would first have to be encouraged by minorities to rebel against the 'dull compulsion' and the 'insatiable drive for expansion' (Luxemburg 1913, p. 443). They would have to risk part of their own security and liberate themselves from fetishisms. Emancipatory-solidary scientists could contribute to this cause and work to reveal the interrelationship between capital accumulation and everyday life – today!

On the Critique of Everyday Life and Financialisation

'Philosophy is in its death throes' (Lefèbvre 1991, p. 84). In 1947, Henri Lefèbvre laments the state of 'Marxist philosophy'. 'Marxists must open their eyes and examine the fact closely: Marxism has become *boring*'

(Lefèbvre 1991, p. 84). According to Lefèbvre, one solution to this miserable state could be to turn to the early writings of Marx, the critique of alienation, the idea of a 'total man' (Lefèbvre 1991, p. 89), the study of processes of appropriation. Proceeding from this assumption, he suggests describing and analysing 'everyday life of society' (Lefèbvre 1991, p. 148). This endeavour productively brings the vitality and humanism of the Marxian legacy into focus. Nevertheless, Lefèbvre's attack on Stalinism only progresses to Marx the Young Hegelian. It does not reach the mature Marx, let alone Luxemburg or Gramsci. He confines himself to a mere return to Marx's unresolved questions and limits his work to providing impulses and describing everyday life. Yet Paul Langley is nevertheless fascinated by this and clearly draws on Lefèbvre (Langley 2010, pp. X, 12, 13, 14). His focus prioritises four elements: networks in the financial sphere, financial power, financial identity, and frictions – or rather resistance – in the financial sphere. Langley embeds these elements into the context of the transformation of saving and borrowing in the Anglo-American world. In his analysis he makes positive reference to Foucault and Butler (see Langley 2010, pp. 125, 240, 242), who effectively distinguish themselves from Marx's and Luxemburg's achievements in the critique of political economy in their respective focus on extra-capitalist power structures. Neither Foucault and Butler nor Langley show much interest in how capital elites mobilise necessary accumulation sources, capital for specific projects, nor for competitive gains, the conquest of areas of influence, 'security', and what consequences this has for individuals and society as a whole. This obscures the interrelationship between structures of socialisation rooted in accumulation, the financial sphere and the way of life itself.

The study of this interrelationship requires a closer look at the capital oligarchy along with the symbiotic relationship between industrial capitalists and financial capitalists at its heart. It is they who organise the major projects of capital accumulation and thereby those of their own power base. There are six particular areas capital oligarchies use as bases to control the overall social context in its entirety and manufacture social consensus. This 'sixfold interrelationship' comprises the mutually intertwined areas of energy, transport and agriculture (or rather agri-business), the military-industrial complex (or rather the security sector), as well as

Table 11.1 Components of the ecological footprint per capita in Hamburg and Germany 2007

	Hamburg		Germany	
Components	gha[a]/person	% of total	gha/person	% of total
Nutrition	1.72	33	1.71	34
Housing	0.78	15	0.75	15
Mobility	1.23	24	1.14	22
Goods	1.12	22	1.20	24
Services	0.32	6	0.29	6
Total	5.17	100	5.08	100

Source: Zukunftsrat Hamburg (2012)
[a]gha = global hectares

the financial sphere and the high-tech sector. Added together, these components involve the greatest use of land and resources and generate both the most pollution[3] and the highest profits. They shape the ecological footprint of the great majority of the population (Table 11.1).

Within capital oligarchies, the owners of finance capital and their managers are surrounded by select industrialists, elite figures from 'politics', 'management', 'security', 'culture and science', communication, consulting and accounting, 'the media', 'the law', and 'civil society'. Their interests and relationships both between one another and to others are in a permanent state of flux. They move and operate with the aid of technical-technological and calculative innovations, business strategies, political reforms, legislative amendments and new laws, with political constellations on various levels, with international and transnational agreements, with crises and wars.

[3]Energy-related activities account for about 63 per cent of total harmful emissions, including around 77 per cent of all carbon dioxide emissions. An estimated 28 per cent of climate-damaging emissions and 36 per cent of carbon dioxide emissions originate in electricity and heating. The transport industry accounts for more than a quarter of harmful emissions. 96 per cent of its energy base is oil, the use of which causes more than 95 per cent of transport emissions. Agriculture produces about 14 per cent of carbon dioxide emissions. If we add harmful emissions released as a result of deforestation, the climate-relevant value rises to 32 per cent. CH_4 and N_2O emissions must also be included in this (EPA 2008). The military represents a force of almost immeasurable destruction of the environment. The Iraq War alone has cost more than the total amount of required global investment until 2030 to halt or effectively slow down global warming. From 2003 to 2007, the war led to the release of more climate-damaging emissions annually than 139 states combined over the same period (Hynes 2014, p. 3).

Over the course of World War II, the USA witnessed the emergence of a military-industrial complex, both product and linch-pin of US-American capital oligarchies, that changed society. Expressions of this included the defeat in Vietnam, the monetary, budgetary, economic and oil crises as well as a shifting global balance of forces. Against this backdrop, three innovations were introduced: (1) microelectronic technologies developed for military purposes were 'released' into the private sphere, revolutionising commerce and finance in particular; they set in motion a new dynamic and dimension of socialisation; (2) in 1974, pension funds faced with rising interest rates were permitted to trade on the stock market; (3) beginning in the mid-1970s, ratings were increasingly funded not by the buyers of stocks, but rather by the sellers. There was a meteoric rise in the economic and political weight of the rating agencies Standard & Poor's, Moody's and Fitch (the 'Big 3') (Rügemer 2012, p. 20). Stimulated by drastically rising interest rates, financial institutions and banks progressively developed products to augment profits – evading applicable laws when necessary. In the course of this development they mobilised financial resources from ever-broader layers of the population. They demanded the deregulation of financial markets, basing their argument on alleged impeded propensity to save and discrimination against small depositors, as well as alleged misallocation of financial resources and obstacles to economic growth. Many banks withdrew from the Federal Reserve System (FED) which had been specifically designed to safeguard the financial system. Correspondingly, FED member banks' share of total deposits of commercial banks dropped from 84 per cent in 1960 to 68.8 per cent in 1984 (Streit 1986, p. 81). As a result, the regulations lost effectiveness while the abolition of interest rate ceilings triggered a process of liberalisation (Streit 1986, pp. 31, 42–43). Vast number of small depositors became investors (Reich 2007, pp. 93 ff.). Capital oligarchies mobilised new accumulation sources, recombined them and utilised them in novel ways. In doing so, they radically transformed both themselves and society along with the economy: widespread use of information technology, the unleashing of 'the economy', or rather of 'the markets' and especially 'financial markets', all-encompassing corporate practices, concentration and centralisation of capital all became the norm. While in 1970 the five largest banks had held just 17 per cent of total deposits in the US banking sector, this figure rose to 52 per cent by 2010 (Federal Reserve Bank of Dallas 2011, p. 7). Adding to this was the growing weight of transnational corporations, the globalisation of the 'sixfold interrelationship' and thus of 'overall globalisation'. A new kind of socialisation and a new type of economic, or rather politico-economic regulation were established.

Capital oligarchies in the USA and the other centres of the global industrial regions provide sufficient space to renew the social consensus, particularly via the interplay between individual lifestyles and work, housing, mobility, education, nutrition, social security and recreational behaviour. A way of life has emerged that buttresses and reinforces the predominance of the capital oligarchies of 'financial market capitalism'. This way of life has a lot to do with exclusion – both in the centres themselves as well as, in particular, globally. It causes violence and environmental destruction. One crucial means of this renewal is capital accumulation through financialisation. Individual and social life is increasingly permeated by financial operations and financial market actors. Financialisation mobilises accumulation sources, the use of which drives socialisation forward. However, it results in the further isolation of individuals. They invest financial means, titles of ownership and payment bonds in order to secure their day-to-day existence, while building up savings to privately ensure their health care and retirement. Their isolation is accompanied both by new freedoms and enormous dependencies. The capital oligarchies who control the everyday life of large parts of the population simultaneously organise a social consensus in their favour. Together with their partners in the state, in the supra-state, and in political life, they constitute a system that accelerates the accumulation of finance capital via deregulation, privatisation, state debt management and fiscal policy, borrowing, as well as free trade, foreign and 'security' policies. This system increasingly shapes social life and it includes:

(a) a new social model, transmitted via mass media – a society of capital owners who independently use their labour and financial resources in an entrepreneurial way to build an appealing lifestyle;
(b) innovations in financial markets and new forms of dealing with debt as the foundation for financing private households;
(c) infrastructures facilitating flexible and mobile consumer behaviour;

(d) demand(s) for workers (or rather citizens) with special abilities, skills, modes of behaviour and living who are able to deal with flexibility and mobility;
(e) renewed privatisation of social services, public enterprises (or rather of the public sector as such).
(f) a new type of manager who orients business management towards the interest of the rentiers – the owners of company shares – and thus towards profit maximisation stimulating speculation (Toporowski 2008, pp. 13–16);
(g) the privatisation and financialisation of natural resources, of pollution and environmental destruction, as well as agreements on ostensible climate protection mechanisms (see Backhouse 2014).

Workforces, business partners, clients and customers, as well as consumers are expected to generate new desires and demands for goods, mobilise their assets and income for the organisation of capital investment, enthusiastically and creatively organise or perform more or less (unpaid) labour by way of social processes of labour, production and reproduction. They are to develop a mindset and behaviour appropriate to the dominant logic(s) of competition and security, and participate in the reproduction of hegemony.

Even the mainstream acknowledges the fact that the modes of production and ways of life prevalent in the centres of the capitalist mode of production cannot be generalised globally, even remotely, neither in social nor in ecological terms. 'We are living beyond our means' is a common refrain in the media. But this 'we' represents a generalisation that abstracts from social exclusion. Here, one group lives 'beyond the means of others [...] even in absolute terms' (Lessenich 2014). Ulrich Brand and Markus Wissen have studied the reasons for this and characterised the 'way of life of the global North' as 'imperial' (Brand and Wissen 2011, p. 24). They identify two dimensions of this way of life: the exploitation of labour forces and resources of the global South by the global North, and the latter's occupation of natural resources. They refer to Clark and Foster, who describe the unequal ecological exchange between North and South as a kind of 'ecological imperialism' with grave social and ecological implications. Brand and Wissen seek to expand 'this concept with the perspective of the Gramscian theory of hegemony' and speak of concrete everyday praxes of the 'imperial way of life' (Brand and Wissen 2012, p. 551). The global industrial centres, as the sites of this way of life, can no longer be viewed as confined to 'the global North' if we consider, say, the BRICS.

If the term of the imperial, of imperiality, means 'the command over the accumulation of capital in space and time' (Rilling 2007, p. 182), then it must be pointed out that those who rule the global industrial and financial centres determine and influence developments on a worldwide scale, thereby affecting living conditions in other parts of the world. The task at hand would be to demonstrate how imperial modes of production and living reproduce and stabilise rulers' control over global capital accumulation. Pension insurance and real estate funds are important tools in this, as even wage-earners pay into them voluntarily (or rather are forced to pay due to social needs like housing and social security). Wage components serve the purpose of generating profits for the fund's largest shareholders from primary and secondary[4] exploitation, as well as preparing the ground for further liberalisation and privatisation.

Based on a different approach and a different focus, Langley summarises: 'In sum, the everyday life of global finance is embedded in transformed networks of saving and borrowing that overlap with the networks of capital markets; situated in the operation of technological, moral, and political power relations; embodied in new and uncertain financial subjects and their self-disciplines; and marked by manifold but problematic practices of dissent' (Langley 2010, p. 40). Langley demonstrates several interrelationships between financial market actors on several different levels. In the past, people went to a bank, opened a savings account, paid money into it and received a certain interest rate that had been agreed upon beforehand. The bank was a capital corporation within networks that were, by and large, concretely defined. Today, investment saving has become a widespread and common practice. People buy into an investment fund or purchase shares of one or several funds. They speculate on short-term price rises or invest long term. They can also enter into a

[4] Primary exploitation occurs in the production process, secondary through the exchange of non-equivalents in circulation (see Marx 1894, p. 745).

fund-based savings agreement to engage in more long-term investment saving. This is especially the case when small depositors seek to secure a private pension, or rather a private pension share. This can be encouraged politically: through cuts in subsidies for public pension schemes, through relieving employers from social security contributions and through incentive for investment saving and pension funds (Langley 2010, pp. 69, 71, 87).

Just as banks in the past had regular customers and customer networks, so do today's banks and funds – only theirs are significantly more dynamic, larger dimensioned and opaque. They consist of globally active members and their networks. For example, swisspartners advertises: "With our globally operating network, we develop tailored future-oriented solutions for asset, tax and inheritance planning. We are convinced that only long-term relationships promise lasting success. [...] On our website you will find information on the core competencies of swisspartners: the prudent care of assets and the organisation of asset structures with consideration for tax aspects and succession planning. [...] As a network of professionals working in six different group companies, swisspartners can mobilize highly qualified experts. Leveraging in-depth know-how and years of experience, we manage the assets of our clients to meet their individual investment goals." (swisspartners 2015)

More than 70 per cent of the swisspartners Investment Network AG belongs to the LLB Group, the Liechtensteinische Landesbank AG with its 100 per cent subsidiaries Lichtensteinische Landesbank (Austria) AG, LLB Asset Management AG and LLB Fund Services. The group is particularly active in Switzerland, Austria and the United Emirates. The country of Liechtenstein owns almost 60 per cent of bearer shares (LLB 2015). For years the Landesbank represented a major tax haven, particularly for Germans. In January 2015 the first Finance Forum Liechtenstein was convened. Those invited to attend included in particular bankers from Germany, the former CEO of Deutsche Bank Josef Ackermann, and Phillip Hildebrand, vice chairman of BlackRock (Finance Forum Liechtenstein 2015).

This example shows that everyday investment saving is linked to global finance. Ethical investment funds and credit projects, social networks and so forth are hardly able to offer sustainable alternatives (Langley

Table 11.2 BlackRock's shares in the 30 DAX companies

DAX company	Share (%)	DAX company	Share (%)
Daimler	9.2	Commerzbank	5.0
Continental	8.7	RWE	5.0
Linde	8.7	Deutsche Post	5.0
Deutsche Börse	7.0	Merck	4.9
BASF	7.0	Lanxess	4.3
BMW	6.5	VW	4.1
Münchner Rück	6.4	Deutsche Bank	3.5
Siemens	5.2	Fresenius	3.0
HeidelbergCement	5.1	SAP	3.0
K+S	5.1	Adidas	3.0
Thyssen Krupp	5.0	Deutsche Telekom	3.0
E.on	5.0	Infineon	3.0
Fresen. Med. Care	5.0	Lufthansa	3,0
Allianz	5.0	Beiersdorf	3.0
Bayer	5.0	Henkel	0.8

Source: Jost (2014)

2010, pp. 113 ff., 208 ff.). The new networks of banks and funds, or rather financial market actors, are networks of members of specific globally active capital oligarchies who develop sources for the accumulation of their financial capital. What puts Langley's abstraction of corporations in the 'sixfold interrelationship' to the test is BlackRock's share of DAX companies (Table 11.2). He pays little attention to the fact that, for example, BlackRock invests in gold, diamonds and rare metals that are obtained under inhumane conditions. Langley addresses the issue of rating agencies (such as in Langley 2010, p. 237), but he does not ask about the politico-economic power of these agencies. And yet the owners of the three major rating agencies own shares in all investment banks and enterprises of the 500 largest corporations worldwide (Rügemer 2012, p. 62). Langley does refer repeatedly, however, to employment and wage problems (e.g. Langley 2010, p. 235). After all, the behaviour of investment savers and borrowers is mainly based on the unknown, regardless of whether they seek to portray themselves as reliable, disciplined customers. They live in economic uncertainty, and the creation of social security is increasingly delegated to the individual responsibility of citizens through targeted policies by the rulers. The former are lured en masse into taking out consumer loans, pressured into taking on credit to pay tuition fees, and stimulated or coerced into mortgage credits for housing – usually for purposes of security in old age. Whoever takes out a loan today can generally assume that it will be securitised and circulated within and via networks of creditors, thus leading to more borrowing.

To develop a better understanding of the most recent financial crisis, it helps to look at a speech by former US president George W. Bush. Here, we find a model illustration of the dominant logic of social policy: according to Bush, US society was to become an 'ownership society'. This goal was to be realised through credit financing. As Bush put it at the time: "Our Government is supporting homeownership because it is good for America; it is good for our families; it is good for our economy. One of the biggest hurdles to homeownership is getting money … and so today I'm honored to be here to sign a law that will help many low-income buyers to overcome that hurdle and to achieve an important part of the American Dream … This administration will constantly strive to promote an ownership society in America … The rate of homeownership in America now stands at a record high of 68.4 per cent. Yet there is room for improvement. The rate of homeownership amongst minorities is below 50 per cent. And that's not right … Many people are able to afford a monthly mortgage payment but are unable to make the down payment, and so this legislation will authorize 200 million per year in down payment assistance to at least 40,000 low-income families … The dream of homeownership should be attainable for every hard-working American" (Bush 2003).[5] The law consisted of three parts: a doubling of funds for housing consultancy services for creditors, potential buyers and associations; new regulations making it easier for buyers to compare prices and to secure the best deal and the best possible service; new regulations that would facilitate credit applications for buyers and owners of residential property and make it easier for them to finalise mortgage loan agreements. The implementation of the law has brought about the emergence of a second-class credit market for those discriminated against because of their income level, ethnicity and/or gender. While black households had

[5] Bush does not name the rulers behind these monetary movements. They are the globally active capital oligarchies. They financialise the life of society as well as its members in order to mobilise capital for new major projects, particularly within the 'six-fold interrelationship', and to gain social acceptance of such projects. This forms the basis of their control over society.

to put up 63 per cent of their net income to secure housing, this figure was at only 38.5 per cent for white households (Young 2013, p. 284 f.). For women, and for black women in particular, access to credit was made significantly more difficult than for men, and white men in particular (Young 2013, p. 284).

On this second-class market, creditors circulated debtors' securitisations and hedgings. One securitisation was followed by another and subsequently circulated within the creditors' networks and beyond. However, the creditors on the subprime market themselves were only poorly hedged. When borrowers (as is now widely known) defaulted on interest and repayment obligations due to wage losses, many creditors ended up equally insolvent as a result. The networks of subprime creditors were not all that came crashing down. After all, these networks were linked to 'global finance', particularly via hedge funds. In late 2012 more than six million residences had been vacated by people unable to pay, while four million others were threatened with eviction (Young 2013, p. 285).

As valid as it is to speak of precarious creditors as well as borrowers in this context (Langley 2010, p. 235), it is nevertheless inappropriate to reduce the housing market to a question of selling and buying residential properties: a glimpse at major transactions by housing portfolios in Germany (Table 11.3) shows the activities of banks and funds as well as 'stock market investors' on this 'market'.

Bulk selling of housing portfolios continued in 2014, significantly exceeding the figures for 2013. For instance, one joint venture involving the real estate company Prelios and Deutsche Bank sold a package of 18,000 residential units to the Austrian firm Buwog (Franke and Lorenz-Henning 2014, pp. 4–6). In the first three quarters of 2014, 79.3 per cent of housing portfolios sold in Germany were sold to German firms, 15.9 per cent to other European investors, 0.8 per cent to buyers from the Middle East and 1.7 per cent to investors in North America. Of all buyers, 59.2 per cent were large real estate corporations, 12.3 per cent special funds, 7 per cent small and medium-sized real estate firms, 4.9 per cent public authorities, 3.4 per cent investment/asset managers, 2.7 per cent pension funds, 2.6 per cent equity/real estate funds (Fritz 2014).

Table 11.3 Housing portfolio transactions starting at 10,000 residential units 2010 to 2013

Year	Res. units[a]	Seller	Company sold	Buyer
2010	No transactions with more than 10,000 Res. units			
2011	29,300	Cerberus/Goldman Sachs	GSW Immobilien AG (60%)	Stock exchange investors
	25,100	BayernLB (Bayerische Landesbank)	DKB Immobilien GmbH (100%)	TAG Immobilien AG
	23,400	Barclays Bank	BauBeCon Immobilien GmbH (100%)	Deutsche Wohnen AG
	22,000	Speymill Deutsche Immob. Company	–	Cerberus
	21,000	Landesbank Baden-Württemberg (LBBW)	LBBW Immobilien GmbH (100%)	Consortium around Patrizia Immobilien AG
	13,000	Archstone (Lehman Brothers)	DeWAG GmbH (100%)	AvalonBay Communities, Equity Residential
	11,400	Bundesanstalt für Immobilienaufgaben (BImA)	TLG WOHNEN GmbH (100%)	TAG Immobilien AG
	53,200	Stock exchange investors	GSW Immobilien AG (91%)	Deutsche Wohnen AG
	44,900	Goldman Sachs	LEG Immobilien AG (50%)	Stock exchange investors
	29,400	BayernLB (Bayerische Landesbank)	GBW AG (92%)	Consortium around Patrizia Immobilien
2013	27,800	Terra Firma Capital Partners	Deutsche Annington SE (16%)	Stock exchange investors
	25,500	Fortress Investment Group	GAGFAH Group (18%)	Stock exchange investors

(*continued*)

Table 11.3 (continued)

Year	Res. units[a]	Seller	Company sold	Buyer
	11,800	Goldman Sachs	LEG Immobilien AG (13%)	Stock exchange investors
	10,100	Fortress Investment Group	GAGFAH Group (7%)	Stock exchange in-vestors

Source: Franke and Lorenz-Henning 2014
[a]Rounded up; in sales of company shares the number of residential units was calculated proportionally

Saving and borrowing to purchase a house has rather complex social and ecological consequences. Among them is the enormous consumption of land involved, which has constituted one of society's most severe environmental problems for quite some time. Germany loses about 90 hectares of natural land surface every day. In return, surface coverage by roads increases by 22 hectares daily. Yet the trend towards owning a 'house in the countryside' continues. Owner-occupied real estate property, comprising roughly 18.2 million residential units, is accounted for mainly by single-family and two-family homes (ifs 2014). This blocks investment in energy-saving renovations urgently required if we are to successfully halt climate change. This places the homeownership rate at about 43 per cent (Statistisches Landesamt Sachsen-Anhalt 2014). While in 1960 an individual in Germany had 14 square meters of living space statistically, this figure had risen to 42 square meters by 2010. Municipalities compete for the resettlement of commercial districts and residential areas. For landowners, the sale of their land for home construction is usually more economically rational than its agricultural or natural use. Both urban and rural land use planning commonly proceeds from a notion of the 'car-owning citzen' (see Bündnis 90/Die Grünen, Kreisverband München-Land 2013). This 'car community' harms the quality of life through pollution and environmental degradation, noise, hazards (especially for children), stress, exclusion of people without cars, aggressiveness, lost opportunities for living in decent conditions in an attractive environment, and for spaces of communication and solidary cooperation throughout the community.

Capital elites are equally confronted with contradictions: in order to stay competitive on a global scale, wages must be depressed. This contradicts the interests of producers of consumer goods, of the providers of human social services as well as those of financial market actors. In order to stay competitive and dominant on a global scale, corresponding economic structures which exude 'security' and attractiveness are crucial. This 'security' and attractiveness are simultaneously connected to resources of power, ideologies, ethics, surveillance, and the weakness of the opposing forces. The development of economic structures requires sources of accumulation. These resources are mobilised and valorised with the involvement of the population – as workforces, consumers, owners, financial market actors, 'silent players'. They are all oriented toward these challenges of capital accumulation, which requires a sufficient general framework: 'the markets' must function properly, 'the state' is to provide for those functioning markets, as well as for skilled and disciplined workforces, consumers, owners, investors, competitive infrastructure and 'security'. The state is expected to guarantee the mobilisation of required accumulation sources while at the same time minimising the costs of this for capital: lowering taxes, awarding public contracts for lucrative investments, only minimally regulating capital flows. And the state obliges: from 1992 to 2013 stock exchange capitalisation within the EU rose from 22 per cent to 65 per cent of GDP (European Commission 2015, p. 7), with poverty increasing during the same period. While in 1992 about 15 per cent of the EU's population were affected or threatened by poverty, this figure reached 25 per cent in 2013 (see Commission of the European Communities 1992; EAPN 2014).

Conflicting interests certainly exist among capital elites. However, their general common interest in Germany and the EU can be summarised as follows: consolidation of public funds, patent and investment protection, active regulation of the economy, unification of capital, banking and energy markets, infrastructural policy, delegation of responsibilities concerning 'employability' and social security to individual citizens, free trade and market deregulation, extensive privatisation, deployment of public funds on behalf of capital valorisation in combination with corporation- and wealth-friendly tax policies. And these things happen – capital oligarchies and their partners ensure that: public-private partnerships,

'European Long Term Investment Fund' (ELTIF), 'Investment Offensive for Europe', 'homeownership', 'private pensions', 'tuition fees' are key terms in this regard. ELTIF and the investment initiative are intended to invest private funds over the long term with the aim of improving infrastructure. Public funds are supposed to stimulate this process and cover the risks. In the eyes of the European Commission, 70 per cent of ELTIF is comprised of net asset values of more than 10 million euros and of companies/projects not traded on the stock exchange: schools, hospitals and prisons, social infrastructure, social housing, roads, public transportation systems, airports, energy infrastructure, climate projects, nuclear power plants, pipelines and power grids, water supplies, sewage and irrigation systems, communications infrastructure, recycling and waste handling systems. The European Commission plans to cover the remaining 30 per cent through new investments. In an effort to make this venture 'worth it' for private investors, pressure to implement more liberalisation and privatisations is heightened (WEED 2014). ELTIF simultaneously represents an important component of the 'Investment Offensive for Europe', which is to mobilise another 315 billion euros for investment. Pension funds are again listed as potential partners in this endeavour. 'Innovative financial instruments' are supposed to have a leverage effect on financial markets with a factor of 15 or 20. This inevitably leads to further speculation. These 'innovative financial instruments' are linked to 'solutions in the form of public-private partnerships' (European Commission 2014, p. 12) and to 'structural reforms' (European Commission 2014, p. 15) – that is to say, to even more market, and more power for the market actors who are already the most powerful. This logic resurfaces in the commission of experts appointed by Minister of the Economy Sigmar Gabriel in the summer of 2014 to devise a 'new investment strategy' for Germany. Furthermore, a study compiled for the German and French Ministers of Economy reads as follows: 'The EU (especially continental Europe) should accelerate the transition from a bank-based and credit-based economy to a market-based and equity-based economy. This transformation is necessary, because Europe's credit-based system is not commensurate with its needs in terms of fostering the emergence of a new growth model' (Enderlein and Pisani-Ferry 2014, p. 24). It is not, however, 'the markets' that invest, but at most those active on the markets, or rather on the stock exchange. Due to the fact that this must be profitable for them, the interests of large population groups – indeed of the global majority – are brought in line with the generation of profit while necessary steps towards socially and ecologically sustainable development are abandoned.

So What? A Few Conclusions

We have established that citizens are included in the mobilisation of accumulation sources through their unpaid labour, through assets, incomes and means of circulation. In the centres of the capitalist mode of production they do so because they must in order to earn an income, to provide for social security, to solve their housing problem; or, rather, they do so because they think they must. They perform labour in the production of goods, the results of which are appropriated privately/by capital oligarchies. Socialised (primary) exploitation takes place. When this surplus value in the form of profit then (partly) comes back to individuals in the form of interest, these individuals share in the results of the same socialised exploitation at whose mercy they also find themselves. This occurs in highly differing ways, both socially as well as regionally, and large parts of the population do not participate at all: because they do not participate actively in commodity production and/or have no skills or means with which to earn money; because interest is essentially a wage portion and thus the received wage is ultimately a reduced wage; or because certain projects simply fail. This is how redistribution, or secondary exploitation operates. In this 'game' the weakest social groups and regions are excluded and exploited most brutally. Resources are plundered, people are subjected to violence, and the natural environment is destroyed.

Individuals take this 'game' as a given. The outcome appears as good or bad luck, as success or failure. Yet what looks like a game of pure chance is really a deeply entrenched way of life. And it is the latter that strengthens the 'sixfold interrelationship' along with the associated capital oligarchies ultimately responsible for ecological destruction and social cleavages, not to mention for continuous pressures to adopt said way of life. Individuals are isolated and honed into particular functions within the accumulation process, while relationships of competition and exploitation are intensified. 'This society' is a globalised 'externalisation society' (Lessenich), in which the rulers in the global industrial regions preserve the imperial way of life with the consent of the majority of local populations, thereby blocking the path to a self-determined and dignified life for the world's weakest. 'Most importantly, the inhabitants of the externalisation society live at their expense, at their cost.' (Lessenich 2014). This 'externalisation mechanism' includes financialisation and the 'free trade' associated with it: behind both lies the accumulation of finance capital driven by profit maximisation and the mobilisation of resources required for this. To the main actors, free trade is about the least regulated access to natural resources, labour products, and labour capacity possible. Financialisation, then, is all about powerful financial market actors' access to all existing and potential (or rather desired) accumulation sources for finance capital. Financialisation and free trade are crucial tools for enforcing the predominance of today's capital oligarchies. The majorities in this globalised 'externalisation society' are unable to translate the will to live a self-determined, ecologically sustainable life in solidarity into actual practice. Often, the will does not even exist.

How, then, can we break out of these relations of socialisation dominated by globalised capital oligarchies, if the day-to-day existence of the vast majority of citizens is so firmly rooted in this way of life, which in turn shapes society's way of life as a whole? Some points of departure can perhaps be found in those parts of this regime that are particularly parasitic, dangerous, destructive, or simply irrational. The task at hand is nothing more and nothing less than to stage a revolt against the daily madness of 'financial market capitalism'. A few simple demands are a good start:

Against military build-ups and arms exports.

Against total surveillance of the citizenry.

Against an investment and infrastructure policy that focuses on major projects that ultimately harm citizens and the natural environment.

Against a fiscal, tax and financial policy that implements redistribution from the bottom to the top and from the public to the private.

Against this kind of free trade; No to EPA, TTIP, CETA, TISA.[6]

---

[6] EPAs: European Partnership Agreements in the sense of neo-colonial free trade agreements with the ACP countries; TTIP: US-EU free trade agreement; CETA: Canada-EU free trade agreement; TISA: agreement on the further liberalisation of commerce in the service sector.

Against the coercion to become a financial market actor merely to attain social security.

Against a political orientation subalternate to the USA.

Against this 'externalisation society' that forces people here to participate in the exploitation of the world's weakest.

Against This Consensus, Against the Notion That There Is No Alternative

Being 'against' so much may seem defensive, but then again, breaking out of 'financial market capitalism' is ultimately the precondition for any real change to occur; secondly, emancipatory-solidary forces are currently on the defensive; thirdly, these points represent starting points for certain alternatives that can begin in everyday life; fourthly, political action as well as the associated political alliances already exist here; and fifthly, given the destructive dynamic of financial market capitalism described above, these 'counter-movements' can also be interpreted in an offensive manner: namely, for a self-determined, dignified, solidary and ecologically sustainable life! This would constitute a radical demand which could serve as an integrative platform for work on socio-political alternatives for reform. It then becomes necessary, however, to stop missing opportunities for action present in both the 'silent and loud' coercions due to a lack of permanent analysis of constellations of interests, a lack of permanent search for such opportunities, and a lack of ongoing solidarity with those who need it most.

Beginning from this self-criticism and this taking a stance 'against', the Left would have to devise strategies that link defensive struggles with opportunities for action. These struggles would turn on the question as to whether or not capital oligarchies are able to mobilise and utilise further sources of accumulation of finance capital. The offensive component of this strategy concerns the everyday life of people. The Left's engagement with strategy would have to be oriented toward everyday life while simultaneously adopting a transformative perspective in terms of a vision of structural roll back or overcoming of a mode of socialisation through capital oligarchies. The aim would be to create the conditions under which humans can socialise themselves as freely associating individuals.

The coming defensive struggles will be about defending democratic, social and ecological standards in order to prevent further privatisations of the public as well as the use of public resources to support corporations. This may allow us to avoid a new 'wave of financialisation'. At the same time, the task at hand is to halt the major projects of an industrial policy fixated on global competitiveness and the 'capacity to act' as well as on 'security', thereby expediting militarisation. Likewise, defensive struggles against (new) free trade agreements must be strengthened.

Of utmost importance is the demonstration of viable perspectives and the mobilisation of the forces needed for their realisation. This starts with local and regional problem solving in the housing economy, the supply of energy and the transport sector, as well as for certain sectors of the construction and agriculture industries. These perspectives may then seep into the life of citizens who could actually challenge the social consensus – as employees, residents, users, consumers, customers, or even as socially, ecologically, politically committed people with their organisations and associations. This would require building local and regional alliances as well as supra-regional, European, transnational networks between these alliances. Logically, then, they must focus on the preservation, democratisation and expansion of the public, as well as on democratic, social and ecological standards and possibilities for alternative local and regional development (Dellheim 2014, pp. 358–62). At the initial stage, political conflicts in the areas of housing/living environment/mobility and social security – along with their corresponding links to social provisions more generally, the commons and a different security policy – are of particular importance; especially because of the struggles occurring here and their significance for capital oligarchies' accumulation and social strategies; because of the potentials for bringing together, activating and creating solidarity among citizens, social actors, and for interesting people in a new way of social life.

Today, the Left's support for the Greek Syriza government has become increasingly important. But here the deficit is still enormous. A Left strategy would have to protect and expand the possibilities of the Greek government and the Greek Left to deal with the humanitarian crisis on the one hand and with the creditors on the other hand. The challenge is to find commonalities in interests, demands and positions and to make them politically effective. This is particularly true of struggles over transparency and the implementation of social, democratic, civil and human rights, tax justice, of dealing with corruption and the debt issue, with repression and militarisation, prescribed social and ecological destruction, privatisation and financialisation. All of these struggles also relate to the sources of accumulation as political issues, and such an approach could indeed aid in productively strengthening the political force of the 'against'. After all, it is the latter's strength that will determine possible scenarios of social development in the EU. These scenarios in turn depend decisively on the balance of forces in Germany. Three different scenarios seem plausible: (1) being even more determined by the interests of capital oligarchies and thus oriented towards financialisation/liberalisation/privatisation/militarisation; (2) continuing on the current path, but with a stronger focus on the interests of the EU's own capital oligarchies; (3) rolling back the power of capital oligarchies, breaking their dominance, and initiating a problem-solving social-ecological transformation.

The weakness of the Left is not least related to the fact that some important issues are approached too narrowly, in terms of 'labour market policy' or the 'socio-political'. If one analyses interests and constellations of interests only sporadically, if a certain policy measure is opposed and/or a guaranteed minimum income advocated as a universal solution 'only' for reasons of jobs, wages, pay scales and prices, then many aspects will be overlooked – for example, if contexts in which the rulers act according to their own accumulation and power interests and launch new attacks are not addressed – then possibilities for self-empowerment and for the exertion of influence on social life, particularly on the 'six-fold interrelationship', remain unutilised. Ultimately, opportunities for action are missed. However, the weakness of the Left is also owed to the fact that little awareness exists of how deeply individuals are afflicted by fetishisations themselves. People of the Left are rarely recognisable by their exhaustion of individual and collective possibilities to live differently and turn such possibilities into a starting point for everyday politics. The focal points of a necessary confrontation with one's own weakness include one's own lifestyle, one's history of criticising fetishism and one's politico-economic education. This would mean that individuals of the Left ought to cease aspiring to homeownership and private social security models, as the latter are designed to foster de-solidarisation and the reproduction of economic and power structures.

In order to identify opportunities for political action and to consolidate and develop promising approaches, the input of Left scholars is required – specifically, to investigate the causes and workings of capitalist 'madness' and the state of its opponents, as partners in the analysis of transformative potential(s), in the development of transformational projects and political strategies. Karl Marx and Rosa Luxemburg wrote first and foremost for those seeking to reshape society and therefore to convince others of the viability of such an endeavour. They worked incessantly to make sense of social development, to substantiate the notion of an association of the free and equal, to strengthen those struggling for such a goal. A serious account of the 'madness' is only truly possible if we 'turn to Marx and Luxemburg' again and again, make use of their legacy and practice our own critical mode of research, thought and behaviour in everyday life. In this endeavour, it is the process that matters and not the actual findings as such (Bourdieu 1991, p. 278). Surely, it is possible to fail in the permanent search for opportunities for political action, but this search may nevertheless produce new opportunities for action as new constellations of interests emerge. As Balibar puts it:

> 'Today we are no longer dealing with the final crisis of an attempt to establish "socialism", but rather with a structural crisis of a (productivist) mode of accumulation and a (finance-driven) capitalist mode of regulation, the outcome of which is unpredictable and causes extremely intense fractures in the consciousness and emotional life of subjects. Yet I still believe, in accordance with Marx, at least as I understand him, that the ethics we require is precisely the one that is split between two irreconcilable social interests, instead of simply assuming that these interests could appear as two sides of the same coin if people only showed just a little bit more goodwill' (Balibar 2013, p. 198).

Acknowledgments The author would like to thank Lutz Brangsch, Michael Brie and Frieder Otto Wolf for their comments and criticisms.

Bibliography

Backhouse, M. (2014). Green grabbing in the Brazilian Amazon. http://kapacc.blog.rosalux.de/2014/02/14/maria-backhouse-green-grabbing-in-the-brazilian-amazon/.

Balibar, É. (2007). *The philosophy of Marx*. London: Verso.

Balibar, É. (2013). *Marx' philosophie*. Berlin: b-books.

Bourdieu, P. (1991). Inzwischen kenne ich alle Krankheiten der soziologischen Vernunft, Pierre Bourdieu im Gespräch mit Beate Krais. In B. Krais (Ed.), *Soziologie als Beruf. Wissenschaftstheoretische Voraussetzungen soziologischer Erkenntnisse* (pp. 269–284). Berlin: de Gruyter.

Bourdieu, P. (1993). *Sociology in question*. London: Sage Publications.

Brand, U., & Wissen, M. (2011). Die Regulation der ökologischen Krise. Theorie und Empirie der Transformation gesellschaftlicher Naturverhältnisse. *Österreichische Zeitschrift für Soziologie, 36*(2), 12–34.

Brand, U., & Wissen, M. (2012). Global environment and the imperial mode of living: Articulations of state-capital relations in the multiple crisis. *Globalizations, 9*(4), 547–560.

Brie, M. (2015). A critical reception of *Accumulation of Capital*. (chapter in this book).

Bündnis 90/Die Grünen Kreisverband München-Land. (2013). Positionspapier Flächenverbrauch. www.gruene-ml.de.

Bush, G. W. (2003). Remarks on signing the American dream downpayment act. http://www.presidency.ucsb.edu/ws/?pid=64935.

Commission of the European Communities. (1992). Towards a Europe of solidarity. COM (542), Brussels http://aei.pitt.edu/4819/1/4819.pdf.

Dellheim, J. (2014). Kapitaloligarchien und Transformation. Zur Entwicklung der Europäischen Union. In M. Brie (Ed.), *Futuring. Transformation im Kapitalismus über ihn hinaus* (pp. 332–367). Münster: Westfälisches Dampfboot.

Enderlein, H. and Pisani-Ferry, J. (2014). Reforms, investment and growth: An agenda for France, Germany and Europe, report to Sigmar Gabriel, Federal Minster for Economic Affairs and Energy, and Emmanuel Macron, Minister for the Economy, Industry and Digital Affairs http://www.bmwi.de/BMWi/Redaktion/PDF/Publikationen/empfehlung-enderlein-pisani-ferry-englisch,property=pdf,bereich=bmwi2012,sprache=de,rwb=true.pdf.

Environmental Protection Agency. (2008). Global greenhouse gas emissions data. http://www.epa.gov/climatechange/ghgemissions/global.html.

European Anti-Poverty Network (2014). *120 million people in European Union at risk of poverty* (Press release, 6 December 2014). http://www.eapn.eu/en/

news-and-publications/news/eu-institutions-news/120-million-people-in-european-union-at-risk-of-poverty.

European Commission (2014). An investment plan for Europe. Communication from the commission to the European parliament, the council, the European Central Bank, The European economic and social committee, The committee of the regions and the European investment Bank. COM, 903.

European Commission. (2015). Building a capital markets union, GREEN PAPER, COM, 63/2, SWD, 13.

Federal Reserve Bank of Dallas. (2011). Choosing the road to prosperity, why we must end too big to fail – now. Annual Report, Dallas.

Finance Forum Liechtenstein. (2015). Finance Forum Liechtenstein zeigt Strategien auf. http://www.finance-forum.li/.

Franke, J. and Lorenz-Henning, K. (2014). Deutlicher Anstieg beim Handel großer Wohnungsportfolios in 2012 und 2013. BBSR-Analysen KOMPAKT, 3.

Fritz, C. (2014). Wohnungspakete bleiben Anlegermagnet', *procontraonline*, 17 October. http://www.procontra-online.de/artikel/date/2014/10/wohnungspakete-bleiben-anlegermagnet/seite/1/.

Hynes, P. H. (2014). The "invisible casualty of war": The environmental destruction of U.S. militarism, *DifferenTTakes, 84*. http://traprock.org/wp-content/uploads/2014/06/Militarism-and-the-Environment.pdf.

ifs–Institut für Städtebau, Wohnungswirtschaft und Bausparwesen (2014). Wohneigentumsquoten in Deutschland und Europa. http://typo3.p165294.webspaceconfig.de/fileadmin/Daten_Fakten/Wohneigentumsquoten_in_Deutschland_und_Europa.pdf.

Jost, S. (2014). EZB lässt sich von Finanzmacht BlackRock beraten, *Die Welt*, 27 August. http://www.welt.de/wirtschaft/article131660696/EZB-laesst-sich-von-Finanzmacht-BlackRock-beraten.html.

Langley, P. (2010). *The everyday life of global finance. Saving and borrowing in Anglo-America*. Oxford: Oxford University Press.

Lefèbvre, H. (1991). *Critique of everyday life, volume I*. London: Verso.

Lessenich, S. (2014). Neben uns die Sintflut, *Süddeutsche Zeitung*, 30 October.

LLB. (2015). Wir über uns. https://www.llb.li/de/die-llb/ueber-uns.

Luxemburg, R. [1913] (2015). The accumulation of capital. A contribution to the economic theory of imperialism. In *Rosa Luxemburg. Complete works, Volume 2*. pp. 7–344. London/New York: Verso.

Marx, K. [1859] (1992). A contribution to the critique of political economy, preface. In *Karl Marx. Early writings*. pp. 424–428. London: Penguin Books.

Marx, K. [1867a] (1982). *Capital. A critique of political economy, volume I*. New York: Penguin Books.

Marx, K. [1864] (1985). Inaugural address of the working men's international association in *Marx/Engels collected works, volume. 20.* pp. 5–13. New York: International Publishers.

Marx, K. [1894] (1993). *Capital. A critique of political economy, volume III.* New York: Penguin Books.

Marx, K. and Engels. F. [1848] (1997). *Manifesto of the communist party.* Moscow: Progress Publishers.

Reich, R. B. (2007). *Supercapitalism. The transformation of business, democracy, and everyday life.* New York: Knopf.

Rilling, R. (2007). Imperialität, US-amerikanische Diskurse seit 9/11. In M. Brie (Ed.), *Schöne neue Demokratie. Elemente totaler Herrschaft* (pp. 141–207). Berlin: Dietz Verlag.

Rügemer, W. (2012). *Rating-Agenturen. Einblicke in die Kapitalmacht der Gegenwart.* Bielefeld: Transcript.

Statistisches Landesamt Sachsen-Anhalt. (2014). Indikator L109 – Wohneigentumsquote (%). https://www.statistik.sachsen-anhalt.de/apps/StrukturKompass/indikator/zeitreihe/37.

Streit, J. (1986). *Finanzinnovationen, Deregulierung und Geldmengensteuerung in den USA.* Tübingen: Mohr Siebeck.

Swisspartners. (2015). The road to success demands care, respect and discipline. http://www.swisspartners.com/lp/en/index_en.

Toporowski, J. (2008). The economics and culture of financialisation. School of Oriental and African Studies working paper, 158. London: SOAS.

WEED (2014). Europäische langfristige Investmentfonds (ELTIF). *Informationsblatt*, January. http://www2.weed-online.org/uploads/infoblatt_europaeische_langfristige_investmentfonds.pdf.

Wolf, F. O. (2012). *Rückkehr in die Zukunft – Krisen und Alternativen. Beiträge zur radikalen Philosophie.* Münster: Westfälisches Dampfboot.

Young, B. (2013). Gender, debt and the housing/financial crisis. In D. M. Figart & T. L. Warnecke (Eds.), *Handbook of research on gender and economic life* (pp. 278–289). Cheltenham: Edward Elgar Publishing.

Zukunftsrat Hamburg (2012). *Der ökologische Fußabdruck der Hansestadt Hamburg. Eine Stadt lebt auf zu großem Fuß.* Hamburg: Zukunftsrat.

Erratum to: Chapter 8, 9 and 10 of Rosa Luxemburg: A Permanent Challenge for Political Economy Judith Dellheim and Frieder Otto Wolf

Erratum to:

Chapter 8 in: *Tove Soiland, A Feminist Approach to Primitive Accumulation*, DOI 10.1057/978-1-137-60108-7_8

The reference “Boltanski, L., & Chiapello, E. (2005a). Te new spirit of capitalism. London: Verso.” has been deleted.

The online version of the updated original chapter can be found under 10.1057/978-1-137-60108-7_8

Erratum to:

Chapter 9 in: *Klaus Dörre, Limits to Landnahme. Growth Dilemma as Challenge*, DOI 10.1057/978-1-137-60108-7_9

The reference is now updated as “Boltanski, L., & Chiapello, E. (2007). *The new spirit of capitalism*. London and New York: Verso.”

J. Dellheim, F.O. Wolf (eds.), *Rosa Luxemburg: A Permanent Challenge for Political Economy*, DOI 10.1057/978-1-137-60108-7_12

The reference is now updated as "Boltanski, L., & Chiapello, È. (2005). The role of criticism in the dynamics of capitalism: social criticism versus artistic criticism. In M. Miller (Ed.), *Worlds of capitalism. Economic performance, governance and economic change in the era of globalization* (pp. 237–266). London/New York: Routledge.

The online version of the updated original chapter can be found under 10.1057/978-1-137-60108-7_9

Erratum to:

Chapter 10 in: *Michael Brie, A Critical Reception of Accumulation of Capital*, DOI 10.1057/978-1-137-60108-7_10

The reference is now updated as "Boltanski, L., & Chiapello, E. (2007). *The new spirit of capitalism*. London and New York: Verso."

The online version of the updated original chapter can be found under 10.1057/978-1-137-60108-7_10

Index

J. Dellheim, F.O. Wolf (eds.), *Rosa Luxemburg: A Permanent Challenge for Political Economy*, DOI 10.1057/978-1-137-60108-7

GPSR Compliance
The European Union's (EU) General Product Safety Regulation (GPSR) is a set of rules that requires consumer products to be safe and our obligations to ensure this.

If you have any concerns about our products, you can contact us on

ProductSafety@springernature.com

In case Publisher is established outside the EU, the EU authorized representative is:

Springer Nature Customer Service Center GmbH
Europaplatz 3
69115 Heidelberg, Germany

www.ingramcontent.com/pod-product-compliance
Lightning Source LLC
Chambersburg PA
CBHW060749150926
51501CB00004B/133
9781137601070